Developments in Russian Politics 6

P9-DGS-225

NO LONGER
the property of
Whitaker Library

Developments in
Russian Politics 6

Edited by

Stephen White
Zvi Gitelman
and
Richard Sakwa

Whitaker Library
Chowan University
Murfreesboro, North Carolina

DUKE UNIVERSITY PRESS
DURHAM 2005

Editorial matter and selection © Stephen White, Zvi Gitelman and
Richard Sakwa 2005

Individual chapters (in order) © Richard Sakwa, John P. Willerton,
Thomas F. Remington, Michael McFaul, Stephen White, Alfred V. Evans, Jr,
Sarah Oates, Robert Sharlet, Gordon Hahn, Darrell Slider, Peter Rutland,
Judy Twigg, Margot Light, Zvi Gitelman 2005

First published in 1990 as *Developments in Soviet Politics*
Second edition (*Developments in Soviet and Post-Soviet Politics*) 1992
Third edition (*Developments in Russian and Post-Soviet Politics*) 1994
Fourth edition (*Developments in Russian Politics*) 1997
Fifth edition (*Development in Russian Politics*) 2001

Published in the United States in 2005 by
Duke University Press
Durham, NC 27708

First published in Great Britain in 2005 by
PALGRAVE MACMILLAN
Houndmills, Basingstoke, Hampshire RG21 6XS

Library of Congress Cataloging-in-Publication Data
    Developments in Russian politics 6 / Edited by Stephen White, Zvi Gitelman, and
    Richard Sakwa.—6th ed.
        p. cm.
    Includes bibliographical references and index.
    ISBN 0-8223-3510-7 (cloth: alk. paper)—ISBN 0-8223-3522-0 (pbk. : alk. paper)
        1. Russia (Federation)—Politics and government—1991– I. Title: Developments in
    Russian politics six. II. White, Stephen, 1945– III. Gitelman, Zvi Y. IV. Sakwa, Richard.
    DK510.763.D48 2005
    320.947'09'0511—dc22

                                                                    2005004619

Printed in China

Contents

List of Maps, Tables and Figures   ix

Preface   x

Notes on the Contributors   xi

List of Abbreviations   xv

Glossary   xvi

1 Politics in Russia   1
Richard Sakwa

Russia enters the new millennium   1
The politics of independent Russia   5
The transition and regime type   8
Regime and administered democracy   10
Politics in Russia today   13
Conclusion   16

2 Putin and the Hegemonic Presidency   18
John P. Willerton

Strong executives past and present   20
The hegemonic presidency   23
Constellation of elements in the Putin team   33
Contending views of Putin's hegemonic executive   36

3 Parliamentary Politics in Russia   40
Thomas F. Remington

The RSFSR transition-era parliament   42
Boris Yeltsin and the crisis of 1993   43
The Federal Assembly   46
The third and fourth Dumas   50
The Federation Council   52
The legislative process in the Federal Assembly   53
The Federal Assembly in perspective   58

4 The Electoral System   61
Michael McFaul

The non-political origins of competitive elections in Russia   61
Elections as certain procedures with uncertain outcomes   64

The development of more certain rules   66
Uncertain electoral outcomes   68
The Putin era: certain procedures and certain outcomes   73
State limits on the electoral playing field   75
Conclusion: do elections still matter?   78

5   **The Political Parties**   80
    Stephen White

    The contemporary party spectrum   81
    Parties and the Russian public   89

6   **A Russian Civil Society?**   96
    Alfred B. Evans, Jr

    Civil society and democracy   96
    Civil society in late tsarist Russia   98
    Social organizations in the Soviet Union   98
    The troubles of civil society in the 1990s   101
    Different types of organizations in civil society in Russia 105
    Civil society under Putin   108
    Conclusion   111

7   **Media and Political Communication**   114
    Sarah Oates

    Media in the Soviet era   115
    The growth of Soviet television   117
    Glasnost and the Russian media   118
    The Russian media in an emerging nation   120
    The future of the Russian media   128

8   **In Search of the Rule of Law**   130
    Robert Sharlet

    Constitutional promises, constitutional ambiguities   131
    Russia's tripartite judicial system   133
    Rule of law reform under Yeltsin: progress and regression   135
    Putin's restoration of constitutional authority and legal
        unity   139
    Law reform continues under Putin   140
    Criminal procedure, the Constitutional Court and due
        process   140
    Continuing obstacles to a unified rule of law system   142
    Conclusion   146

9   Reforming the Federation   148
    Gordon Hahn

    Federalism and multi-communal states   149
    The legacy of the Soviet state and Russia's revolution from
        above   151
    Putin's federative counter-reforms   156
    Eliminating Russian federalism's asymmetry   159
    Federal–regional inter-budgetary relations   163
    Eliminating consociational mechanisms   164
    The Chechen quagmire and Putin's federative
        counter-revolution   164
    Conclusion: assessing Putin's federative reforms   166

10 Politics in the Regions   168
    Darrell Slider

    Regional political institutions   169
    Components of governors' power   172
    Putin and regional politics   174
    Local government   179
    Conclusion   182

11 Putin's Economic Record   186
    Peter Rutland

    The legacy of the Yeltsin years   187
    Putin takes the helm   190
    Economic performance   193
    An unfinished agenda   197
    Future prospects   203

12 Social Policy in Post-Soviet Russia   204
    Judy Twigg

    Poverty   205
    Crime   209
    Health and demographic concerns   211
    Education   216
    Separate and unequal   219

13 Foreign Policy   221
    Margot Light

    The domestic context of Russian foreign policy   222
    Russian policy towards the 'near abroad'   229

Russia and internal and interstate conflicts in the CIs   232
Russian policy towards the 'far abroad'   235
Conclusion   240

14   The Democratization of Russia in Comparative Perspective   241
      Zvi Gitelman

What is democracy?   242
Transition, democratization and consolidation   243
The prospects for democracy in Russia   245
Democratization in Russia in comparative perspective   251

Guide to Further Reading   257
References   263
Index   281

List of Maps, Tables and Figures

Map

Map of Russia and the former Soviet republics   xvii

Tables

1.1   Soviet and Russian leaders since 1917   2
2.1   Post-Soviet Russian presidents and prime ministers
       (including acting)   30
3.1   Factional composition of the State Duma, 1994–2004   42
3.2   Legislative activity of the State Duma, 1994–2003   51
4.1   Elections to the Russian State Duma, 1993–2003   69
5.1   Trust in parties and other institutions, 1997–2004   90
5.2   Party preferences, 1994–2004   90
5.3   Political party memberships (selected parties, 2003)   92
7.1   Patterns of media consumption, 2004   124
7.2   The major television channels   124
9.1   Russia's republics and regions (according to the 1993
       constitution)   150
11.1   The Russian central government budget, 1996–2003   189
11.2   Basic economic indicators, 1998–2003   194
13.1   Russian foreign ministers, 1990–2004   224
13.2   The Russian foreign policy decision-making process   226

Figures

2.1   Major institutions of the second-term Putin presidency   26
2.2   Major informal groups of the second-term Putin
       presidency   34
3.1   The legislative process: overview   54
3.2   The legislative process: bill introduction   54
3.3   The legislative process: three readings   55

Preface

The sixth edition of this book finds Russia, once again, at a new stage in its political development. We began life as *Developments in Soviet Politics*; soon we were *Soviet and Post-Soviet Politics*, then *Russian and Post-Soviet Politics*, and then simply *Russian Politics*. We kept the same title in the fifth and keep it again in this sixth version, but we deal with a political system that is undergoing further changes as Vladimir Putin moves into his second term, most dramatically a series of changes in the electoral and representative systems that followed a hostage-taking crisis in the North Caucasus in the late summer of 2004. For many, these and other changes have placed in question the political liberties that had been won under Mikhail Gorbachev and Boris Yeltsin, and a recurring theme in our chapters is the nature of the Putinist system: is Russia a 'democracy' (because there are competitive elections), or a hybrid 'partial democracy', or no more than a form of 'competitive authoritarianism' of a kind that exists in many developing countries and indeed in some other former republics of the USSR?

As before, we have attempted to provide an account of a changing system that covers events and institutions but goes on to explore such issues of interpretation. Reflecting a changing system, *Developments 6* has four first-time authors and three more not featured in its immediate predecessor. In some other cases, the same authors have tackled new subjects; we also welcome a new coeditor. As before, all chapters are written specially for this edition, and they draw not just on a wealth of classroom and specialist experience but upon first-hand research, some of which is reported on these pages.

We hope that all those who are familiar with earlier versions of this book will find at least as much that is of interest and value in this new edition.

STEPHEN WHITE
ZVI GITELMAN
RICHARD SAKWA

Notes on the Contributors

Alfred B. Evans, Jr is Professor of Political Science at California State University, Fresno. His publications include *Soviet Marxism–Leninism: The Decline of an Ideology* (Praeger, 1993), and more recently a coedited volume on *The Politics of Local Government in Russia* (with Vladimir Gel'man, Rowman & Littlefield, 2004). He is also an editor (with Laura Henry and Lisa McIntosh Sundstrom) of the forthcoming volume, *Change and Continuity in Russian Civil Society: A Critical Assessment*. His current research deals with local government and civil society in Russia.

Zvi Gitelman is Professor of Political Science and Preston Tisch Professor of Judaic Studies at the University of Michigan. His most recent books, all published in 2003, are (edited) *Jewish Life after the USSR* (Indiana University Press); *New Jewish Identities in Contemporary Europe* (Central European University Press); and *The Emergence of Modern Jewish Politics* (University of Pittsburgh Press).

Gordon Hahn has taught Russian domestic and foreign policy and international and comparative politics at Stanford, St Petersburg State, Boston, American, and San Jose State Universities. He is author of *Russia's Revolution from Above, 1985–2000: Reform, Transition and Revolution in the Fall of the Soviet Communist Regime* (Transaction, 2002) and has been published in numerous scholarly journals, including *Post-Soviet Affairs* and *Europe–Asia Studies*. In 2003–04, Dr Hahn was William J. Fulbright Visiting Professor at St Petersburg State University's Faculty of International Relations. His current research examines federalism, democratization, and inter-ethnic and inter-confessional relations in Russia.

Margot Light is Professor of International Relations at the London School of Economics and Political Science. Her publications include *Internal Factors in Russian Foreign Policy* (with others, Oxford University Press, 1996), and, more recently, 'US and European perspectives on Russia', in John Peterson and Mark A. Pollack (eds), *Europe, America, Bush: Transatlantic Relations in the Twenty-First Century* (Routledge, 2003), 'In Search of an Identity: Russian Foreign Policy and the End of Ideology', *Journal of Communist Studies and Transition Politics* (September 2003), and (with Stephen White and Ian McAllister) 'Enlargement and the New Outsiders', *Journal of Common Market Studies* (March 2002). Her current research is on EU and NATO relations with Russia, Belarus and Ukraine.

Michael McFaul is the Peter and Helen Senior Fellow at the Hoover Institution and an Associate Professor of Political Science at Stanford University. He is also a non-resident Senior Associate at the Carnegie Endowment for International Peace. He has coauthored, with Nikolai Petrov and Andrei Ryabov, *Between Dictatorship and Democracy: Russian Post-Communist Political Reform* (Carnegie Endowment for International Peace, 2004); with James Goldgeier, *Power and Purpose: American Policy toward Russia after the Cold War* (Brookings Institution Press, 2003); with Timothy Colton, *Popular Choice and Managed Democracy: The Russian Elections of 1999 and 2000* (Brookings Institution Press, 2003); and as coeditor, with Kathryn Stoner Weiss, *After the Collapse of Communism: Comparative Lessons of Transitions* (Cambridge University Press, 2004).

Sarah Oates is a Lecturer in Politics at the University of Glasgow, and has served as an international media analyst for elections in Russia and Kazakhstan. She was the recipient of a research fellowship from the Leverhulme Trust to conduct a cross-national study of data on media performance in elections in nine former Soviet countries, and is currently studying the framing of terrorist threats in Russian and US elections. Her publications include the coedited volume *Elections and Voters in Post-Communist Russia* (Elgar, 1998) and a forthcoming coedited collection on *Civil Society, Democracy and the Internet* as well as other studies of the mass media, elections and public opinion in postcommunist Russia.

Thomas F. Remington is Professor of Political Science and Chair of the Political Science Department at Emory University. Among his publications are two books on the Russian parliament: *The Russian Parliament: Institutional Evolution in a Transitional Regime, 1989–1999* (Yale University Press, 2001) and *The Politics of Institutional Choice: Formation of the Russian State Duma* (coauthored with Steven S. Smith) (Princeton University Press, 2001). His research focuses on the development of representative institutions in postcommunist Russia, particularly the legislative branch and legislative–executive relations.

Peter Rutland is Professor of Government at Wesleyan University in Middletown, Connecticut. He is the author of two books on Soviet planning – *The Myth of the Plan* (Hutchinson, 1985) and *The Politics of Economic Stagnation in the Soviet Union* (Cambridge University Press, 1993) – and editor most recently of *Business and the State in Contemporary Russia* (Westview Press, 2001). He writes about Russian politics and economics for the Jamestown Foundation's *Eurasia Review*.

Richard Sakwa is Professor of Russian and European Politics at the University of Kent. He has published widely on Soviet, Russian and postcommunist affairs. His recent books include *Contextualising Secession: Normative Aspects of Secession Struggles*, coedited with Bruno Coppieters (Oxford University Press, 2003), and *Putin: Russia's Choice* (Routledge, 2004). His current research interests focus on problems of democratic development and the state in Russia, the nature of postcommunism, and the global challenges facing the former communist countries.

Robert Sharlet is the Chauncey Winters Research Professor of Political Science at Union College in Schenectady, New York. He has published extensively on Russian law and politics, most recently in the forthcoming volume *Public Policy and Law in Russia* coedited with Ferdinand Feldbrugge, to which he contributed three chapters. Other recent publications include 'Russia in the Middle: State Building and the Rule of Law' in Donald R. Kelley (ed.), *After Communism: Perspectives on Democracy* (University of Askansas Press, 2003), and 'Resisting Putin's Federal Reforms on the Legal Front', *Demokratizatsiya* (2003). He is presently working on Russian constitutional politics under Yeltsin and Putin.

Darrell Slider is Professor of Government and International Affairs at the University of South Florida, Tampa. In 2004–05 he was a Visiting Fulbright Professor at the Higher School of Economics in Moscow. For the last ten years most of Dr Slider's research has centred on regional politics and federalism in Russia; his publications include *The Politics of Transition* (co-authored with Stephen White and Graeme Gill, Cambridge University Press, 1993), and contributions to *Slavic Review*, *Europe–Asia Studies* and other journals.

Judy Twigg is Associate Professor of Political Science and Director of Undergraduate Programs at the L. Douglas Wilder School of Government and Public Affairs at Virginia Commonwealth University, Richmond. Her research interests include social and health policy in the Russian Federation, with a particular interest in health system restructuring and medical insurance reform. She is the coeditor of *Russia's Torn Safety Nets: Health and Social Welfare during the Transition* (with Mark Field, Macmillan, 2000), and *Social Capital and Social Cohesion in Post-Soviet Russia* (with Kate Schecter, Sharpe, 2003). She recently completed an evaluation for the World Bank of its efforts to assist Russia in its fight against HIV/AIDS, and advises the US government on an array of Russian health and social issues.

Stephen White is Professor of International Politics and a Senior Research Associate of the School of Central and East European Studies at the University of Glasgow, and Visiting Professor at the Institute of Applied Politics in Moscow. He was President of the British Association for

Slavonic and East European Studies in 1994–97, and is chief editor of the *Journal of Communist Studies and Transition Politics*. His recent publications include *Russia's New Politics* (Cambridge University Press, 2000), *The Soviet Elite from Lenin to Gorbachev* (with Evan Mawdsley, Oxford University Press, 2000), and *Postcommunist Belarus* (coedited with Elena Korosteleva and John Lowenhardt, Rowman & Littlefield, 2005). He is currently working on the implications of EU and NATO enlargement for Russia, Ukraine and Belarus, and on patterns of political disengagement within and beyond the region.

John P. Willerton is Associate Professor of Political Science at the University of Arizona, Tucson. He is the author of *Patronage and Politics in the USSR* (Cambridge University Press, 1992) and three dozen articles and chapters dealing with various facets of Soviet and post-Soviet Russian domestic politics and foreign policy, including recent contributions to the *Journal of Politics* and *International Politics*. His current research focuses on post-Soviet political elites, the Russian federal executive, and Russia's relations with the Commonwealth of Independent States and former Soviet Union countries.

List of Abbreviations

ABM	Anti-Ballistic Missile Treaty (1972)
BMD	Ballistic missile defence
CFE	Conventional Forces in Europe treaty
CIS	Commonwealth of Independent States
CPRF	Communist Party of the Russian Federation
CPSU	Communist Party of the Soviet Union
CSTO	Collective Security Treaty Organization
EU	European Union
FO	Federal district
FSB	Federal Security Service
GDP	Gross domestic product
GUUAM	Treaty embracing Georgia, Ukraine, Uzbekistan, Azerbaijan and Moldova
IMF	International Monetary Fund
KGB	Soviet security police
LDPR	Liberal Democratic Party of Russia
MFA	Ministry of Foreign Affairs
MVD	Ministry of Internal Affairs
NATO	North Atlantic Treaty Organization
NDR	Our Home is Russia party
NMD	National missile defence
OSCE	Organization for Security and Cooperation in Europe
OVR	Fatherland–All Russia party
PCA	Partnership and Cooperation Agreement
PR	Proportional representation
RSFSR	Russian Soviet Federative Socialist Republic
SPS	Union of Right Forces
UNAIDS	United Nations lead agency on AIDS
USSR	Union of Soviet Socialist Republics
WTO	World Trade Organization

Glossary

Duma	Lower house of Federal Assembly (parliament)
Glasnost	Openness, publicity
Ispolkom	Executive committee
Kompromat	Smear tactics
Komsomol	Young Communist League
Krai	Territory
Matryoshka	'Nested-doll'
Nomenklatura	List of party-controlled posts
Oblast	Region, province
Perestroika	Restructuring
Politburo	Key decision-making body in the Communist Party
Polpred	Envoy
Praktik(i)	Practical worker(s), persons(s)
Raion	District
Sobranie	Assembly
Zemskii sobor	Assembly of nobility, clergy and merchants

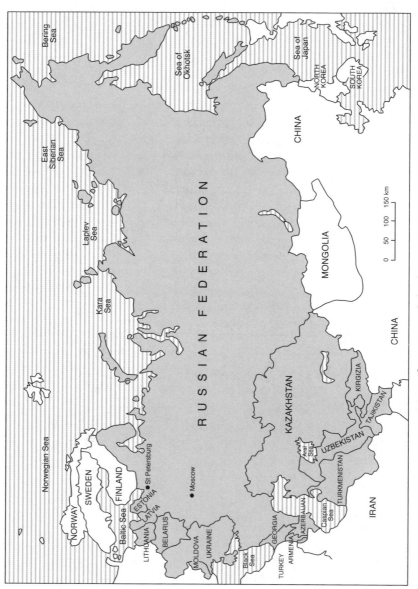

Map of Russia and the former Soviet republics

Chapter 1

Politics in Russia

RICHARD SAKWA

Democratization in Russia has endured a troubled journey since the country became an independent state on the dissolution of the USSR at the end of 1991. No one thought that it would be easy to create the institutions of representative democracy and the rule of law, together with the mechanisms of market capitalism and national cohesion, but few could have anticipated quite how difficult these processes would be. The formal establishment of democratic institutions, symbolized above all by the adoption of a new constitution in December 1993, was the relatively easy part. Making them work and imbuing them with the spirit of legality, accountability and pluralism is something else. Russia's postcommunist development has been marked by some spectacular failures, yet overall the picture is not quite so bleak as some would suggest. This chapter will present an overview of political developments in the recent past, and suggest some ways of evaluating the contemporary situation.

Russia enters the new millennium

Russia has been undergoing a complex process of accelerated political change for over two decades. The appointment of a reforming General Secretary of the Communist Party of the Soviet Union (CPSU) in March 1985 set in motion changes whose outcome is still not clear. Mikhail Gorbachev came to power with a clear vision that the old way of governing the Soviet Union could no longer continue, but his plans for change swiftly came up against some hard realities. He achieved some significant success in democratizing the Soviet system, but by 1991 the communist order was dissolving and the country disintegrating.

The dominant rule of the Communist Party had been established by Vladimir Ilich Lenin soon after coming to power in October 1917, and for Lenin (once victory in the Civil War of 1918–20 was assured) development became the priority of Soviet power rather than more general emancipatory goals. For Joseph Stalin, who after a struggle following Lenin's

1

death in 1924 achieved dictatorial power, accelerated industrialization became the overriding aim, accompanied by the intensification of coercion that peaked in the terror of the late 1930s. Victory in the Great Patriotic War of 1941–45 over Nazi Germany and its allies appeared to vindicate all the sacrifices of the early Soviet period, yet the prevalence of terror remained. A first step towards de-Stalinization was taken following Stalin's death in 1953 by his successor, Nikita Khrushchev, in his 'Secret Speech' of February 1956 at the Twentieth Party Congress. Khrushchev provided a devastating critique of Stalin himself but failed to give a systemic critique of how he had been able to commit so many crimes for so long.

During the long reign of Leonid Brezhnev (1964–82) the question of the political renewal of the Soviet system was placed firmly on the back burner. The attempt to renew the communist system by establishing a more humane and democratic form of socialism in Czechoslovakia in 1968 was crushed by Soviet tanks in August of that year. Instead, the last years of Brezhnev's rule gave way to what later was called a period of stagnation (*zastoi*) as the high hopes of the period of détente with the West

Table 1.1   *Soviet and Russian leaders since 1917*

Date	Name of leader
1917–24	Vladimir Ilich Lenin (Chairman of the Council of People's Commissars or prime minister, and also de facto party leader until his death in January 1924)
1924–53	Iosif (Joseph) Vissarionovich Stalin (General Secretary of the Communist Party from 1922 and de facto leader from the late 1920s; also prime minister from 1941 until his death)
1953–64	Nikita Sergeevich Khrushchev (First Secretary of the Communist Party and also prime minister after 1958)
1964–82	Leonid Ilich Brezhnev (First, later General Secretary of the Communist Party, and from 1977 Chairman of the USSR Supreme Soviet Presidium or de facto head of state)
1982–84	Yuri Vladimirovich Andropov (General Secretary of the Communist Party and Chairman of the USSR Supreme Soviet Presidium)
1984–85	Konstantin Ustinovich Chernenko (General Secretary of the Communist Party and Chairman of the USSR Supreme Soviet Presidium)
1985–91	Mikhail Sergeevich Gorbachev (General Secretary of the Communist Party and also successively Chairman of the USSR Supreme Soviet Presidium, Chairman of the USSR Supreme Soviet and USSR president)
1991–99	Boris Nikolaevich Yeltsin (RSFSR and later Russian president, re-elected 1996 but resigned prematurely at the end of 1999)
2000–	Vladimir Vladimirovich Putin (prime minister 1999–2000, acting president and then from March 2000 Russian president; reelected in 2004)

gave way to an intensified and extremely dangerous renewed phase of the Cold War.

With his quick mind and political flexibility, Gorbachev was clearly a contender for top office. In 1979 he achieved candidate membership of the Politburo and full membership in 1980, and he was one of the nation's top figures when Brezhnev died in November 1982. Following the brief leadership of Yuri Andropov until February 1984, the Brezhnevite Konstantin Chernenko managed to hang on to power for a brief period despite many illnesses, with Gorbachev effectively acting as second in command. Chernenko's death in March 1985 finally allowed a new generation to assume the reins of leadership.

Gorbachev did not come to power with a clear set of policies; but he did have an attitude towards change to which he remained loyal to the bitter end. Gorbachev was convinced that the communist system could not continue to manage the economy and society in the old way, and he intended to achieve its modernization through a process that he called *perestroika* (restructuring). For him the aim was not to transcend the Soviet system but to achieve its reform. He had no detailed blueprint about how this was to be achieved, but he knew it had to be done. In the economic sphere he got off on the wrong foot right away: the policy of acceleration (*uskorenie*) sought to achieve economic transformation and increased output at the same time, and in the event was unable to gain the long-term achievement of either. This was accompanied by an anti-alcohol campaign that deprived the country of nearly one-third of its tax revenues. Soon after came *glasnost* (openness), intended at first not to be freedom of speech but to be used as a way of exposing the failings of a corrupt bureaucracy, and thus to strengthen the Soviet system. However, *glasnost* soon became a devastating search for the truth about Leninist and Stalinist repression and took on a life of its own, escaping from the instrumental constraints that Gorbachev had at first intended.

Gorbachev's own views about the past were filtered through a romantic Leninism, believing in an allegedly more democratic and evolutionary late Leninist model of the New Economic Policy of the 1920s. By the end of 1987 democratization came to the fore, with the gradual introduction of multi-candidate elections accompanied by a relaxation of the Leninist rule against the formation of groups in the Communist Party. Gorbachev's own views at this time were eloquently developed in his book *Perestroika: New Thinking for Our Country and the World* (1987), in which he talked of *perestroika* as a revolution both from above and from below. The 'from below' element was by now taking hold in the form of thousands of 'informal' associations, representing the rebirth of an independent civil society.

The changes begun by Gorbachev began to outrun his ability to control them. The high point of Gorbachev's hopes that a humane and democratic socialism could replace the moribund system that he inherited was the Nineteenth Party Conference in June–July 1988, where he outlined a programme of democratic political change and a new role for the USSR in the world. Soon after institutional changes weakened the role of the party apparatus, and constitutional changes later in the year created a new two-tier parliament, with a large Congress of People's Deputies meeting twice a year and selecting a working Supreme Soviet. The first elections to this body took place in March 1989, and revealed the depths of the unpopularity of party rule. The early debates of the parliament riveted the nation, as problems were openly discussed for the first time in decades. The Congress stripped the Communist Party of its constitutionally entrenched 'leading role' in March 1990, and at the same time Gorbachev was elected to the newly created post of president of the USSR. His failure to stand in a national ballot is often considered one of his major mistakes. Lacking a popular mandate, he was sidelined by those who did – above all Boris Yeltsin, who became chair of the Russian Congress of People's Deputies in May 1990 and then went on to win a popular ballot in June 1991 to become Russia's first president.

What was called the 'nationalities question' now began to threaten the integrity of the country. Although Gorbachev was responsive to calls for greater autonomy by the fifteen union republics that made up the Union of Soviet Socialist Republics (USSR), he had no time for any talk of independence. Through an increasingly desperate attempt to negotiate a new union treaty, Gorbachev hoped to transform what was in effect a unitary state into a genuinely confederal community of nations. These hopes were dashed by Lithuania's declaration of independence in 1990, followed by that of Georgia and other republics in 1991. In foreign affairs Gorbachev advanced the idea of 'new political thinking', based on the notion of interdependence and a cooperative rather than confrontational relationship with the West. On a visit to the European Parliament in Strasbourg in September 1988 he talked of the establishment of a 'common European home', but it was not clear what form this would take. By 1989 the East European countries in the Soviet bloc took Gorbachev at his word when he called for change, and from later that year, one after another, their communist regimes fell. Gorbachev facilitated the unification of Germany, although he is much criticized for failing to guarantee in treaty form the demilitarized status of the eastern part of the new country.

At home resistance to his aims and his policies grew to the point that a group prepared to seize power in a coup. The specific issue was the planned signing of the new union treaty on 20 August 1991, but the plotters were also concerned about economic disintegration and the loss of political control. For three days in August (19–21) Gorbachev was isolated in his dacha in Foros in the Crimea, while his nemesis, Yeltsin, emerged much strengthened. In the days following the coup Yeltsin put an end to communist rule by banning the party in Russia. Attempts to save the Soviet Union in the last months of 1991 failed. The pressure for increased sovereignty for republics grew into demands for independence, and following the creation of the Commonwealth of Independent States (CIS) on 7–8 December comprising Russia, Ukraine and Belarus, the USSR was clearly on its last legs. The CIS was broadened on 21 December to include the other former Soviet republics, apart from the Baltic republics and Georgia. Gorbachev formally resigned as president on 25 December 1991, and on 31 December the USSR formally ceased to exist.

Gorbachev's reform of the Soviet system provoked its demise. The debate over whether the Soviet Union could have been reformed while remaining recognizably communist continues to this day (see, for instance, Cohen 2004). Gorbachev's *perestroika* clearly showed the system's evolutionary potential, but this was an evolution that effectively meant the peaceful transcendence of the system it was meant to save. The fundamental question remains whether Gorbachev's reforms were a success or a failure. The issue depends on the definition of both. In one sense, they were a triumphant success. By 1991 the country had become relatively democratic, it was moving towards becoming a market economy, the union was changing into a community of sovereign states, and the Cold War had been overcome largely by Gorbachev's efforts. However, the terminal crisis of the system in 1991 revealed deep structural flaws in Gorbachev's conception of reform and in the system's capacity for change while remaining recognizably communist in orientation.

Gorbachev remained remarkably consistent in his commitment to a humane democratic socialism with a limited market in a renewed federation of Soviet states. However, his attempts to constrain the process of change within the framework of his preconceived notions soon collided against some harsh realities: the aspirations for independence in a number of republics, notably of Estonia, Latvia and Lithuania, forcibly incorporated into the USSR by Stalin; the inherent instability of a semi-marketized system – it either had to be one thing or another, a planned or a market economy; and ultimately the lack of popular support for any socialism, irrespective of how humane or democratic it may have been. The attempt to reform the Soviet system brought into the open its many contradictions, and these ultimately brought the whole system crashing down.

The politics of independent Russia

Russia emerged as an independent and sovereign state in 1991. The

Yeltsin administration was committed to Russia becoming a democratic market state allied with the advanced Western nations and integrated into the world economy. There was far less agreement, however, on how these three goals – democratization, marketization and international integration – were to be achieved. Bitter debates raged throughout the 1990s over all three, and aspects of these controversies will be discussed in later chapters of this book. On one thing, however, there was broad agreement: the borders of the Russia that emerged as an independent state in 1991 should not be changed, however unfair and arbitrary many considered them to be. Some 25 million ethnic Russians found themselves scattered across the fourteen other newly independent states, yet Yeltsin's refusal to exploit the real and imagined grievances of the Russian diaspora to gain cheap political capital must forever stand as one of his major achievements. Politics in the postcommunist era would be *in Russia*, and not in some mythical reestablished Soviet Union in whatever guise.

The nature of these *politics* is less clear. For the first two years following independence Russian politics was wracked by the struggle to adopt a new constitution (Andrews 2002). The two-tier parliament that Russia inherited from the Soviet Union was clearly an unworkable arrangement, and ultimately provoked an armed confrontation between the Congress of People's Deputies and the president in October 1993. The constitution was finally adopted in December 1993, and has given Russia a degree of political stability ever since. Politics moved off the streets and into constitutional channels. Although the constitution is a fundamentally liberal document, proclaiming a range of freedoms that would be expected of a liberal democratic state, the balance drawn in the separation of powers between the parliament and president remains controversial. The presidency emerged as the guarantor not only of the constitutional order, but also of a reform process that under Yeltsin was driven forwards with a single-mindedness that at times threatened to undermine democracy itself (Reddaway and Glinski 2001). This was most vividly in evidence when it came to elections. Fearing that neo-communists and other opponents of moves towards the market and international integration would come to power in the 1996 presidential elections, some in Yeltsin's entourage urged him to cancel the elections altogether. In the event, although in ill health, he won a second term and dominated politics to the end of the decade.

Although Yeltsin formally remained committed to Russia's democratic development, there were features of his rule that undermined the achievement of his ambition. The first was the unhealthy penetration of economic interests into the decision-making process. Rapid and chaotic privatization from the early 1990s gave birth to a new class of powerful economic magnates, colloquially known as oligarchs. Their support for

Yeltsin's reelection in 1996 brought them into the centre of the political process, and gave rise to the creation of what was known as the 'family', a mix of Yeltsin family members, politicians and oligarchs. Most notorious of them was Boris Berezovsky, who effectively used political influence as a major economic resource. Many others at this time could exploit insider knowledge to gain economic assets for a fraction of their real worth. It was in these years that the empires of Mikhail Khodorkovsky (preeminently the Yukos oil company), Roman Abramovich (with Berezovsky, at the head of the Sibneft oil company), Vladimir Potanin at the head of Norilsk Nickel, Vladimir Gusinsky at the head of the Media-Most empire, and many others were built. Their heyday were the years between the presidential election of 1996 and the partial default of August 1998, and thereafter oligarchical power as such waned although as individuals they remained important political players.

The second feature was the exaggerated power of the presidency as an institution. Granted extensive authority by the 1993 constitution as part of a deliberate institutional design to ensure adequate powers for the executive to drive through reform, the presidency lacked adequate constraints and accountability. Too many decisions were taken by small groups of unaccountable individuals around the presidency, notably in the case of the decision to launch the first Chechen war in December 1994. We will return to this question below, but associated with that is the third problem, the weakness of mechanisms of popular accountability. Although far from powerless, the Duma (see Chapter 3) was not able effectively to hold the executive to account. This is related to the weakness of the development of the party system (see Chapter 5). The fourth issue is the question of the succession. While all incumbent leaders try to perpetuate their power or to ensure a transfer to favourable successors, in Yeltsin's case the stakes were particularly high: he feared that a new president could mean a change of system in its entirety, with the possibility of personal sanctions being taken against him and his family. For this reason the Kremlin engaged in a long search for a successor who would be able to ensure continuity and the personal inviolability of Russia's first president and his family. They found this guarantee in the person of Vladimir Putin, nominated prime minister on 9 August 1999, acting president from Yeltsin's resignation on 31 December, formally elected to a first term on 14 March 2000, and to a second term on 14 March 2004.

Russia entered the twenty-first century and the new millennium a very different country from the one that had entered the twentieth. The tsarist empire had disintegrated, the autocracy had been overthrown, the Soviet communist system had been and gone, and the USSR had also disintegrated leaving fifteen independent republics. Independent Russia was for the first time developing as a nation state rather than as an empire; its economy was severely distorted by the Soviet attempt to establish a planned economy and by the subsequent privatization of the 1990s with its oligarchs; and the country was engaged in an extraordinary act of political reconstitution intended to establish a liberal democratic system. The key point is that politics, defined as the procedural contest for political power accompanied by a public sphere of debate, criticism and information exchange, had come to Russia. Whether the so-called transition had actually achieved democracy is another question, and one to which we will now turn.

The transition and regime type

The scope of transformation in the postcommunist world has been unprecedented. Monolithic societies are being converted into pluralistic ones, economies are being reoriented towards the market, new nations are being born, and states are rejoining the international community. Since 1989 the countries themselves and the scholars studying them have accumulated a wealth of experience, much of it hard and painful, about the problems of transition. The actual course of transformation proved more complex than was assumed in the early postcommunist days. The reform process itself generated new phenomena that raise questions about the received wisdom of the political and social sciences. There has been rapid divergence in the fate of postcommunist countries, with the majority of Central and East European countries joining the European Union in May 2004, while the twelve former Soviet states grouped in the CIS look ever more different from each other. At one extreme thoroughly authoritarian systems operate in Turkmenistan and Uzbekistan, while at the other Russia and Ukraine remain engaged in what is recognizably a transition agenda – the establishment of the legal and practical arrangements of a market economy and the development of the normative and juridical framework of constitutional democracy.

The 'third wave' transitions, to use Huntington's (1991) term to describe the mass extinction of authoritarian regimes since the fall of the dictatorship in Portugal in 1974, prompted a renewed interest in problems of democratization. The fall of communism encouraged political scientists to look again at the theoretical literature on democratization and to compare the current transitions in the former communist bloc with earlier transitions in Latin America and Southern Europe. The insights garnered in the study of the democratization process elsewhere provide a theoretical framework to study the problem of the reconstitution of central political authority on principles of democratic accountability. The degree to which this literature has anything to offer when political regime change is accompanied by economic transformation, state and nation building and societal reconstruction remains a moot point (Bunce 1995, 2003).

The view that democracy is the inevitable outcome of postcommunist transition is clearly mistaken. There is far too much that is contingent in processes of systemic change to allow any firm teleological view to be convincing. While about a hundred countries have set out on the path of democracy during the 'third wave', at most three dozen have achieved functioning democracies (Carothers 2002). The contrary view – that the legacy of communist and even precommunist authoritarian political cultures, economies and social structures doom the attempt to build democracies where there had at best been weak traditions of pluralism, toleration and political competition – is equally wrong. Deterministic views of democratization leave out of the account national political cultures, levels of economic development, strategic concerns, leadership choices and elite configurations, economic dependencies, and proximity to zones of advanced capitalist democratic development (above all the European Union). Robert Dahl's preference for the term 'polyarchy' rather than 'democracy' recognizes the problem of making democracy an absolute (Dahl 1971). Questions of political order, constitutionalism, state building, social structure and social justice must play their part in any discussion of democratization, together with the practice of democratic norms and good governance. Despite the best efforts of political scientists, there is no agreement on one single factor that determines the success or failure of a democratization process.

The relationship between liberalism, democracy and constitutional order remains contested in a postcommunist context. Some of Putin's supporters have seized on the argument that security should come before democracy. Russia, they suggest, should not be expected to achieve a high-quality democracy, given its authoritarian past, its political culture and the weakness of civil society. Immediately following the Beslan school massacre of September 2004, Putin's speech announcing a range of reforms to the state system, including the appointment of governors and wholly proportional parliamentary elections, was seen as reflecting this strategy of authoritarian modernization. The best that Russia can do at this point is to be satisfied with some form of 'managed democracy' – at least, so the supporters of this approach argue, the country remains a democracy, however limited. This is not an argument that is satisfactory in the long run. One reason is the lack of contemporary legitimacy for developmental discourses or for those suggesting that 'order' must take priority over democracy. Russians and others who have lived in the shadow of authoritarian regimes are well aware how often the notion of 'order' can be used to subvert political freedom. Unless elites and political leaders strive for genuinely liberal, democratic and constitutional rule, there is no knowing where the back-sliding will end.

The question of the quality of democracy is particularly acute in Russia, where the very 'givenness' of a structured society is in question. Implicit in many discussions is the view that in the transition from authoritarianism to democracy, society can spring back into shape; whereas in the transition from totalitarianism, society is destroyed to such a degree that it has to become an object of the transition process itself. This tends to justify the displacement of sovereignty from the people to some agency that can carry out the necessary transitional measures. In the Russian case this was the elite group around Yeltsin, and under Putin the institutions of the administrative system.

Regime and administered democracy

It has become popular to call Russia a 'managed democracy', and there are undoubtedly elements of this, although the system remains flexible and open-ended enough to suggest that while the democracy may be managed, it retains a democratic core. To help characterize the present system we will first look at two substantive approaches before providing our own analysis of the system.

Fareed Zakaria distinguishes between *liberal* democracy, defined as 'a political system marked not only by free and fair elections, but also by the rule of law, a separation of powers, and the protection of basic liberties of speech, assembly, religion and property', what he calls constitutional liberalism, and *illiberal* democracy. In the latter, 'Democratically elected regimes, often ones that have been reelected or reaffirmed through referenda, are routinely ignoring constitutional limits on their power and depriving their citizens of basic rights and freedoms' (1997: 23). For Zakaria, the regular staging of relatively fair, competitive, multiparty elections might make a country democratic, but it does not ensure good governance. In practice, even relatively free elections 'have resulted in strong executives, weak legislatures and judiciaries, and few civil and economic liberties' (1997: 28). In a later work Zakaria (2003) developed his argument that while constitutional liberalism can lead to democracy, democracy does not necessarily lead to constitutional liberalism. The Central European postcommunist states are negotiating the passage to democracy more successfully than the former Soviet states, it is argued, because they went through a long phase of liberalization without democracy in the nineteenth century that grounded the rule of law and property rights into social practices.

In a similar vein, Giullermo O'Donnell has argued that in weakly established democracies a leader can become so strong that he or she can ignore those whom they are meant to represent. O'Donnell characterizes these countries as having 'delegative' rather than representative democracy, with the electorate allegedly having delegated to the executive the right to do what it sees fit, 'constrained only by the hard facts of existing power relations and by a constitutionally limited term of office' (1994: 59). Thus a government emerges that is 'inherently hostile to the patterns of representation normal in established democracies' by 'depoliticising the population except for brief moments in which it demands its plebiscitary support' (O'Donnell 1993: 1367). This sort of democracy is, according to O'Donnell, underinstitutionalized,

> characterised by the restricted scope, the weakness, and the low density of whatever political institutions exist. The place of well-functioning institutions is taken by other nonformalized but strongly operative practices – clientelism, patrimonialism, and corruption. (O'Donnell 1994: 59)

The notion of delegative democracy has clear application to Russia, and has been used fruitfully in analysing regional politics. However, the concept has limitations when applied to the post-Soviet world. Although the powers of the executive everywhere have been enhanced, these are not classical presidentialist regimes of the Latin American type although they do share some of the characteristics of Latin American *democraduras* ('hard democracies'). Politics in Russia is too unstructured, institutions too fluid, and the personages too constrained by the emerging class system, ethnic contradictions and regional forces to allow the full delegation of authority.

In terms of regime type Russia is a semi-presidential democracy, but this does not tell us much about how the constitution works in practice. The entwining of institutional and personal factors in a weak constitutional order and underdeveloped civil society gave rise to the dominance of a power system centred on the presidency that relies on administrative ways of managing conflict and of reducing the uncertainty engendered by the electoral process. Decisions and leadership do not emerge out of the untrammelled operation of politics but out of an administrative elite positioned between state and society. This is what we call regime politics.

Russia's fledgling democracy is characterized by the gulf between a system with a constitution and one governed by genuine constitutionalism. According to Max Weber (1995), Russia's 1906 constitution represented sham constitutionalism in that it was not able effectively to establish accountable government. Even less effective in this respect were the various Soviet constitutions of 1918, 1924, 1936 and 1977, since they signally failed to define and thus to limit the powers of the leadership. They were pseudo-constitutions since they did not even attempt to fulfil the classic functions of a constitution, let alone foster the practices of constitutionalism (that is, the impartial exercise of the rule of law, limited government and a division of powers). Russia's 1993 constitution finally does what a constitution is supposed to do: establish the basic principles of the polity, define the roles of the institutions of government, and entrench the practice of the rule of law. At the heart of the idea of modern constitutionalism is the separation of powers, and this is indeed embedded in the 1993 document, although this separation in various aspects is unbalanced.

The contrast between the informal relations of power established within the framework of regime politics, on the one hand, and the institutionalized competitive and accountable politics characteristic of a genuinely constitutional democratic state, on the other, is typical of many countries in the postcommunist era. In Russia, as elsewhere, particularistic informal practices have been in tension with the proclaimed principles of the universal and impartial prerogatives of a constitutional state. Under Yeltsin personalized leadership came to the fore, with the administrative regime and its oligarchic allies operating largely independently of the formal rules of the political system, whose main structural features were outlined in the constitution. Behind the formal façade of democratic politics conducted at the level of the state, the regime considered itself largely free of genuine democratic accountability and popular oversight. These features, as Hahn (2002) stresses, were accentuated by the high degree of institutional and personal continuity between the Soviet and postcommunist systems, a finding confirmed by Kryshtanovskaya and White's research (1996, 2003). While a party-state ruled up to 1991, the emergence of a presidential state in the 1990s fostered the creation of a system that perpetuated in new forms some of the arbitrariness of the old order. Both the administrative regime and the constitutional state succumbed to clientelist pressures exerted by powerful interests in society, some of whom (above all the so-called oligarchs) had been spawned by the regime itself.

Instead of government being accountable to the representative institutions of the people and constrained by the constitutional state and its legal instruments, the government assumes an independent political existence. It is at this point that a politically responsible and accountable government becomes a regime; formal institutions are unable to constrain political actors and informal practices predominate (North 1990). In Russia the *administrative regime* can be contrasted with the *constitutional state*. The outward forms of the constitutional state are preserved, but legality and accountability are subverted. In an administrative regime a set of para-constitutional behavioural norms predominate that while perhaps not formally violating the letter of the constitution undermine the spirit of constitutionalism. Para-constitutional behaviour gets things done, but ultimately proves counterproductive because it relies on the mechanical armoury of leadership politics rather than the self-sustaining practices of a genuinely constitutional system. The regime is constrained by the constitutional state but the system lacks effective mechanism of accountability.

Politics in Russia today

The attempt to characterize regime type only gets us so far. It is undoubtedly important to provide some sort of handy label to mark down a system, and it has become part of the staple of transition studies, where there is a great proliferation of 'democracy with adjectives' (Collier and Levitsky 1997). The concept of 'managed democracy' is just one of several hundred terms that have been applied to describe the realities of postcommunist Russian politics. However, this approach remains relatively passive and tends to homogenize the complexity of political processes. Contemporary Russia is characterized by a number of competing, and not always compatible, strategies of ruling groups, with the advocates of 'managed democracy' being no more than one group among many (Bjorkman 2003: 61). The administration remains torn between various approaches, and thus to apply the concept of 'managed democracy' as a single encompassing ideology of a single united ruling elite misses far too much of the complex reality of contemporary Russian politics to be convincing.

For Fish, Russia's 'low-caliber democracy' is a result of a particular institutional design, namely an excessively strong executive that he and others call 'super-presidential' (Fish 2001). The regime in Russia is focused on the presidency but is broader than the post of president itself. The regime system can be seen as a dynamic set of relationships that include the president, the various factions in the presidential administration, the government (the prime minister and the various ministries), and the informal links with various powerful oligarchs, regional bosses and other favoured insiders. The so-called 'family' represented the dominant faction in the regime under Yeltsin; under Putin the *Pitertsy* (those from his hometown of St Petersburg) were brought in to establish a power base of his own. The *Pitertsy* in turn are divided between the *chekisty* (the representatives of the security apparatus), lawyers and liberal economists.

Our model of Putin's presidency suggests that it is caught between the constitutional state and the administrative regime, and seeks to draw on the resources of both to retain its own freedom of manoeuvre and independence as a political actor. It is for this reason that Putin's administration appears always to have two faces. On the one hand, Putin appeals to the 'dictatorship of law' and the unimpeded writ of the constitution throughout the country, something used to reduce the autonomy of regional governors (see Chapter 8). On the other hand, Putin was not averse to using the whole range of instruments at the disposal of the administrative regime to consolidate his rule and to achieve his government's goals. Too often neo-Soviet methods were used to achieve post-Soviet goals. In his attempt to reduce the power of over-mighty subjects, above all regional bosses and oligarchs, Putin was in danger of re-establishing an over-mighty state.

A presidential regime system allows great room for manoeuvre for the chief executive and, paradoxically, can foster the development of the autonomy of the constitutional state. This at least was the philosophy that underpinned the establishment in 1958 of the Gaullist Fifth Republic in France, and Putin himself acknowledged de Gaulle as one of his role models (Putin 2000: 194). The presidency under Putin sought to free itself from societal pressures (above all in the form of oligarchs, regional barons and parliamentary faction leaders) by appealing to the normative framework of the constitution. The framers of the Russian constitution had quite explicitly drawn on the experience of the Fifth Republic in France, and thus it was not surprising that a Gaullist system (which itself is in the Bonapartist tradition) emerged in Russia. However, unlike in France, where there is the possibility of flipping between parliamentary and presidential predominance (cohabitation), in Russia such a rotation is far more difficult, although theoretically not impossible and elements of this were seen during the premiership of Yevgenii Primakov between September 1998 and May 1999. Russian-style Gaullism perpetuates some traditional Soviet patterns in which the relationship between the state and administration is based on an exclusive claim to expertise.

Putin was able to reduce some aspects of state capture by reasserting the constitutional prerogatives of the state (what he called the 'dictatorship of law'), a project that we call the reconstitution of the state: the attempt to reassert the prerogatives of the constitutional state *vis-à-vis* the administrative regime. In pursuing a policy of reconstitution by reasserting state autonomy from societal actors, Putin at the same time sought to reassert the political independence of the presidency from the informal practices of the administrative regime. This twofold struggle for autonomy was intended to be mutually reinforcing: a constitutional state would be crowned by a free president defending the universal application of constitutional norms.

From the very first days of his presidency Putin drew on constitutional resources to reaffirm the prerogatives of the state *vis-à-vis* segmented regional regimes and the excesses of oligarchical capitalism. The selective (although not arbitrary) approach to the abuses of the Yeltsin era, the attack on segmented regionalism that threatened to undermine the development of federalism, and the apparent lack of understanding of the values of media freedom and human rights suggested that Putin's reforms could become a general assault on the principles of federalism and democratic freedom. The struggle for the universal application of the rule of law, however, threatened to intensify at the federal level the lawlessness that characterized so much of regional government. Yeltsin's personalized regime represented a threat to the state, but its very diffuseness and encouragement of asymmetrical federalism allowed a profusion of media, regional and other freedoms to survive.

Putin's statism carries both a positive and a negative charge: the strengthening of the rule of law was clearly long overdue; but enhancing the powers of the administrative regime and the presidency was not the same as strengthening the constitutional rule of law. The weakening of the federal pillar of the separation of powers was not likely to enhance the defence of freedom as a whole. The rhetoric of the defence of constitutional norms and the uniform application of law throughout the country threatens the development of a genuine federal separation of powers, media and informational freedoms, and establishes a new type of hegemonic party system in which patronage and preference are disbursed by a neo-*nomenklatura* class of state officials. There were many indications that United Russia sought to become the core of a new patronage system of the type that in July 2000 was voted out of office in Mexico after 71 years. The key test is whether the revived presidency will itself become subordinate to the new emphasis on 'the dictatorship of law', and thus encourage the development of a genuinely ordered rule of law state; or whether it will attempt to remain outside of politics and thus once again perpetuate the traditions of displaced sovereignty and sham constititutionalism.

While the presidency under Putin sought to carve out greater room for manoeuvre, Putin was hesitant to subordinate the administrative regime entirely to the imperatives of the constitutional order or to the vagaries of the popular representative system (elections). Yeltsin earlier had feared that the untrammelled exercise of democracy could lead to the wrong result, the election of a communist government that would undo the work of building market democracy, threaten Russia's neighbours in pursuit of the dream of the reunification of the USSR, and antagonize the country's Western partners. The dilemma was not an unreal one, and reflected the administrative regime's view that the Russian people had not yet quite matured enough to be trusted with democracy. A neo-traditional type of paternalism replaced the purposiveness that had characterized the Bolshevik and early Yeltsin years. However, we know that whenever the military acts against democracy as the 'saviour of the nation' the results are usually the opposite of those intended. The administrative regime stymied the development of an independent political order robust enough to allow the autonomous operation of democratic constitutional norms.

In a constitutional state the activist presidency would itself be constrained, and all history demonstrates that such an act of subordination is not normally voluntary but derives from the constraining effect of conflicts within the political elite or from the pressure of social forces. Putin's state-building project, following the French Jacobin tradition of establishing a homogeneous legal space and the universal application of governmental norms, sought only ambivalently to achieve the associated development of the republican concept of an active citizenry. Putin's sovereignty struggles – restoring the autonomy of the constitutional state, challenging the autonomy of regional bosses, weakening the ability of economic magnates to impose their preferences on the government, and freeing the presidency from the administrative regime – neglected one important element: the sovereignty of the people in a federal state.

Conclusion

A democratic transition is usually considered to be over when democracy becomes the only game in town and where there is 'definiteness of rules and indefiniteness of outcomes'. According to Kulik (2001) Russia's transition is indeed over, but instead of democratic consolidation Russia's 'managed democracy' has reversed the formula to ensure 'definiteness of outcomes and indefiniteness of rules'. This is true to a degree, but the scope for democratic development in Russia remains open. The government does seek to deliver a set of public goods, and it does not appeal to an extra-democratic logic to achieve them. The regime is legitimate precisely because it claims to be democratic. Putin's government is undoubtedly considered legitimate by the great majority of the Russian people, as evidenced by the December 2003 Duma elections and his reelection in March 2004, together with his consistently high personal ratings throughout his first term, although painful social reforms in the second undermined his popularity. Whether the system is becoming an illiberal or delegative democracy is more contentious. Too much is settled not in the framework of competitive politics but within the confines of the administrative regime, leaving the administration only weakly accountable to society and its representatives. Nevertheless, the sinews of constitutionality are developing, and politics is not yet entirely subsumed into the administrative order.

This leaves us with the question: is Russia a liberal democracy? The answer is far from unambiguous. The power that was lost by the communist system in 1991 was not effectively gained by the people, and instead a reconfigured elite came to the fore. A new democratic equilibrium has not yet replaced the equilibrium destroyed in the course of Gorbachev's reforms from 1985. Liberal freedoms have been introduced and are defended (however fitfully) by the rudiments of a system of the rule of law and constitutionalism. The quality of the democracy, however, has gone little further than the basic Schumpeterian version of electoral choice, and even there the administrative system interferes in the competitive political process. Dahl's polyarchy has not been achieved; and as far as more substantive versions of democracy are concerned, with active participation by the population in processes of self-government, political emancipation and governmental accountability, there is still a long way to go. But so there is in much of the West. The problems of achieving a full-blooded substantive liberal democracy in Russia are only a more extreme form of the crisis affecting modern democratic politics in general. Just as the price of freedom is eternal vigilance so, too, the struggle for democracy is never a single act but must be advanced daily. This struggle is far from over in Russia.

Chapter 2

Putin and the Hegemonic Presidency

JOHN P. WILLERTON

Vladimir Putin, in his second presidential term, governs a Russian Federation that has made considerable progress in the establishment of a democratic polity and a regulated market economy. Easily reelected in March 2004 and working with a parliament dominated by his supporters and allies, Putin is institutionally well-positioned to promote his power and policy agenda. With a broad public consensus for accelerated system transformation, Putin has set out an ambitious programme that – if implemented – will further consolidate Russia's transformation, bolster the power of federal authorities, and reinforce the mounting sense of 'normalcy' in Russia's second post-Soviet decade.

Putin had come to power as acting president at the end of 1999 when Russia was sorely lacking a strong central authority that could fully channel the country's reform processes. His predecessor and Kremlin mentor, Boris Yeltsin, had overseen the destruction of the Stalinist system and the laying of the foundations of a democratic market system. But Yeltsin had grown frail and ineffectual in advancing a reformist agenda, his administration racked with internal struggles and rife with cronies suspiciously connected with the new capitalist elite. With oligarchic business elements and regional elites greatly influencing the implementation of root-and-branch economic reform, there was widespread public disillusionment with many of the initial results of the country's democratic and market transformation. Putin confronted a universal public desire not only to reestablish the federal government's authority, but also to bolster the country's legal order and to focus and refine the processes of economic reform. Although preoccupied with his own power consolidation and formation of a new governing team during his first term, Putin acted on these public desires, and in his projected persona, governing style and articulated goals provided Russian society with the leadership and policy responses that garnered him consistently high public approval ratings (in the 60–70 per cent range) and easily earned him a second term.

18

Central to Russia's continuing political and socioeconomic transformation is the federal presidency, with its vast organizational resources and its constitutionally legitimated preeminence in the decision-making process. While Russia has a semi-presidential political system with formally independent and separately elected executive and legislative branches, the 1993 Yeltsin constitution vests overwhelming – indeed 'hegemonic' – power in the federal presidency. In Vladimir Putin, Russia has a highly popular president whose first term entailed a further strengthening of the executive branch's power position *vis-à-vis* other federal and subfederal actors. A relative unknown just six months before assuming the country's highest office, Putin quietly and effectively consolidated power over the executive branch, expanded its powers, and in the process was able to begin to implement his own ambitious policy agenda. Since Putin's ascent to the presidency, all major policy initiatives have come from the federal executive, with institutional reforms and policy achievements further bolstering the position both of the man and of the office he presently holds.

We focus in this chapter on the federal executive and the presidency, examining key institutions, their functions and roles in the Russian polity, and influential politicians who direct policy-making and implementation. We also consider the relationship of the presidency to other actors, federal and subfederal, in the process detailing the hegemonic decision-making position the executive has carved out for itself. To better understand the realities of contemporary Russian politics and to appreciate the complex dilemmas inherent in system transformation, we must draw a number of distinctions about factors affecting the current political process.

First, we must differentiate between the institution of the Russian presidency and the office-holder standing at its helm. The 1993 constitution invests the presidency with considerable powers, but these are separate from the abilities, intentions and authority of the individual holding the country's highest office. Putin, like his predecessor, has devoted considerable energy to consolidating his power as he advances his agenda; his institutional presidential power is distinguishable from his personal authority as the country's leader. In this regard, the personal authority of the president, grounded in such factors as public approval and policy success, can augment institutional prerogatives, making the chief executive and his team all the more politically potent.

Second, we must distinguish between the formal duties and prerogatives of the presidency and the informal arrangements that affect its operation and permit it to so dominate the Russian political landscape. A governing 'team' composed of identifiable groups with potentially different interests and perspectives manoeuvres around the president and is the human conduit through which institutionalized interests and programmatic goals are realized. And finally, we must consider the logic of the Russian institutional design, grounded in a tradition of executive assertiveness and dominance. Perspectives on this design, a semi-presidential system with a hegemonic executive, vary greatly as we distinguish between arguments that see the powerful presidency either facilitating or obstructing both the building of viable democratic institutions and the emergence of a civil society. Overall, the Russian federal executive is central to policy creation and implementation, and under both Yeltsin and Putin it has assumed the decisive institutional role in guiding the country's post-Soviet transformation.

Strong executives past and present

The centrality of the hegemonic presidency to Russian political life must be considered in the context of a long tradition of powerful leaders supported by both elites and the mass public. The size and diversity of Russia have been seen by many as necessitating some degree of power concentration and public deference to the political leadership to ensure political order, societal stability and economic well-being. Meanwhile, with a Russian public that has traditionally been deferential to authority, state coercion – whether massive or targeted, overt or more subtle – has often reinforced the decision-making prerogatives of the supreme leader. Today, the power concentration and often heavy-handed behaviour of the federal executive have not dimmed Russian citizens' preferences, consistently revealed in opinion surveys, for a strong, stabilizing hand guiding the democracy. (It is telling that in an opinion survey conducted just weeks before the March 2004 presidential election, 50 per cent of Russian respondents viewed the forceful Putin as a president 'without deficiencies': Rosbalt, 28 February 2004.)

Past Russian political systems have had a strong political executive as power was concentrated with a small ruling elite. In tsarist times, the centralized autocracy was organized on the basis of a steep power hierarchy. Peter the Great, a historical figure especially inspiring to President Putin, reined in restive regional elites and consolidated the position of the country's chief executive and his immediate coterie. The tsar was the ultimate decision-making authority, he stood atop a massive state bureaucracy, and he was legitimated by his position as the formal head of the Russian Orthodox Church. Meanwhile, the tsar was assisted by an impressive array of government ministries and advisory councils: bodies that assumed critical information-gathering, consultative and policy-coordinating roles. In contrast, representative bodies such as the Zemskii sobor (first selected in the mid-sixteenth century) and the State Duma (created in 1905) only occasionally functioned, and they never constrained the actions of the tsar. Indeed, they were ignored and even dissolved when the tsar deemed appropriate.

The Soviet period (1917–91) entailed a continuation of the tradition of a strong chief executive directing a massive state bureaucracy. The core feature of the Soviet political system was its centralized, hierarchical structure, with a massive set of interlocked bureaucracies linking all institutions and interests into an apparatus ruled by a small communist elite. Chief executives such as Joseph Stalin, Nikita Khrushchev and Leonid Brezhnev, serving as the Communist Party General or First Secretary, devoted primary attention to consolidating and maintaining power within the party-state apparatus. These leaders' ability to promote their policy agendas was dependent upon their organizational prowess.

Growing systemic and policy problems eventually necessitated fundamental reform of the political executive and reconfiguration of the centralized party-state bureaucracy, with the reform efforts proving central to the ultimate collapse of the Soviet system in 1991. Mikhail Gorbachev's reforms (1985–91) shifted power away from the party and state bureaucracy to new federal-level executive and legislative institutions, including a federal presidency. It was intended that a broad political consensus would arise through a viable legislature, guided by a president with an independent base of authority. These federal-level changes were copied at lower levels, including Russia, where Boris Yeltsin and other politicians used the new arrangements to advance their agendas as they challenged Soviet federal authorities. The executive–legislative struggles of the late Soviet period in turn set the stage for the institutional conflicts of the post-Soviet era.

Boris Yeltsin, Russia's first freely elected president, was the critical transitional figure bridging the late Soviet authoritarian system and a fledgling democratic polity. A one-time regional Communist Party official of peasant origin, he became a champion of the rights and economic interests of common citizens. Reaching the zenith of power in Gorbachev's regime, his freewheeling and iconoclastic style earned him the Soviet establishment's wrath while simultaneously garnering him strong public support. Yeltsin successfully competed in the USSR's first elections to a newly reconstituted parliament (1989) and ultimately assumed the newly established and directly elected Russian presidency in June 1991. The collapse of the Soviet system and Communist Party, with the forced retirement of a politically compromised Gorbachev, left Yeltsin fully in control of the federal executive – and an independent Russia – at the end of 1991.

The hallmarks of Yeltsin's leadership style, determinative in the crafting of the Russian presidency, were evident throughout his tenure (Aron 2000). While a political opportunist, Yeltsin was a pragmatist who engaged in both decisive reform and compromise. He exhibited a strong willingness to navigate around formal rules to advance his personal and policy agenda, and he often proved authoritarian in pursuing his own ends. Yet Yeltsin's policy legacy as Russian president has proven complex. He oversaw the destruction of the Soviet Communist Party and instituted the rules and organizational changes for the construction of a democratic political order. He was a leader who promoted a radical economic reform programme that would transform the Stalinist command economy, moving Russia towards a regulated market system even as that programme resulted in increased inequality, crime and corruption. But his use of force against parliamentary opponents in 1993 and in Chechnya in 1994–96 compromised his standing as a democratic reformer, with mounting health problems, policy dilemmas and decision-making inertia after his June 1996 reelection leaving him a much weakened leader more beholden to the advice of his protégés. The strong federal executive itself was compromised by Yeltsin's weakness, regime in-fighting and constant turnover of personnel. In the nine years of Yeltsin's tenure, Russia went through eight governments, over two hundred government ministers, and six heads of the presidential administration. Moreover, the politics of this putative Yeltsin democracy were dominated by members of the so-called 'Family', a group of friends, associates and even relatives who controlled access to the president and heavily influenced the decision-making of his administration.

Yeltsin's handpicked successor, Vladimir Putin, represented a study in contrast to Yeltsin both in career background and leadership style. Born to a working-class family and a product of the post-Stalinist era, Putin made a career in the Soviet security-intelligence services (KGB) that entailed a more elite education, travel and work abroad, and a broader awareness of both the Russian society and the outside world (Putin 2000). His life experiences of the late Soviet and immediate post-Soviet periods left him subject to divergent and conflicting influences that would continue to be evident both in his rise to power under Yeltsin and in his own presidency. As a security official, Putin was well conditioned to a chain-of-command culture that emphasized loyalty and strict subordination, the value of order, and commitment to a strong state. Working as a key associate of the reformist St Petersburg mayor Anatolii Sobchak, however, he personally experienced the need for root- and-branch system change, and became sensitive to bottom-up societal pressures, notions of elite and governmental accountability, electoral procedures and the messiness of democracy-building. Taken in its totality, Putin's life and career experience provided him with a mounting awareness of the complexities of system change and of governmental administration, and not only of commercial life but of civil society.

Both of post-Soviet Russia's chief executives have proven to have forceful leadership styles and each has used the formidable powers of the presidency to advance his power and policy ends (Shevtsova 1999, 2003). However, political authority, connoting a leader's ability to augment the brute force of the state with public and elite support, is advantageous to decision-making, and in just a few years Putin has amassed an enviable level of authority that is core to his longer-term policy success. Where Yeltsin left office with single-digit approval levels, Putin began his presidency at well over 50 per cent approval, building on this in his early years and maintaining a level of 70 per cent or more well into his second term (Mishler and Willerton 2003). Given the matching of this leader's forcefulness and high public approval with the considerable institutional powers of the federal executive, Russia now has its most powerful chief executive in decades.

The hegemonic presidency

Russia's hegemonic presidency embraces not only a vast array of institutions and officials that comprise the federal executive, but also a set of formal and informal arrangements that define and reinforce the president's decision-making primacy *vis-à-vis* competing political and societal actors. While the president was given extensive powers and prerogatives under the 1993 constitution, Vladimir Putin has initiated additional institutional changes that have only bolstered the position and decision-making authority of the country's chief executive. The federal presidency is hegemonic not only because its position is legally superior to that of other institutions, but because it possesses considerable independence and freedom of manoeuvre. The president, through decrees, legislative proposals and vetoes, can direct the federal decision-making process. Moreover, he appoints and guides the work of the prime minister and government, with top cabinet members (such as the ministers of defence and internal affairs) appointed by and directly accountable to him. He is supported by a large set of agencies and officials that link him to all federal and major subfederal institutions and actors.

The 1993 constitution specifies that the president 'defines the basic directions of the domestic and foreign policy of the state', while he also represents the country domestically and internationally (see Articles 80–93). As the head of state and commander-in-chief of the armed forces, he has the right to declare a state of emergency and martial law, call for referenda, and even suspend the decisions of other state bodies if their actions violate the constitution or federal laws. The presidency is the key institution responsible for the conduct of centre–periphery relations in a country that is as vast as it is varied in its regional and ethnic make-up.

Russia has a semi-presidential political system that entails a separately elected president and parliament, with the government formed by a prime minister appointed by the president and approved by the lower house of parliament, the State Duma. In reality, the president guides the federal government through the appointment and supervision of the prime minister and other top officials, with the parliament needing to formally approve the prime minister designate but operating more as a constraint on presidential and government actions. The president, acting through his vast apparatus of supporting agencies and officials, initiates legislation, reporting annually to a joint parliamentary session on his government's domestic and foreign policy. There are conditions under which the president can dissolve the lower house, the State Duma, but these entail unusual circumstances that to date have not materialized. Meanwhile, the ability of the rival legislative branch to remove the president for malfeasance is extremely limited. Procedures for impeaching the head of state are cumbersome and involve numerous federal bodies including the Supreme Court, the Constitutional Court and the upper house of parliament, the Federation Council. The probability of a president's removal from office is remote, since two-thirds majorities in both houses are needed. The only close case of an impeachment came against the unpopular President Yeltsin in spring 1999, yet even with considerable pent-up frustration with the president's actions and real doubts about his competence in office, all five opposition-sponsored counts failed. The more real constraint on the president's tenure in office comes with the constitutionally mandated two-term limit (each term of four years' duration). Yeltsin's surprise December 1999 resignation from office came only six months before the end of his second term, while President Putin has consistently indicated he will retire at the end of his second presidential term in 2008.

Much of the chief executive's ability to manoeuvre unilaterally stems from the ability to make institutional and policy changes through presidential decrees (*ukazy*), which have the force of law. The constitution (Art. 90) grants the president extensive leeway in issuing decrees that, while inferior to laws, are binding throughout the country so long as they do not contradict the constitution or federal laws. Given the massive size of the state bureaucracy, with its numerous and often conflicting ministries and agencies, there is a need for powerful top-down mechanisms such as presidential decrees to direct its activities. Although policy-setting decrees may be overridden by parliament, a two-thirds vote of both legislative houses is needed, and this is unlikely to occur given the weakness of the party system and the parliament's highly fragmented structure.

Presidential decrees have had a significant impact on Russian politics, in particular when the president lacked strong parliamentary support or desired to move expeditiously in promoting an institutional or policy change. President Putin, like his predecessor, has used decrees to advance both major reforms and more parochial interests. During his first term, Putin issued more than five hundred normative (or policy-setting) decrees, including important initiatives involving the establishment of the country's seven federal districts and restoration of the system of presidential envoys, efforts to 'normalize' the Chechen situation, and energy and economic reforms. During his nearly nine years in office, and in the midst of generally conflictual relations with the parliament, Boris Yeltsin had issued over two thousand policy-relevant decrees spanning the range of institutional and policy concerns. Yet as the political gap between president and parliament narrowed in Putin's first term, reliance on decrees lessened and the executive increasingly advanced its agenda through the legislative process. This tendency is likely to continue with Putin's consolidation of power and high public approval and in the wake of the December 2003 emergence of a two-thirds majority of Putin supporters in the State Duma.

Presidential administration and advisory bodies

A vast presidential administration supports the activities of the country's chief executive and supervises the implementation of presidential decisions. Built upon the organizational resources of the defunct Soviet Communist Party central apparatus, this extensive set of institutions is composed of dozens of agencies and includes approximately 2,500 full-time staff members, a number much larger than the comparable support bodies and employees of the US president. The array of presidential executive bodies reflects both the decision-making and supervisory prerogatives of the country's chief executive, with the complex and often hidden manoeuvrings of the varied organizational actors and numerous informal groups of officials constituting a sort of 'checks and balances' system within the federal executive. Since the Russian constitution is silent on the organization and functioning of this all-important administration, it is up to successive presidents to structure it in accordance with their own power and policy interests (Huskey 1999).

The presidential administration has been reorganized several times during the Russian Federation's brief history, with institutional and personnel changes accomplished by presidential decree. President Putin once again reorganized this administration at the outset of his second term, merging dozens of support organizations into twelve directorates, their titles reflecting their domains of institutional and policy responsibility (see

Figure 2.1). These directorates address the full range of policy concerns comprising the Putin agenda while undertaking the considerable organizational and administrative tasks required in 'guiding' the work of the government and its ministries. This most recent reorganization was said to be inspired by the executive arrangements of the French Fifth Republic, which entails a developed system of counsellors and advisory bodies. More than a dozen years after the Soviet collapse and laying of democratic and market foundations, this renovated presidential administration is said to be more streamlined and conducive to addressing the policy challenges of fine-tuning a political and socioeconomic transformation already well under way. Concomitant with the presidential administration reorganization has been a recasting of the government's role which, led by the prime minister and Cabinet of Ministers, is intended to play a larger role than in the past in the administration of the country and in its all-important economic revitalization.

The head of the presidential administration, the president's chief of staff who oversees both personnel and administrative matters, operates as a sort of *éminence grise* of the federal executive. He is well-positioned to influence all matters of state since he is not only a top aide but also the key conduit linking the president to all subordinate political actors. The real

Figure 2.1   *Major institutions of the second-term Putin presidency*

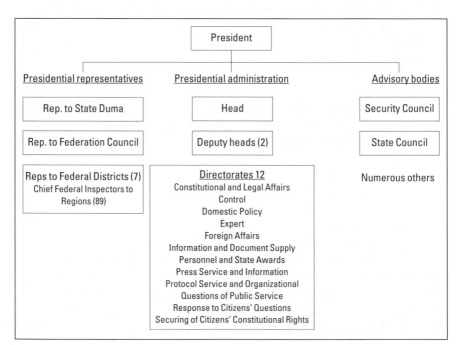

decision-making powers of the head of the presidential administration vary depending upon presidential needs and preferences. Thus, Yeltsin's long-serving administration head, Anatolii Chubais, was a powerful political player (as in the crafting and application of the privatization programme) whose position was only bolstered by the president's illness, while Yeltsin's final head, Aleksandr Voloshin, also transformed himself into an influential behind-the-scenes player who helped to weaken certain oligarchs and regional elites, restructure the administration's relations with the parliament, regroup party arrangements and tighten control over the electronic media.

Dmitri Medvedev, who replaced Voloshin in October 2003 near the end of the president's first term, is a long-time Putin confidant from St Petersburg whose legal background and wide-ranging administrative experience signify that he will be well-positioned to address the variety of policy areas – from civil service reform to the restructuring of state control over the energy sector – that are key to Putin's second-term agenda. Having only come to Kremlin power politics with Putin's political ascent, Medvedev's political savvy should not be underestimated: he had headed Putin's electoral headquarters in 2000 and had helped to consolidate the presidential administration's influence over the all-important energy conglomerate Gazprom. Other senior members of the presidential administration, notably the deputy heads, are also influential in the federal executive, with Putin appointing deputies tapping different components of his broader presidential 'team' (for example, former St Petersburg officials and officials drawn from the security services, the so-called *siloviki*).

The federal executive includes numerous presidential representatives to most federal and subfederal bodies, with these representatives serving as liaisons to help coordinate those bodies' actions with presidential preferences. It also includes numerous advisory bodies that deal with selected policy areas while formally linking the president and his executive team to other institutional actors. These bodies do not have a constitutional status, they operate at the president's pleasure, and similar to the presidential administration can be reorganized or abolished as the chief executive sees fit. Several of these bodies have now acquired some institutional history, encompass senior officials and facilitate the president's handling of high-level policy matters. This is true of the Security Council (created in 1994), which deals with foreign and security issues and includes the prime minister, relevant ministers and the heads of the seven federal districts. Putin's first-term foreign minister Igor Ivanov now serves as the Security Council's secretary, and Putin – like his predecessor – has regularly used the Security Council to legitimate his decisions and to coordinate government actions.

A more recent advisory body, the State Council (created in 2000), includes the heads of Russia's 89 regions and is the main institutional setting where regional leaders can deal directly with the president. Created by Putin to compensate regional leaders for the loss of their seats – and power – in the upper house of the parliament, the Federation Council, the State Council addresses centre–periphery and subfederal policy issues and meets every three months. Continuity in centre–periphery consultations is ensured through a smaller presidium or governing council of seven regional leaders – one from each of the federal districts – who are selected by the president and who meet monthly. A comparable advisory body, the State Council of Legislators, was created in 2002 for heads of regional legislatures and addresses similar issues. Meanwhile, Putin's creation by decree during the run-up to the 2004 presidential election of the Anti-Corruption Council is a more recent illustration of the political utility of advisory bodies as a chief executive attempts to institutionally address a high-profile policy area.

Prime minister and government

The president's power and authority are also grounded in his direct influence over the prime minister and cabinet, which form the government. While the constitution does not specify which ministries shall be formed, leaving it to the president and prime minister to make the desired choices, it does identify the policy areas with which the government will deal. The government crafts the federal budget and implements fiscal and monetary policies. It is responsible for the conduct of the economy and has oversight of social issues. The government implements the country's foreign and defence policies, administers state property, protects private property and public order, and ensures the rule of law and civil rights.

At the government's helm stands the prime minister, who is nominated by the president and must be approved by the Duma. While the Duma can remove the prime minister through the passage of two no-confidence votes within three months, there are political constraints on the parliament doing so; indeed, the Duma can be dissolved by the president if it does not approve his prime minister designate. In reality, the prime minister's power is grounded in presidential approval rather than parliamentary support. The prime minister chairs the Cabinet of Ministers, which oversees the state bureaucracy and has both political and law-making functions. Individual ministers set objectives for their ministries, craft their own subordinate bodies' budgets, and oversee policy implementation, but they do not have independent power bases. While all ministers report to the prime minister, those heading the so-called 'power ministries' (such as foreign affairs, defence and internal affairs) are also directly accountable to the president. The president, working with the prime minister, sets out the particular institutional constellation by which his government will be organized and will operate.

Putin and his second-term prime minister, Mikhail Fradkov, have established a vertical, top-down administration arrangement which is said to streamline the policy process and to better address the inter- and intra-ministerial struggles which have often overwhelmed Russian administration. The second-term government consists of the prime minister, one deputy prime minister, fifteen ministers (each with two deputies), and approximately sixty services and agencies; this in place of several deputy prime ministers, several dozen ministries, and dozens of other federal agencies, services and committees. Time will tell whether this new organizational arrangement will radically reduce the size of government and make it more efficient, but in forming the second-term government Putin and Fradkov assembled a diverse set of ministers who looked to be competent and reliable managers and not just political watchdogs.

The prime minister is the key administrator of presidential preferences and, accordingly, the presidential–prime ministerial relationship is an important and complex one. Some prime ministers have brought rich careers and considerable political standing to the office (such as Yeltsin's long-serving prime minister, Viktor Chernomyrdin), but more have risen to this post little known and with little independent political clout (see Table 2.1). Putin himself was a relative unknown who had only been working in the federal executive for a few years when he was surprisingly chosen to be Yeltsin's last prime minister in August 1999. Likewise, both of Putin's prime ministers have been officials of modest standing who were presented as technically able to run the government while enjoying the president's trust. Putin's first prime minister, Mikhail Kasyanov, who lasted nearly the entirety of the first term (March 2000–February 2004), bridged the Yeltsin and Putin political circles, worked effectively with bureaucrats and oligarchs, and proved to be a competent administrator who continued the economic reform programme while adopting a cautious approach to the reform of Russia's social infrastructure. Cosy with tainted business elements even as he promoted economic and administrative reform, Kasyanov – subject to constant rumours of his impending ouster throughout his tenure – finally succumbed to the pressures of Putin's reelection needs even as the president pronounced his general satisfaction with the government's performance.

Mikhail Fradkov, appointed in March 2004 to lead the second-term government, was a surprise choice, yet Fradkov brought extensive experience as a trade official and tax enforcer as well as a reputation – rare among long-serving officials – of being 'clean' and not compromised by business or bureaucratic intrigue. A reliable pragmatist who publicly shared Putin's vision of Russia's accelerated socioeconomic development,

Table 2.1 *Post-Soviet Russian presidents and prime ministers (including acting)*

	Tenure in office	*Background*
Boris Yeltsin (b. 1931)	June 1991–December 1999	Communist Party official
Yegor Gaidar (b. 1956)	January–December 1992	Liberal economist
Viktor Chernomyrdin (b. 1938)	December 1992–March 1998	Energy official
Sergei Kiriyenko (b. 1962)	March–August 1998	Security forces official
Yevgeny Primakov (b. 1929)	September 1998–May 1999	Diplomat
Sergei Stepashin (b. 1952)	May–August 1999	Security forces official
Vladimir Putin (b. 1952)	August 1999–March 2000	Security forces official
Vladimir Putin (b. 1952)	Since January 2000	Security forces official
Mikhail Kasyanov (b. 1957)	March 2000–February 2004	Government bureaucrat
Mikhail Fradkov (b. 1950)	Since March 2004	Trade official

Fradkov's nomination was characterized by Anatolii Chubais as 'upgrading Russian politics to European class' (RIA Novosti, 1 March 2004). His experience and non-corrupt reputation would be critical to two top-level priorities of Putin's second term: the continued integration of Russia into the global capitalist mainstream and the further upgrading of an increasingly effective system of taxation. Fradkov's initial decision-making style signalled that ministers would focus on strategic planning and leave bureaucratic tasks to subordinate agencies, while his early programmatic posturing suggested continued privatization with an accelerated dismemberment of Russia's remaining social infrastructure (including the end of free healthcare and an expansion of market-based utilities).

The recomposition of the second-term government included other senior officials who, like Fradkov, were administratively competent, free of questionable pasts, and seemingly committed to accelerated reform. Aleksandr Zhukov, the sole deputy prime minister, was an economist who had worked with Fradkov in Soviet economic organizations, had experience in Russia's emergent private sector, studied at the Harvard Business School and spent ten years in the Duma, including service as the chairman of its budget committee. A political independent until he joined Putin's United Russia, he has worked well with a wide array of politicians and interests, spanning liberal reformers (Yabloko) to right-wing nationalists (the Liberal Democratic Party). Zhukov also has a reputation as a 'clean' politician, and he will play an important role in promoting two Putin priorities, tax reform and budgetary change. Dmitri Kozak, who began Putin's second term as chief of government staff, is a legal expert from St Petersburg who worked under its reformist mayor Anatolii Sobchak and with Putin. Coming to Moscow in 1999 when Putin became prime minister, he went on to head Putin's 2004 election campaign office. A policy 'trouble-shooter' who has dealt with judicial and administrative reform as well as the restructuring of centre–periphery relations, Kozak was chosen by Putin in the wake of the September 2004 Beslan school seizure to head the Southern Federal District, guide the Federal Commission on the Northern Caucasus, and serve as the de facto liaison between the federal executive and Russia's most troubled region. Sergei Naryshkin, another one-time St Petersburg official with connections to Kozak and Putin, ascended to the post of government chief of staff, promising to continue his predecessor's efforts at streamlining and further integrating the increasingly powerful federal executive branch. Finally, with the reappointments of well-regarded senior ministers such as German Gref (economic development) and Aleksei Kudrin (finance), the Fradkov government appeared primed to tackle the reform agenda of the country's increasingly impatient chief executive.

Parliament and periphery

Major political changes initiated by Putin in his first term fundamentally altered the federal executive's relationships with leading institutional rivals, notably the parliament and regional governments, further reinforcing Russia's hegemonic presidential framework. The Soviet collapse and early Yeltsin years had entailed a significant weakening of both the federal government and the executive branch, with the late 1993 executive–legislative crisis and subsequent publicly approved Yeltsin constitution bolstering the presidency's formal position but leaving its legislative and regional rivals as formidable competitors. With the December 1999 electoral success and emergent power of the pro-Kremlin Unity bloc, and subsequent March 2000 single-round election of Putin, the presidential administration was better able to effectively manipulate rival Duma factions, secure influence with standing committees, and coopt the legislative leadership to reorient legislative action in a direction more compatible with Kremlin interests.

The December 2003 electoral triumph of Unity's successor party, United Russia, with its securing of two-thirds of all Duma seats, further consolidated the position of the pro-Putin forces. With Putin ally (and former Internal Affairs minister) Boris Gryzlov at its helm and United Russia members chairing all Duma committees, the stage was set for a pliable parliament anxious to move Putin's agenda with little hesitation. Meanwhile, the parliament's upper chamber, the Federation Council, was subdued by Putin initiatives early in his first term: the regional governors, who were members, were moved into the advisory State Council and replaced with less prominent representatives selected by the regions. With a new membership, a revamped committee system and a chamber leadership more responsive to presidential concerns, government proposals moved more smoothly through the legislative process. At the outset of Putin's second term, the parliament could be said to be in the hierarchy of presidential governance, leaving presidential administration head Dmitri Medvedev to observe that political stability had been 'confirmed and legitimated by the Russian people' (*Financial Times*, 22 January 2004).

Meanwhile, centre–periphery relations were restructured through the May 2000 creation of seven federal administrative districts directed by presidential envoys (see Chapter 9). Selecting five generals and two senior government officials (including former prime minister Sergei Kiriyenko) to head these macro-districts, Putin expressed the hope that the new system would 'restore effective vertical power in the country' (*Rossiiskaya gazeta*, 19 May 2000). With squeaky clean reputations and offices staffed by security services personnel, the presidential envoys were important conduits of information for the federal executive, ensuring regions complied with federal legislation and directives, inserting themselves into regional-level conflicts, and assuming a role in regional economic development. Indeed, while the seven envoys meet regularly with Putin, the once powerful leaders of the 89 regions must now operate through those envoys in organizing contacts with the president. Beneath the seven envoys are chief federal inspectors, one each for the 89 regions, who are more intimately involved in the daily political affairs of their domains of responsibility.

Meanwhile, the political reforms proposed by Putin immediately after the September 2004 Beslan school seizure (though in the planning for months before this tragic event) further consolidated the federal executive's position as the president sought parliamentary approval for the power to nominate all regional governors (with those nominations then subject to the approval of regional legislatures rather than popular vote). The Kremlin justified these changes by claiming that many governors had put the interests of their own regional economies first and had advanced too many of their associates and even relatives, leaving them with little ability to address national-level policy problems such as public security and threats of terrorism. Overall, the restoration of the presidency's power over the periphery during the Putin period has occurred simultaneously with the reassertion of the federal government's own authority in the conduct of political and economic life throughout the country.

Constellation of elements in the Putin team

Russia's hegemonic presidency involves not only the formal institutions that comprise the federal executive and the arrangements that tie the presidency and executive to other political actors, but also the officials and interests that form the president's 'team' and the informal mechanisms by which those actors operate and the chief executive governs. The reality of Russian decision-making is that much occurs behind the scenes and involves more informal relationships among both governmental and private actors. Such informal operations are nearly impossible to observe and evaluate definitively, but we know they affect governmental actions and policy outcomes. The high-level political intrigues and hidden manipulation of resources and ideas that were at the heart of the Soviet system have found resonance in the Yeltsin–Putin era. 'Court politics' and manoeuvring *vis-à-vis* the president are especially important when power is so concentrated with the chief executive and a hierarchical federal executive. It is important to be sensitive to the inner operations of the presidency, albeit with a concomitant need to be sceptical in drawing firm conclusions.

Consolidation of power within the hegemonic presidency was a major goal – and arguably the most important achievement – of Putin's first term. Putin had come to power with few protégés or long-term associates, meaning he would have to balance various competing elements even as he carefully crafted his own team. In contrast with the tumultuous Yeltsin years, a hallmark of Putin's regime was personnel stability, accommodation of already entrenched interests, a gradual but constant elevation of trusted associates, and coalition-building across competing interests both within the presidential administration and with other political actors. The diversity of elements within the emergent Putin team was at least as great as that of Yeltsin, with a balancing of interests that precluded any single factional or sectoral element from becoming dominant. Throughout his presidency, Putin has exhibited a remarkable finesse in juggling competing interests, and his mastery of the hegemonic presidency proved an achievement that could not be assumed at the unexpected onset of his tenure.

The diversity of elements forming the Putin team reflects the varied forces that have been influential in the formation of the president's career and worldview (see Figure 2.2). With Putin a product of Russia's security services, it is not surprising that a substantial cohort of officials from this area have become influential figures in the federal executive (Kryshtanovskaya and White 2003). Meanwhile, with most of Putin's political career grounded in late Soviet and post-Soviet reformist efforts – especially as advocated by one of Putin's mentors, the reformist St

Figure 2.2   *Major informal groups of the second-term Putin presidency*

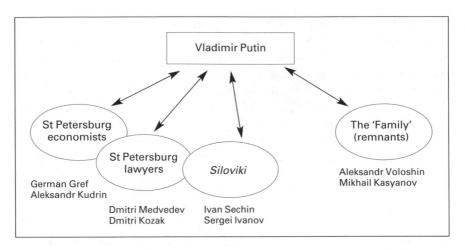

Petersburg mayor Anatolii Sobchak – it is understandable that many economic and political reformers have assumed senior posts in his administration. Many officials came to the Kremlin from St Petersburg with Putin; indeed, most of his senior presidential personnel began their executive work early in the first term.

Much foreign attention has been given to the security–intelligence elements – what Russians refer to as the *siloviki* (derived from the Russian word for force) – who represent a significant component in the senior leadership. The *siloviki* began coming to power under Yeltsin, but this accelerated with Putin's rise to the prime ministership and presidency. It is challenging to draw a broad description that accurately captures a common interest or shared set of perspectives for all officials drawn from the security–intelligence community. Many assume the *siloviki* have a natural preference for the reemergence of a strong Russian state and may be less sensitive to the niceties of the democratic system. Putin regime *siloviki* present themselves as disciplined professionals, they are generally well-educated, and some bring past commercial experience to their government posts. If they are committed to continued political and economic reform, they may also have a decided preference for investigations and prosecution: actions viewed as necessary in restoring the state order deemed necessary to reform success. A common view of many – in Russia if not in the West – is that these *siloviki* are generally non-ideological, are not corrupt, have a pragmatic law and order focus and have Russian national interests at heart. Some *siloviki* stress the critical importance of state institutions being independent from economic – notably the oligarchs' – influence. They may represent the sort of dependable cadres

Putin says are critical to the reinvigoration of the administrative elite. Overall, the *siloviki* do not form a cohesive group, they do not have a single leader, and there are influential figures with presumed rivalries who advance their own policy (and career) agendas. Indeed, there is no common, articulated *silovik* agenda, but the security–intelligence officials bring the work ethic and skills that Putin apparently favours. Thus, senior *siloviki* such as Sergei Ivanov (Minister of Defence), Viktor Ivanov and Igor Sechin (top presidential administration officials) and Boris Gryzlov (former Minister of Internal Affairs and current Duma Speaker) – all of whom have had close working relationships with Putin – are key members of the second-term team, but whether their common security–intelligence background and presumed similar worldviews translate into common policy preferences is difficult to assess. Observers, however, have been impressed by the rise in the number of security–intelligence elements, not just in top federal executive posts but in watchdog deputy ministerial posts, among the seven federal district envoys (five of the original envoys) and prominent members of their staffs, and among regional governors (including those of Smolensk and Voronezh).

The reformist St Petersburg economists and lawyers – many of whom have career and personal ties to the president dating back to the early 1990s – represent two other groups that are prominent in the Putin team. Many leading members of the economic reform team – both in the presidential administration and the government – are drawn from the St Petersburg group, while the same is true of many senior officials focused on political–legal reforms. Once again it is tricky to generalize about the backgrounds and policy preferences of these reformers. A reasonable description, however, would include that they are academically qualified and have significant administrative experience, are often focused on the technical complexities of the country's system transformation, and are – in general – committed to market development, privatization and the continued diminution of the state's role in the country's socioeconomic life. The liberal economists have pressed for a normal market economy, fully engaged with the global system and nested in a democratic political system. They contend that the consolidation of democracy comes with improving the population's standard of living and developing the private sector. In a related vein, the St Petersburg lawyers focus on constitutional–legal–administrative arrangements to bolster an efficient democratic system, favouring reforms that strengthen simultaneously the market economy and political stability. Putin's so-called 'managed democracy' depends upon the development of laws and legal safeguards essential to the judicial processes and rights of both individuals and corporate actors. Prominent St Petersburg economists include the influential senior government ministers Aleksei Kudrin (Finance) and German

Gref (Economic Development and Trade) and Putin's iconoclastic economic adviser Andrei Illarionov. Among the St Petersburg lawyers we find presidential administration head Dmitri Medvedev and trouble-shooter Dmitri Kozak. There are reported personal-career rivalries among such elements (notably the reputed struggles involving Kudrin, Gref, and now their boss, Prime Minister Fradkov), but it is difficult to assess their dynamics, while all these officials in their public utterances and actions appear fully committed to Putin's power and policy agenda.

A final identifiable group involves remnants of the so-called 'Family' – a term originally referring to relatives and associates of former President Yeltsin – who survived the Putin first term and continue, generally from the margins, to influence the policy process. Most senior 'Family' members have left the highest corridors of power, but some have 'golden parachuted' into respectable elite positions that permit them to influence important policy matters even as they maintain immediate access to the senior leadership. Thus, former presidential administration head Alexander Voloshin now chairs the Unified Energy System's Board of Directors and plays a critical role in the reform of the country's all-important power monopoly, while former prime minister Mikhail Kasyanov oversees a major financial project in creating a new international bank to help expand Russia's export infrastructure (especially in exporting energy to the European Union). Major players from the Yeltsin regime are now out of top echelon offices, but many retain the skills, connections and elite standing that allow for important inputs to the Putin policy agenda.

Contending views of Putin's hegemonic executive

A review of the Russian hegemonic presidency reveals the presence of a set of institutional means fully capable of directing the country's complex policy-making and policy-implementing processes. Meanwhile, the two forceful occupants of the country's highest political office have had the personal commitment and leadership skills necessary to dominate Russia's politics. At the time of writing, with second-term President Vladimir Putin fully in command, we find a federal executive able to structure all aspects of Russia's political and economic reality, but what are the policy consequences to date of such concentrated power and what do they say about the evolving Russian democracy? Major issue areas and related policies of Russia's post-Soviet democratic system are discussed in subsequent chapters, but we conclude this examination of the federal executive by assessing its policy results and considering the contrasting ways observers judge its role in Russia's transformation and democracy-building.

At the heart of the Yeltsin–Putin policy agenda has been Russia's successful economic transformation, with the Putin regime recording impressive economic growth rates without an undue reliance on the energy and minerals sector. Unemployment is down, wages are now paid, personal consumption is up, and the growth in living standards now outstrips the increase in gross domestic product. While these changes are grounded in systemic changes dating back to the early 1990s, they are products of Putin's economic stabilization and reform programme; at the very least, these changes have occurred on Putin's watch and he has benefited significantly. The federal executive, working with a more cooperative (or pliable) parliament, has crafted more balanced budgets, introduced a simpler tax system that has yielded considerably more revenues, and implemented numerous significant administrative reforms that have not only bolstered the economy, but citizens' and foreigners' confidence in that economy, and most observers' confidence in the Russian political process itself. Meanwhile, the federal executive's focus on restoring stability and order – especially in confronting Yeltsin-era 'oligarchical capitalism' – has lessened the power of some influential business figures (such as the country's richest citizen, oligarch Vladimir Khodorkovsky), while channelling the political activities of others (such as oligarch and Chukotka governor Roman Abramovich). Meanwhile, the whole country has become increasingly subject to federal preferences, while a forceful yet diplomatically astute President Putin has effectively engaged the West and outside world.

These advances notwithstanding, Putin and the federal executive have confronted a number of high-profile challenges, including the *Kursk* submarine disaster (August 2001), the Dubrovka Theatre hostage ordeal (October 2002) and the continuing seemingly unsolvable Chechen war, which took an even more disturbing turn with the Beslan school seizure of September 2004. Yet such dilemmas, whether short-term or continuing, have not weakened Putin's standing (reinforcing his reputation as a 'Teflon president') and have enhanced his efforts to strengthen the federal executive. The widespread support for the president after more than four years in office was tellingly revealed in one public opinion survey conducted on the eve of the March 2004 presidential election: 50 per cent of all respondents indicated they trusted Putin, whereas only 9 per cent trusted the government and 1 per cent trusted political parties. Moreover, in another revealing spring 2004 survey, only 10 per cent of respondents would characterize their country as a 'democracy', citizens being more concerned about sociopolitical order and economic advance – perceived achievements of the Putin presidency (*Ogonek*, 19–25 April 2004). Indeed, only a month after the Beslan school tragedy, Putin's popularity still stood at a strong 72 per cent (*Kommersant*, 10 October 2004). In these and other comparable public opinion results lies the challenge of weighing divergent understandings of the hegemonic presidency, its current occupant, the future direction of Russia's transformation and the prospects for accelerated democracy-building.

Putin's hegemonic presidency has entailed policy successes and mounting pubic confidence. Yet how should one understand the complexities and nuances of these perceived successes, especially as they influence system-building and the setting of long-term precedents? To take some priority executive initiatives as examples, what are the deeper significance of political attacks on the oligarchs and the further assertion of the government's regulatory role in the country's economic life? Are corruption and cronyism fatally weakened, or do new forms of authoritarianism emerge? In a related vein, does the federal executive's promotion of the notion of 'natural rent' taxes on energy and mineral companies – those tax revenues 'redistributed' from corporations to the citizenry – signify the championing of citizens' rights and social justice? Or does it constitute a nuanced form of demagogic pandering that weakens fundamental conditions of a free market system? What are the 'logic' and implications of Putin's uncompromising 'scorched earth' approach to Chechen secessionist efforts, and will this be conducive to the long-term integration of national minorities into a more tolerant Russian society?

Finally, what are the systemic implications of the second-term Putin initiative to consolidate the country's 89 regions into two or three administrative units and to have the federal president for all intents and purposes appoint regional governors? Are there unforeseen ramifications of simultaneously streamlining federal governance and further bolstering Moscow's centralizing control? Combined, will all these and related Putin initiatives result in better legal and policy conditions, bolster the war on crime, reinforce the integrity of the Russian Federation, and improve the investment climate and foster the opening of the federal, regional and local economies to small and medium business? Or will they undercut the foundations of a viable democratic system and independent market, stifle the emergence of a civil society and move Russia back towards its traditional highly centralized decision-making proclivities? Essential to all these initiatives and their successful implementation is the powerful presidency, a resolute chief executive, and a Russian citizenry overwhelmingly supportive of the country's policy direction.

Serious observers – both inside and outside Russia – can and have drawn very different conclusions about this state of affairs with a 'hyperpresidency'. For some, especially those outside the country and in the West, a concentration of power with the head of state and executive branch is fundamentally threatening to a viable democracy and a flourishing civil society. Certainly, the Western scholarly literature on democracy-building points to the dilemmas inherent in presidential systems lacking viable checks and balances (Linz and Valenzuela 1994; Mainwaring and Shugart 1997). For others, the undue dependence of the system on one office-holder and one limited set of executive institutions represents a constant threat to stability and policy continuity over time. These types of views are counterposed to the predominant Russian view – held by the overwhelming majority of political elites as well as the citizenry – of the necessity of a strong head of state and federal executive not only in assuring stability and order, but in addressing the excesses and inequities of the country's socioeconomic transformation in its first post-Soviet decades. Outsiders' scepticism about Putin's hegemonic presidency and first-term record certainly did not influence the 71 per cent of voters who reelected him in the first (and only) round of the 2004 election.

In the final analysis, the hegemonic executive brings the political–institutional potential for continued profound system transformation, but possible long-term outcomes vary greatly with the leadership's intentions and policy measures. Today Russia has a politically unified federal government – executive, legislative and judicial – which is more influential *vis-à-vis* the periphery than at any time since the heyday of the Soviet system. In assessing the likely future impact of the Putin hegemonic presidency, we must focus on the governing elite's overriding vision of the desired Russian polity, economy and society, the types of priorities emphasized in the second term, and the specific policies that are intended to address the stated issue agenda. President Putin, in his May 2004 inaugural address, offered the following perspective on his second term: 'Now the main objective of the next four-year period is to turn the potential we have already accumulated into the new energy of development, to achieve through this a fundamentally better quality of life for our people, to bring about a real, tangible increase in their well-being' (BBC Monitoring, 7 May 2004). Putin and his allies now have in place all of the necessary organizational means to advance their ambitious agenda. By 2008, with two completed Putin terms and close to two decades of post-Soviet system-building, we should be in a better position to judge the powerful presidency's longer-term consequences and the related prospects for a vibrant Russian democracy.

Chapter 3

Parliamentary Politics in Russia

THOMAS F. REMINGTON

The place of parliament in Russia's political system has come full circle in the last fifteen years. Gorbachev's democratizing reforms in the late 1980s transformed the Soviet parliament from a ceremonial adornment of communist rule into an arena of stormy debate and tense political confrontations in the Yeltsin era; under Putin, however, parliament has largely retreated to its earlier role as docile rubber stamp for the leadership's proposals. In this process of transformation are reflected the hopes, contradictions and failures of democratic reform. Still, while parliament is not the source of political legitimacy and authority for the state in Russia that it is in democracies, neither is it quite the decorative window-dressing that it was in the Soviet era. Today, under Putin, parliament remains a site of bargaining and deal-making among organized interests over the distribution of benefits and liabilities and serves, even in its much-reduced state, as a forum for the articulation of public opinion. The rise and decline of parliament's status as a political institution over the transition period tells us a great deal about the dynamics of the Russian political system.

To understand parliament's structure and role today, it is useful to begin with a brief summary of the place of elective representative bodies in the Soviet Union. Although they exercised little actual power, they symbolized the idea that the people were sovereign in the state. Legally, the Soviet political system rested on the fiction that state power resided in the hierarchy of soviets (or councils). Soviets were popularly elected bodies in which, according to Soviet doctrine, legislative and executive power were fused. Each village and town, region and republic, had its nominally elected soviet (elected in the characteristic, uncontested elections for which the regime was famous), while at the apex of the system, the USSR Supreme Soviet was the equivalent of a parliament for the Soviet Union as a whole. At the same time, it was understood that actual political power lay with the Communist Party of the Soviet Union, which exercised its power through the soviets and through the executive bodies that were nominally accountable to the soviets. Therefore the few votes that

soviets were called upon to take were exercises in the unanimous affirma-
tion of decisions that had been made by the Communist Party. Both Soviet
political thought and practice rejected any notion of a separation of
powers, and thus reinforced the older Russian tradition of an absolutist
state.

This system changed significantly when Mikhail Gorbachev launched
his political reforms in the late 1980s. Gorbachev used new expanded
parliamentary structures and open elections as instruments for awaken-
ing popular political energies. His goal was to channel the country's newly
active political life into a new set of legislative structures where he would
be able to guide decision-making. Gorbachev created a cumbersome four-
tiered parliament for the USSR, consisting of a huge, 2,250-member
Congress of People's Deputies, which elected a smaller, full-time parliament called the Supreme Soviet. In turn, the Supreme Soviet was guided
by its Presidium, which was overseen by a Chairman. Elections of
deputies to this new parliamentary structure were held in 1989; in 1990,
elections were held for the equivalent bodies at the level of the union
republics and in regions and towns throughout the Soviet Union.

Gorbachev's strategy was to give *glasnost*, his policy of open political
communication, an institutional base. He sought to incorporate many
diverse groups into the new parliamentary arena while ensuring that he
would have the ultimate power of decision over policy. But liberalization
of politics under Gorbachev had unanticipated consequences. Not only
did it mobilize radical democrats against defenders of the old order, it also
encouraged coalitions of democrats and nationalists in the republics,
including Russia, to rally around demands for national independence. As
a result, the new USSR parliament and its counterparts at lower-levels
represented reasonably well the political divisions existing in the country
between defenders and challengers of the old order. But they were
woefully unsuited to *deciding* the grave policy questions that the country
faced. They lacked even the most rudimentary institutional means to
generate and debate coherent alternative policy options. They depended
heavily on the executive to set their agendas and guide their decision-
making. Sessions of the new USSR parliament, and the parliaments in the
union republics and lower level territories, were frequently the sites of
passionate but inconclusive debate, dramatic walk-outs by embattled
minorities, and deep frustration as the deputies found themselves unable
to reach majority decisions on difficult issues. Little wonder that they
were never able to resolve the most serious crises that the Soviet Union
faced.

Gorbachev's awkwardly remodelled parliament did achieve some
notable results, passing some major new legislation and stimulating the
formation of proto-parties. But faced with the fundamental conflict

between radical reformers and hardliners over market-oriented reform, the parliament simply ducked: it created a state presidency for the USSR, a curiosity that was logically incompatible with the principle of CPSU rule. Then it delegated extraordinary powers to President Gorbachev, who fell into a trap of his own making by constantly expanding the nominal powers of the president. What he failed to recognize at the time was that by doing so, he only encouraged the presidents of the union republics to follow suit at their own level of jurisdiction, thus deepening the disintegration of the Soviet state. The more power Gorbachev claimed for himself as president of the USSR, the less power he had in actuality, and the more he undercut the possibility that *any* central-level institution – president, parliament or Communist Party – could have held the union together.

The RSFSR transition-era parliament

A round of elections was held in 1990 for the parliamentary bodies in the union republics and for the soviets at regional and local levels. Russia (formally the Russian Soviet Federative Socialist Republic), the largest of the republics making up the Soviet Union, created a four-tiered legislative structure consisting of Congress, Supreme Soviet, Presidium and Chairman which was very similar to the structure that Gorbachev devised at the USSR level. In Russia, the 1990 election brought about a new surge of democratic mobilization among voters. A large group of reform-oriented deputies was elected to the Russian parliament, but a nearly equal number of pro-communist conservatives won mandates as well. This Russian parliament then underwent a history rather similar to the USSR parliament. Unable to cope with the mounting crises of political and economic order, the Russian Congress created a presidency, delegated emergency powers to it, then almost immediately regretted its own decision and tried to win back its prerogatives. Confrontation between parliament and president then intensified to a final, violent peak in October 1993, when Russian president Boris Yeltsin dissolved parliament and called new elections.

Like the USSR parliament, the RSFSR parliament of 1990–93 was ill-adapted institutionally to form a decisive majority, especially on contentious issues; its structural problems were exacerbated by the deep and intense gulf separating communist and nationalist forces from radical democrats. Once Russia was faced with the need to choose policies to deal with the most fundamental questions of its constitutional and economic order, these partly inherited, partly improvised legislative institutions were unable to cope. Although the parliament was formally endowed with vast constitutional authority, it was unable in fact to wield it.

Still, the RSFSR Congress and Supreme Soviet in the 1990–93 period succeeded in passing some important legislation on matters where its communist and reformist camps could find common ground. Among these were laws on taxation and budget formation, privatization and property relations, banking, bankruptcy, and land relations. Other legislation reformed regional government and the state's territorial–administrative structure. Perhaps of still greater importance were the laws reforming the justice system, including the law creating the Constitutional Court. The Supreme Soviet also passed legislation on social welfare, creating a mandatory medical insurance system, as well as on civil liberties, including a law guaranteeing freedom of religion. Often the legislation was broad and vague, leaving loopholes that executive agencies could fill (as had long been the practice in Russia) with administrative instructions and regulations. These often had the effect of distorting and weakening the intent of the law. The scope of the legislative record of the Supreme Soviet suggests, nonetheless, that many deputies took their law-making responsibilities seriously, and used the institutional resources at hand to fulfil them. The laws passed by the USSR and RSFSR parliaments then were inherited by the new Russian Federation when it became independent following the USSR's dissolution.

Boris Yeltsin and the crisis of 1993

The 1990–93 period was marked by the rise of Boris Yeltsin, who made Russia's parliament his initial base of power. Yeltsin led a coalition of radical democrats and Russian nationalists in a struggle for greater autonomy for Russia within the union. Yeltsin's own position was strengthened, rather than weakened, by Gorbachev's clumsy attempts to undermine him. In 1990, Yeltsin was elected by a narrow margin to the position of Chairman of the RSFSR Supreme Soviet, enabling him to use the parliament as his institutional base for challenging Gorbachev. In spring 1991, Yeltsin rallied a majority of deputies and won their endorsement of his proposal for a powerful, directly elected Russian president. In June 1991, he was elected president of Russia in a nationwide election.

Once the presidency was established, however, it led to a contest between the legislative and executive branches within Russia itself. The leadership of the RSFSR Congress and Supreme Soviet began to challenge Yeltsin for supremacy, claiming that the legislative branch was the supreme seat of state power. Yeltsin claimed that as popularly elected president, he embodied the Russian people's desire for a decisive break with the communist past. The August 1991 coup attempt further solidified Yeltsin's political position. The surge of popular resistance to the coup in Moscow, Leningrad and other Russian cities, and his own uncompromising opposition, gave Yeltsin a substantial political bonus. Many of his communist opponents in the Russian parliament lost their political bases through a series of decrees Yeltsin issued which suspended, and later outlawed, the activity of the CPSU and confiscated its considerable property. In October 1991, at the Fifth Congress, Yeltsin sought and received special powers to enact economic reform measures by decree; he won the congress's consent to put off elections of local heads of government until 1 December 1992; he won approval of constitutional amendments giving him the right to suspend the acts of lower authorities in Russia if he found they violated the constitution and to suspend legal acts of the union if they violated Russian sovereignty; and the congress approved his programme for radical economic transformation. A few days later Yeltsin assumed the position of prime minister himself, named a new cabinet dominated by young economists committed to rapid liberalization, and issued a package of decrees launching a radical 'shock therapy' of the economy.

Making full use of his expanded powers, Yeltsin pursued his programme of reform throughout 1992. Although the impetus of 'shock therapy' fizzled out as the year proceeded, opposition to Yeltsin grew, and the majority in the parliament shifted further and further away from him. Yeltsin was also unable to win legislative approval of a new constitution that would formalize his powers *vis-à-vis* the government and the legislative branch. Under the old constitution, however, only the Congress had the power to amend the constitution or adopt a new one. Confrontation between Yeltsin and the Congress–Supreme Soviet intensified. In March 1993 the Congress attempted to remove Yeltsin from power through impeachment but fell slightly short of the required two-thirds majority. Yeltsin responded by holding a popular referendum on support for his policies in April, which gave him a surprisingly strong vote of confidence. However, the constitutional crisis continued to deepen.

Finally, on 21 September, Yeltsin issued decrees that lacked constitutional foundation but offered a political solution to the impasse. He shut down parliament, declared the deputies' powers null and void, and called elections for a new parliament to be held on 12 December. He decreed that there was to be a national vote on adopting the draft constitution that had been developed under his direction. In the December referendum, Yeltsin's constitution was approved. It has remained in effect ever since.

Yeltsin's constitution created a two-chamber Federal Assembly. The upper chamber, the Federation Council, allocated two seats to each of Russia's 89 constituent territories (called 'subjects of the federation'). The lower house, the State Duma, introduced a fundamentally new principle into Russian legislative institutions: proportional representation (PR). Half of the Duma's 450 seats were filled by candidates on parties' electoral lists according to the share of votes that party received in the election in a single federal-wide district. To receive any seats, however, a party or electoral association had to win at least 5 per cent of the PR votes. The other half of the seats were filled by plurality voting in 225 single-member districts. In the first election held under this plan, in 1993, voters were also given the opportunity to elect their two representatives to the Federation Council.

Not surprisingly, Yeltsin's draft constitution provided for a very strong presidency. The president could issue decrees with the force of law, as well as veto laws passed by parliament. Yet the constitution also provided for the 'separation of legislative, executive and judicial powers' (Article 10). Contradictions between the powerful presidentialist elements in the constitution and the principle of separation of powers have been resolved very differently at different times since the adoption of the constitution. Under Yeltsin, the president shared some power with the parliament; since Putin has been in office, however, parliament has been pushed to the sidelines of the political system. The changes in the balance of power between president and parliament reflect both changes in the organizational arrangements within parliament itself and shifts in the larger institutional environment in which parliament and president operate.

It is often said that the 1993 constitution was imposed by Yeltsin and reflected his demand for a presidential (or even super-presidential) system. There is some truth in this. Yet Yeltsin and his advisers were shrewd enough to recognize that they needed to provide just enough political concessions to other powerful political interests in the country to keep them in the game. Moreover, Yeltsin's constitution incorporated some ideas that had become generally accepted in political circles. Most political groups agreed, for instance, that the parliament should comprise two chambers: a lower, popular chamber and an upper house giving equal representation to each region making up the federation. In the past, bicameralism had been part of USSR parliaments but had been purely nominal. Both Gorbachev and Yeltsin had tinkered with advisory councils made up of the leaders of the regions. The plan that Yeltsin initially intended to put to the voters in the 1993 referendum called for a Federation Council made up of two representatives from each territorial unit of the federation. But at the last moment, Yeltsin also decided that the two representatives should come from the executive and legislative branches – a casual constitutional improvisation that has led to endless difficulty since then. However, most of the 1993 constitution's elements were not the arbitrary interventions of a capricious president; they were the products of struggle and deliberation. Some reflected Yeltsin's calculations about how much power he could give himself without provoking an open revolt by the groups he wanted to participate in the system. Some issues were left unresolved.

After the new parliament convened in 1994, its organizational arrangements reflected other points of consensus among the political elite about what institutional forms were appropriate. One widely accepted notion was that political parties should have a significant place both in the elections and in the lower chamber. Many politicians agreed that something other than a Presidium should be the steering committee for the new parliament. Most agreed that the post of chairman should be substantially weakened in comparison to the previous system, with the power to manage the chamber residing in a collective council of parliamentary leaders. The system of standing legislative committees with specialized jurisdictions that had been used in the previous parliaments aroused no controversy. Thus, to design the new parliament, the deputies drew upon experience with earlier forms as well as international experience, adapting models according to their political aims and ambitions (Remington 2001).

The Federal Assembly

One of the most important determinants of the balance of power between president and parliament is the outcome of elections. The first elections held under the new electoral system in 1993 gave no one political party or coalition a majority of seats in the Duma. Reform-oriented deputies occupied about a third of the seats; centrist forces about a quarter; and opposition deputies about 40 per cent (Table 3.1 lists the distribution of seats by political faction in each Duma). Winning voting coalitions in the 1994–95 Duma often were 'left-centrist' – that is, they included the votes of the Communists, the Agrarians, the centrist 'Women of Russia' group and, nearly as often, Zhirinovsky's Liberal Democrats and the Democratic Party of Russia. As a result, parliament fought Yeltsin over much of the legislation he proposed, with the result that Yeltsin sometimes simply bypassed parliament by issuing presidential decrees. Yet both Yeltsin and the parliamentary leadership generally sought to avoid the sort of mutually destructive confrontations that had brought the country to the brink of civil war in 1991 and 1993. Regular bargaining and consultation between the executive and legislative branches succeeded in working out compromises on numerous pieces of legislation.

This pattern continued in the second Duma, which sat from 1996 to 1999. Yeltsin had decreed that the Duma elected in 1993 would serve for only two years and that elections would be held again two years later, in December 1995, for a new Duma serving a four-year term. The December 1995 election was characterized by a huge number of political groups

Table 3.1 *Factional composition of the State Duma, 1994–2004: party factions and registered deputies' groups as of beginning of each convocation**

	Faction	No.	Per cent
2004 (May)	United Russia	306	68.0
	CPRF	52	11.6
	LDPR	36	8.0
	Motherland	39	8.7
	Unaffiliated	14	3.1
2000 (January)	Russia's Regions	38	7.9
	CPRF	89	18.6
	People's Deputy	58	12.1
	Unity	81	16.9
	Yabloko	21	4.4
	Union of Right Forces	32	6.7
	Fatherland–All Russia	45	9.4
	Agro-Industrial Group	41	8.6
	LDPR	17	3.5
	Unaffiliated	18	3.8
1996 (January)	CPRF	149	32.8
	LDPR	51	11.2
	Our Home Is Russia	65	14.3
	Yabloko	46	10.1
	Russia's Regions	41	9.0
	Agrarian	35	7.7
	People's Power	37	8.1
	Unaffiliated	26	5.7
1994 (January)	Agrarian Party of Russia	56	12.6
	LDPR	64	14.3
	Democratic Party of Russia	15	3.4
	CPRF	46	10.3
	Women of Russia	23	5.2
	Russia's Choice	72	16.1
	Party of Russian Unity and Accord	29	6.3
	Yabloko	29	6.5
	New Regional Policy	65	14.6
	Liberal-Democratic Union of December 12	23	5.2
	Russia's Way	11	2.5
	Unaffiliated	13	2.9

* Under Duma rules, any party receiving seats as a result of winning at least 5 per cent of the valid party list vote in parliamentary elections automatically forms a political faction consisting of those deputies elected on its list together with any other deputies who join it. In addition, a deputy 'group' may be registered and given the same rights and privileges as a party faction if it has a sufficient number of members to qualify. In the convocations of the Duma that sat in 1994–95, 1996–99 and 2000–03, this threshold number was 35. In January 2004, the new Duma raised the minimum threshold for a group to gain registration to 55. As a consequence, no deputy groups were registered.

running: 43 parties registered and ran lists – far more than could be accommodated in view of the 5 per cent threshold rule for receiving seats. Four parties succeeded in winning seats on the PR ballot, and divided the 225 party list seats among themselves: the Communists, Zhirinovsky's Liberal Democratic Party of Russia, the 'Our Home is Russia' bloc formed around Prime Minister Chernomyrdin, and the Yabloko bloc led by Grigorii Yavlinsky. Of these, the Communists were by far the most successful. Russia's Democratic Choice, which had been the major reform faction in the previous Duma, failed to receive even 4 per cent. Altogether, half of the votes were cast for parties that failed to win any seats on the party list ballot. These votes were redistributed to the parties that did clear the threshold. As a result, each of the four winners gained about twice as many seats as they would have been entitled to had there been no wasted votes. Moreover, the Communists were quite successful in winning district seats, taking more than 50. Combined with the seats they won through the party list vote, they wound up with one-third of the seats in parliament, the highest share that they or any party had held in the previous Duma.

The Communists and the factions allied with them came close to commanding a majority of seats in the new Duma. The Communists therefore became an indispensable member of many majority coalitions. However, their position was not secure. To win majorities, they generally needed to offer concessions to other factions or to moderate their policy stance. The Communists refrained from seeking full control over the chamber, although whether it was in their power to gain a clear and lasting majority is uncertain. In any case, they abided by the previous working arrangements in such matters as the distribution of committee chairmanships among factions, and the practice of forming task forces and legislative commissions by recruiting members from all factions. Most important, they retained the rule under which the Duma's steering committee, the Council of the Duma, comprised the leader of every faction, one leader per faction.

Likewise, President Yeltsin devoted considerable effort to bargaining with the Duma over legislation. Both the president and the government maintained permanent representative offices in the Duma, working closely with deputies to ensure the passage of key legislation. Altogether, around one hundred executive branch officials were detailed to liaison duty with the Duma. Much of the bargaining within the Duma and between the Duma and the executive went on out of public view; public attention instead tended to focus on the histrionic displays of temper on the floor and high-stakes brinkmanship between president and Duma. One of the most memorable confrontations between the branches came as the Duma tried to remove the president through impeachment. The deputies were well-aware that removal of the president by means of impeachment was a long and complicated process of which a two-thirds parliamentary vote was only the first step, and that even if they succeeded in passing a motion to impeach, the odds of actually removing Yeltsin were remote indeed. The action thus served largely symbolic purposes for the parliamentary opposition.

The Communists in the Duma had long tried to put impeachment on the agenda. They finally succeeded in June 1998, when the chamber agreed to form a commission to examine five accusations against Yeltsin: that he had committed treason by signing the agreement in December 1991 to dissolve the Soviet Union; that he had illegally initiated the war in Chechnya in 1994; that he had illegally dissolved the Russian Congress and Supreme Soviet in 1993; that he had destroyed Russia's defence capacity; and that he had committed genocide against the Russian people through the effects of the economic policies of his government since 1992. In March 1999 the commission approved all five charges and submitted them to the full chamber for its consideration. On May 15 the deputies voted on the five charges. None gained the required 300 votes, although the charge that Yeltsin had illegally initiated and conducted military operations in Chechnya came close. Yeltsin used the full range of carrots and sticks at his disposal to avert impeachment, promising material rewards to some deputies in return for their support, and reminding the Duma that he still had other trump cards in his hand.

Yet spectacular as this pyrotechnic display of president–parliament conflict was, it was already a sideshow by 1999. The polarization between democratic and communist forces, real enough in the early 1990s, had faded in importance by the end of the decade in guiding actual alignments in parliament. Although episodes such as the impeachment vote continued to attract public attention, actual parliamentary politics increasingly came to centre on distributive issues – how the benefits of government spending should be allocated; on whom the burdens of taxes should be imposed; who should control the privatization of state enterprises; to whom access rights to the exploitation of lucrative mineral resources should be granted. The Duma became a central arena for wheeling and dealing among powerful organized interests, including firms, business associations, regional governments, federal ministries, and shadowy bureaucratic 'clans' linked to senior figures in the presidency and government. The fine details of legislation were the object of acute interest; vast sums of money were at stake, not a little of which wound up in the pockets of those drafting and voting on the legislation itself (Barnes 2001).

This era ended in December 1999. Elections to the third Duma were held on December 19; five days later the second Duma held its final session. On 31 December, Yeltsin resigned as president. He was succeeded as acting president by his prime minister, Vladimir Putin, whose powerful political appeal had been demonstrated by the remarkable electoral success of the party he was loosely affiliated with, Unity, in the parliamentary election. Putin's accession to the presidency, combined with the outcome of the parliamentary election of December 1999, produced a fundamentally new dynamic in legislative–executive relations. After January 2000 the Duma was neither the arena for confrontations between the president and the opposition, nor the main site for distributive politics, but became an instrument for legislative endorsement of nearly any initiative offered by the president. This trend grew still more marked following the 2003 parliamentary election, when the president's allies gained an overwhelming majority in the Duma, and the president had succeeded in taming or suppressing nearly every source of independent political initiative in the country.

The third and fourth Dumas

The 1999 election gave the party most closely allied with Putin – Unity – a strong plurality in the Duma. Unity had to work to build majority coalitions that could pass legislation proposed by the president and government. Its success in forming a fairly reliable cross-factional majority coalition reflects the skill with which the presidential administration manipulated parliamentary politics.

Working in close cooperation with the president's parliamentary managers, Unity assembled a coalition of four parliamentary factions that coordinated voting on major legislation proposed by the president and government. Faction leaders did not succeed in enforcing pure party discipline in all cases (two of these factions were made up of deputies elected in single-member districts, who had to pay close attention to powerful local interests back home), but by drawing votes as needed from other factions, they ensured that the president's legislative agenda almost never suffered a defeat. The result was that Putin and his government were able to pass an ambitious legislative agenda, and that almost none of the legislation the Duma passed was vetoed by the president. As Table 3.2 indicates, only 61 per cent of the legislation that passed the Duma in the third (final) reading was signed by the president in the 1994–95 period, and only 74 per cent of the legislation passed in the 1996–99 period was signed. But over 95 per cent of the laws passed in the 2000–03 period were signed by the president. It is notable that whereas Yeltsin had often resorted to his presidential decree powers to enact major decisions, Putin almost never did: thanks to his commanding base of support in the parliament, he was able to pass a far more sweeping legislative agenda than

Table 3.2   *Legislative activity of the State Duma, 1994–2003*

	1994–95	*1996–99*	*1999–2003*
Laws examined in first reading	n.a.	1,693	2,053
Laws passed in third (final) reading	461	1,036	772
Laws signed by president	282	771	737

Source: *Informatsionno-analiticheskii byulleten'* *2000–2003 gg.: Itogovyi*, http://wbase. duma.gov.ru:8080/law?d&nd=981600984 (accessed 29 September 2004; data as of 31 December 2003).

Yeltsin had proposed. Putin's legislative achievements include significant changes to the tax system, legalization of a market for transactions in land, foundations for a system of mortgage lending for land, sweeping changes in the pension system, overhaul of the labour market, major changes to federal relations, substantial liberalization of the judicial system, and break-ups of major national monopolies. Painful as many of these changes were for the deputies to swallow, they ultimately passed them, albeit in some cases with modifications making them more politically palatable.

The 2003 elections produced a decisive victory for the president's forces and a humiliating defeat for the opposition both on the right and the left. The liberal democratic forces failed entirely to win party list seats and the communists' share of the party list fell nearly by half, while the party backed by the Kremlin, United Russia (the successor to Unity, which had performed so well in 1999), took 37.5 per cent of the party list vote. Together with deputies elected in single-member districts, United Russia wound up with two-thirds of the seats in the new Duma. Since the advent of democratization in the late 1980s, no party had ever held so dominant a position in parliament. United Russia used its commanding majority to make sweeping changes to the way parliament was run. They replaced the old power-sharing, proportional arrangements of the previous three Dumas with a new majoritarian system in which their members held nearly all the committee chairmanships and seats on the governing Council of the Duma, and their leader was elected the Duma's chairman. They quickly moved to impose a gag rule on their members, demanding that no member speak to the press without party approval. But for all their ability to control the Duma, theirs was a pyrrhic victory, because all the power to make policy decisions lay in the Kremlin. As total as United Russia's influence was in the Duma, the Kremlin's monopoly on policy-making was just as absolute. As a result, United Russia placed itself in a position of complete subservience to the Kremlin for its power and privileges, with no independent base of support in society. This is a mixed blessing for the Kremlin as well, however: if President Putin's political support should drop, parliament cannot offer him an independent political mandate.

The Federation Council

The Russian upper house is designed as an instrument of federalism in that every constituent unit of the federation is represented in it by two deputies. Thus the populations of small ethnic-national territories are greatly overrepresented compared with more populous regions. Members of the Federation Council were elected by direct popular vote in December 1993 but since the constitution was silent on how they were to be chosen in the future, requiring only that one representative from the executive branch and one from the legislative branch from each region be members of the chamber, new legislation was required to detail how members of the Federation Council should be chosen. Under a law passed in 1995, the heads of the executive and legislative branches of each constituent unit of the federation were automatically given seats in the Federation Council, and this was the system in force between 1996 and 1999. Under President Putin, however, new legislation was passed in 2000 which provided that the governors and legislatures of the regions were to choose full-time representatives to occupy their regions' seats in the Federation Council. This change yielded a new and heterogeneous body of members. Some regions chose prominent national political figures to serve as their voices and lobbyists in Moscow; others designated high-ranking business executives; others still sent former governors and legislators with deep roots in their regions home to represent them. About half of the members were Moscow-based, the other half came from the regions that sent them. Observers agree that the selection process is closely monitored by the Kremlin.

The Kremlin also manages the legislative process in the Federation Council. Although the Federation Council has rejected the use of political factions to organize political bargaining, its committees process a great volume of legislation efficiently. Under the constitution, some legislation is not required to be considered by the Federation Council, although the Federation Council can choose to take up any bill it wishes to consider. Actual voting in the Federation Council routinely produces lopsided majorities favouring the president's position; the chamber spends very little time on floor debate, since the decisions have been agreed upon beforehand in consultations among committee chairs and the president's representatives. Often members of the Federation Council involve them-selves in shaping legislation while it is still being considered by the Duma, so that by the time it has passed the Duma it already reflects their interests. Federation Council members also spend a good deal of time in lobbying with federal government agencies on behalf of their home regions or business interests (Remington 2003).

Constitutionally, the Federation Council has important powers. It approves presidential nominees for high courts such as the Supreme Court and the Constitutional Court. It approves presidential decrees declaring martial law or a state of emergency, and any actions altering the boundaries of territorial units in Russia. It must consider any legislation dealing with taxes, budget, financial policy, treaties, customs and declarations of war. In the Yeltsin period, the Federation Council defied the president's will on a number of issues, rejecting some of his nominees for the Constitutional Court as well as his candidates for Procurator-General. Since President Putin entered office, however, the Federation Council lost any independence it once had enjoyed. Its members, although often caught between the conflicting imperatives of their home regions and the president's domination of the political system, have rarely had much difficulty deciding to take the president's side. Although some have subsequently been recalled for defying their governors' instructions, the high degree of centralization of the Putin era means that it is far more costly to members to oppose the president than to side with the president against their home regions.

The legislative process in the Federal Assembly

Basic legislative procedure

The State Duma originates all legislation except for certain categories of policy which are under the jurisdiction of the upper house, the Federation Council. Upon final passage in the State Duma, a bill goes to the Federation Council. If the upper house rejects it, the bill goes back to the Duma, where a commission comprising members of both houses may seek to iron out differences. If the Duma rejects the upper house's changes, it may override the Federation Council by a two-thirds vote. Otherwise it votes on the version of the bill proposed by the commission (see Figures 3.1–3.3). When the bill has cleared both chambers of the Federal Assembly, it goes to the president for signature. If the president refuses to sign the bill, it returns to the Duma. The Duma may pass it with the president's proposed amendments by a simple absolute majority, or override the president's veto, for which a two-thirds vote is required. The Federation Council must then also approve the bill, by a simple majority if the president's amendments are accepted, or a two-thirds vote if it chooses to override him.

Figure 3.1 *The legislative process: overview*

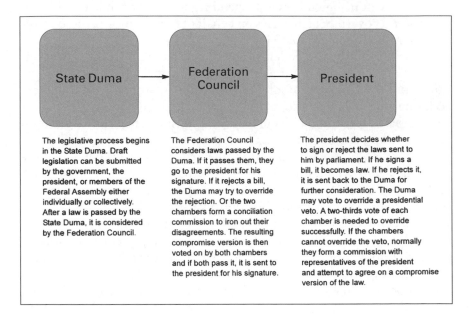

The legislative process begins in the State Duma. Draft legislation can be submitted by the government, the president, or members of the Federal Assembly either individually or collectively. After a law is passed by the State Duma, it is considered by the Federation Council.

The Federation Council considers laws passed by the Duma. If it passes them, they go to the president for his signature. If it rejects a bill, the Duma may try to override the rejection. Or the two chambers form a conciliation commission to iron out their disagreements. The resulting compromise version is then voted on by both chambers and if both pass it, it is sent to the president for his signature.

The president decides whether to sign or reject the laws sent to him by parliament. If he signs a bill, it becomes law. If he rejects it, it is sent back to the Duma for further consideration. The Duma may vote to override a presidential veto. A two-thirds vote of each chamber is needed to override successfully. If the chambers cannot override the veto, normally they form a commission with representatives of the president and attempt to agree on a compromise version of the law.

Figure 3.2 *The legislative process: bill introduction*

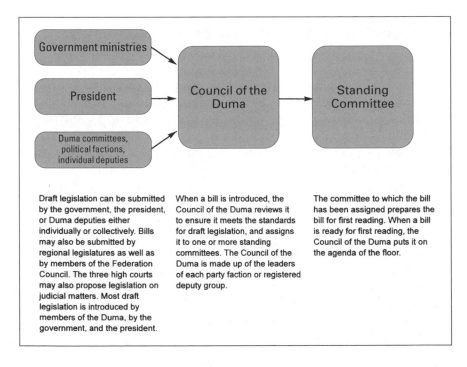

Draft legislation can be submitted by the government, the president, or Duma deputies either individually or collectively. Bills may also be submitted by regional legislatures as well as by members of the Federation Council. The three high courts may also propose legislation on judicial matters. Most draft legislation is introduced by members of the Duma, by the government, and the president.

When a bill is introduced, the Council of the Duma reviews it to ensure it meets the standards for draft legislation, and assigns it to one or more standing committees. The Council of the Duma is made up of the leaders of each party faction or registered deputy group.

The committee to which the bill has been assigned prepares the bill for first reading. When a bill is ready for first reading, the Council of the Duma puts it on the agenda of the floor.

Figure 3.3   *The legislative process: three readings*

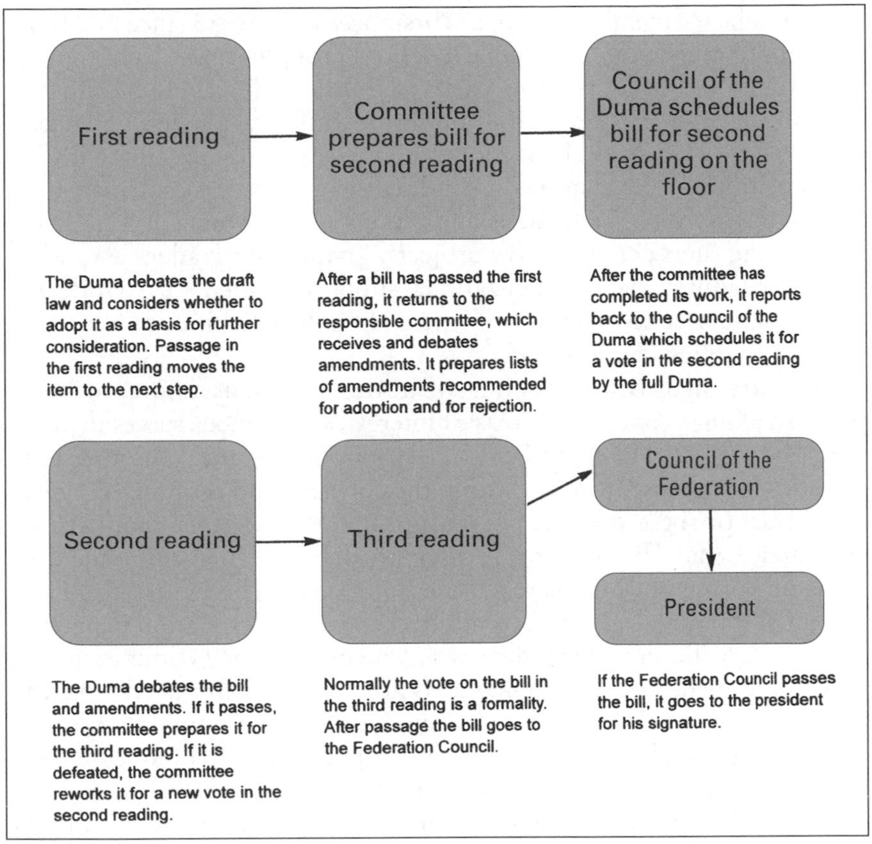

First reading	Committee prepares bill for second reading	Council of the Duma schedules bill for second reading on the floor
The Duma debates the draft law and considers whether to adopt it as a basis for further consideration. Passage in the first reading moves the item to the next step.	After a bill has passed the first reading, it returns to the responsible committee, which receives and debates amendments. It prepares lists of amendments recommended for adoption and for rejection.	After the committee has completed its work, it reports back to the Council of the Duma which schedules it for a vote in the second reading by the full Duma.
Second reading	Third reading	Council of the Federation / President
The Duma debates the bill and amendments. If it passes, the committee prepares it for the third reading. If it is defeated, the committee reworks it for a new vote in the second reading.	Normally the vote on the bill in the third reading is a formality. After passage the bill goes to the Federation Council.	If the Federation Council passes the bill, it goes to the president for his signature.

State Duma

The steering committee of the Duma is the Council of the Duma. The Council of the Duma makes the principal decisions in the Duma concerning the agenda, and acts on occasion to overcome deadlocks among the political groups represented in the Duma. Until the sweeping changes of 2004, it was made up of the leader of each party faction or registered deputy group regardless of size, and thus served to diffuse political power in the chamber. Since 2004, however, it has been dominated by the United Russia faction, whose members hold eight of its eleven seats.

Nearly all deputies in the Duma belong to a political faction or deputy group, and these factions exercise considerable influence in determining voting alignments on the floor. Each party that has won at least 5 per cent of the party-list vote in the proportional representation half of the ballot is entitled to form a faction in the Duma made up of its elected deputies, together with any of the deputies elected in single-member districts who wish to join. Moreover, any group of deputies that can assemble a minimum number of members (35 in the first three Dumas; 55 since 2004) has the right to register as a recognized deputy group in order to obtain the same rights and benefits as the party factions obtain. These benefits are valuable to deputies: they include funds for staff, office space, and procedural rights. Moreover, the factions and groups divide up all the leadership positions in the chamber, including the committee chairmanships, among themselves. The factions and groups see the Duma as a means of showcasing their pet legislative projects, giving their leaders a national forum, obtaining crucial organizational support for their party work, and providing service to their constituents. These benefits induce almost all deputies to join a faction or group.

Deputies also form a number of informal caucuses to coordinate policy-making in particular areas of interest. One caucus serves deputies strongly interested in oil and gas legislation, for instance. Another links deputies from Moscow. Even within the cohesive and centralized United Russia faction there are loose internal groupings linked to individual leaders. Factions have been relatively disciplined, however, in enforcing decisions on voting once items reach the floor stage. The Duma also has a system of standing legislative committees to handle legislation in particular issue jurisdictions. Each deputy is a member of one committee. The work of drafting and developing legislation goes on in the committees, and committees report out legislation along with recommendations on amendments that have been proposed. Members join committees according to the issues areas in which they wish to specialize.

Formally, bills are considered in three readings (see Figure 3.3). In the first reading, the Duma simply decides whether or not to approve the basic conception of a piece of legislation. If so, then the bill goes back to the committee, which then sifts through the amendments which are offered to the bill by deputies (sometimes thousands of amendments are offered to a single bill). When the committee has agreed on its recommended version of the bill, it reports it out again to the floor for a second reading, and the whole chamber decides on which amendments to approve and which to reject. At that point the floor votes on the bill in its entirety, and sends it back to the committee for a final editing and polishing. The third reading then gives the Duma's final approval to the bill and it goes to the Federation Council.

In the Putin era, a practice evolved whereby much of the bargaining over legislation occurred in the so-called 'zero reading' stage. This refers to the consultation between the government and its supporting factions in the Duma before a bill is ever formally submitted to the Duma. A number of taxing and spending bills are dealt with in this way, so that by the time the legislation is voted on in first reading, all the major decisions regarding its provisions have already been agreed to between the government and those factions that can ensure the bill's passage on the floor. The zero reading stage also gives the Federation Council an opportunity to weigh in well before the bill has been sent from the lower chamber to the upper.

Deputies have the right to initiate legislation and actively avail themselves of this opportunity to publicize their position on a particular issue. However, most major legislation originates in the executive branch, a pattern that has become much more marked since Putin's accession. Much of the development of legislation occurs through ad hoc working groups tasked with drafting bills to accomplish policy purposes decided on by the government or president. The president's annual message to parliament is considered the most authoritative statement of the president's legislative agenda. Legislative working groups typically include representatives of the federal ministries directly involved, the presidential administration, interest groups, and expert organizations. Each draft law such groups produce is then referred to a full meeting of the government (consisting of all the cabinet-level government officials) for approval before being formally submitted to parliament. Notwithstanding the dominance of the presidential administration in Russian politics, it remains the case that a great deal of inter-agency bargaining and consultation goes on in developing policy and building consensus for it. In this respect, however, the Putin era political system is not so different from the highly bureaucratized Soviet political system of the 1970s and 1980s, where most significant policy decisions were the product of lengthy intrabureaucratic deliberation.

Disagreements within the Duma, between the Duma and Federation Council, and between legislative and executive branches in the 1990s – a phenomenon much more typical of the Yeltsin era than under Putin – are typically handled by forming ad hoc commissions to resolve differences. In instances of disagreement between the branches, three-way commissions are created, consisting of Duma deputies, Federation Council members, and representatives of the president and government. In the Yeltsin period, the work of these bodies is one reason so many legislative compromises were eventually found. Over the 1996–99 period, almost 300 such inter-cameral or inter-branch commissions were created. Two-thirds of all bills that were rejected either by the Federation Council or the president on the first round were eventually passed and signed after such commissions worked out mutually acceptable language. Under Putin, however, the president enjoys such dominance in both the Duma and the Federation Council that it is unheard of for either chamber to reject a legislative initiative of the executive branch.

The 1993 constitution did not give the Federal Assembly a formal power of 'oversight' over the executive, such as the United States Congress has. Parliament has, however, other formal powers which it can use to monitor and check executive power if it is so inclined and if the executive allows it to do so. One of its instruments is the Audit Chamber, which reviews the accounts of state bodies including federal ministries, regional governments, and even private companies. Another is the practice of inviting government officials to parliament to respond to deputies' questions during 'government hour'. Committees frequently organize hearings to gather public testimony on matters of public policy and assist in developing legislation. Parliament can also conduct investigations of allegations of executive branch misconduct. All of these powers, however, can only be exercised to the extent that parliament chooses to wield them and the executive branch consents to their being used. Moreover, parliament's ability to use the results of hearings, investigations and reports is contingent on its own ability to form a collective will independent of the executive branch. In the Putin era, when political power in the state is highly concentrated in the presidential administration, parliament's independence has been reduced to virtually nil.

The Federal Assembly in perspective

The ability of a legislature to exercise its constitutional prerogatives depends both on its own internal rules and structures and on features of its institutional environment. One critical aspect of that environment in Russia is the degree to which the president dominates political processes. Yeltsin and Putin offer sharply contrasting models in this regard. Yeltsin's political and physical weakness, and, undoubtedly, his own fitful but sincere political instincts, allowed parliament to play a stronger role than has been the case under Putin. Although under Yeltsin the balance between the branches was asymmetric, with the presidency still possessing the upper hand over parliament, parliament still managed to check the president's power and influence public policy in a number of significant issue areas. This was because parliament found its own institutional means to overcome fragmentation and to produce majorities on legislative issues, and because the presidential administration and government were often divided, encouraging bureaucratic interest groups to compete for support in parliament. Putin has reversed both patterns. He has centralized and disciplined policy-making within the executive branch, and he has succeeded in reengineering the internal procedures of both chambers of parliament in such a way as to ensure him consistent and reliable majorities. In the Duma this has come about through the formation of a pro-Kremlin coalition of factions in the 2000–03 period, and since

2004 through the massive domination of United Russia. In the Federation Council Putin's reforms of 2000 deprived the Federation Council of any political independence, allowing him to shape the chamber's majorities as he chose. Thus neither chamber has the means or inclination to challenge the president. This state of affairs is not necessarily permanent, but a shift to a more balanced relationship between the branches will require significant changes on both sides. The president would need to give up much of the informal power he presently possesses, and parliament would need to win an independent political mandate from the electorate.

The series of terrorist attacks in Russia in 2004, culminating in the shocking school seizure in Beslan in September, prompted President Putin to propose still more far-reaching political reforms affecting the balance of power between the executive and legislative branches, and between the central government and the regions. He urged three changes. First, in place of directly elected governors, he proposed that the president nominate governors and have them confirmed by regional parliaments. Second, he proposed eliminating all single-member district seats from the Duma and instead filling all the 450 seats through the national party-list contest. Third, he called for the creation of a new 'public chamber' that would serve to filter and review all legislative proposals before they were submitted formally to the Duma. Taken together, these changes will severely reduce the ability of members of parliament to develop any independent base of political support: lacking local constituencies, they will have to rely on ties to the leaders of national parties; governors will have little opportunity or ability to influence deputies from their regions; and the Duma will find it more difficult to engage in legislative entrepreneurship in order to influence public policy.

The rise and fall of parliamentary power in Russia clearly illustrates the point that a given constitutional framework can accommodate substantial variation and evolution, depending on the distribution of power and preferences among key actors in the institutional environment. In Russia the place of parliament has varied significantly over time. For a period of several months in late 1998 and early 1999, Russia's political system even gravitated toward a parliamentary system, in that the head of government (at that point Yevgenii Primakov) derived his power from the support of a parliamentary majority rather than from the president. Yeltsin soon became resentful of Primakov's growing power and unceremoniously replaced him in early 1999. Yet the episode suggests that Russia's political system is still susceptible to evolution in the way its constitutional structures operate. If political parties in Russia one day become more effective in aggregating the interests and preferences of large sections of Russia's voters, then parliament will again become a more important arena for deliberation and decision. Likewise, if the mass media, national interest groups and judicial bodies gain greater independence, they will encourage members of parliament to stake out policy positions independent of the president and to position themselves as counterweights to the executive branch. Finally, if the president himself comes to recognize that a system in which the government is accountable to parliament makes it a more reliable, disciplined and effective instrument for exercising power, Russia's political system may eventually see a greater balance in the relationship between its legislative and executive branches.

Chapter 4

The Electoral System

MICHAEL McFAUL

Competitive elections are the most dramatic institutional change that distinguishes the old Soviet dictatorship from the new Russian political system. During the Soviet period, elections occurred on a regular basis. But since the ballot offered no choice and Soviet citizens faced sanctions if they did not vote, these elections lacked real political consequences. Beginning in 1989, however, Soviet leader Mikhail Gorbachev introduced reforms that allowed for semi-competitive elections to the USSR Congress of People's Deputies. This reform, in combination with others, brought about a fundamental transformation of the Soviet political system, which eventually led to the collapse of the USSR and the emergence of the Russian Federation as an independent state at the end of 1991.

The function of Russian elections has evolved over time. Since 1993, the formal institutions, rules, and regulations governing the practice of elections in Russia have changed very little. However, the political implications of elections have changed considerably. If elections in the early 1990s constituted the main political drama of post-Soviet politics, they no longer play that role today. In particular, under President Putin, the outcomes of elections have become more certain, less competitive, and therefore less meaningful in Russian politics. This change occurred in part because Putin is so popular and has faced few serious challengers during his time in office. Additionally, Putin's own political 'reforms' – that is, changes in the political system that have made Russian politics less pluralist during his reign – have also contributed to the lessening importance of elections. This result threatens the very essence of Russia's nascent democracy. If competitive elections no longer determine who governs Russia, then Russia can no longer be considered a democracy (Diamond 2002).

The non-political origins of competitive elections in Russia

In many transitions to democracy over the last two decades, competitive elections mark the culmination of a political process of change (O'Donnell and Schmitter 1986). Before these first or founding elections, incumbents in the old authoritarian regime and challengers from the democratic movement negotiated the basic contours of a new political system. At a minimum, an interim set of 'rules of the game' is codified, which spells out the rights and responsibilities of those who win the first competitive elections. Of course, the rules often change after the first elections, especially if the country in question needs to draft a new constitution. In a sense, these negotiated transitions become democracies *before* first elections take place.

The Russian transition from communist rule followed a different sequence. The last General Secretary of the Central Committee of the Communist Party of the Soviet Union, Mikhail Gorbachev, assumed when he took office that his first and principal responsibility was economic reform. He soon concluded that he needed political reform as well in order to succeed on his economic agenda. In particular, Gorbachev wanted to weaken the conservative mid-level bureaucrats in his own party, whom he perceived as the main impediments to his economic reforms. Gorbachev decided to try to give the system of elected soviets real power to counter the strength of party bureaucrats. His method of empowerment was competitive elections.

Through semi-competitive elections in the spring of 1989, Gorbachev aimed to give more legitimacy to the USSR Congress of People's Deputies. They were only partially competitive because a third of the 2,250 seats in the Congress were allocated to 'social organizations', such as the Communist Party of the Soviet Union (CPSU). The remaining seats were in principle open for contestation. Communist Party officials enjoyed unfair advantages, since the cumbersome electoral procedures made the nomination of non-communist challengers near impossible, and no substantial sources of independent financing or media existed. Nonetheless, these elections exposed Soviet voters to a competitive electoral process for the first time. It was clearly a welcome change, as one of its effects was to stimulate an unprecedented level of public participation.

In several republics including Russia, this expansion of civic activism continued until the next round of elections in the spring of 1990, when voters went back to the polls to select deputies to soviets at the republic, regional, city and district levels. The 1990 elections for the Russian Congress of People's Deputies were more democratic and more competitive than elections to the Soviet Congress the previous year. Most importantly, the Russian electoral law did not set aside any seats for 'public organizations'. Instead, all seats were filled in first-past-the-post elections in two kinds of electoral districts – one defined by the status of the region

(168 seats) and the other by number of voters (900 seats). If no candidate won 50 per cent approval in the first round, a run-off between the top two finishers occurred two weeks later.

In this election, two main camps formed: the 'democrats' and the 'communists'. The 'democrats' – a label that both their enemies and friends adopted – had begun to organize as a united political force well before the spring of 1990. In January 1990, these leaders met to plot campaign strategy for the upcoming spring elections. They founded a new organization, Democratic Russia, which assumed primary responsibility for coordinating candidate recruitment and campaign activity for Russia's nascent democratic movement. Anti-communism, anti-*status quo* and even anti-Gorbachev were the common themes of Democratic Russia's 'ideology of opposition'. The articulation of concrete alternative programmes or appeals to special ethnic or class interests did not occur.

The Communist Party constituted the second main player in the 1990 elections. However, the CPSU did not participate as an electoral party, but as the representatives of the *ancien régime*, or the incumbent 'party of power' in contemporary Russian parlance. Moreover, because the CPSU leadership was split between reformists and conservatives, the party did not orchestrate a national electoral campaign. Under the banner of the Democratic Platform, many CPSU officials actually competed in these elections as challengers and opponents to the 'party of power'.

Compared to the 1989 elections, the 1990 elections were not only freer and fairer, but they also produced a different result – a surprisingly strong showing for Russia's 'democrats' who were no longer loyal to Gorbachev. These challengers to the status quo won roughly one-third of the 1,068 seats in the Russian Congress. Communists won roughly 40 per cent of Congress seats, while 'centrists' occupied the *boloto* (or 'swamp') in the middle.

The 1990 vote was a referendum on the Soviet system and Gorbachev's attempt at reform. In urban areas where people wanted more change, 'democrats' won decisively. In rural areas where people feared change, communist candidates won. This dichotomous spectrum marginalized candidates or political groups, such as nationalists or social democrats, that attempted to carve out third positions or raise different political issues. The 1990 elections underscored the depth of public dissatisfaction with the status quo. The incumbents controlled the media, state or administrative resources (cars, phones, faxes, lists of voters, printing houses and so on), and enjoyed access to formal organizations affiliated with the Communist Party such as trade unions, women's organizations and youth groups. Yet, these advantages were not enough to counter the demand for change among a solid minority in Russia.

The 1990 elections marked a pivotal turning point for the fate of the

Soviet Union. After the 1990 elections, several republics in the Soviet Union finally had parliaments with majorities that were anti-Soviet, anti-Moscow and anti-Gorbachev. In the Russian parliament, the distribution of power between 'democrats' and 'communists' was relatively equal and polarized. But the surprising strength of the challengers to the status quo in this election propelled Boris Yeltsin to power as the chairman of the Russian Congress. He just squeezed by, winning this position after several votes and by a minuscule majority of just four votes. But once in power as the chairman, Yeltsin used his new position to directly confront Gorbachev and the Soviet state. The votes that occurred during this period, including most importantly the March 1991 referendum on the fate of the Soviet Union in which a solid majority inside Russia voted in favour of preserving the Union and the June 1991 Russian presidential election won by Yeltsin in a landslide, were events organized as part of this polarized struggle.

In this drama, Gorbachev and his government had control over all the traditional levers of power such as the state finances, the military, the police, the KGB and the media. Yeltsin and his allies had only one advantage – an electoral mandate – which proved to be critical in helping him face down the coup attempt in August 1991. Because he was elected and therefore sat physically in the 'White House', the building that housed the Russian Congress and Russian government, the democratic opposition had a place to defend when seeking to resist the coup. Yeltsin's electoral victories, in 1989, 1990, and 1991, gave him legitimacy among the Russian people that the coup plotters lacked. At this period in Soviet and Russian history, elections were playing a critical, transformative role in the destruction of the Soviet *ancien régime* and the construction of a new Russian regime.

Elections as certain procedures with uncertain outcomes

Between June 1991 and December 1993, Russia did not hold elections for national office. In the tumultuous period between the failed August 1991 coup attempt and the dissolution of the Soviet Union later that year, organizing new elections was the last item on Yeltsin's agenda. First and foremost, he concentrated on breaking up the Soviet Union in a peaceful manner, a mammoth project that involved dismantling the Communist Party of the Soviet Union and splitting into pieces the Soviet army and intelligence services while keeping his own Federation from experiencing a similar fate. His other great priority was jump-starting Russian economic reform. Yeltsin believed that he already had secured an electoral mandate from the people as recently as June 1991. His allies in the Russian Congress were elected in the spring of 1990, just a year earlier. New elections in post-Soviet Russia, therefore, seemed distracting, dangerous, and unnecessary. Yeltsin even postponed local elections scheduled for December 1991.

Yeltsin's failure to secure a new electoral mandate had destabilizing consequences for the new state. The combination of major economic dislocation, in part fuelled by Yeltsin's reforms, and poorly defined political institutions created ambiguity, stalemate and conflict both between the federal and subnational units of the state, and then, more consequentially, between the president and the Congress of People's Deputies. After price liberalization and the beginning of radical economic reform in January 1992, the Congress, once loyal to Yeltsin, began a campaign to reassert its superiority over the president. The disagreement about economic reform in turn spawned a constitutional crisis between the parliament and the president. With no formal or even informal institutions to structure relations between the president and the Congress, political polarization not unlike the stand-off between Gorbachev and Yeltsin in 1990–91 reemerged.

In this newly polarized context, both sides claimed to represent the will of the people. In the heat of the stalemate Yeltsin and the Congress agreed to ask the voters directly which political institution and what reforms they supported. In the April 1993 referendum, voters went to the polls to give answers to the following questions:

- Do you trust Russian President Yeltsin?
- Do you approve of the socioeconomic policy conducted by the Russian president and by the Russian government since 1992?
- Should a new presidential election be conducted ahead of schedule?
- Should a new parliamentary election be conducted ahead of schedule?

On the first question, despite the serious economic hardship that most people endured at the time, 58.7 per cent of voters affirmed their trust in Yeltsin, compared with 39.3 per cent who did not. Even more amazingly, 53 per cent expressed their approval of Yeltsin's socioeconomic policy, while 44.5 per cent disapproved. Regarding questions three and four a plurality (49.5 per cent) supported early presidential elections, while a solid majority (67.2 per cent) called for new parliamentary elections.

These results reflected the highly divided and polarized nature of Russian politics at the time. In essence, voters were being asked their opinion about the revolution midstream in the revolution: half supported it, half did not. This electoral result, therefore, did little to defuse the constitutional crisis in Russia. On 21 September 1993, Yeltsin issued

Presidential Decree Number 1400, which dissolved the Russian Congress of People's Deputies and called for a referendum to adopt a new constitution. The Congress rejected Yeltsin's decree as unconstitutional and instead impeached him and appointed his vice-president, Aleksandr Rutskoi, as the new president. In a replay of August 1991, the crisis only ended when one side – Yeltsin's side – prevailed in a military conflict.

The development of more certain rules

After Yeltsin's successful use of force against the Congress, which ended on 4 October 1993, the president sent mixed signals about his commitment to elections and the democratic process. Obviously, the dissolution of the Congress was a blatant violation of both the constitution and the spirit of democracy. The deputies, after all, had been elected by the Russian people. Yeltsin showed the same disregard for the electoral process by dissolving the regional soviets. He also removed three out of eight regional heads of administration who had been elected several months earlier. At the same time, Yeltsin seemed eager to establish new political rules in which elections would play a central role. He published a draft constitution and called for a referendum to approve it in December. After 4 October, Yeltsin also announced that elections for a new bicameral parliament would take place in December.

Without parliament in place, Yeltsin used decrees to establish new electoral laws. As we saw in Chapter 3, he dictated that the new lower house of parliament, the State Duma, would be elected according to a mixed system: half of the 450 seats would be determined by a first-past-the-post system in newly drawn-up electoral districts, while the other half would be allocated according to a system of proportional representation. Parties had to win at least 5 per cent of the popular vote to win seats on the proportional representation ballot. For the Federation Council, the upper house, Yeltsin decreed that voters in each of Russia's 89 regions would cast two votes for their senatorial candidates on one list. The top two finishers in each region would win.

The December 1993 elections served as the founding elections for Russia's new political system. A majority of Russian voters ratified Yeltsin's draft constitution, giving popular legitimacy to a set of political rules for governing Russia. (While it seems clear that a majority of voters did support the constitution, it is not clear that the 50 per cent of eligible voters participated in the referendum, the required minimum to make the election valid. Some electoral observers amassed serious evidence suggesting that the turnout numbers had been falsified (Sobyanin and Sukhovolsky 1995)). The new constitution outlined difficult procedures for amending it, meaning that adoption of this constitution was likely to produce a lasting set of political institutions for postcommunist Russia. Since 1993, the constitution has not been amended. The December 1993 vote was also the first election in Russia's brief democratic history in which political parties had the opportunity to participate fully, with proportional representation being an additional incentive for stimulating party participation and development.

The basic rules of the game for elections to the Duma established during this tumultuous period in the autumn of 1993 have endured more than a decade. Eventually the newly elected Duma codified Yeltsin's mixed electoral system into law, meaning that four parliamentary elections (1993, 1995, 1999 and 2003) occurred using the same electoral system. Electoral districts have been redrawn, but not in a radical way. Since 1993, all parliamentary elections occurred as scheduled, as prescribed by law. The 2000 presidential vote occurred three months earlier than planned because Boris Yeltsin suddenly resigned from his office on the last day of the millennium. As outlined in the law on presidential elections, a new election had to be held three months after Yeltsin's resignation, meaning the vote was held in March instead of June. All other major rules and practices governing presidential elections, however, have remained stable over the last decade. If examining the formal rules and procedures, elections in Russia have become normal, certain events. The predictability of elections and the stability of those institutions run by elected officials in Russia during the last decade stand in sharp contrast to the earlier electoral history from 1989 to 1993, when not a single elected legislative body served out its full term. Formally, the Russian president has the power to disband the Duma under certain circumstances spelled out in the constitution. Since the end of 1993, however, the Russian parliament has never been dissolved.

The Federation Council is the one government body that has experienced volatility in how it is constituted. Originally, as just discussed, deputies to this upper house of parliament were elected in double-mandate districts: in each region in Russia the top two finishers won seats in the Federation Council. After the 1993 vote, however, the rules governing the formation of the Federation Council twice changed dramatically. Before the parliamentary election in 1995, regional executives (presidents in republics and governors in *oblasts* and *krais*) and heads of regional parliaments pushed hard for and succeeded in winning the right for direct elections to their regional offices, followed by automatic appointment to the Federation Council rather than direct elections. Such a formulation gave governors increased local legitimacy and greater autonomy from Yeltsin and Moscow, because elected governors were harder to dismiss than appointed ones. This new formulation also gave governors a direct voice in national legislative affairs, blurring the divisions both between executive and legislative powers and between national and subnational units of the federal system. This formulation lasted until Vladimir Putin was elected president in the spring of 2000. In one of his first acts as president, Putin pressed for and eventually succeeded in changing the constitution of the Federation Council. Instead of elected governors and head of regional parliaments, the Putin formulation called on regional executive and legislative heads to appoint representatives to the Federation Council from their regions. In effect, this new procedure for selecting 'senators' made the upper house less powerful, since those serving did not have an electoral mandate.

Uncertain electoral outcomes

Since 1993, Russia's electoral rules have become increasingly certain. At the same time, throughout the 1990s, the outcome of these elections remained uncertain. For those interested in the development of Russia's electoral democracy, this was good news, as the presence of stable electoral rules and unpredictable electoral outcomes is the essence of genuine democracy (Przeworski 1991).

The constitutional referendum in December 1993 produced predictable if somewhat contentious results (these and later results are set out in Table 4.1). Not surprisingly, a majority of Russians approved the new constitution. But the vote for the Duma did produce a shocking, unexpected result. The pro-reform party affiliated with Yeltsin, Russia's Choice, won only 15 per cent of the popular vote, only a third of what pollsters and analysts had predicted just two months earlier. Even more amazing was the strong showing of Vladimir Zhirinovsky's Liberal Democratic Party of Russia (LDPR), a xenophobic, nationalist organization that was neither liberal nor democratic. In essence, Russian voters remained divided in rather equal proportions between those who supported Yeltsin's 'reforms' and those that did not. Zhirinovsky's supporters were simply a new, non-communist expression of dissatisfaction with Yeltsin's course. Zhirinovsky's sudden splash created the impression that Russian voters yearned for a fascist resolution to the tumultuous times in which they lived.

The results of the 1995 parliamentary vote were also surprising (the parliament elected in 1993 was an interim body whose term expired after two years, instead of the normal four years as stated in the constitution). In the two-year interval between the first and second Duma elections, Zhirinovsky's star had waned. Taking advantage of Zhirinovsky's demise was the Communist Party of the Russian Federation (CPRF), which

Table 4.1 *Elections to the Russian State Duma, 1993–2003*

	1993				1995				1999				2003			
	List (%)	List seats	SMC seats	Total seats	List (%)	List seats	SMC seats	Total seats	List (%)	List seats	SMC seats	Total seats	List (%)	List seats	SMC seats	Total seats
LDPR	22.9	59	5	64	11.2	50	1	51	6.0	17	0	17	11.5	36	0	36
RC	15.5	40	27	67	3.9	0	9	9	–	–	–	–	–	–	–	–
CPRF	12.4	32	16	48	22.3	99	58	157	24.3	67	46	113	12.6	40	12	52
WR	8.1	21	2	23	4.6	0	3	3	2.0	0	0	0	–	–	–	–
AP	8.0	21	11	33	3.8	0	20	20	–	–	–	–	–	–	–	–
Yabloko	7.9	20	6	26	6.9	31	14	45	5.9	16	4	20	3.6	0	2	2
PRUC	6.7	18	1	19	0.4	0	1	1	–	–	–	–	4.3	0	4	4
DPR	5.5	14	1	15	–	–	–	–	–	–	–	–	–	–	–	–
NDR	–	–	–	–	10.1	45	10	55	1.2	0	7	7	0.2	0	0	0
Unity	–	–	–	–	–	–	–	–	23.3	64	9	73	–	–	–	–
FAR	–	–	–	–	–	–	–	–	13.3	37	31	68	–	–	–	–
SPS	–	–	–	–	–	–	–	–	8.5	24	5	29	4.0	0	3	3
UR	–	–	–	–	–	–	–	–	–	–	–	–	37.6	120	105	225
Rodina	–	–	–	–	–	–	–	–	–	–	–	–	9.0	29	8	37
Others	8.7	0	8	8	34.0	0	32	32	12.2	0	9	9	17.2	0	33	33
Independents	–	–	141	141	–	–	77	77	–	–	105	105	–	–	69	69
Against all	4.2	–	–	–	2.8	–	–	–	3.3	–	–	–	4.7	–	–	–

Party abbreviations are: LDPR: Liberal Democratic Party of Russia (competing in 1999, as the Zhirinovsky Bloc); RC: Russia's Choice (in 1995, Russia's Democratic Choice); CPRF: Communist Party of the Russian Federation; WR: Women of Russia; AP: Agrarian Party; PRUC: Party of Russian Unity and Concord; DPR: Democratic Party of Russia; NDR: Our Home is Russia; FAR: Fatherland–All Russia; SPS: Union of Right Forces; UR: United Russia.
Source: Central Electoral Commission.

reemerged as the leading force of the anti-Yeltsin coalition. The CPRF made impressive gains, winning almost a quarter of the popular vote and reclaiming its role as the leader of the opposition. Buoyed by party identification on the ballot, CPRF candidates also dominated the single-mandate races. Zhirinovsky won less than half his 1993 total, but still came second, and Prime Minister Viktor Chernomyrdin's Our Home is Russia (NDR) was the only reformist party to break through to double digits. Grigorii Yavlinsky's Yabloko, the self-proclaimed leader of Russia's democratic opposition, dropped almost a full percentage point, and former acting prime minister Yegor Gaidar and his Democratic Choice of Russia (a modified reincarnation of Russia's Choice from 1993) suffered the greatest setback, winning less than a third of its 1993 total. The Kremlin did not orchestrate this election result. On the contrary, Yeltsin aides created, generously funded, and provided massive media coverage to Our Home is Russia, yet the pro-Kremlin bloc placed a distant third, while outright opponents of those in power scored major gains.

Coming just six months after the communist comeback in the December 1995 parliamentary elections, the 1996 presidential election also exhibited great uncertainty, especially in the early months of the campaign. President Yeltsin began the New Year with a single-digit approval rating. Support for his policies, such as the Chechnya war, hovered in the low double digits. Russia seemed poised to follow the electoral trajectories in other postcommunist countries in which first-generation reformers lost their second election to left-of-centre parties.

Yeltsin, however, still enjoyed several advantages over his opponents that eventually helped him win a second term. Perhaps most importantly, Yeltsin was offered the opportunity to campaign yet again against an old-style communist, CPRF leader Gennadii Zyuganov. The reemergence of the Communist Party as the main opposition force allowed those in power to frame the 1996 election as a referendum between communism and the past versus anti-communism and the future. With the contest framed in this way, Yeltsin could assert that he was the only reform candidate capable of defeating the communist challenge (McFaul 1997).

Yeltsin enjoyed the additional advantage of controlling Russia's two major television stations, ORT and RTR. Both channels broadcast relentlessly pro-Yeltsin and anti-Zyuganov ads, news, talk shows and 'documentaries'. Russia's third national channel at the time, NTV, was a private company, but its owner, Vladimir Gusinsky, backed Yeltsin as did all the other business tycoons – the so-called oligarchs – who had made their fortunes during the Yeltsin era. Yeltsin also employed the more traditional tactics of distributing government pork to obtain support from regional heads of administration (Treisman and Gimpelson 1998). During the campaign, Yeltsin raised pensions and increased the salaries of government employees. For the first time since 1989, the administrative resources of the state were playing an instrumental role in deciding the outcome of a national election.

In a field of a dozen candidates, Yeltsin barely managed to win more votes than his communist opponent: in the first round he took 35 per cent of the vote, while Zyuganov captured 32 per cent. However, when the vote became a binary choice between the 'communist' and the 'reformer', the vast majority of Russians still favoured moving forward, not backwards. In the second round, Yeltsin's entire campaign message painted him as the lesser of two evils. Yeltsin won easily in the second round, winning 54 per cent of the popular vote compared with Zyuganov's 40 per cent. In contrast with electoral trends in many parts of postcommunist Europe, Russian voters opted to retain their first democratically elected leader for a second term.

The 1999 Duma elections continued to exhibit the same mix of certainty about the procedures, but uncertainty about the results. In fact, the December 1999 parliamentary election may have been Russia's most competitive in the 1990s, since the ruling elite was openly divided. In the prelude to the 1999 campaign, the combination of the August 1998 financial crash, the subsequent instability in the government and Yeltsin's declining health created the appearance of weakness and disarray in the Kremlin. Those in power looked vulnerable. Just a year before the presidential election, they had not produced a candidate to replace Yeltsin. The Kremlin's lack of a game plan for staying in power eventually triggered the defection of many considered to be part of the ruling party of power. Moscow mayor Yuri Luzhkov planned to participate in the next electoral cycle as an opposition candidate. Former prime minister Yevgenii Primakov joined Luzhkov's coalition, Fatherland–All Russia (OVR), as a step towards winning the 2000 presidential election. At the beginning of the 1999 campaign, Primakov was ahead of all other presidential contenders by a large margin. For the first time in its postcommunist history, Russia appeared poised to hand over presidential power from one political group to another through the ballot box.

Those close to Yeltsin in the Kremlin were not going to vacate their fortress without a fight. Because Primakov decided to compete in the 1999 parliamentary vote as a way to build momentum for 2000, his enemies in and close to the Kremlin decided to join the battle against the former prime minister in the parliamentary election as well. As a result, the 1999 election was the first time the federal government became actively involved in a parliamentary contest.

As in 1996, the state played a tremendous role in shaping the outcome of the 1999 election. Working closely with figures in the presidential administration, Russian tycoon Boris Berezovsky helped to invent a new pro-presidential electoral bloc, Unity. State resources contributed to this new electoral bloc, often referred to in the Russian press at the time as a 'virtual' party. Berezovsky hired the best electoral consultants money could buy and then deployed the full force of his ORT television station to promote Unity and destroy OVR. To a lesser degree, RTR assumed a similar mission. ORT newscasters and commentators unleashed the most vicious personal attacks of any Russian campaign against OVR leaders (White *et al.* 2005).

Indirectly, another arm of the state – the armed forces – contributed to the rise of Unity and the eventual presidential winner, Putin. Russian armed forces responded to an attack by Chechen rebel forces against Dagestan and alleged terrorist attacks against Russian civilians in Moscow and elsewhere by invading Chechnya in September 1999. At the time, Prime Minister Putin had a negligible approval rating; however, the war effort – especially as portrayed on ORT and RTR – was popular, and soon catapulted Putin's popularity into double digits and above all other presidential contenders. Putin in turn endorsed Unity. The blessing of the popular prime minister helped the virtual electoral bloc win nearly a quarter of the popular vote.

The results of the 1999 parliamentary vote radically altered the balance of power within the Duma and determined the winner of the 2000 presidential race. As in 1995, the CPRF won the largest percentage of any party, 24 per cent, an outcome that ensured Zyuganov a second-place finish yet again in the presidential contest the next year. Unity came second with 23 per cent, followed by OVR in a distant third place with a vote that was so disappointing that Primakov decided not to run in the 2000 presidential election. The newly revamped liberal coalition, the Union of Right Forces, surprised many by winning more than 8 per cent of the popular vote, almost double the total of its chief liberal rival, Yabloko. Zhirinovsky's Liberal Democratic Party of Russia continued to fade, winning only 6 per cent of the party list vote and just barely crossing the 5 per cent threshold.

When the distribution of seats from single-mandate races was added into the equation, the balance of power within the parliament had moved in a decisively pro-Putin direction. The Communist Party still controlled a solid minority of seats, but it could not construct opposition majorities to Kremlin initiatives. The combination of a loyal Unity, a divided and weakened Communist Party, a sometimes supportive SPS (Union of Right Forces), and strong backing from independents and other smaller factions produced a parliament supportive of Putin on major issues – an outcome that few would have predicted just a year earlier.

The Putin era: certain procedures and certain outcomes

The results of the 1999 parliamentary election made clear that Putin was going to win the 2000 presidential election. Upon naming Putin prime minister in August 1999, Yeltsin had hinted that he hoped Putin would replace him as president the following year. Yeltsin gave his heir one last boost by resigning as president on 31 December 1999, an act that moved the date of the presidential election from June to March. As Putin's popularity peaked in January and slowly declined until election day in March, Yeltsin's decision to resign was critical in helping Putin win the 2000 presidential election in the first round.

During the abbreviated campaign period in 2000, Putin continued to enjoy the unequivocal support of ORT and RTR. Though Putin did not run an official campaign, which he considered demeaning for a sitting president, these television stations continued to document his every move in glowing terms. His opponents, by contrast, received no attention at all from these Kremlin-friendly media outlets. Most oligarchs and regional heads of administration also stumbled over each other in trying to show their support for Putin, since everyone knew he was going to win. And they were right to jump on board since Putin won in a landslide, winning more than half of the popular vote in the first ballot, compared to 24 per cent for the runner-up, communist candidate Zyuganov.

Unity's surge in 1999 and then Putin's victory in 2000 marked the beginning of the Kremlin's dominance over national electoral politics in Russia. Throughout the 1990s, electoral support for Yeltsin and his allies always seemed precarious. Yeltsin orchestrated a dramatic comeback to win reelection in 1996, but parliamentary votes both before and after 1996 demonstrated that support for Yeltsin's policies was soft. The volatility in voter preferences in 1999, expressed in opinion polls during the campaign, suggested that the traditional cleavage among voters between 'democrats' and 'communists' had faded as the central driver of Russian electoral politics. Beginning in the 1999–2000 electoral cycle, Putin offered a different reason to support his party and his candidacy – stability. After a decade of chaotic revolutionary change, Russian citizens yearned for it. With the exception of the ongoing war in Chechnya, Putin delivered it. The Russian economy grew more in each year of Putin's first term in office than in all of the previous decade. Voters did not care whether this growth was due to Putin's economic reforms, which were substantial, or to the combination of high oil prices and low international interest rates. Putin got the credit regardless. More generally, Putin's positive rating as a leader hovered well above 70 per cent for his entire first term. In contrast to Yeltsin, Putin appeared to be a young and able leader who showed up for work every day and made Russians proud again of their president and their country.

It was not surprising, therefore, that Putin and his allies won again in the 2003 parliamentary elections and the 2004 presidential elections. In December 2003, his party – United Russia (the latest incarnation of Unity from 1999) – won a major victory, capturing more than a third of the popular vote on the party list and winning more than a hundred of the single-mandate contests. Two other parties close to the Kremlin also performed well beyond expectations: Zhirinovsky's LDPR doubled its total from the 1999 parliamentary election, winning 11.5 per cent of the popular vote. The other Kremlin-friendly party to cross the threshold on the party list, with 9.2 per cent of the popular vote, was Rodina (Motherland), a loose coalition of nationalist and left-of-centre politicians that the Kremlin helped to organize and then advertise over the course of the campaign. After the vote and after independents lined up behind different factions in the Duma, United Russia and its allies controlled the two-thirds majority needed to pass amendments to the constitution.

While the pro-Kremlin parties surged in 2003, the main opposition parties on both the left and right faltered. On the left, the CPRF lost half of its party-list vote from 1999, and managed only eleven victories in single-member districts. As a result, the CPRF faction in the Duma shrank by 61 seats, falling from 113 in 1999 to 52 in 2003. Liberal opponents of the Kremlin fared even worse than their comrades on the left. Both Yabloko and the Union of Right Forces (SPS) failed to cross the 5 per cent threshold. In the single-mandate contests, Yabloko won only four seats, while candidates affiliated with SPS won three seats. For the first time since competitive elections began in 1990, the liberals had no faction in the parliament. To varying degrees, all three parliamentary parties that increased their share of the popular vote since the last election supported Putin and enjoyed support from the state. All three parties that criticized Putin (and hence did not enjoy state support) fared worse in 2003 than they had in 1999.

The overwhelming victory of United Russia in the Duma elections made it clear that Putin would win the presidential ballot without any difficulty. Indeed, Putin's reelection was so certain that none of the party leaders who competed in the December parliamentary vote ran as presidential candidates in March. Zhirinovsky, Communist Gennadii Zyuganov, Yabloko leader Grigorii Yavlinsky and SPS leader Boris Nemtsov all stepped aside, and let other lesser-known figures in their parties run in vain against Putin. In March, Putin won on the first ballot, capturing more than 71 per cent of the popular vote. The Communist Party candidate Nikolai Kharitonov came a distant second with 13.7 per cent. Former Motherland leader Sergei Glazev came in third with 4.1 per cent; Irina Khakamada of the SPS garnered only 3.8 per cent; the LDPR candidate, Zhirinovsky bodyguard Oleg Malyshkin, managed just 2.0 per cent; and Putin backer and Russian Party of Life candidate Sergei Mironov trailed the field with 0.7 per cent, well behind 'against all', the choice of 3.4 per cent of those who went to the polls.

State limits on the electoral playing field

Given the president's popularity, it is hard to imagine how Putin and his surrogates could have lost free and fair elections in 2003 or 2004. We can only speculate about the results of free and fair elections, however, because the actual elections in December 2003 and March 2004 took place in a context that did not offer a level playing field. Instead, Putin's regime limited opportunities for political challengers while at the same time it provided the president and his supporters with virtually unlimited 'administrative resources' to wield during the campaign. To be sure, Putin did not inherit a consolidated democracy from Boris Yeltsin. At the end of Yeltsin's rule, Russia's democratic institutions were still weak (McFaul 2001). Nonetheless, Putin did little to strengthen democratic institutions and much to weaken them (McFaul *et al.* 2004).

First, Putin and his government initiated a series of successful campaigns against independent media outlets. When Putin came to power, only three television networks had the national reach to really count in politics – ORT, RTR and NTV. By running billionaire Boris Berezovsky out of the country with a politically motivated criminal prosecution, Putin effectively acquired control of ORT, the channel with the biggest national audience. RTR was always fully state-owned, and so it was even easier to tame. Controlling the third channel, NTV, proved more difficult since its owner, Vladimir Gusinsky, decided to fight. But in the end, he too lost not only NTV but also the daily newspaper *Segodnya* and the weekly *Itogi* when prosecutors pressed charges. When the parliamentary campaign started, the Kremlin de facto controlled all television networks with a national reach.

At the same time, the independence of electronic media eroded on the regional level. Heads of local state-owned television stations continue to follow political signals from regional executives, and most regional heads of administration stood firmly behind Putin in the last electoral cycle. Private and cable stations steer clear of political analysis altogether. Dozens of newspapers and web portals have remained independent and offer a platform for political figures of all persuasions, but none of these platforms enjoys mass audiences. Moreover, Putin has changed the atmosphere for doing journalistic work. When journalists have criticized his policies, such as the war in Chechnya or his handling of the sinking of the submarine *Kursk* in 2000, he has called them traitors. As we note in Chapter 7, media independence eroded so significantly during Putin's first term that Freedom House downgraded Russia's media from 'partly free' to 'not free'. Reporters without Borders, which published their first worldwide press-freedom index in 2002, ranked Russia 121st out of 139 countries assessed (just one ranking above Iran), making it one of the worst performers in the postcommunist world. The Committee to Protect Journalists accorded Russia the dubious distinction of being one of the ten worst places in the world to be a journalist.

Given these changes, the media played a very different role in the 2003–4 electoral cycle than they had four years earlier. During the campaign for the 1999 parliamentary elections, Russian elites supported different electoral blocs: OVR or Unity. Russia's national media outlets lined up on both sides of this divide. ORT and RTR backed Unity, while Gusinsky's NTV as well as Luzhkov's Moscow television station TV–Centre and several other regional stations backed OVR. The playing field was not equal, but opposing points of view were represented in the national electronic media. In the 2003 parliamentary vote and 2004 presidential election, by contrast, the Kremlin controlled all the major national television stations, and because most regional elites were now united behind Putin, the vast majority of regional stations (including Moscow's TV–Centre) also sided with pro-Kremlin candidates.

A second important political change carried out on Putin's watch was 'regional reforms'. Almost immediately after becoming president in 2000, Putin made reining in Russia's regional barons a top priority. As we discuss more fully in Chapters 9 and 10, he began his campaign to reassert Moscow's authority by establishing seven supraregional districts headed primarily by former generals and KGB officers. These new super-governors were assigned the task of taking control of all federal agencies in their jurisdictions, many of which had developed affinities if not loyalties to regional governments during the Yeltsin era. These seven representatives of federal executive authority also investigated governors and presidents of republics as a way of undermining their autonomy and threatening them into subjugation. As already discussed, Putin also emasculated the Federation Council, and regional leaders who resisted his authority found elections rigged against them. In the most recent gubernatorial elections in the Kursk, Saratov and Rostov regions, as well as in the presidential races in Chechnya and Ingushetia, the removal of the strongest contenders ensured an outcome favourable to the Kremlin.

These reforms regarding the distribution of power between Moscow and the regions had important consequences for national elections in

2003 and 2004. Wielding carrots and sticks, the Kremlin eliminated the serious divisions among regional elites that had created the main drama of the 1999 parliamentary elections. By late 2003, almost all regional leaders were supporting Putin and United Russia. These regional executives also deployed their local resources to support United Russia candidates in the single-mandate district races.

A third context-changing initiative by the Putin regime was a crackdown on the oligarchs. Very early in his first term, Putin made clear that the oligarchs could no longer treat the state as simply another tool to be used for their personal enrichment. Instead, Putin implied that the oligarchs had to get out of politics altogether. Eventually, he arrested or chased into exile three major oligarchs – Boris Berezovsky, Vladimir Gusinsky, and Russia's richest man, Mikhail Khodorkovsky, head of the oil conglomerate Yukos. All three had previously played significant roles in funding and supporting political parties and individuals not deemed loyal to the Kremlin. The marginalization of these three sent a chilling message to other tycoons. In the 2003 parliamentary campaign, oligarchs continued to contribute significant resources to political campaigns, but only as sanctioned by the Kremlin. Compared to the previous electoral cycle, big business in 2003 was relatively united in backing United Russia and other pro-Kremlin candidates. In 2004, everyone backed Putin.

The effect of these political 'reforms' on the 2003–4 electoral cycle occurred well before the votes were actually cast. The absence of independence or internal divisions within media, regional elite and oligarchic ranks reduced the freedom to manoeuvre for opposition political parties and candidates. At the same time, the state's larger role in this electoral cycle gave incumbents enormous advantages, be it positive, continuous and free national television coverage, massive logistical and administrative support from regional executives, or enormous financial resources from companies like Gazprom and Lukoil. Before the legislative balloting, the Organization for Security and Cooperation in Europe (OSCE) issued its first-ever critical preliminary report on a Russian election, stressing that the

> State Duma elections failed to meet many OSCE and Council of Europe commitments for democratic elections. In addition, important safeguards in domestic legislation were not enforced by the Russian authorities. This is a worrisome development that calls into question Russia's fundamental willingness to meet European and international standards for democratic elections. (OSCE 2003)

Although none of Russia's previous elections were wholly free and fair, the most recent ones have been the least free and fair of all.

Conclusion: do elections still matter?

In the last years of the Soviet Union and the first years of independent Russia, elections helped to weaken or remove communist incumbents and open political opportunities for non-communist challengers. In the context of social, political and economic upheaval, elections in the USSR and then Russia often were convoked to serve an immediate political purpose. They were not simply ways to choose leaders, but were used and manipulated in the heat of battle over such major issues as the fate of the Soviet Union or the course of economic reform. The ad hoc nature of these elections underscored the political motivations behind them; the dates of the first six national multiparty elections in the Soviet Union and then in Russia were all determined just months before the vote.

Since 1993, national elections have become more regular and antici-pated events conducted in the context of a widely accepted constitutional system and guided by electoral laws approved through a democratic process. However, stability in the electoral calendar and electoral proce-dures has been paralleled by increasing stability in the outcomes of elec-tions. The most powerful office in the country – the presidency – has not seen a turnover of power. The landslide victory of the party of power in the 2003 parliamentary elections and the 2004 presidential election marked a new milestone in demonstrating how incumbents could use elections to help strengthen their power.

In democracies all over the world, incumbents enjoy tremendous elec-toral advantages. For instance, in the 2002 elections for the US House of Representatives, incumbents seeking reelection won 98 per cent of the time. Before the election, fewer than 30 of the 435 races were even consid-ered competitive. Parties of power have remained in power for decades in countries widely regarded as liberal democracies.

Nonetheless, the way in which Russian elites have begun to deploy state resources to stay in power represents a greater challenge to the democratic process than some of these other examples of incumbent entrenchment in liberal democracies. The imbalance in resources of the state compared to resources controlled by society give those already in power a tremendous and unfair advantage. The state's growing role in determining who gets on the ballot and who does not is an especially disturbing trend. The trajectory over the last decade has been clear – a growing role for the state in determining electoral outcomes.

At the same time, the elimination of elections is unlikely, since too many actors are interested in preserving the process. The political elite need elections in their present form to legitimize their rule. International norms also place pressure on the Russian elite to continue the formal practice of elections. Moreover, polls indicate that very solid majorities of

Russian citizens believe that their leaders should be elected (Colton and McFaul 2003).

Consequently, elections are likely to perform a quasi-democratic function in Russia for the foreseeable future. Elections in which several parties and multiple candidates participate will continue to occur, though the party of power – currently called United Russia – is likely to win these contests thanks to monopoly control over national television, unstinting support from the oligarchs, and solid backing from most regional elites. In close elections they also are likely to benefit from the control of those state institutions that have demonstrated a capacity to falsify elections.

Elections of limited consequence, however, are better than no elections at all. And as dictators in Kenya and Serbia recently learned, elections can unexpectedly change from a charade into a much more meaningful procedure during periods of crisis. In Russia today, elections have less meaning than they did several years ago. In a time of crisis, they might acquire meaning again.

Chapter 5

The Political Parties

STEPHEN WHITE

The Bolshevik revolution of October 1917 ushered in more than two generations of single-party dominance. Formally, there was no limit on the number of parties that could be formed; the Bolsheviks were in coalition with the radical Left Socialist Revolutionaries for some months after the revolution, and other parties continued a de facto existence until the mid-1920s. But fairly soon, the boundaries of political contestation began to be narrowed: factions were banned in the Bolshevik party itself in 1921, and opposition leaders were marginalized or in a few cases (in 1922) put on trial. According to the new orthodoxy, the working people had a single interest; that single interest was expressed in the Communist Party, which had a scientific understanding of the laws of social development; and with the establishment of public ownership of productive resources there could be no social basis for the kind of political divisions that were to be found in capitalist countries.

Formally speaking, the Communist Party was one of the USSR's many 'voluntary associations', although it was clearly the dominant political institution from a very early stage. The 1936 'Stalin' constitution spelt out its role more fully when, for the first time, it acknowledged the Communist Party as the 'vanguard of the toilers' and the 'leading core of all organizations'. The 1977 constitution, adopted during Leonid Brezhnev's leadership, made still more comprehensive provision for the party's political dominance when it defined the Communist Party in its sixth article as the 'leading and guiding force of Soviet society, the core of its political system and of state and public organizations', and as a body that gave a 'planned, scientifically grounded character to the struggle [of the Soviet people] for the victory of communism'.

The Gorbachev years, in the later 1980s, saw the dissolution of the Communist monopoly and the emergence of an 'informal' and then an organized opposition. The first largely competitive elections took place in 1989, with a choice of candidates in most seats if not a choice of parties. Then in February 1990 the Communist Party agreed to relinquish its guaranteed leading role, and the constitution was amended accordingly the following month. In October 1990 a new law 'On public organizations' provided a formal basis for what had already become a multiparty society, although it was one within which the CPSU remained the most important source of political authority; and in April 1991 a second political party was officially registered, the Liberal Democratic Party, after it had completed the necessary formalities. The collapse of the attempted coup in August 1991 led meanwhile to the suspension and later the banning of the CPSU entirely (Gorbachev had already resigned as leader), and then in December 1991 the state itself dissolved into fifteen independent republics.

The Russian Federation was by far the largest of the successor republics, and the constitution it adopted in 1993 committed the new state to 'ideological diversity' and 'multiparty politics' provided the constitutional order was respected and that no attempt was made to incite social, racial, national or religious animosity (Art. 13). What kind of multiparty politics this would be remained unclear and, indeed, remains somewhat unclear more than a decade after the transition to postcommunist rule. For some, it was best described as a 'floating party system' (Rose *et al.* 2001), one in which the turnover of parties was so rapid that they offered no opportunity for an electorate to pass judgement on their performance. Others (for instance, White 2005) have called it a 'client party system', heavily dependent on the support of the central authorities or other sponsors, and focused around a 'party of power' that is sponsored by the regime itself. Whatever the label, there has been little sign to date of a party system that performs the classic functions of its Western counterparts: recruiting a political leadership, offering alternative programmes of government, and linking citizens more generally with the political process.

The contemporary party spectrum

The Russian party spectrum in the early years of the twenty-first century hardly conformed to a 'classic' left–right formation. Many parties avoided designating themselves in these terms, and in any case about half of the electorate typically found it difficult to place themselves on the same kind of scale, a level much lower than in Western Europe (Colton 2000: 144–8). Several other classifications have been suggested: parties, for instance, might be 'bureaucratic' or 'charismatic' (following Max Weber); alternatively, they could be 'parties of power' or 'parties of the elite' (Kryshtanovskaya 2003: 144–59). Another, more elaborate classification distinguished between 'parties of the leader' (such as the Liberal Democrats, who have been all but indistinguishable from their long-standing chairman, Vladimir Zhirinovsky, or Yabloko, headed from the outset by economist Grigorii Yavlinsky); 'parties of values' (such as the Communist Party, or the Union of Right Forces); and 'parties of power' (such as United Russia, which was virtually defined by its support of the president, or before it the pro-Kremlin party Our Home is Russia) (*Izvestiya*, 31 March 2003: 3).

As of the start of 2005 there were 43 parties registered with the Ministry of Justice, and which were accordingly permitted to put forward candidates at elections. Some 23 parties or blocs of parties put forward candidates in the party-list contest for seats in the State Duma in December 2003, although only four won enough votes to clear the 5 per cent threshold and secure representation in their own right. Another four parties secured 2 per cent or more, which was enough to avoid repayment of the state funds they had received for their campaign publicity but short of the threshold, and a total of eleven parties won seats in contests for the single-member constituencies of which the Duma is also composed (the Liberal Democrats won a share of party-list seats, but not a single one of the single-member constituencies; accordingly, twelve parties won seats in either of the two sets of contests). The largest share of the vote in the single-member constituencies, however, more than 26 per cent, was cast for independents rather than for the candidates that had been nominated by any of the political parties (see Table 4.1).

Of the six parties that won the largest share of the party-list vote, the closest to a political party of the conventional kind was the Communist Party of the Russian Federation (CPRF), which was the successor to the Communist Party of the Soviet Union and, much earlier, the Russian Social Democratic Workers' Party that had been formed in 1898 and which had subsequently led the October Revolution. The CPRF had a substantial grassroots membership and a functioning national structure, both of them largely inherited from Soviet times; and it had the best established party press, with three national newspapers (including *Pravda*) and two oppositional papers that were broadly supportive. Its leader was Gennadii Zyuganov, a party official from the late Soviet period, whose booming voice and homely features ensured his nationwide recognition. He was the party's standard-bearer in the 1996 presidential election, when he took Boris Yeltsin to a second round, but was less successful in 2000 (when Putin won on the first round), and did not compete in 2004.

The party programme, as amended in 1997, reflected nationalist as well as socialist concerns. It took issue with the 'barbaric and primitive' form of capitalism that had been established in Russia after 1991, rather than with private property as such, and it warned of the dangers that this implied for 'Russian civilization' as well as for the living standards of ordinary people. The party's more specific aims were 'people's power', expressed through the elected soviets; social justice, including guaranteed employment and social benefits; equality, based on the elimination of exploitation and the primacy of state ownership; patriotism; the responsibility of individuals to society; a renewed form of socialism; and communism as the 'historic future of humanity'. Internationally, the party suggested, the choice lay between a divided world in which a few rich countries dominated an impoverished periphery, or one in which more emphasis was placed on the stable and equitable development of all of its members on the basis of their own circumstances and historical experience (*Programma*, 2001: 4–8).

Communists, in spite of these ambitious objectives, were losing ground in the early years of the new century. Part of the problem was an ageing and dwindling membership; and another part of the problem was their ambiguous attitude towards Vladimir Putin – they supported the Russian president in so far as he was a 'patriot', but could hardly approve his moves towards the private ownership of land and the reduction or elimination of state subsidies for housing, transport and other public services. A more immediate problem was fragmentation, as leading members found themselves tempted to retain their positions in the Duma even if the party instructed them to do otherwise, or as entire parties were encouraged by the Kremlin to compete for a share of the vote that might otherwise have gone to their most serious opponents. The Kremlin had enormous resources to commit to such purposes, including its ability to offer public employment as well as to control access to state television, and it drew upon the advice of its own pollsters and 'election technologists' in elaborating and then conducting its strategy.

The first serious split was in April 2002, after the Duma, acting apparently at the instigation of the Kremlin, voted to remove all communist committee chairmen from their positions. Seven were voted out, and two others resigned in protest; but Duma Speaker Gennadii Seleznev, a communist of long standing who had been second only to the party leader on its list of candidates in the December 1999 Duma election, refused to follow them although he was instructed to do so. The Central Committee voted in late May to expel him, together with two other members who had similarly refused to surrender their Duma chairmanships. Seleznev had already formed his own centre-left movement, 'Russia', in the summer of 2000, with what appeared to be the Kremlin's encouragement; it later became the Party of Russia's Rebirth and in that capacity competed in the December 2003 Duma election in association with the Russian Party of Life, taking nearly 2 per cent of the party-list vote and three single-member constituencies. Seleznev himself won a single-member seat in St Petersburg and sat as an independent.

There were further difficulties in late 2003 when the party's list of candidates for the Duma election was approved. Controversially, two employees of the Yukos oil giant were included on the central list in what appeared to be winning positions. According to newspaper reports, Yukos had paid the party $30 million for its places on the list, and individual businessmen anything from $1 to $3 million for an advantageous position (*Izvestiya*, 23 September 2003: 3). Another financier, Gennadii Semigin, was included in the list at the expense of a well-known and ostentatiously proletarian deputy from the outgoing Duma, Vasilii Shandybin. Semigin, chairman of the People's Patriotic Union of Russia, a left-patriotic coalition of which the Communist Party was itself a part, was later accused of undermining party unity in the spring of 2004 and expelled. At the same time there were accusations that party leader Zyuganov had sold out to the oligarchs, and that he was more interested in Hugo Boss suits than the concerns of ordinary workers (*Argumenty i fakty*, no. 4, 2004: 4). Indeed, in late 2004 a left-wing rival was established, the All-Russian Communist Party of the Future, led by Ivanovo governor Vladimir Tikhomirov, which claimed to be more genuinely Leninist.

A more serious rival, Rodina (Motherland), appeared in the summer of 2003 based on a bloc of more than thirty parties of a broadly left-nationalist orientation. It was headed by economist and former minister Sergei Glazev, who had been a member of the communist fraction in the outgoing Duma although not formally a party member, and Dmitri Rogozin, who had been leader of the nationalist Congress of Russian Communities and Putin's special representative. Rodina came fourth, with a remarkable 9 per cent of the vote, in the December 2003 election. In a familiar pattern, its two leaders parted company soon after the election; Glazev went on to stand as a candidate in the presidential election under different auspices, and Rogozin became head of the party faction in the Duma and, in the summer of 2004, was confirmed as party chairman. His aim, he told journalists, was to make 'social justice' and 'patriotism' the centre of the party's appeal (*Nezavisimaya gazeta*, 7 July 2004: 2); the party programme, in the version that was adopted at the same time, insisted that without a 'strong, effective Russian state' there could be no prospect of resolving the country's 'systemic crisis' (www.rodina.ru).

The 'centre' was occupied by United Russia, the 'political force that [he had] relied upon throughout these four years', as President Putin told television interviewers in November 2003. Putin was not a member of this or any other party, but he lost no opportunity to make clear his personal commitment to United Russia, which in turn virtually defined itself by its support of the Russian president. He attended United Russia's party congress in September 2003 so that he could 'signal his gratitude', and the list of candidates that went forward in December 2003 was heavy with governors and other representatives of the administration. It was also representative of the country's largest companies, not just so that they could exercise influence in the new Duma but so that they could demonstrate their political loyalty. United Russia won 223 seats in the December 2003 election, but had 300 by the time the Duma convened as independents and candidates of other parties transferred their loyalties to the winning side. With a majority of this size, United Russia could guarantee the adoption of any legislation that required a 'qualified' or two-thirds majority, and it took charge of all the Duma committee chairmanships.

United Russia had officially been formed in 2001, but its origins lay in the 'Unity' party that had been formed a few months before the December 1999 Duma election. The Unity list was also heavy with government ministers and governors, and the party defined itself publicly as the 'party of Putin' (who made clear that, in his private capacity, he would be voting for it); with the help of the media, particularly state television, it came a close second in the party-list contest, just behind the Communists. Unity held its founding congress in February 2000, and established itself as a political party in May 2000. The following year, it began to merge with the Fatherland–All Russia party that had opposed it at the December 1999 election: in April 2001 the two party leaders issued a joint declaration that announced the start of the process of unification, in July 2001 a 'Union of Unity and Fatherland' held its founding congress, and in December 2001 it became the 'All-Russian Party of Unity and Fatherland', or more briefly United Russia. In March 2003, at its second congress, emergencies minister Sergei Shoigu stood down and was replaced by interior minister Boris Gryzlov; the party, he told the congress, could already claim 400,000 members (Popov 2003: 140).

It was less clear what the new party stood for, other than support for the president and his policies. Gryzlov told the party's preelection congress in September 2003 that the party's ideology was 'common sense'; government should simply 'do what [wa]s good for the majority of citizens' (*Izvestiya*, 22 September 2003: 2). A more elaborate manifesto, 'The Path of National Success', was adopted at about the same time, in an attempt to map out a coherent and distinctive strategy. The manifesto called for a 'new nationwide recovery', based on an 'ideology of success'. It claimed to unite the 'responsible political forces of the country', aiming to minimize the differences between rich and poor, young and old, state, business and society. The economy, at the same time, should combine state regulation and market freedoms, with the benefits of further growth distributed for the most part to the less fortunate. The party rejected left-wing and right-wing ideologies in favour of a 'political centrism' that could unite all sections of society and which was expressed in the policies of President Putin, whose reforms were 'vital for Russia' (www.edinros.ru).

The more ideological, liberal or pro-market 'right' suffered a heavy defeat in the December 2003 election, and neither of its two main representatives, Yabloko or the Union of Right Forces, was able to reach the 5 per cent threshold and take part in the allocation of party-list seats (although they both won single-member constituencies). Yabloko, formed as an electoral bloc in late 1993, was one of the oldest of the new Russian parties (see Manikhin 2003). The party was led from the outset by economist Grigorii Yavlinsky and indeed incorporated the first two letters of his surname, as well as letters from the surnames of the other two founders. Yabloko identified itself as 'democratic', or broadly supportive of the political and economic changes that had taken place since 1991; but it was strongly critical of the 'corrupt oligarchy' that had taken power, and outspoken in its defence of all who depended on the state for their employment or social support. Yabloko rejected the communist system that had 'brought the country to a dead end', but it also rejected the 'vulgar economic policies' of the postcommunist years, which had led to a fall in living standards, deepening social divisions, and a crisis in education, healthcare and science. Business and government had meanwhile become so closely associated that corruption was endemic, and a bureaucratic authoritarian system had been established that served the interests of a small minority.

Yabloko's own proposals were broadly social democratic – indeed its entire strategy was modelled on the values of Russia's European neighbours. The party aimed to establish a 'stable democratic order, including a state based on the rule of law'; a 'socially oriented market economy'; a 'civil society'; a 'contemporary system of security'; and a 'postindustrial strategy within the framework of the European path of development'. It favoured a 'society of equal opportunities, based on the principles of social justice and social solidarity of the strong and the weak'; private initiative was important, but the market was not an end in itself, and it had to be associated with a set of measures that would protect the less fortunate. Yabloko, alone among the major parties, referred not only to the need to combat terrorism but to do so by engaging in political dialogue, in Chechnya as elsewhere. Russia, Yabloko believed, was a 'European country in its historical destiny, its cultural traditions, [and] its geographical situation', with a potential that could only be realized by 'making creative use of the values of European civilization'. Yabloko was accordingly a supporter of Russian membership of the EU (not, admittedly, an immediate prospect), and of other European organizations (www.yabloko.ru).

Yabloko had been supported by the media magnate Vladimir Gusinsky over many years, and by the oil giant Yukos, which had four representatives on the party's central list at the December 2003 Duma election. It was accordingly placed in some difficulty by the takeover of Gusinsky's media outlets, particularly (in 2001) of its NTV television channel, and by the series of actions that began to be taken against Yukos from late 2003 onwards including the arrest of its chief executive Mikhail Khodorkovsky, who had made no secret of his intention to support Yabloko and the Union of Right Forces at the forthcoming elections. Yabloko's failure to reach the 5 per cent threshold led to further difficulties, in that it lost most of its access to the resources that parliament provided for elected members, and sponsors had little interest in a party that could wield so few votes on its behalf, and which was clearly unpopular with the Kremlin. Many of the party's central staff lost their jobs, and those that remained had to depend on the lecture fees and other earnings of the party leader himself. Yabloko put forward no candidate at the 2004 presidential election, and in the view of some outside observers was heading for 'political oblivion' (*Izvestiya*, 22 December 2003: 3).

Yabloko's companion on the liberal margins of the political spectrum was the Union of Right Forces (SPS), formed in August 1999 shortly before the Duma election of that year. Its leaders were the former prime minister Sergei Kirienko, former deputy premier Boris Nemtsov, and businesswoman Irina Khakamada. The party programme, as modified in 2001, committed the party to 'liberal values', including freedom of speech and association, the separation of powers, decentralization, the rule of law, democratic control of society over the state, private property, equality of rights and opportunities for all citizens, and tolerance of diversity. Only a liberal market economy, in their view, would be able to ensure the accumulation and proper distribution of the national wealth; there was less emphasis than in the case of Yabloko on redistribution, and more on cutting taxes and respecting the rights of private property (www.sps.ru). The Union of Right Forces, however, was even less successful than Yabloko at the December 2003 Duma election, its three leaders stood down, and although Khakamada stood in the 2004 presidential election it was not as the party's official candidate (she left the URF immediately afterwards).

The oldest of the new parties was the Liberal Democratic Party of Russia (LDPR), led by its outspoken chairman Vladimir Zhirinovsky. The party, despite its name, was usually seen as right-wing nationalist or even fascist. It had been the surprise winner of the party-list contest in 1993, and took party-list seats again in 1995, 1999 and 2003 – the only party, apart from the Communists, to do so. The Liberal Democrats were very closely identified with their leader, an effective media performer who had himself stood with some success for the presidency. Zhirinovsky had supported the attempted coup of 1991, and opposed the agreement that brought the USSR to an end later that year. He was particularly successful in identifying the problems of ordinary Russians and suggesting simple remedies, such as shooting the leaders of organized crime or forcing all the Chechens over the border and then closing it. In spite of the party's oppositional rhetoric it was broadly pro-government in its voting behaviour in the Duma, and the Kremlin appeared to offer the party its covert support so as to ensure that it regularly reached the party-list threshold.

The LDPR programme aimed squarely at the 'revival of Russia as a great power'. It called for the restoration of a unitary Russian state and for a simplification of the federal system into a smaller number of 'provinces', each of which would be headed by an appointed governor who would in turn appoint subordinates at lower levels. The LDPR opposed communism, but also the 'wild capitalism' that had been constructed over the postcommunist period. It favoured a society of social justice in which there would be no hungry, homeless or workless people. The LDPR was also concerned about 'anti-Russian and amoral' programmes on television, and it opposed the presence of 'non-traditional' sects in Russia, whose activities were 'as a rule' directed by the espionage services of foreign states whose aim was to undermine Russian power and stability. The LDPR favoured a mixed economy with a variety of forms of ownership, but the state should be responsible for the management of the economy as a whole, and it should maintain a substantial manufacturing sector of its own. The state should also monopolize the sale of tobacco, sugar and alcohol, and land should be left in the hands of those who cultivated it.

The Liberal Democrats took a distinctive position in foreign affairs, with a strong, almost Huntingtonian emphasis on 'civilizations'. The LDPR supported the restoration of a Russian state within its 'natural boundaries', including Belarus, Ukraine and parts of other former Soviet republics, and welcomed the union treaty that had been concluded with Belarus as a first step in this direction. It favoured a more distant relationship with the United States and its allies, which represented the 'main threat' to Russian interests, and better relations with 'traditional partners' such as Iran, Iraq, Cuba, Libya and North Korea. More generally, Russia should take the side of Islam against the USA and 'Western–Christian civilization' as a whole, and its claims to global domination in particular. The LDPR championed the rights of Russians abroad, for instance in the Baltic states, and demanded that they be allowed to take out Russian citizenship and protected against discriminatory legislation. Economic, political and cultural relations should be restored with the countries of the former socialist community, especially the Slavic states of Eastern Europe; and the party welcomed the national security doctrine of 2001, which authorized the use of nuclear weapons in the event of a serious security risk to the national territory (www.ldpr.ru).

Parties and the Russian public

So far, there has been little evidence that Russia's parties have engaged the loyalties of Russia's people. In part, this simply reflects the fact that there has been a high level of turnover in the parties themselves. In all, more than 80 parties or blocs contested at least one of the Duma elections between 1993 and 2003, but only three (the Communists, Liberal Democrats and Yabloko) contested all four of them, only two (the Communists and Liberal Democrats) won party-list seats in every case, and only one (the Communist Party) won single-member as well as party-list seats in each of them. To put this another way, all the parties or movements that contested the 1993 party-list election, taken together, won no more than 32 per cent of the party-list vote in 2003 (only five of the original thirteen appeared on the ballot paper). Conversely, more than half the parties that competed in December 2003 had not fought a previous election, and nearly two-thirds (63 per cent) of the party-list vote was won by parties or blocs that had not contested a single previous election; this included two of the four parties that reached the 5 per cent threshold, Rodina and United Russia.

A more direct measure of party legitimacy is the extent to which respondents are willing to 'trust' political parties as compared with other institutions. The national public opinion research centre has asked questions of this kind since the early 1990s (see Table 5.1). Consistently, the church and the armed forces enjoy the highest levels of confidence. The presidency, after a bad patch in the later Yeltsin years, exceeded them both in the early years of the new century, but might not continue to do so indefinitely. Local government was normally more widely respected than central government, and the media were more widely respected than the agencies of law enforcement, which were more often associated with corruption and maltreatment than with the administration of justice. Political parties, however, have consistently come at the bottom of the list, below even the parliament within which they are represented. And these are findings that are replicated in other investigations; the only case in which political parties have not been the least trusted civic institution appears to have been when respondents were asked, on a single occasion, to express their confidence in a list that included the investment funds that had (for the most part) defrauded ordinary citizens of the vouchers they had obtained as a result of the privatization of state property (Rose 1998: 59).

Table 5.1   *Trust in parties and other institutions, 1997–2004*

	1997	1998	1999	2000	2001	2002	2003	2004
President	13	2	2	45	54	61	59	62
Church	38	32	37	39	38	40	37	41
Army	28	28	35	35	33	28	27	28
Media	26	24	25	26	24	23	22	26
Security organs	19	18	20	21	23	23	23	20
Regional government	20	15	19	20	22	19	13	19
Local government	23	18	22	19	21	21	15	18
Courts	13	12	11	12	14	16	13	13
Government	10	4	8	20	22	24	16	12
Trade unions	11	11	9	11	11	13	13	10
Parliament	7	7	4	10	11	11	9	9
Parties	4	4	4	7	6	7	5	5

Note: 'Courts' from 1997 to 1999 refers to law enforcement generally (courts, police and procuracy); references to 'parliament' from 2001 are for the State Duma. Figures report percentages who 'completely trust' a given institution.
Source: derived from All-Russian Public Opinion Research Centre (VTsIOM) and (in 2004) Levada Centre data as reported in *Monitoring obshchestvennogo mneniya*, various issues.

A further set of questions has asked respondents at regular intervals to choose among the parties that currently exist, also allowing them to choose 'none' or 'hard to say'. The results are set out in Table 5.2. The figures show the strong but weakening base of the Communist Party of the Russian Federation, a decline in popular support for Yabloko, and a low but more stable level of support for the Liberal Democrats. United

Table 5.2   *Party preferences, 1995–2004 (percentages)*

	1995	1999	2001	2002	2003	2004
Communist Party	6.9	19.7	18.2	19.6	18.2	8.0
Liberal Democrats	8.0	5.7	4.5	5.7	8.2	6.0
Union of Right Forces	–	0.8	4.0	3.9	3.2	2.0
United Russia	–	–	11.9	13.1	8.2	24.0
Women of Russia	4.7	3.7	3.1	3.8	2.5	–
Yabloko	8.1	10.1	5.1	4.0	4.8	2.0
None/DK	38.3	37.5	50.2	45.9	48.2	49.0

Source: As Table 5.1 (figures are normally for May in each year). The question wording was 'Which of the currently existing parties and associations to the greatest extent reflects the interests of people like you?

Russia, formed in late 2001, had lost some of its support by the spring of 2003, but recovered strongly to win more than a third of the party-list vote in the December election, and was still popular – although losing ground again – the following year. Some of these variations stemmed from differences in question wording, and still more so from the changes that took place in the politicians that were identified in each case as party leader (United Russia's vote, for instance, appeared to have fallen when Boris Gryzlov took over from the charismatic emergencies minister Sergei Shoigu). These minor variations hardly diminished the most striking result of all, which was the very large and growing proportion of the electorate who refused to identify with any of the parties on offer: clear evidence, on the face of it, of a Russian *Parteienverdrossenheit* (or general disaffection from parties).

There have been different views about the extent to which partisan identifications have developed in postcommunist Russian politics. These variations stem, again, from different question wordings, and from the different time-periods in which surveys have been conducted (post-election surveys, in particular, tend to measure reported vote rather than a more enduring loyalty). Miller and his colleagues, at one extreme, found that as many as 61 per cent of Russians thought of themselves as 'supporters of a particular party' (Miller *et al.* 2000). Others have reported much lower measures: the present author and associates, for instance, found in a 2001 survey that just 27 per cent indicated there was a party that was 'closer to you in its policies than others', and Evans and Whitefield (1995: 500) have reported a figure of 13 per cent, lower than anywhere else in the postcommunist world. Measures of partisan identification have not been uncontroversial in the established democracies, and here too much depends on the wording of the question (see, for instance, Bartle 2003). When all allowances have been made, it remains difficult to contest that Russia has low levels of partisanship in broadly comparative terms, still more so in comparison with established democracies such as the UK (where 86 per cent have some form of partisan identification) and the USA (where nearly 92 per cent identify with either of the two main parties) (Webb *et al.* 2002: 20, 318).

Another measure of identification is membership of the political parties (see Table 5.3). Overall, just under 1 per cent of the adult population regarded themselves in our 2001 survey as a member of one or other of the political parties; this compared with 2 per cent who were members of a cultural society or a residential association, 8 per cent who were in a sports club, and 19 per cent who were members of a trade union. Comparatively considered, these are very low levels. The figures made available by the parties themselves vary widely and are often problematic. Indeed there is some evidence that parties maintain three different lists of members: one

Table 5.3   *Political party memberships (selected parties, 2003)*

Party (date of foundation)	Claimed membership	Party cards issued	Leader
Liberal Democratic Party (1990)	600,000	475,000	Vladimir Zhirinovsky
Communist Party (1993)	500,000	500,000	Gennadii Zyuganov
United Russia (2001)	257,000	50,000	Boris Gryzlov
Agrarian Party (1993)	100,000	100,000	Mikhail Lapshin
People's Party (2001)	81,400	64,000	Gennadii Raikov
Party of Russia's Rebirth (2000)	40,000	n.a.	Gennadii Seleznev
Social Democratic Party (2001)	30,000	30,000	Mikhail Gorbachev
Yabloko (1993)	26,500	n.a.	Grigorii Yavlinsky
Union of Right Forces (2001)	20,000	10,000	Boris Nemtsov
Party of Life (2002)	15,000	n.a.	Sergei Mironov

Source: Derived from *Nezavisimaya gazeta*, 13 January 2003: 1–2.

for public consumption, another for the Ministry of Justice, and a third for internal use (*Nezavisimaya gazeta*, 13 January 2003: 1–2). The Liberal Democratic Party, for instance, told the Justice Ministry it had 19,100 members, but claimed 600,000 in its public statements. The Communist Party, similarly, claimed 19,300 in its registration documents, but 500,000 in its official statements. United Russia appeared to maintain another, fourth column, for reporting to its Kremlin masters (it had promised a million members by the end of 2002 but had evidently fallen short).

Independent estimates were similarly varied. The Communist Party, by general consent, was the largest of the parties, with between 500,000 and 800,000 members (*Izvestiya*, 5 August 2002: 4). It tended to have a more elderly membership than its competitors, but was making considerable efforts to recruit from a younger age group: in the three years up to 2000 more than half of its new members were aged under 30, many of them students (*Spravochnyi* 2000: 47). United Russia claimed a membership of 300,000, all of whom had been enrolled since its foundation at the end of 2001 (*Izvestiya*, 20 February 2003: 3); there were reports, however, that many had been recruited in a somewhat 'Soviet' manner, on the basis of instructions from above. In a shopping complex in the Moscow region, for instance, each retail unit had been told it would have to provide two members (*Izvestiya*, 3 March 2003: 1); in the town of Velikie Luki, local employees were being fired or had their wages withheld unless they took out membership (*Novye izvestiya*, 3 July 2003: 1). By late 2004 United Russia was claiming as many as 840,000 members, and the Communists were down to 250,000; but these were still the two largest totals (*Nezavisimaya gazeta*, 5 October 2004: 2).

There were several reasons for the relatively low salience of parties in the Russian governmental process. One was certainly the constitutional framework. Government was accountable not to parliament, but to the president: which meant that Russian parties were unable to 'win power' at a parliamentary election, and were in no position to compel the formation of a government that reflected the composition of a new Duma. When Prime Minister Chernomyrdin's party, Our Home is Russia, won just over 10 per cent of the party-list vote in the 1995 parliamentary election, he did not resign but made clear that the election result would have no consequences whatsoever for the composition of the government or the policies it pursued (*Segodnya*, 20 December 1995: 1). When Boris Yeltsin dismissed the entire government three times in 1998–99, equally, it had nothing to do with a change in party balance in the Duma, still less a national election. Under the terms of the law on state service that applied until 2003, indeed, ministers were not allowed to have a party affiliation, and under the law on the government until it was amended in 2004 they were not allowed to hold office in a party or public organization. This reflected the Soviet view that the business of government was to administer the affairs of state, but not set national priorities.

There were some signs, as the postcommunist system consolidated itself, that the strongly presidential nature of the constitution might at least be reconsidered. Yeltsin, and then Vladimir Putin, gave little indication that they thought their considerable powers should be restricted. But there was considerable support in other sections of the political class and among Russian jurists for a constitutional change that would balance an overpowerful presidency by strengthening the position of parliament. The Duma, these commentators suggested, had too little influence on the conduct and composition of government. Appointments to important ministries, such as defence and foreign affairs, should require its approval. The Duma, in its turn, should have the right to question ministers and to express its lack of confidence in individuals, not just the government as a whole; and it should be required to give its approval to the dismissal of the prime minister, not just to his appointment (White 2000b: 101–6).

The logic of these changes was a semi-presidential system, along the lines of the French system in which the president appointed the government but the government required the support of a parliamentary majority (see Elgie 1999). There was some indication that, as a first step, the president might in future consider the appointment of a prime minister

who commanded the confidence of deputies (Putin spoke of the formation of a 'professional, effective government relying on a parliamentary
majority' in his address to the Federal Assembly in the spring of 2003:
Rossiiskaya gazeta, 17 May 2003: 4). At least implicitly, this was a step
towards party government; but it was only a modest step so long as it
reflected no more than a change in political conventions, and one that
applied only if there was a parliamentary majority that was supportive of
the president and his policies.

Political parties in modern Russia operate within what is perhaps a
uniquely adverse environment. The long experience of misrule by the
Communist Party of the Soviet Union was scarcely an encouragement to
the development of the multiparty politics for which the 1993 constitution provided; indeed it seemed to have discredited the very word 'party',
as was apparent in the way in which so many Russian parties found other
labels by which they could describe themselves. As we have seen, parties
are viewed with scepticism, or even hostility, by the mass public. There is
only a loose relationship between election outcomes and party representation in the Duma; and the Duma itself has little influence on the conduct
and composition of government apart from its ability to reject nominations to the premiership and to declare its lack of confidence in the
government as a whole, either of which would normally lead to an early
general election. Parties, moreover, have relatively few members, and they
can draw on relatively few human or material resources apart from the
covert support of the Kremlin itself.

Indeed, so far from representing the interests of voters in their dealings
with government, parties were becoming an increasingly important part
of Putin's top-down 'managed democracy'. Parties, for instance, were
given a monopoly of the right to nominate candidates under the law on
political parties that was adopted in 2001. But parties could register only
if they had a substantial membership drawn from a large number of
republics and regions, and to secure representation within the Duma they
had to secure at least 5 per cent (from 2007, 7 per cent) of the party-list
vote, from which, from the same date, all the seats in the Duma would be
drawn. The largest parties were also the main beneficiaries of the system
of state funding that was established by the parties law, because payments
were directly proportional to the number of votes that parties won at each
election. The larger parties were still further advantaged by changes in the
parties law itself, which was amended in late 2004 so as to require a minimum of 50,000 members – five times as many as before – in order for a
party to obtain registration (*Rossiiskaya gazeta*, 15 October 2004: 2).

But how far could a party system be shaped from above, in the interests
of the regime itself? Across Europe, there was a generalized crisis of political engagement: turnouts were falling, parties were losing members, and

political institutions were losing the trust of ordinary citizens. In the former communist countries, and particularly in the former Soviet republics, memberships remained very low, parties were more distrusted than all other institutions, and substantial numbers at elections were voting 'against all' candidates where they had an opportunity to do so, or not voting at all. Russia had a number of factors that might ordinarily have been expected to encourage political engagement, including high levels of education and a substantial pool of professionals. But the long experience of communist rule had choked off the development of a civil society, and there was little sign of its emergence in the first decades of the new century. It was possible, even probable, that the continuation of a 'top down' approach to the development of Russia's postcommunist parties would deny them the organizational autonomy that would be necessary if an authentic citizen politics was to develop.

Chapter 6

A Russian Civil Society?

ALFRED B. EVANS, JR

A large body of scholarly literature supports the thesis that a vigorous civil society greatly increases the chances of success of democracy in the political sphere. Though the tsarist state was far from democratic, in Russia during the late nineteenth century and early twentieth century civil society had begun to emerge, as citizens generated a growing variety of voluntary associations. After 1917, however, the Bolsheviks gradually suppressed independent social organizations, and attempted to establish a network of pervasive party-state control of all social structures. Only in the Gorbachev period did 'informal' groups created by the independent initiatives of citizens enjoy encouragement from the top leadership. Thus by the time of the disintegration of the Soviet regime, there was a burst of optimism concerning the prospects for the growth of civil society and democracy in Russia. The boom of informal social groups during the years of *perestroika* was followed by a slump of organized, independent activities of Russian citizens during the 1990s, however, so that it seemed clear that civil society was quite weak by the end of that decade. Nevertheless, a substantial number of social organizations managed to survive and continued to provide services to a variety of clients. If civil society organizations were marginalized during the first years of independence for Russia, they have been subjected to efforts to integrate them into a centralized, coordinated system of control since Vladimir Putin came to power. Putin's success in expanding his domination of the Russian political system and his efforts to integrate social groups into the regime's base of support have left the prospects for autonomous organizations of citizens very uncertain.

Civil society and democracy

In this chapter, civil society will be considered to refer to the sphere of organizations formed primarily by the independent efforts of citizens who mobilize their resources and efforts in cooperative endeavours aimed at the achievement of common goals. Civil society is often thought of as the 'third sector' of organized human structures, distinct from the state, with its exercise of political authority, and the realm of business, filled with profit-seeking enterprises, though it is in close interaction with the state and the economy. We may also identify civil society as functioning on the level of intermediate social organization, between families and the state. There is considerable debate concerning the types of groups that should be included in civil society; most scholars would exclude criminal organizations and extremist ideological groups that resort to violence, while some are inclined to regard all religious organizations as outside civil society. There is also discussion of the degree of independence from the state that is inherent in civil society; though the scholarly literature (and the rhetoric of many publicists and politicians) has often assumed an adversarial relationship between the state and civil society, some recent works have emphasized that even in Western democracies, government leaders and agencies frequently have played a significant role in encouraging the growth of organizations of citizens.

The primary reason for the proliferation of scholarly writings on civil society during the last few decades is the widespread acceptance of the thesis of a relationship between civil society and democracy. The vast majority of the scholars who study the subject believe that without a vibrant civil society, the chances for the survival of an established democracy, or for the success of a transition to democracy in a country formerly under authoritarian rule, are severely diminished. Those scholars argue that strong organizations of citizens provide channels for the representation of popular interests, furnish a potential check on a government that might disregard democratic rights, and invite citizens to learn habits of cooperation in reaching common goals. In Poland and some other countries in Eastern Europe under communist rule, by the 1970s, certain circles of dissident intellectuals began to articulate the hope that the quiet growth of elements of social organization outside the control of the state would bring gradual progress towards democratic transformation. Those anticommunist dissidents proved to be correct in their supposition that most regimes in their region would tacitly tolerate a degree of unofficial independence in society; on the other hand, they were as surprised as everyone else by the rapid disintegration of those regimes by the early 1990s. When apparently similar events took place in the Soviet Union around the same time, both Russian and foreign scholars were moved to reexamine some elements of Russian history.

Civil society in late tsarist Russia

Before the mid-1980s, most Western historians had stressed the continuity of Russia's authoritarian political legacy from the tsars to the Soviet period, and thus perpetuated the view that tsarist Russia had been characterized by a dominant state and a submissive society. Indeed, there is at least partial validity in that argument in relation to the main tendencies in the long sweep of Russian history. There is no doubt that the tsarist state was essentially autocratic, and that under the tsars Russian society never enjoyed the degree of protection of individual rights and associational independence that was found in some Western countries. Nevertheless, in recent decades a growing body of writing based on scholarly research by a variety of historians has converged on the conclusion that a genuine civil society had begun to emerge during the last decades of the Russian empire. With the Great Reforms of the 1860s and 1870s under Tsar Alexander II, the general attitude of the state towards independent social organizations became more favourable (though instances of petty harassment by some ministries and regional officials persisted), and the elected local governments that were created by new legislation stimulated increases in social activism.

During the last decades of the nineteenth century, the number of voluntary associations formed by the initiative of citizens grew steadily, and those associations provided badly needed services of various kinds (Bradley 2002). The beginning of industrialization, rapid urbanization and broader access to education ensured the expansion of those strata of society that were the main sources of recruits to professional, civic and philanthropic organizations (Clowes *et al.* 1991), though participation in such endeavours was coming from wider segments of the population. It seems clear that by the end of the nineteenth century a nascent civil society had come into existence in Russia (Conroy 2005), and had the potential eventually to match the level of social organization that had been reached in Western democracies. Most of the highest officials in the tsarist state became more suspicious of independent social activism by the later years of the century, however, while the most radical segment of the intelligentsia disdained the 'small deeds' and good works of the civil activists. Though social associations continued to provide vital services during the turbulent years of the First World War, the Bolshevik Revolution of October 1917 would sound the death knell for civil society in Russia.

Social organizations in the Soviet Union

At first glance it might seem that the October Revolution was not unfavourable to the future of independent social organizations in Russia, since in the years immediately following the takeover of power by the Bolsheviks there was a burst of independent social activity, reflected in the appearance of a large number of new clubs and societies (Evans 2005). That trend was not to last, however, since the intentions of the dominant elements in the Bolshevik leadership from an early time favoured the eventual elimination of all previously existing associations, except for a very few that would be coopted into the state's system of control, and the creation of a network of new organizations that would be subordinated to direction by the Communist Party and state. In December 1919 the Soviet Communist Party adopted a rule that specified that when three or more party members belonged to any organization, they would be required to form a party cell to assist in supervising it. From its inception the Bolshevik regime was particularly hostile towards religious organizations, above all the Russian Orthodox Church, which bore the brunt of violent attacks during the Russian Civil War (1918–21). The state banned religious instruction of children outside the family, and by 1929 charitable work by religious groups was prohibited. Il'ina (2000) and other Russian historians have documented the manner in which the party leadership gradually but deliberately tightened its control over social organizations from this time onwards. The Bolsheviks derided the notion of 'civil society' as a product of bourgeois consciousness, and they rejected the notion of competition among diverse social interests. As Lenin said of trade unions in Soviet Russia, all social or non-state organizations were to be 'transmission belts', assisting in carrying out the tasks that history had entrusted to the party.

By the middle of the 1920s, as Joseph Bradley (1994: 37) puts it, 'a new network of organizations' began to appear, comprising the new mass membership organizations that had been created by the Communist Party and would be subjected to its control. For example, the political regime managed to eliminate all previously existing organizations for children and youth, and to replace them with the Communist Youth League (Komsomol) and its affiliates for children. Even an institution like Proletkult (the Proletarian Cultural–Educational Institutions), which hoped to realize the dream of giving the working class the opportunity to create a new proletarian culture, proved to be too independent from the point of view of the single-party leadership, and thus its activities were soon curtailed and eventually brought to an end. After Stalin consolidated his dominance of the Soviet regime control of social organizations was tightened, and by the middle of the 1930s almost all associations that had been founded before 1929 were eliminated. The period of the First Five-Year Plan in the late 1920s and early 1930s was also a time of renewed and intensified persecution of religious institutions, when tens of thousands of clergy were killed. During the Second World War Stalin changed course in his policy towards religion and reached an accommodation of sorts with the Orthodox Church, but the new arrangements gave the Soviet state greater control of the church, so that it was assimilated into the pervasive network of support for the Stalinist regime.

It may be said accurately that there was no civil society in the Soviet Union by the end of the Stalin years, because no formal organizations in society were sufficiently independent of control by the party-state regime to be considered essentially self-governing. All legally permitted *obshchestvennye* ('social' or 'public') organizations primarily carried out the function of assisting the regime in attempting to achieve its goals. At the same time, however, to one degree or another each social organization in the Soviet system was also likely to perform some services of practical value to its members, and to make some cautious efforts to exert influence on behalf of their interests. That dualistic functioning of most Soviet social organizations is worth noting, because it has affected their activities and the prospects for their survival in the postcommunist period. Nevertheless, the results of survey research in the former Soviet Union confirm that most citizens had a low level of confidence in such organizations as the Komsomol and trade unions.

In the decades after Stalin's death in 1953, detailed control over some institutions, such as the natural science institutes of the Academy of Sciences of the USSR, was loosened perceptibly, and informal attempts to influence official policies, such as the efforts of scientists who advocated protection of the natural environment, became permissible if the interests at stake were not deemed too sensitive. Many scholars and journalists have also reported that after the early 1960s low-level, informal groups of citizens began to form in gradually growing numbers, as the authorities quietly looked the other way instead of suppressing such entities. Groups formed by citizens were more likely to survive if they did not seek explicitly political objectives; those who tried to challenge the official ideology and the party's monopoly over the public articulation of values suffered a harsh fate. By the middle of the 1960s an organized movement of dissidents had taken shape, and its participants resorted to letters, petitions, self-published manifestos, and occasionally public demonstrations. The Communist Party directed the KGB to move with increasing thoroughness and brutality to suppress such activities, and the dissident movement was reduced to a shadow of its former existence by the late 1970s, though the regime was never able to stamp out dissent entirely. The dissidents never threatened to constitute a mass movement, as they drew their participants mostly from the scientific and creative intelligentsia (and mobilized only a fraction of those in such strata) and never had much connection with the majority of workers and peasants.

Mikhail Gorbachev brought a sharp change in the leadership's attitude toward the dissenters as part of his drive for the radical restructuring (*perestroika*) of the Soviet system. He sought to enlist the discontented elements of the intelligentsia into his base of support for *perestroika*, and he invited competition among contending points of view in accordance with his conception of 'socialist pluralism'. The political component of Gorbachev's programme of restructuring was called 'democratization', and one implication of radical political reform was the tolerance and even encouragement of the open forming of 'informal' groups of citizens, which were generated by the initiative of citizens without seeking permission from the Communist Party. Though many lower-level officials remained suspicious of independent associations, such groups proliferated rapidly in the late 1980s. By 1989 the central Communist Party newspaper *Pravda* reported that there were about 60,000 'informal groups' in the USSR, though that estimate may have been exaggerated (White 1999: 12). Some of the new groups openly demanded changes in government policies, as they raised issues that had not been made public for decades. By the beginning of the 1990s some optimistic scholars argued that a civil society had already begun to emerge in the Soviet Union, and that the retreat of the Stalinist state and the advance of independent, assertive social interests had become irreversible. In short, such analysts as Moshe Lewin and S. Frederick Starr expected the imminent flourishing of civil society and the triumph of democracy in the Soviet Union.

The troubles of civil society in the 1990s

Before the end of the 1990s a wide range of works by Russian and Western scholars testified to the disappointment of the hopes for the rapid growth of civil society in Russia that had been stimulated by the creation of a myriad of informal groups during the last years of the Soviet regime. In 1998 K. G. Kholodkovsky and his colleagues noted that the 'takeoff' of social organizations in the late 1980s had been followed by a 'relative slump' in the 1990s (1998: 150). Another Russian scholar, Z. T. Golenkova (1999: 15), suggested that only 'small oases of autonomous social life' had survived. V. G. Khoros and his colleagues observed discouragingly that the institutions of the third sector were 'only a thin film on the surface of society', arguing that Russia not only would not follow the path of the West in the growth of independent social organizations, but also lagged far behind many countries in Asia and Latin America with respect to the basic criteria of civil society (Khoros *et al.* 1998: 208, 291). A large number of non-governmental organizations (the number varies greatly among contending estimates, from as few as 70,000 to as many as 350,000) still existed in Russia by the end of the twentieth century, and it is generally agreed that some new organizations had been created after 1991, but the condition of the base of support, political influence, and social impact of most such organizations was discouraging, particularly in relation to the euphoric hopes of the beginning of the 1990s.

The sources of the weakness of civil society in postcommunist Russia that became evident during the 1990s seem to fall into three categories: cultural, economic and political. In the first place, attitudes that were formed within the Soviet system still present obstacles to attracting citizens to active participation in voluntary associations. Students of comparative communism have described the cultural legacy of Leninist regimes as a widespread habit among the population of dichotomizing society into two spheres: the private sphere of relationships with family members and close friends, where people can be trusted and they genuinely try to help each other, and the public sphere, where mistrust prevails, as each can expect the conduct of others to be motivated by narrow self-interest and statements of ideological or ethical principle to be essentially hypocritical. In line with that assessment, some Russian scholars see the 'new Russian individualism' of the postcommunist period as a direct continuation of the opportunistic individualism of Soviet society, reflecting scepticism not only towards the stated norms of the old, socialist order, but also towards the principles of democracy and civil society. The assumption that almost all others are engaged in amoral individualism leads to a low level of trust in fellow citizens, which discourages a commitment to voluntary associations that seek positive social change.

The reluctance of most Russian citizens to give active support to voluntary associations was reinforced by the consequences of the severe decline of the Russian economy in the 1990s. Though there were sporadic protests such as periodic strikes and demonstrations by coal miners, the predominant response to the collapse of earlier hopes for the success of political and economic reforms was a growing tendency towards apathy and alienation from public activism. While a few got rich quickly, the majority of Russians were plunged into a struggle for economic survival that left most of them without the time or energy for activities that did not bring immediate material benefits for them or their families. Participation in civic-minded or charitable social groups seemed a luxury that most could not afford, even if they had believed in the possibility that such organizations were genuinely dedicated to filling legitimate needs. The economic catastrophe experienced by most Russians during the years after the disintegration of the Soviet Union also impoverished the middle strata of the population, marginalizing and demoralizing the groups that would have presented the strongest potential for involvement in the development of civil society. In addition, many who had been leaders in groups that had been part of the movement for democracy in Russia sought positions in government or business in the 1990s, in part to gain economic security.

The third set of factors that helped to explain the weakness of civil society in the period following the end of communist rule could be found in the political sphere. As president of independent Russia, Boris Yeltsin actually discouraged the stimulation of mass social and political activism as he sought to introduce radical economic transformation from the top down. As other chapters in this book demonstrate, Yeltsin was successful in concentrating preponderant power in the institution of the Russian presidency, creating a system that Steven Fish (2000) has dubbed 'super-presidentialism'. Yeltsin neglected the strengthening of political parties or the national parliament, which would have provided channels of potential influence for organized interests to reward the mobilization of support from large numbers of citizens. Within the presidential administration, central government and regional and local centres of authority, a premium was placed on personal relationships with key officials, or in many cases on direct involvement in insider politics by the representatives of particular interests. In such an environment, the most successful strategy for gaining benefits was winning the favour of powerful patrons rather than combining the voices, votes and financial contributions of many citizens of various ranks in society. In the aftermath of the privatization of most previously state-owned enterprises, the process of representation of interests was dominated by a few people who became wealthy primarily though the ingenious use of connections within the state – those who soon were called 'oligarchs' – and the great weight of their influence made attempts by ordinary citizens to gain satisfaction for their demands seem hopeless.

The unfavourable environment of the 1990s not only shaped the means by which social groups attempted to achieve influence in government, but also conditioned the manner of operation of those groups in performing the services to which they were committed. Valerie Sperling's extensive research on women's organizations in the 1990s found that the organizations she studied did not do many of the things that non-profit or non-governmental organizations (NGOs) in the West considered essential for success. Sperling (1999) learned that most of the women's groups that had formed independently were created by a few dedicated activists who drew support from friendship networks or colleagues in their places of work. Many of the organizations that she studied remained small, with each still consisting mainly of its original circle of founders. (Other scholars who have studied non-governmental organizations in Russia have remarked that some of them are little more than 'NGIs' – non-governmental individuals.)

It may seem surprising that most of those groups did not even attempt to attract larger numbers of members or recruit many volunteers to assist in their projects. Sperling points out that although most women's groups 'are practically devoid of income, they lack membership-building strategies', and show almost no interest in attracting new members (1999: 42). The fact that many of those organizations do not collect dues from their members helps to explain why they are not interested in expanding their membership roles. Many of the groups that Sperling investigated have very limited financial resources, surviving largely because of the dedication and enthusiasm of small circles of activists, while they get by with minimal office space, equipment, and means of communication and travel. In Russia it is very common for a social organization to operate out of the business or professional office of its main leader and use the telephone, computer and other equipment in that office. As Sperling notes, the lack of facilities and paid staff further discourages women's organizations from engaging in outreach activities. Most of the groups that she encountered do not carry out fundraising campaigns, partly because of a lack of means to take on such a task, but mainly because of an appreciation of the futility of asking most Russian citizens to make donations to any cause.

For the leaders of non-governmental organizations that are starved for funding, assistance from Western governments and foundations may appear to be life-saving support, especially since there are still very few domestically based foundations in Russia. Many women's organizations have turned to international sources for their funding in these circumstances, with mixed results. Sperling's research shows that the women's organizations that were successful in winning grants from foreign agencies did acquire better offices and equipment, and their leaders did improve their professional skills, including skill at submitting grant applications, organizing conferences and writing reports. On the other hand, another effect of the pattern of foreign funding was to increase divisiveness among women's organizations, as the gulf between those with foreign funding and those without such support widened. A similar argument is presented by the research of Sarah Henderson (2003: 165), who found that a relationship of 'principled clientelism' often developed between Western donors and the Russian women's organizations to which they regularly awarded grants, so that both the donor and the funded groups were able to justify each other's continued existence. Sperling argues that Russian women's organizations that had consistently won grant funding from abroad tended to concentrate their attention on the issues that were important to Western donors, rather than on the problems that were important to most Russian women. Writings by a number of scholars, both Western and Russian, confirmed that by the end of the 1990s, most groups in civil society in Russia were marginal in terms of their base of popular support, their financial resources, their political influence, and their impact on the lives of most citizens of their country.

Different types of organizations in civil society in Russia

A large proportion of Western research on civil society in postcommunist Russia has focused on a narrow range of organizations, principally those devoted to the causes of human rights, environmental protection and women's rights. Those are the types of organizations that have had little influence on the policies of their government, that have a slender base of domestic support, and that have depended heavily on moral support and material assistance from Western donors. Those organizations are, however, only a few of the large number of social organizations in Russia that draw on the work of hundreds of thousands of citizens and directly serve about 20 million people (Hudson 2003: 217). Many of those organizations have survived from the Soviet period, so they bear the legacy of having served the goals of the party and state under the old order. We should recall that a substantial body of research showed that most of those organizations functioned dualistically in the Soviet system, as they filled some genuine needs of their members while being careful to subordinate their activities to the goals of the political regime. Since 1991 little research has been directed to those 'holdover' or 'survivor' organizations, so our information about most of them is limited (Russian trade unions are an exception, since they have been studied by highly competent scholars in recent years).

We know that many of these organizations have survived, sometimes with changed names, and it is certain that government funding for most of them has been reduced sharply. We also know that for many of them, assistance from one level or another of government (national, regional or local) is vital for their continued existence, and that while funding from government officials is usually meagre, the provision of office space and other facilities by local or regional government gives such organizations a crucial advantage. In some cases those organizations gain modest revenue by renting a part of their office space to commercial firms or operating their own subsidiary, income-producing enterprises. It is widely reported that friendly relationships with powerful political officials are important for securing continued benevolence from government for such NGOs, so their independence is distinctly limited. It should also be added, however, that personal observation by this author and some other Western scholars, along with reports by Russian scholarly and journalistic sources, suggest that the fundamentally cooperative character of the relationship between the leaders of a social organization and the patrons in government does not preclude persistent striving by the most dedicated NGO leaders to represent the interests of their members, even if that introduces an element of contention into their relationships with government officials. It is likely that the balance of cooperation and conflict, and of subservience and assertiveness, varies from one case to another.

By the end of the 1990s, despite the problems that social organizations had encountered over the decade, and despite the fact that the network of such organizations had not assumed the proportions of those in any Western country (and apparently did not have the potential to do so in the near future), civil society had survived, and many of the organizations that made up the mosaic of civil society did play useful roles, taking advantage of their limited resources as much as possible. Western research since the 1990s has identified a wide range of organizations in postcommunist Russia, promoting a diverse pattern of activities. Henry (2005) has identified three distinct kinds of environmentalist groups: professionalized organizations, grassroots organizations, and government affiliates. The professionalized groups rely more on foreign grant funding, and usually do not have strong ties with their potential base of support among the Russian population. They are usually led by scientists who do not seek active support from the general public and frequently oppose state policies, though they still want to work through the state to achieve their objectives. Their leaders have a cosmopolitan outlook and are well connected with the international environmentalist movement.

Grassroots organizations, on the other hand, are less likely to receive grants from foreign sources, and tend to be based on local administrative, cultural or educational institutions that have been carried over from the Soviet era. Those groups are more likely to gain assistance from officials of local government (so they tend to avoid confrontation with local authorities), and to emphasize issues that are important to their local communities. Grassroots organizations often carry out educational programmes for children and engage in other local projects. They usually work inside the system, seeking gradual, incremental change in institutions and policies. Government affiliates are closely aligned with political officials; indeed, many of their leaders occupy administrative positions in the state while they serve as officers of NGOs. Such groups see their role as implementing the policies of a state that they trust to be committed to environmental protection. Henry has found that, while the limitations of professionalized environmentalist organizations and government affiliates are well-recognized, the grassroots environmentalist movement continues to grow in Russia, quietly gaining increased support and participation. Her research suggests the importance of distinguishing the particular strategies pursued by different types of social organizations, and also implies that an organization's strategy and its chances for success may be conditioned by the relationship between its goals and the prevailing values in the domestic society.

Like Sperling, Sundstrom (2002) affirms that most Russian women's NGOs do not seek broad public support and rarely engage in outreach activities. Sundstrom emphasizes that such self-imposed limitations are especially evident for Western-style women's organizations with a strongly feminist orientation that seek major social and political change. A basic factor conditioning the strategy of such groups (and helping to explain why they search for assistance from Western sources) is their detachment from their own society, 'due to an enduring level of hostility to feminist ideals among Russians' (Sundstrom 2002: 215). The traditional values of Russian society do not support across-the-board equality of men and women in the home and at work, and thus make it difficult to muster public backing for campaigns against such injustices as sexual harassment and gender-based discrimination in employment. That is the main reason that organizations 'that are more critical of government policies and insist on their autonomy from the state tend to be marginalized and discouraged in their attempts to exert any influence on public policy' (Sundstrom 2002: 221).

On the other hand, Sundstrom (2005) points out that the Committees of Soldiers' Mothers, which first sprang up in Russia in 1989, have been able to establish branches in many cities, have received much favourable coverage from their country's media, have won widespread sympathy from the population, and are treated with respect by the government, even though it does not always acquiesce in their demands. She argues convincingly that the traditional norms of Russian culture, which strongly value the role of mothers as protectors of their sons, provide a favourable framework for the goals of the Committees of Soldiers' Mothers. On the other hand, groups that have taken an openly pacifist, anti-militarist stance have gained little support from the Russian public, and have not received a friendly hearing from the government, apparently because of the disparity between the outlook of those groups and the generally pro-military orientation of the majority of Russians. Sundstrom's analysis underlines the importance of values and attitudes in the prevailing national culture in influencing the chances that a social organization may gain widespread support for its activities.

Civil society under Putin

After Vladimir Putin became president, scholars debated the nature of his intentions for the Russian political system. A consensus concerning the general character of Putin's goals has gradually formed, as his actions have increasingly made his goals clear. For a while some analysts tried to come up with terms such as 'managed democracy' or 'virtual democracy' to try to capture the complexity of Putin's design. Now more would find Gordon Hahn's description of Putin's 'stealth authoritarianism' (2004) or Aleksei Zudin's concept of Putin's 'monocentrism' (2003) to be more appropriate. The real question is no longer whether Putin wants to decrease the degree of pluralism in the Russian polity, or whether he can be successful in manipulating political forces to make that possible, since the answers to both those questions are obviously affirmative; the real question for researchers is the precise contours of the structures that Putin seeks to construct.

There is no evidence that Putin has a detailed blueprint of the political system that he wants to shape, and he has explicitly disavowed the idea of an official state ideology. Putin's style is to implement his plans cautiously and gradually, often using indirect methods of discouraging independent criticism, while ostensibly endorsing democracy and the rule of law. Hahn (2004) is also correct in observing that Putin seeks 'a hegemonic rather than a monopolistic centralization of power', so that many groups and institutions that retain token independence, remaining formally outside the vertical executive hierarchy of the state, have become (or will become) part of the base of support for the presidential administration that he heads. It is also part of Putin's mode of operation to offer rewards for organizations that are integrated into his pyramid of support, while he also makes it clear, usually by deeds rather than words and often in a manner that makes it possible for him to deny responsibility for the punishment, that there will be penalties for resisting subordination to centralized authority.

Within a few years after becoming president, Putin was able to decrease pluralism in the mass media in Russia, curtail the independence of the regional governors, ensure that the national parliament would accept his leadership with docility, and intimidate the super-rich 'oligarchs' so that they would not stand in the way of his political moves. Already during Putin's first term in office it became clear that journalists and environmentalists who were too critical of the government's actions in the most sensitive areas of policy would be subject to harassment or prison sentences. Most recently Putin has stepped up his efforts to integrate non-governmental organizations into his system of comprehensive control. A portent of Putin's wishes was the announcement in 2001 that a Civic

Forum would be convened in Moscow in November of that year, so that 5,000 representatives of NGOs could meet with government officials. The original purpose of that gathering apparently was to integrate 'civil society organizations throughout Russia into a single corporatist body that would allow them an official consultative role with the government' (Squier 2002: 177). In other words, social organizations would sacrifice their independence in order to gain institutionalized representation of their interests and a share of state benefits.

After vocal complaints from many activists, the government backed away from efforts at the immediate implementation of this particular plan, and while some NGO leaders refused to take part in the conference, others saw it as an opportunity to bring their concerns to the attention of the political leadership. If the Civic Forum was a temporary setback for Putin and his lieutenants, it did not deter them from a patient attempt to use the means at their disposal, including the legal, administrative and financial tools in the hands of the state, to make it gradually more difficult for existing NGOs to operate independently of government domination. At the same time, as some social organizations resisted cooptation by the state, an increasing number of groups which were informally dubbed 'government-organised nongovernmental organisations', or GONGOs, appeared (Nikitin and Buchanan 2002: 149). While Putin has made many statements giving token endorsement to the development of civil society, it is now apparent that his vision is of a pseudo-civil society in which social organizations are subordinated to the authority of the state and express demands that are consistent with the programme of the regime itself. While groups that resist integration into the centralized system may risk prosecution in the courts or denial of registration, for most of them the real penalty will be irrelevance, as they are consigned to a marginal political status and denied a voice in influencing the shaping of policies.

Putin has shown a strong preference for organizations that share his enthusiasm for a strong state, nationalistic themes, and traditional Russian values. In his state of the nation address to the national parliament in May 2004, though he endorsed the idea of civil society and acknowledged that 'many citizens' associations in Russia are working constructively', Putin complained that for some social organizations the priority was 'obtaining funding from influential foreign or domestic foundations', and for others it was 'servicing dubious group and commercial interests' (Putin 2004a). His words seemed to be directed against NGOs that were supported by international funding sources and organizations that received support from oligarchs who had earned the disfavour of the Kremlin. He implicitly linked criticism of the Russian state by domestic human rights groups with the machinations of external forces that allegedly were inimical to Russian national strength and independence. It should be noted that Putin's speech highlighted a previously tacit policy of putting pressure on human rights groups with foreign ties that had been in effect for at least two years before his pronouncement. The Russian government had already terminated the US Peace Corps programme, expelled the head of the American Federation of Labor and Congress of Industrial Organizations affiliate in Moscow, and pressed dubious charges against Russian researchers and journalists who were accused of having revealed state secrets to foreign governments.

The pressure on groups that were seen by the political leadership as troublemakers was intensified perceptibly after Putin's remarks. The speech was soon followed by a statement from public relations consultant Gleb Pavlovsky (who often serves as an adviser to the government), who accused human rights advocates of a conflict of interests, saying that their striving for Western grants had led them to accept foreign conceptions of rights and forget about protecting the interests of Russian citizens. A few weeks later, in an interview in the government-sponsored paper *Rossiiskaya gazeta*, Pavlovsky (2004) rejected the idea that civil society should be a force opposing the political regime and characterized Russian human rights groups as 'dissident organisations' that were archaic, since in his view they did not solve any social problems. The Ministry of Foreign Affairs meanwhile accused humanitarian organizations in Chechnya of using their missions to cover up anti-Russian activities. The Ministry of the Interior, which commands the regular police, announced a plan to assign police representatives to all rights groups, ostensibly to promote cooperation and prompt responses to citizens' complaints, but in the view of officers of such groups, with the implicit purpose of placing them under the supervision of the government. In a further development, foreign minister Sergei Lavrov met representatives of 48 NGOs in June 2004, including a number known for their support of the government and none highly critical of official policies, to call on them to work with the government to promote Russian interests abroad and 'help create a positive image of Russia outside the country'(*Moscow Times*, 25 June 2004, p. 1). While ostensibly calling for dialogue and cooperation with civil society, Lavrov clearly suggested that non-governmental organizations should serve Russia's national interests as interpreted by the regime itself, and should refrain from actions that would tarnish Russia's image abroad.

In July 2004 the government had submitted draft legislation to the Duma that would regulate the process by which domestic and foreign donors might assist non-governmental organizations. The proposed law would require foreign governments and foundations to register each grant made to a Russian NGO with a special government commission. Russian organizations that wanted to support NGOs would have to be included on a government list of approved donors, or their grants would be subject to a 24 per cent tax. Leaders of some Russian NGOs saw the proposed legislation as another step toward tightening the state's control of social organizations. Putin's 'public chamber', a consultative body that was proposed in his package of political reforms of September 2004, was conceived as a 'platform for extensive dialogue, where citizens' initiatives could be presented and discussed in detail'. It would apparently be a forum for the controlled articulation of demands, and a substitute for genuinely independent social groups, political parties and parliamentary representatives. Putin also proposed that as part of the work of the security agencies, the state should 'support citizens' initiatives in setting up voluntary structures to maintain public order' (*Rossiiskaya gazeta*, 14 September 2004, pp. 1, 3). It seems likely that the security organs, including the FSB, would play a role in giving direction to such 'citizens' initiatives', and that the new 'voluntary structures' would operate under the guidance of those state organs. Recent statements and actions by the political leadership have reinforced the evidence that the Putin administration speaks of the need for a vigorous civil society, but interprets civil society as a network of organizations that, while remaining technically outside the state, will be coopted to assist the leadership of the political regime in pursuing the objectives that it has chosen for society.

Conclusion

As the trends of the 1990s that brought a greater measure of democracy to Russia are being reversed by these manoeuvres, it would be easy to return to the familiar assumption that Russia has never known any tradition other than that of rule by an authoritarian regime. Yet though one of the main themes in Russian political history has been the autocratic character of the state that has wielded authority throughout the country's history with brief interruptions, many Western and Russian scholars now recognize that in the late nineteenth century and early twentieth century, a young civil society was emerging in Russia through the efforts of citizens who formed a growing variety of associations to tackle many of the problems of the cities and countryside. Though independent social organizations were suppressed by the Bolsheviks, who substituted a web of mass organizations controlled by the Communist Party, the memory of the social activism of the prerevolutionary period was never completely erased, and informal, largely non-political groups quietly came into being in growing numbers during the post-Stalin years, not yet constituting a civil society, but indicating the potential for self-generated organizations of citizens. When Gorbachev loosened the state's restraints, independent organizations – the so-called 'informal groups' – proliferated with surprising rapidity, and some of them began to voice political demands with new-found boldness.

The hopes for the imminent flourishing of a civil society that would be as developed as those in established democracies were disappointed in the 1990s, as non-governmental organizations struggled to continue their existence under extraordinarily different conditions. Nevertheless, civil society did survive the first postcommunist decade in Russia, and though most organizations of citizens were starved for material resources and did not seek to recruit a wide base of membership, the number of such groups remained large, and was probably increasing by the late 1990s. Many organizations that had been part of the Communist Party's web of control before *perestroika* continued to provide services of value to their members, and new groups were founded in response to unfilled needs. Since Vladimir Putin's ascent to power at the beginning of the twenty-first century, he has sought to decrease the degree of pluralism in the Russian political system, and it has become increasingly apparent that he wants civil society to be an adjunct to a monocentric state that will be dedicated to his version of the Russian national ideal. Of course, the concept of a civil society whose component organizations are subordinate to the state is a contradiction in terms, and in that contradiction we may find the principal flaw in Putin's design for relations between state and society. Putin seems to hope that social organizations will mobilize the initiative of citizens and provide institutionalized representation for their interests, while being subjected to control by the political regime in order to coordinate social groups' activities within the framework of the leadership's conception of the national interests.

Lenin's aspiration of combining enthusiasm from below with direction from above ultimately proved to be self-defeating, and the same may be expected of Putin's model, even though his methods of control are precisely the same as Lenin's. (Putin, indeed, does not want the state to assume the degree of financial responsibility for the functioning of social organizations that Lenin was willing to embrace.) In the final analysis, for all of Putin's political skills he remains a product of the Soviet system, and his methods of pursuing his goals characteristically involve the introduction of mechanisms of control strongly influenced by a mentality inherited from the Soviet experience. Whether he is successful in imposing his essentially state-centred design for non-governmental organizations in Russia remains to be seen. We may expect that the process of interaction between Putin's administration and the non-governmental organizations that are led by inventive and resourceful social activists will produce a pattern of relationships that we cannot foresee in detail. The contest will be an unequal one, however, because key elements of the political infrastructure of civil society, such as political party competition, the rule of law, and free mass media, are weak or absent in Russia. There is meanwhile no doubt that Putin is moving Russian politics and society in a direction that is diminishing autonomy for social organizations, and one that promises to narrow the range of interests that they express.

Chapter 7

Media and Political Communication

SARAH OATES

Both international and domestic observers have noted a significant decrease in Russian media freedom in recent years. In 2004, media freedom in Russia was ranked worse than that of Iraq or Angola, falling to 148th place out of the 193 countries surveyed by Freedom House. In fact, for the first time since the Soviet Union collapsed, the Russian media were judged as 'not free' by the non-profit organization Freedom House in its 2004 report. At the same time, the International Committee to Protect Journalists reported that Russia was one of the ten worst places in the world to work as a journalist, not only because of the dangers of covering the Chechen war, but particularly because journalists in the provinces 'continue to be murdered with impunity'. In the summer of 2004, the last high-profile television shows that promoted open discussion about the Russian state ceased transmission and yet another prominent journalist – this time the editor of the Russian edition of *Forbes* business magazine – was slain by unknown assailants. This compounded the fact that the two main nationwide commercial television stations are now controlled by state interests and one is now a sports-only channel with no political content.

There are two particularly puzzling factors about the abuse of media freedom in the Russian Federation. First, the Russian media do not have a staid authoritarian face. There are still media outlets that reflect a wide range of points of view, particularly among the well-loved newspaper sphere in Russia as well as on the internet websites that have emerged more recently. In addition, the Russian audience has not turned away from their media, nor do they now hold them in disdain. Rather, there is compelling evidence that many Russians approve of the return to more control and less wide-ranging content in the media. Even as there is a vague appearance of a free media, however, those with differing opinions from the Putin regime are harassed and sometimes silenced. The most popular and influential television station is run by the state and is strongly

114

biased toward the Putin administration. The regime has used dubious
financial tactics to oust outspoken news producers, notably to wrest
control of commercial television stations from those unsupportive of the
Putin administration in 2001 and again in 2003. Those legal manoeuvres
are underlined by the widespread violence against journalists, many of
whom have been killed trying to report on stories ranging from corruption to the war in Chechnya. The ability of the Russian public at large to
get information and make informed political decisions dwindles every
year. Yet, neither the majority of journalists nor most Russians seem
particularly concerned about their shrinking access to information in the
political system.

This chapter will present data and information in an attempt to understand how the Russian mass media, critical in formulating public opinion
during the *glasnost* era, have become a tame lapdog of the state. Although
the media spectrum in Russia is quite broad, this chapter will focus on
television and its news coverage as a critical part of the political process.
What emerges from the study of Soviet and Russian journalism is the
notion that the media have never managed to establish independence
from the state and, as the regime becomes less free, the media are forced
to follow suit. While it would appear that the media became more 'free'
during the *glasnost* era in Soviet times and in the early days of the Russian
state, in fact the media never switched their role from champion of political causes from the Soviet era to watchdog in service of the public in
Russia. As political control tightened with the election of President Putin
in 2000 and again in 2004, the Soviet model of media in service to a
regime has become clear once again. Certainly, contemporary Russian
media are more lively, modern and varied than their Soviet counterparts.
Yet, the type of information control engendered by a lack of respect for
the role of free media in civil society by politicians, journalists and many
citizens does not bode well for the future of the small amount of media
freedom that remains.

Media in the Soviet era

Except for the youngest journalists, most of the current Russian media
profession was educated and inculcated into the journalism system of the
Soviet Union, which collapsed in 1991. Soviet leaders were quick to identify the importance of the media to educate the public about communist
values and to encourage support of the regime itself. In addition to control
through censorship and direction from party officials, the Soviet authorities fostered a journalistic culture that demanded total support of the
ideology and policies espoused by the leaders of the Communist Party of

the Soviet Union. The development of the 'internal censor' on the part of journalists was very effective at controlling the media. In order to get and keep their jobs, journalists had to prove their ability to produce stories and broadcasts that were completely supportive of the party line. Thus, the regime did not really rely on censoring the journalistic output; rather the journalists themselves obediently produced articles and broadcasts supportive of the party line.

Both print and broadcast media were considered critical propaganda tools by the party authorities. As a result, the Soviet Union had newspapers with some of the largest circulations in the world. For example, in 1980, the party daily *Pravda* (Truth) had a circulation of nearly 11 million while another important central newspaper called *Izvestiya* (News) had a circulation of 7 million. Certainly, much of what was printed was ignored or merely put to use in other ways by consumers (most notably as toilet paper when that commodity was scarce). Nonetheless, recent research indicates that people who lived through Soviet times retain two important characteristics of that period: they enjoy reading a wide range of print media, and they are quite good at extracting useful information from even relatively banal statements by officials. In addition, many were pleased that the media, both print and broadcast, supported a positive image of the great Soviet state, something in which they took a great pride even while they were aware of its shortcomings.

Aside from the huge circulations of the biggest newspapers, more than 8,400 newspapers, magazines and periodicals were published in 1990. Despite the lack of objectivity and unadulterated news, sociological studies showed that many adults were eager consumers of newspapers. For example, a survey in Leningrad (now St Petersburg) in the early 1970s found that 75 per cent of those surveyed read a newspaper every day and a further 19 per cent did so three to four times a week, suggesting that virtually every adult in the city was a regular newspaper reader (Firsov and Muzdybaev 1975). In addition, people energetically wrote and sent millions of letters to the editors of newspapers, particularly as this was one of the few effective ways to complain about minor issues and problems in the Soviet state. The total postbag of the national press was estimated at 60–70 million in the early 1980s, and the letter department was often the largest section of the paper (White 1983).

While media content varied over the course of the Soviet regime, it always mirrored the policy of the state. Thus, the media were most conservative under Joseph Stalin, but there was a brief period of relative openness during the later years of the leadership of Nikita Khrushchev. This 'thaw' period saw the publication of some dissident writers, including Alexander Solzhenitsyn's account of prison camp life, *A Day in the Life of Ivan Denisovitch*. Tighter censorship returned after Leonid

Brezhnev took over as party leader. There was a wide variety of periodical titles for different readerships, from chess players to female peasants and football fans, but all of them supported the regime and its policies – and all of them ultimately came under the control of party officials.

The growth of Soviet television

Television also supported the positive image of the Soviet state, but was more monolithic than the print media. Initially far behind the West, the Soviet authorities aggressively developed the availability of television. While only about 5 per cent of the Soviet population could watch television in 1970, at least one channel was available to about 99 per cent of the country by the 1990s. This was a remarkable technological achievement in a country as vast as Russia, in which 13 per cent of homes still lacked running water and 60 per cent had no telephone lines by the 1990s (according to official statistics). The availability of television, both through a satellite system of broadcasting and massive output of television sets, shows that the Soviet administration very much valued the ability of television to inculcate the masses with a positive view of the policies they were promoting. According to official data, at least three-quarters of all households across its vast territory had television sets by the later years of Soviet rule, and the typical audience for the main nightly news programme *Vremya* (Time) reached 80 per cent of the adult population, including the entire armed forces (Mickiewicz 1988: 8).

By the early 1980s, there were two dominant national television networks: Ostankino on Channel 1 (now called the First Channel) and Russian State Television on Channel 2. In addition, much of the country could see either the Moscow channel on Channel 3 or Leningrad television on Channel 4. Local news programmes had slots on the national channels. Soviet television was not, of course, all news reports about record-breaking harvests and the achievements of the Soviet space industry (the fullest account of television content at this time is Mickiewicz 1988). It also featured nature programmes, sports programmes, cultural programmes such as ballet and opera, and reports from overseas, albeit with an ideological slant. There were even game shows, including a popular show called *Let's Go, Gals!* and *Let's Go, Lads!* that featured young people showing off their skills in games, such as competing to see who could build a wall with the fewest bricks while being driven around on a city bus by another contestant. One of the most popular shows then – and now – is an amateur talent show that features teams of young people competing in a series of skits, jokes and singing performances called *The Club of Happy and Resourceful People*. The love of this type of light-hearted programme, complete with an irreverent host, would reemerge in the post-Soviet years when Russian television began serious competition for viewers. For example, participants in focus groups, conducted under the author's direction in Moscow and the regions in 2000, recalled with particular fondness Soviet-era programmes on travel and animals. Many others expressed nostalgia for films and news programmes that celebrated Soviet achievements and a glorified view of the Soviet way of life.

What Soviet leaders failed to appreciate was that the mass media, particularly television, were powerful weapons, but one that could *either support or subvert* the ruling regime. Secure in the knowledge that they controlled the journalists as well as the broadcast signals, Soviet party leaders seemed unaware that the attentive audience spread across the country would be very responsive to even the most subtle suggestions for change. They had created both an impressive media network and a well-primed audience, educated and with a lively interest in the wider world. During the mid-1980s, both of those elements in society began to work against the long-term survival of the Communist Party as it sought to cling to power in a changing society.

Glasnost and the Russian media

The introduction of *glasnost* by Soviet leader Mikhail Gorbachev after his rise to power in 1985 prompted change at an exponential rate in the Soviet media. *Glasnost* literally translates from Russian as 'publicity' but it is better understood as 'transparency'. Gorbachev's new policy was to launch a more honest and unconstrained discussion of the shortcomings of the communist system in the mass media. Gorbachev did not plan for this to be freedom of the press and, in fact, the Communist Party intended to keep control of all of the mass media. Not surprisingly, many Western observers and Soviets themselves were suspicious of the introduction of any sort of openness into the Soviet media system, perceiving it as an attempt by the Communist Party to increase its hold on power or as a cynical exercise in public relations. However, while the initial changes in the mid-1980s were quite modest and restrained, they had far-reaching effects in a society that previously had very tight information control. *Glasnost* started what became an unstoppable process that moved from slight openness on a narrow range of topics to full freedom of speech within the course of a few years.

While Soviet citizens had been writing letters to newspaper editors for decades, *glasnost* allowed more generalized complaints to be covered in regular articles and editorials. The earliest ventures into more 'transparent' press coverage, in retrospect, seem very tame. For example, *Pravda* created a sensation in February 1986 by referring to special shops and other facilities reserved exclusively for Communist Party members. Far greater revelations were to follow. By the late 1980s, the media were running stories revealing Second World War atrocities by Soviet troops, challenging Soviet rule in the Baltic states, questioning the war in Afghanistan, and even criticizing the ideals of Leninism. While some newspapers clung to a more conservative party line, others emerged with an openly pro-Western ideology. A former propaganda outlet aimed at foreigners, *Moscow News* became one of the most aggressive supporters of the new scope that the printed media had begun to enjoy at this time. Another paper that had formerly been the mouthpiece of an official public education society, *Argumenty i fakty* (Arguments and Facts), was similarly outspoken.

In its eagerness to make up for decades of bland, feel-good coverage, Soviet television began to produce almost unremitting images of the failures of the communist regime. The stories they carried included an anguished Russian mother talking about losing her son in the military, an exposé of mental hospitals and coverage of open revolt against Soviet rule in Eastern Europe and even in the Soviet Union itself. New shows and presenters started to gain immense popularity, often trading in the staid, measured tones of traditional announcers for a fast-paced, challenging style that featured more jeans and T-shirts than suits and ties. Youth programmes moved from bland presentations to asking searching questions about the unfairness and emptiness many Soviet youth found in their lives.

When Gorbachev tried to continue to use television as a propaganda tool, he found he had lost control of its immense power. For example, Gorbachev pushed for the live broadcast of the first session of the new Soviet parliament in 1989. The Soviet leader thought the broadcasts would strengthen his image as a liberal communist leader. Instead, viewers saw members of the new Congress – many of whom had been chosen in the first relatively free elections in Soviet history – stand up to challenge Gorbachev, the party, and even the tenets of communism itself on live national television. One of those who challenged Gorbachev was the former dissident physicist Andrei Sakharov, who was instrumental in developing the nuclear bomb for the Soviet Union and had only shortly beforehand been released from internal exile. Short of a return to a much stricter authoritarian regime, it would have been hard for Gorbachev and his supporters to reestablish control after broadcasts of this kind. Yet, many still felt that the debate in the media did not signal an empowerment of Soviet citizens but rather an 'unprecedented freedom to complain about an almost unprecedented drop in living standards and a particularly tyrannical history' with no real power to change the system (Wedgwood Benn 1992: 49).

The media's new freedom reached a peak in August 1991, when a National Emergency Committee attempted to seize power and reinstate the authoritarian controls of the Soviet system. The coup plotters, who held Gorbachev under house arrest in his Black Sea vacation home, managed to order the military into Moscow and seize control of the central media buildings. However, journalists quickly defied the coup and even the presence of armed soldiers in their newsrooms could not stop them from opposing the return to repressive methods. The journalists defied the coup plotters, at first in small ways by failing to cooperate fully and finally through direct defiance in reporting on the resistance at the barricades in Moscow. Even as the coup plotters were holding press conferences claiming that the country would return to authoritarian rule, Channel 1 was broadcasting images of street protests in major cities and putting out calls for resistance. The coup collapsed in a matter of days. In the end, Soviet-created television had the scope and power to contribute significantly to the downfall of the regime itself.

The Russian media in an emerging nation

The dramatic end of Soviet rule in 1991 brought enormous change for all of Russia, including the media. The state no longer had a monopoly on the mass media, which meant that commercial or social groups could start their own publications, radio stations or even television networks. In a practical sense, however, this was enormously difficult because of the economic problems of the young Russian state. In addition, the complex and unwieldy Soviet norms of doing business remained in place, stifling both Russian entrepreneurs and foreign investors interested in the media sphere. Soviet mass media equipment had become badly outdated as the regime ran out of money and failed to invest in new technology. The circulation of the print media plunged, due to both a lack of funding to produce the publications and an inability of Russian consumers to afford them. Even newspapers such as the once mighty *Pravda* floundered in the new market economy, escaping closure only by investment from a Greek tycoon.

Even as the media outlets struggled with a chaotic economy, the Russian audience remained active and engaged. Russians have not dropped their habit of heavy media consumption from the Soviet era, remaining a nation of television watchers and newspaper readers. A 2001 survey commissioned by the University of Glasgow found that about 80 per cent of Russians tune into television seven days a week and almost 70 per cent of them watch for at least two hours a day on weekdays and even more on their days off. In addition, 57 per cent of them pick up a local paper several times a week and 36 per cent of them read a national newspaper at the same rate. In addition, more than 80 per cent of Russians tune into radio daily. It should be noted, however, that radio content has become progressively less political since Putin's initial election in 2000 and the two major radio networks are owned by the state. Finally, Russia has seen an enormous growth in internet use, although the country still lags significantly behind its Western neighbours. According to a 2004 survey, about 30 per cent of urban Russians log on at least once a month.

On paper, Russia has effective laws to protect media freedom and independence. Censorship was formally abolished by the Soviet media law of 1990 and freedom from censorship is now enshrined in the 1993 Russian constitution (Article 29). However, the same article of the constitution places some limits on freedom of speech by forbidding the dissemination of propaganda that spreads social, religious or national hatred. Government secrets are banned from publication. Despite the fact that Article 29 also guarantees the 'freedom of mass information', significant problems remain in the legal protection of the media and journalists in Russia. This includes the lack of a law on broadcasting as of 2004, despite several years of discussion about the details of this legislation.

Yet, it is more the lack of tradition of a free media than any dearth of written law that creates problems for media development in Russia. The country has neither the British tradition of public television with significant editorial independence, nor the type of independent competitive commercial media found in the United States. While these media systems are quite divergent, both serve the public interest by providing service to either citizens or consumers. After the collapse of the Soviet regime, many groups of journalists wanted to take over and run their own newspapers, magazines or even television stations. However, the primary television channels with the largest reach – Channels 1 and 2 – remain under government control. Although many publications attempted to run themselves as commercial enterprises, it soon became clear that a shaky market economy could not support the plethora of publications that had thrived in the Soviet era. Those that did survive have had to deal with twin pressures from funding sources in the government and the demands of their advertisers. Even if advertisers have no direct interest in editorial content, they do demand popular content, a desire that can run counter to the government's need to inform or even propagandize the viewers and readers. In this sense, the Russian media have the worst of both worlds, beholden to both government and commercial sponsors.

The majority of the Russian mass media remains heavily subsidized by the state, including the two prime television channels (the First Channel on 1 and Russian State Television on 2). However, there was strong commercial interest in television in the young Russian state, which was consolidated primarily in the holdings of two powerful Russian 'oligarchs', Vladimir Gusinsky and Boris Berezovsky. Gusinsky, head of the banking concern Media-Most, founded the NTV television channel in 1993. By 1995, the station was broadcasting several hours a day on the former St Petersburg channel and claiming a significant market share. In particular, the station was noteworthy for its aggressive coverage of the first Chechen war (1994–96), in which its editorial team refused to report only the official government line of easy victories and grateful Chechens. Rather, the journalists presented the more harrowing side of the war, including airing the voices of rebel Chechen leaders and showing disturbing footage from the front lines. As a result, state-run television and other media outlets were forced into a less sanitized coverage of the war (Mickiewicz 1999).

Nor was Gusinsky's media influence limited to the NTV channel, which swiftly came to reach about 75 per cent of the Russian public by making use of arrangements with local stations. The Media-Most group also controlled the influential *Segodnya* (Today) newspaper, the weekly news magazine *Itogi* (Results) and the Echo of Moscow radio station. While NTV and Media-Most's commitment to objectivity and fairness in reporting was not absolute – the television station colluded with state television to get Yeltsin reelected in 1996 – in general NTV had a more independent and balanced approach to the news than state-run stations. Berezovsky, a former Soviet official turned Russian entrepreneur, owned a substantial share in the First Channel (then called Public Russian Television) as well as controlling interests in the commercial TV-6 station and three major newspapers.

What has happened to these more diverse voices in the Russian media? Probably the most notable evidence is that both Gusinsky and Berezovsky are now in exile from Russia and under threat of arrest if they ever return. In 2001, the Russian authorities wrested financial control of Media-Most and its media empire from Gusinsky, charging him with fraud and tax evasion. While the financial underpinnings of Media-Most were complex, it was clearly a case of using the law selectively to silence the more critical aspects of the editorial staff. In fact, many prominent journalists immediately left NTV and the editorial line has shifted. (TV-6, which briefly inherited some of the NTV journalists, became an all-sports channel in 2003.) An analysis of NTV news coverage in the 2003 Russian parliamentary elections by the author found that while the flagship evening news programme *Segodnya* remains somewhat more ironic and detached from the government, it has dropped any direct or serious criticism of the Putin regime. In a broader analysis of the Russian media that included five television channels, the Organization for Security and Cooperation in Europe found significant bias across the media spectrum during the 2003 election campaign, with most channels supportive of pro-government parties and providing more negative coverage of the Communists. And although it was a parliamentary election, President Putin dominated the news throughout the campaign.

In terms of war coverage, it should be said that there is evidence from recent Russian focus groups and interviews with journalists themselves that it is less of a conspiracy that keeps Chechnya out of the news than weariness with the story. For journalists, it is a double-edged sword: not only do they perceive the audience as uninterested in seeing more violence in Chechnya and particularly unconcerned about the Chechen point of view, but stories on the Chechen war are politically sensitive as well as hard to report. Although NTV has a Chechen war correspondent who appeared live on air during the 2003 election campaign, the physical risks for the reporters covering the war are quite high. Several journalists (Russian and foreign) have died covering the current war and the lack of a cohesive Chechen opposition that can offer safe passage or protection has made it much more dangerous for journalists since the first war in 1994–96. In addition, there would appear to be little interest in debate about the issue in society.

This leaves the Russian media, and television in particular, dominated by state interests. As many Russians can no longer afford newspapers, television has become even more important as an information source (see Table 7.1). While Russia has a mix of state-run and commercial television channels, almost a quarter of the country cannot receive NTV (see Table 7.2). The state-controlled Channel 1 (now called simply the First Channel) and Russian Television (RTR) on Channel 2 reach virtually all of the country. The Russian government owns just 49 per cent of the First Channel, but controls its editorial policy. The Russian state owns 100 per cent of Channel 2. NTV remains a national commercial channel with regular news programmes, but it has relatively little power to challenge the information hegemony of the Putin regime. TV-Centre is broadcast on Channel 3 and is funded mostly by the Moscow administration. Content analysis of Channel 3 finds it particularly supportive of Moscow Mayor Yuri Luzhkov and his political interests. According to a 2001 survey conducted by the author and associates, 87 per cent of regular television viewers in Russia watched the First Channel daily, 83 per cent watched RTR, 72 per cent watched NTV, 51 per cent watched TV-6 and 35 per cent watched TV-Centre. The preference for news programmes seems to have remained relatively unchanged, although focus groups conducted by the author in 2004 voiced less support for NTV than those in 2000.

It is important to note that there are dissenting voices within the Russian media, particularly on internet sites and in the small weekly newspaper *Novaya Gazeta*. For example, *Novaya Gazeta* continues to

Table 7.1   *Patterns of media consumption, 2004 (rounded percentages)*

	Television	National papers	Local papers
'Routinely'	82	22	31
'Sometimes'	13	36	35
'Seldom'	4	27	23
'Never'	1	16	11

Source: A nationwide survey of 2,000 Russians conducted in December 2003 and January 2004 by Russian Research for Stephen White and associates.

report regularly from Chechnya, at considerable risk to the newspaper's future and the safety of its correspondents. Until mid-2004, some television shows continued to explore controversial issues, notably *Namedni* (Recently) and *Svoboda Slova* (Freedom of Speech) on NTV. Both shows featured live chat with politicians and figures from a wide range of the political spectrum as well as offering a substantially broader range of

Table 7.2   *The major television channels*

Channel	Name	Ownership	Orientation
1	First Channel	Fifty-one per cent owned by the state, rest by mix of public and private corporations	Supports Putin and his administration
2	Russian Television	State-owned	Supports Putin and his administration
3	TV-Centre	Funded primarily by the City of Moscow	Supports mayor and his administration
4	NTV	Commercial, but controlled by interests friendly to the Putin administration	Mildly supportive of Putin, now steers clear of controversial topics and shows
5	Culture	State-owned, cultural channel created by presidential decree in 1997. Only television channel that does not carry paid advertising	No political content
6	TV-6	Commercial/all sports	No political content

opinions than that found on *Vremya* or even *Segodnya*. However, both *Namedni* and *Svoboda Slova* broadcast their last programmes in mid-2004. *Namedni* was forced off the air after broadcasting an interview with a slain Chechen leader's widow who accused the Russian authorities of being involved in the assassination of her husband. The producer and host of *Svoboda Slova*, also under considerable pressure from station executives, stopped producing his programme just weeks later. And while more and more Russians are using the internet each year, it lacks the reach and influence to make it a reasonable challenger to the dominance of state-run television.

What objective evidence is there to measure the state of media freedom in Russia? The most compelling data are from the study of media performance in elections, conducted by the European Institute for the Media, the Organization for the Security and Cooperation in Europe and scholars from the 1993–2004 elections (European Institute for the Media 1994, February 1996, September 1996, March 2000, August 2000; Oates and Roselle 2000; Oates 2004; OSCE 27 January 2004). These reports have consistently shown that the state-run First Channel and Russian Television on Channel 2 give biased, positive coverage to incumbent presidents and pro-government parties. While incumbent politicians tend to attract disproportionate coverage in elections around the world, the coverage given by state-run television in Russia has been excessive and unduly positive. For newspapers, a particular problem has been 'hidden advertising', in which candidates bribe journalists into writing positive articles about them that appear as regular articles rather than advertisements.

At the same time, serious contenders for political power are victims of heavy-handed 'black' propaganda campaigns, in which half-truths, innuendoes and downright lies are broadcast about them. This particular practice, often called *kompromat* (compromising materials) in Russian, was particularly widespread in the 1999 parliamentary elections (White *et al.* 2005). On Channel 1, a large amount of *kompromat* was used against Moscow mayor Luzhkov and his allies as they attempted to challenge Putin and his allies in a nationwide political contest. For example, a popular Sunday news show on Channel 1 devoted itself to smearing Luzhkov, including broadcasting aerial shots of his vast country home and suggesting that embezzlement supported Luzhkov's admittedly extravagant lifestyle. It was particularly disappointing that state television, with a responsibility to serve the public, has been the leader in terms of poor journalistic practices and black propaganda. Meanwhile, media analysts claim it is common for politicians and parties to bribe journalists for everything ranging from a favourable mention on the news to a better slot for a political advertisement. Understandably, few journalists admit even to being offered bribes.

What role has the commercial media played in election campaigns? To a degree, the commercial NTV station has balanced the coverage. The studies cited above have shown that it generally has been less biased and fairer in its political coverage. Yet, NTV and other commercial media outlets have not been objective and professional in the Western sense. First, NTV openly favoured 'its' candidates in elections, particularly by promoting Luzhkov and his allies in 1999. Even worse, during President Boris Yeltsin's faltering bid for reelection in 1996, NTV executives decided to distort the truth about the president's failing health and helped Yeltsin's aides to design and conduct a successful campaign. NTV heads justified the act as necessary because the Communist Party seemed ready to seize control of the country – and the media – once again if Yeltsin had lost his reelection bid. However, the lack of professionalism did little to enhance the reputation of commercial television.

The narrowing of media freedom has been most apparent in the most recent election cycle in Russia, with parliamentary elections in December 2003 and the presidential elections three months later. A large pro-government party, headed by government officials and clearly funded from government coffers, won easily in the parliamentary contest. In turn, Putin dominated in the presidential election, winning easily with 71 per cent in the first round. Unsurprisingly, state-run television coverage paralleled the results at the polls. An analysis of the 2003 parliamentary election prime-time news coverage by the author shows that the government-backed United Russia party received an inordinate amount of coverage on *Vremya*. For example, during the month-long campaign before the December 1999 parliamentary elections, United Russia was mentioned 14 times on *Vremya* and just five times on *Segodnya*. Despite the takeover of its channel by government interests since the last election cycle, *Segodnya* provided more balance and less bias in its coverage, choosing generally quite different stories from *Vremya* to broadcast on the nightly news. However, despite the fact that *Segodnya* paid less attention to pro-government parties, there was much less pointed criticism of Putin and his regime than in earlier elections. A funny and satirical NTV show called *Puppets*, which featured figures lampooning the president and other political leaders, was noticeably absent in the 2003 and 2004 elections. Thus, commercial television provided an information alternative, but it was muted and ironic, rather than pointed and clear. This was a far cry from the station that had challenged the government with its Chechen war coverage during the 1995 parliamentary election.

If the changes in television content are obvious to foreign observers, what do Russians think about the narrowing of media freedom and how are they reacting to this abridgement of their civil rights? Focus groups and opinion surveys that have examined public attitudes to the media in

Russia suggest that Russians do not universally value a pluralistic media that provides for strong criticism of the government. In the turbulent times since the collapse of the Soviet system, much of the Russian public look to the media for stability and reassurance rather than criticism of the regime. As one focus-group participant from Ulyanovsk in 2000 said in a study conducted by the author, 'you watch in pain' as the bad news about the economy and Chechnya are shown on television screens. Other participants echoed this sentiment, finding the relentless negativity of the news, as well as the general hopelessness engendered by the Russian economic problems, difficult to watch on a regular basis. As a result, many focus-group participants favoured the more optimistic tone of state-run Channel 1, even though they were aware of distortions and omissions in its political coverage. These sentiments were echoed in focus groups in 2004, in which very few participants expressed a desire for more unbiased information on the Chechen war. In particular, due to their anger at a recent bombing of the Moscow metro that had been attributed to Chechen terrorists, focus-group participants in the Russian capital were particularly uninterested in hearing the Chechen side of the story.

National surveys make it clear that the preference for authority over truth is relatively widespread among the Russian public. In our 2001 survey, television emerged as the most trusted public institution in the country. Fifty-seven per cent of the 2,000 respondents from across Russia said they had 'full' or 'considerable' confidence in state television, compared with 52 per cent for radio, 50 per cent for the armed forces, 48 per cent for the church, 47 per cent for the print media, 38 per cent for commercial television and 30 per cent for the government. In addition, 65 per cent of the respondents picked national state television as one of the 'most unbiased and reliable sources of information' – far more than those who selected local newspapers (20 per cent), national newspapers (18 per cent), Russian radio stations (16 per cent), commercial television (13 per cent) or even relatives and friends (14 per cent). It is particularly surprising that Russians have such a high level of trust in state television even though propaganda and the obvious manipulation of the news have increased steadily in recent years and even months. Despite this – and many Russians clearly show they are aware of government interference – they believe in state television more than any other media outlet in the country.

In our 2001 survey, the commercial NTV channel was almost as popular as state-run Channel 1. Just over a third of the respondents (37 per cent) selected the First Channel as their favourite and 26 per cent picked NTV. However, in places in which NTV was available it ran head-to-head with ORT in terms of popularity: NTV and ORT each were favoured by about a third of the population. Even as the 2001 survey was being conducted, however, the forced change of ownership ousted the more liberal news team. Over the past three years, the content of NTV has become more cautious, although it still offers more controversial fare than ORT. NTV seems also to have lost some of its popularity. In another survey commissioned by the author and associates and conducted in December 2003 and January 2004, twice as many Russians (76 per cent) reported that they watched *Vremya* regularly compared with those who regularly tuned in to *Segodnya* (38 per cent).

The future of the Russian media

It is clear that the main aim of most of the media in Russia is not unbiased or even balanced reporting; rather they seek to maintain the current elites in power. As a result, the news is remarkably unbalanced when covering domestic politics, using every opportunity to showcase current leaders while ignoring or even vilifying those seeking to contest that power. Focus-group discussions in 2000 and 2004 as well as survey results suggest that Russian viewers are comfortable with trading fairness and objectivity – a concept they regard in any case with scepticism – for the notion of 'strong', stable rule offered on the First Channel.

While there is a range of opinions and information in some newspapers and on internet sites, they have little impact on general public opinion in Russia. Although the liberal newspaper *Novaya Gazeta* continues to cover the Chechen war in depth, it is virtually the only media outlet to send correspondents to the area. Other media outlets have practically ceased covering the war, citing lack of audience interest in the Chechen view or the dangers of sending correspondents to southern Russia. Thus, there are voices offering alternative information and opinions to the dominant state-run media, but few people are listening. If any of these outlets overtly threaten the state, they risk closure. NTV's original owners, who were challenging President Putin in many areas, were forced to hand over the company to other owners in 2001. While NTV remains less sycophantic towards the Putin regime than the First Channel, there is little real challenge to its authority from this single dominant commercial news station. When more outspoken journalists from the original NTV attempted to broadcast on Russia's commercial station TV-6, the channel lost its licence and was turned into an all-sports broadcasting outlet.

Will the Russian media system follow the Soviet model? Certainly there are some clear links between the Soviet media and the Russian system today, particularly in the degree to which Russian journalists practise self-censorship. Russian journalism has managed to parallel some divisions within the political class; however, it has not managed to bridge the gap between the rulers and ruled. This is in many ways an unfair judgement, for most journalists in Russia were never truly given the editorial or economic freedom to pursue goals of objectivity, balance or unbiased reporting. Against a background of threats to their jobs, their security and even their lives, it is difficult to imagine how Russian journalists could have created a relatively independent Fourth Estate. Yet, it is disappointing that there was little effort in this direction, as media outlets and journalists continued to support a range of leaders or causes rather than attempt to serve as a conduit between the elites and the masses. An independent media would have been a very valuable asset for the development of civil society in Russia. The lack of an independent media, particularly television, makes it even more difficult than it would otherwise have been for citizens to remain informed and engaged in a democratic process. Those who oppose Putin's administration are either excluded from media coverage or covered in a biased, unfair fashion. If existing politicians have so little access to the mass media and can have little confidence they will be treated fairly, what about the voices of emerging groups or common citizens in Russia? It would appear that they have no access, and no expectation that the media will allow them to become better-informed, empowered citizens.

Chapter 8

In Search of the Rule of Law

ROBERT SHARLET

In late 2003, the Russian constitution reached its tenth anniversary, no doubt a surprise to some. When the country's first post-Soviet constitution was ratified in 1993 not long after the fiery demise of the first Russian Republic, expectations for its longevity were not high, either in Russia or abroad. The document was seen as a victor's constitution, the product of President Boris Yeltsin's triumph over implacable parliamentary foes in a final military showdown the previous October. During the power interregnum that followed, the constitution, which bore the traces of earlier competing drafts, had been redrafted by trusted Yeltsin advisers. The result reflected a definite pro-executive tilt, as well as a clear slant towards a strong central state.

Yeltsin's draft was based on his desire to avert a repetition of the elite conflict and political fragmentation that had been so fatal to Russia's initial post-Soviet experience. Formally, the draft was designed to replace the heavily amended, Soviet-era RSFSR constitution of 1978. Its incompatible graft of an executive presidency onto a system of parliamentary supremacy had wreaked havoc in Russian politics. As president and parliament duelled for power during 1992–93, many of the constituent parts of the Russian Federation, regions and republics alike, had played the power branches off against each other, gaining a great deal of local autonomy in the process. Thus, the centrist bias of the Yeltsin draft was intended to check this centrifugal trend.

In addition, Yeltsin was convinced that only a strong executive hand could carry out the necessary economic transformation from a state-owned economic system to a capitalist market economy. He believed that a democratically elected, representative legislature more tightly tied to the electorate would have neither the political will-power nor the steady policy nerves to do the job. Hence, in December 1993, Yeltsin's draft constitution went before the public in a constitutional referendum run in parallel with elections for a new streamlined parliament. A majority voted for the Yeltsin draft, and although the authorities marginally fudged the turnout numbers for a legally valid referendum, the new constitution was declared ratified.

Gloomy predictions about Russia regressing to authoritarianism under Yeltsin's constitution were not borne out, neither during his two terms, nor during the first term of his successor, President Vladimir Putin. However, Russia's ongoing political and economic transition during the 1990s as well as the early years of the twenty-first century abounded in difficulties. By the constitution's tenth anniversary, the country's quest for a consolidated democratic polity, a well-functioning market and a fully institutionalized rule of law system still remained a work in progress. Nevertheless, the first decade of constitutional government in Russia had provided a period of relative political stability in which elections became routinized, economic growth finally got under way, and myriad law reforms towards a liberal, modern legal system were accomplished. These were no small achievements for a young country.

This chapter focuses on Russia's uncertain journey towards a rule of law system, namely a society in which the constitutional supremacy of law prevails throughout the land.

Constitutional promises, constitutional ambiguities

By their nature, constitutions promise much, and the Russian constitution is no exception. Such promises are frequently cast in the form of mandates or the expectation that one or more laws, or even a veritable thicket of rules, will be subsequently created to ensure fulfilment of the promises. The promissory clauses of a democratic constitution represent the bedrock of the document as a social compact between citizen and state, while other parts are devoted to delineating the institutions and proce-dures of the governmental system. Therefore, the cynosure of democratic constitution-making is the individual and his or her political, socio-economic and due-process rights and freedoms; hence the many promises. In stark contrast, in the last constitution of the USSR, the citizen remained a stepchild to the all-powerful state with rights limited accordingly.

With the new constitution in place, the position of individual citizens in Russian society and their rights and liberties changed dramatically. Two of the most important promises to the citizen are the right to own prop-erty, as well as the guarantee of a cluster of due-process rights as buffers against the direct power of the state should anyone be called before the criminal justice system. Later, we will review to what extent these promises have been fulfilled.

In its opening chapter on fundamental rights, the constitution proclaims, 'The individual and his rights and freedoms are the supreme value' (Art. 2). To this are added the citizen's right to own private prop-erty (Art. 8.2), including property in land (Art. 9.2). Chapter 2 on human rights spells out a person's property rights in more detail. Private owner-ship is protected by law, property may be bought and sold freely, and the state may only take private property for public use ('eminent domain') with or without the permission of the owner if full compensation is paid in advance (Art. 35). Citizens may freely use their abilities as well as prop-erty to engage in entrepreneurial activities (Art. 34.1). Because of the reverential Russian attitude towards land pre-dating the 1917 Bolshevik Revolution, the constitutional draftsmen thought it wise to single out the individual's right to own property in land in a separate clause (Art. 36.2), Finally, in another notable departure from Soviet practice, Russian citi-zens are guaranteed the right to strike (Art. 37.4), an action which in the past would have brought forth troops and landed one in jail.

While the concept of private property was regarded as bourgeois heresy, the Soviet constitution did include due-process rights for criminal defendants, albeit very imperfect ones subject to state interests. These included a vague presumption-of-innocence rule compromised in practice by the courts' accusatory bias, and the right to counsel which, however, applied only very late in the proceedings. Needless to say, acquittals were non-existent. Soviet due process was further subverted by the ruling Communist Party's behind-the-scenes role in the legal system. Judges and prosecutors were normally party members and all were subject to its disci-pline should the phone ring. Further, in cases of political interest, party officials issued secret directives called 'instructive law' on how a particu-lar law was to be applied, and even how certain cases were to be decided. In practice, this meant that in prosecutions of dissidents beginning in the 1960s the political defendant's due-process rights were routinely violated. Even in ordinary criminal cases, a Soviet defendant's rights were miti-gated by various constitutional caveats which relegated the individual and their interests to an inferior position.

The new Russian constitution of 1993, in contrast, presents an array of greatly enhanced due-process rights, including a 48-hour habeas corpus rule (Art. 22.2), an explicit presumption of innocence (Art. 49), the right to counsel 'from the moment of his detention' (Art. 48.2), and the right to trial by a jury of one's peers (Art. 47.2). Elsewhere, the fundamental law affirms the independence of the judiciary and its subordination solely to the constitution and Russian federal law (Art. 120.1). Finally, a defen-dant's enumerated rights should not be construed to exclude other due-process rights recognized by international human rights law (Art. 55.1). The latter provision, subject to an enabling law, made possible an ultimate appeal to the European Court of Human Rights in Strasbourg.

As mentioned, the final version of the constitution put before the voters was hurriedly drafted with the result that certain difficult issues which had bedevilled the long drafting process were papered over rather than resolved. Most notable was the division-of-powers issue between the central state or federal government, and its 89 subnational or constituent parts, called subjects of the federation. Thus, one finds a wide swathe of constitutional ambiguity under the heading 'Joint Jurisdiction' (Art. 72) in the chapter on the federal system.

Exclusive jurisdiction was assigned to the federal government over a wide array of policy areas (Art. 71), while sole jurisdiction was granted to the federation subjects over a much narrower range of issues (Art. 73). Joint federal–subject jurisdiction fell between these areas of exclusivity (Art. 72). However, in the constitution writers' rush to ready the draft for the referendum, this important clause became merely a list of fourteen areas of co-responsibility between the central and subnational governments of the Russian Federation. Notably, the joint jurisdiction clause was silent on mandates that would address the parameters and specifics of joint policy cooperation on such topics as the collection and sharing of tax revenues (Art. 72.i), federal judicial appointments to the lower courts (Art. 72.k), and the coordination of international economic agreements between Russia's subjects and foreign states (Art. 72.n). Despite constitutional silence, one can logically assume that an implied mandate was intended to direct the vast legislative undertaking of drafting, deliberating and passing a virtual forest of enabling laws necessary to bring to life this constitutional clause at the intersection of Russia's federal system.

Meanwhile, no doubt mindful of the extensive concessions made in Article 72, at least on paper, the constitution's authors in subsequent clauses clawed back and delimited some of the powers devolved to the subjects by expressly asserting the superiority and precedence of federal law (Art. 76.1 and 5), while declaring the federal government a 'unified system of executive power' from Moscow to the most remote local parts of the country (Art. 77.2).

Russia's tripartite judicial system

The constitution provides for a tripartite judicial system at the federal level. Its three parts are the courts of general jurisdiction or general courts, the commercial courts and the Constitutional Court. The largest system is the general courts, headed by the Supreme Court, which along with its personnel was grandfathered from the late Soviet system. Next is the commercial court system led by the Supreme Commercial Court. The commercial courts were set up in post-Soviet Russia based in part on a non-judicial antecedent from the Soviet period. The federal Constitutional Court represents a major institutional innovation in

Russian legal history, and first convened in the days immediately following the collapse of the Soviet Union.

Most of the day-to-day business of Russian legal process occurs in the general court system, particularly in the approximately 2,000 federal district courts throughout the country, the basic trial venue. Their jurisdiction includes all criminal cases, and most civil suits. As in most modern legal systems, civil cases outnumber criminal cases by a ratio of three or four to one, and frequently include property disputes, employee suits under labour law, and divorce proceedings under family law. Beginning in 1993–94, jury trials at the district court level were introduced on an experimental basis in nine federation subjects. In those jurisdictions, defendants facing charges that could incur long prison terms or death have had the choice of a bench trial or the option of exercising their constitutional right to trial by jury.

Caseloads in the district courts are extremely heavy, and further compounded by the many judicial vacancies. Of the general system's 15,500 judgeships, more than a thousand are usually unfilled. The district bench gained some relief from the introduction of a new judicial stratum below it, the justice of the peace (JP) courts. Legislation on the JP courts passed in the late 1990s, but federal budgetary constraints delayed their establishment until 2000. The jurisdiction of these courts includes minor criminal cases, simple divorce proceedings, and cases covering a range of petty administrative offences such as disturbance of the peace and traffic violations. By late 2001, the first 3,500 new justices of the peace had heard over 1.3 million civil suits and 163,000 criminal cases which significantly reduced the overall caseload of the district courts, allowing the judges to concentrate on the more complex and serious cases.

In the general court system, appeals go up from the JP courts to the district bench, from the district courts to the regional courts or the supreme courts of the republics, and from the intermediate level to the Supreme Court in Moscow. The high court is staffed by 111 judges, and divided into civil, criminal and military divisions. All levels are subject to the supervision of the Ministry of Justice, while the Judicial Department of the Supreme Court administers the lower courts in terms of personnel assignments, salaries and materiel support. In addition to the shortfall of judges, the general courts have for years suffered from insufficient funding, shortages of support staff, dilapidated courthouses, periodic wage arrearages, staggering caseloads, and judicial turnover with experienced judges leaving for more remunerative opportunities in the private sector. Most acute under Yeltsin, some of these deficiencies are being addressed by Putin, himself a law graduate, but the general court system remains a judiciary beset by serious problems.

The commercial court system deals primarily with disputes between businesses, commonly cases of failure to perform contracts, as well as administrative complaints against state agencies, frequently over tax assessments. A smaller, more specialized institution, there are 82 federal commercial courts of first instance throughout the Russian Federation along with an intermediate appellate level of ten federal circuit commercial courts. The Supreme Commercial Court in Moscow comprises 22 judges, and is divided into civil and administrative divisions to hear appeals from below. In 2001, the high commercial court reviewed over 18,000 cases. In recent years, the Russian business community's confidence in the commercial court system has grown as more and more enterprises have turned to the courts for remedies.

While the Supreme Court (Art. 126) and the Supreme Commercial Court (Art. 127) each only warrant brief paragraphs in the constitution, a long, seven-part article is devoted to the Constitutional Court, befitting its status at the apex of the Russian judiciary (Art. 125). The Constitutional Court was created in 1991, and except for a hiatus of nearly 18 months from 1993 to 1995, has functioned continuously as the supreme arbiter of Russian constitutional doctrine. The first Constitutional Court got caught in the political crossfire of the first Russian Republic. Under its statute, the court could initiate proceedings at its own initiative, and frequently found itself in the middle of zero-sum separation of power disputes between president and parliament. Yeltsin suspended the court in October 1993.

Under the new constitution, a new court statute was passed which limited the second Constitutional Court to adjudicating cases brought to it by way of petition. The second court convened in 1995 and, with only a few exceptions, has since navigated a careful course between the power branches. The court has gradually gained the respect of the political class and the informed public as it has steadily gained political capital and moral authority. Divided into two roughly equal panels manned by 19 justices, the court accepts only a limited number of case petitions annually, mainly those it deems important in terms of constitutional interpretation. The Constitutional Court has been led by four chief justices since 1991 – Valerii Zorkin, Vladimir Tumanov, Marat Baglai and, recently elected for a second time by his brethren, Zorkin again as the current Chief Justice.

We return later to the subject of specific Constitutional Court decisions pertinent to the question posed at the beginning of the chapter.

Rule of law reform under Yeltsin: progress and regression

A series of legal reforms was enacted under the Yeltsin presidency, and there was some regression from the ideal of a unified rule of law system. Many of the origins of these changes lay in the legal systems of the capitalist West. The legal comparativist Alan Watson (1974: 95) has written that transplanting legal institutions is 'the most fertile source of [legal] development'. By this, he meant the transfer of a rule or system of law from one country to another. As the Cold War came to an end, the United States and Europe believed the way to promote international harmony between erstwhile enemies was to assist Russia in liberalizing and modernizing its political, economic and legal systems. To this end, the US through its Agency for International Development (USAID), as well as non-governmental organizations, and the European Union through its foreign aid programme TACIS, began to pour money and technical advisers into Russia to provide assistance in its transition from Soviet authoritarianism to political democracy, a market economy and the rule of law.

The author, as a principal of the Rule of Law Consortium (ROLC) under the aegis of USAID, was part of this flow of ideas from West to East. ROLC provided major assistance for the development of the then relatively new Russian commercial court system, the drafting of the market-oriented civil code, and the reconstruction of Russian legal education, among other projects. Various European legal teams also played key roles, including the Dutch on the Civil Code, the Germans on the Constitutional Court, and the French on the initial jury trial experiment. In addition, Russia's then new membership of the Council of Europe, the country's need for loans from the IMF, the World Bank and private lenders, and, more recently, its aspiration to join the World Trade Organization, all helped drive the law reform process.

The main law reform achievements of the Yeltsin years were the passage of the new Russian Federation Civil Code beginning in 1994, a massive legislative undertaking, and the recodification of criminal law in 1996 which had been a more conflicted project.

The drafting, enactment and implementation of the new Civil Code to facilitate Russia's transition to a market economy was considered second in importance only to the constitution. In fact, the new code, which was legislated in three parts over a period of eight years, was considered the economic constitution of the country. Part One of the Civil Code was passed in late 1994 and went into effect on 1 January 1995. President Yeltsin signed Part Two into law in early 1996, while Part Three was enacted during Putin's first term in 2001, entering into force in 2002.

The Civil Code represented the realization of the constitution's property mandates. It effectively served as the enabling legislation for implementation of the framers' intent on private property and the right of entrepreneurship. Thus, gone was the former Soviet Civil Code provision that any transaction concluded contrary to the interests of the socialist state and society was deemed void. Instead, Article 1 of the Russian code proclaims the essential freedom of contract without which marketization is inconceivable. Other features foreign to Soviet civil law in the new code included a legal mechanism for bankruptcy, a law on lease, and provisions for the ownership and protection of intellectual property, all prerequisites for a viable market economy.

Passage of a post-Soviet criminal code, essential for the liberalization of society, proved to be a more difficult undertaking. While the issues were being debated, the much amended but heavily punitive Soviet-era RSFSR Criminal Code of 1960 remained operative. In its original form, the Soviet code's declared purpose was to protect the social system of the USSR, its system of socialist ownership of property and, last in priority, the interests of its citizens. In sharp contrast, the new Russian Federation Criminal Code of 1996 proclaims as its first priority the protection of the individual and their liberties and freedoms including ownership, maintenance of public order, protection of the environment and the safeguarding of the constitutional system.

The new Criminal Code differs radically from its Soviet predecessor. Some sixty crimes peculiar to state socialism were dropped. Gone are the political crimes used to curb dissidents, as well as 'economic crimes' intended to stifle forbidden market practices. These included prohibitions against 'anti-Soviet agitation and propaganda' or subversion with a maximum sentence of seven years, anti-regime sedition (three years), and 'private entrepreneurial activity' (five years). Similarly, the new code's emphasis on protection of the person and property of the individual has displaced the Soviet code's opening chapter on 'crimes against the state.' Instead, Russia's Criminal Code now includes among the 70 new definitions of criminal activity many offences familiar to market societies, such as an array of white-collar crimes, computer-related crimes, and a new crime related to Russia's rough transition which appears intended to stem money laundering through façade commercial structures, a serious problem given the country's extensive organized crime networks.

One area of contention in drafting the new code was whether or not to include the death penalty. In the end, it was included although sharply delimited from Soviet times when major economic crimes could result in capital punishment. However, just months after the new Criminal Code took effect in early 1997, Russia's international obligations trumped death penalty advocates. Consistent with the Council of Europe's prohibition against capital punishment in member states, the application of the measure to those already sentenced was put into abeyance. Then, in a decision on a 1999 case, the Constitutional Court went even further, ordering a moratorium on courts' further imposition of the death sentence until the constitutional right to trial by jury in capital cases had been extended throughout the Russian Federation.

Concurrently with these progressive rule of law reforms, the Yeltsin administration was making a series of political concessions to various regions and republics that would vitiate the goal of creating a unified rule of law system throughout the country. The background to this turn of events was that a number of federation subjects had gained considerable autonomy from the centre during the short-lived period before the adoption of the 1993 constitution, either as a consequence of Moscow elites bidding against each other for provincial support, or simply by appropriating more local authority while raging power struggles distracted the capital. The Chechen Republic had already asserted its independence from the Russian Federation even before the collapse of the USSR. The republics of Tatarstan and Bashkortostan, both led by experienced politicians, were restless and often disregarded by central authority. A similar situation prevailed in some of the economically stronger regions. In order to ensure calm and buy civil peace in the fledgling second Russian Republic, Yeltsin invoked an obscure subclause of the constitution to cut deals with potentially troublesome federation subjects.

Invoking authority implied in Article 11.3, President Yeltsin negotiated individual 'treaties' between the federal government and many subjects, beginning with Tatarstan and Bashkortostan in 1994. The thrust of these bilateral treaties was power-sharing between centre and periphery, the most common issues being how much tax revenue could be retained locally versus the share to be sent to the state treasury, and the question of control, marketing, and division of revenues for valuable natural resources such as diamonds, oil and rare metals on the territories of various republics or regions. Actually, the treaties tended to legitimize what the provincial entity had already gained, or taken for itself during the turbulent first Russian Republic.

Other treaties followed with regions as well as republics, each document and its annexes customized on the basis of local factors. In the course of Yeltsin's 1996 reelection campaign, the treaty process was used quite freely to buy support in vote-rich areas. By the end of his tenure in the late 1990s, the centre had signed bilateral treaties with 42 of the 89 federation subjects. In effect, Yeltsin's individualized and ad hoc implementation of Joint Jurisdiction (Art. 72) violated the constitution's fundamental principle of the equality of subjects of the Russian Federation (Art. 5.1) and represented a broad retreat from the objective of a unified rule of law system. As a result, the country began to resemble a mosaic of quasi-independent principalities with political authority severely fragmented, and legal unity deeply compromised.

Putin's restoration of constitutional authority and legal unity

Vladimir Putin's first priority in early 2000 as Russia's new president was to revive Moscow's sagging political authority in the provinces, and restore much needed unity in the field of law. A crucial step was the creation of seven federal districts encompassing the disparate 89 subjects, each district headed by a Putin appointee with plenipotentiary powers. The initial tasks for the president's envoys were to bring republican constitutions and regional charters into compliance with the federal constitution, and to bring subnational legislation into conformity with federal law. In the course of the 1990s, many provincial constitutions and charters had acquired clauses at variance with federal constitutional law, a common one being the assertion of sovereignty within the Russian Federation. Similarly, provincial chief executives and legislative assemblies had produced thousands of laws at odds with federal legislation.

In effect, for the next few years, the envoys undertook the implementation of the constitution's fundamental supremacy clause, from which flowed the express precedence of federal law over local legislation (Art. 15.1). With the assistance of various federal institutions and agencies, the envoys carried out a two-pronged campaign to shore up the integrity of the Russian constitutional system. Republic constitutions and regional charters were harmonized with Russia's fundamental law through the excision of offending clauses, while errant subnational laws were brought into compliance with federal legislation either by means of legislative repeal, or extensive amendment.

The enormous effort to restore constitutional authority and legal unity in Russia was not, however, without difficulties. A number of republic presidents and regional governors put up stiff political resistance as well as resorting to the courts as a delaying tactic, while many provincial assemblies dragged their feet under various pretexts. In some of the federation subjects favoured with bilateral treaties, it soon became apparent that their fallback position in defending retention of local sovereignty clauses and non-conforming legislation was to invoke the authority conferred upon the republic or region through its compact with the federal government. In response to that line of resistance, the president dispatched a senior aide on a special mission to roll back the treaties as obstacles to the legal unity and constitutional integrity of the Russian Federation. Towards the end of the treaty battle two years later, the Kremlin had succeeded through a combination of political persuasion, fiscal pressure and judicial recourse in abrogating 30 of the 42 bilateral treaties, while striking compromise deals with the remaining outliers.

Law reform continues under Putin

While presidential envoys were reestablishing a unified space for rule of law development, the reform process continued in Moscow. Even after the considerable progress of the Yeltsin years, there were still new codes of law to be drafted, as well as numerous special statutes to be enacted if Russia was to continue on the road towards a rule of law society. During Putin's first term, the federal legislature was highly productive in replacing much amended, still extant Soviet law with new legislation consistent with the requirements of democracy, market economics and the rule of law. The output included new codes on land, labour, tax and administrative law, and criminal, commercial and civil procedural law, as well as a major statute on the Bar.

Two areas where legal reform had stumbled in the 1990s were the codification of land law and tax law, both of which are vital to an efficient market economy. Although the constitution promised the right to private ownership of land, the strong Communist Party opposition in the State Duma had consistently blocked President Yeltsin's efforts to push through the legislation. Added to this was the anomaly that land law is a sub-branch of civil law, most of which had been successfully codified. That is, with one major exception. Chapter 17 of Part One of the Civil Code, entitled 'Land Law', remained blank until it was finally included in 2001 thanks to skilful political manoeuvring and legislative compromise by Putin and his parliamentary allies. Codification of modern tax law had also been a fitful process under Yeltsin. Parts of a new tax code had been passed, but other tax reforms were stalled by the obstructive lobbying of Russia's influential business oligarchs and, no doubt, through collusion by the Kremlin as well. Under Putin, who had reduced the business elite's involvement in the political process, Part Three of the Tax Code finally became law.

Criminal procedure, the Constitutional Court and due process

A particularly contentious area of law reform was the recodification of Soviet criminal procedural law. Certain issues – arrest warrants, plea bargaining and jury trial – were controversial among the legal and law enforcement communities, and divided the legislators. In the latter half of the 1990s, several draft criminal procedural codes were put forward to bridge the differences, but none succeeded. Meanwhile, the old Soviet code with its statist bias, in spite of being considerably amended, remained in effect. In practice, this caused disparities between the defendant's constitutional rights and the actual due process of law in the criminal justice system. While lawyers, prosecutors and legislative drafters continued to argue over a successor code, the Constitutional Court was frequently called upon to narrow the gap between theory and practice of criminal due process. Over a ten-year period, of the thirty cases concerning criminal procedure, the court decided an absolute majority of them in favour of defendants.

In one politically fraught case that gave rise to a number of petitions to the Constitutional Court concerning violations of constitutional due process, the court from 1996 to 1999 declared unconstitutional several articles of the extant RSFSR Code of Criminal Procedure which blatantly favoured the state at the individual's expense. These decisions included affirming the defendant's right to a lawyer of his or her own choice, establishing a defendant's equal standing with the prosecutor in appealing certain actions of the trial court, and denying judges the right to remand cases for further investigation rather than render decisions, a long permitted practice which greatly delayed trials while defendants remained under investigation in detention facilities. In another case, the court affirmed defence counsel's right to confer with their clients without the permission of prison officials. In effect, the Constitutional Court introduced significant innovations in Russian due process while judicially amending existing law.

Even after passage of the new Russian Federation Criminal Procedural Code in late 2001, and as it awaited entry into force in mid-2002, the Constitutional Court continued its vigilance on behalf of constitutional due process. The new code shifted from the prosecutor to the court the right of arrest and detention, but deferred its application for 18 months. In defence of the constitutional right of habeas corpus (Art. 22.2), the Constitutional Court directed the parliament to immediately amend the new code to eliminate delayed application. In the same decision, the court also limited to six months the administrative deferral of the new code's provision for expanding jury trial throughout the entire national territory. In the months following the entry into force of the new code, the court continued its oversight, affirming the right of a prisoner to apply for parole, and sending back to the parliament for reconsideration a loosely drafted article permitting an appellate bench's summary reversal of a trial court's decision to acquit.

Beyond issues raised by the Constitutional Court, the new Code of Criminal Procedure is mainly consistent with relevant provisions of the European Convention on Human Rights and, hence, a positive step further in the direction of the rule of law. Several of the code's salient and most progressive features are worth noting, including transferring the power to issue arrest and search warrants from the prosecutor to the judge, restricting custody without charge to a maximum of 48 hours without consent of the court, allowing a suspect to meet with an attorney before talking to the police as well as having their attorney present during interrogation, and a prohibition against conveyor-style interrogations designed to wear down suspects and induce confessions. Once a suspect is formally charged, the new code places limits on the length of pre-trial detention, requires the obligatory participation of defence counsel in all phases of proceedings, and expands the right of jury trial in serious cases from the original nine regions to all 89 subjects of the federation. Still, there are lingering problems with the new Code of Criminal Procedure, which will be discussed in the next section.

Continuing obstacles to a unified rule of law system

In spite of steady progress during the constitution's first decade, Russia continues to be plagued by a number of problems in its drive to diffuse rule of law relations throughout society. I will comment briefly on the four main areas where further attention and corrective action are necessary, as well as a very recent concern.

Imperfect legislation

After 1991, all aspects of the Soviet legal system had to be either replaced or extensively renovated, which meant introducing new institutions and legal norms on a massive scale. The legislative agenda writ large included well over a dozen major law codes as well as hundreds of specialized statutes. In addition to enacting this great volume of law, there was also the constant task of integrating each new code and statute with still extant law from the past as well as new law. A single new statute would have a ripple effect, as various codes and numerous other laws had to be amended accordingly. A bill comprising each piece of amended legislation, in turn, had to be steered through the legislative process to become new law.

Hence, a certain amount of legal drafting and legislative fine-tuning was inevitably done hastily and imperfectly by inexperienced and under-staffed legislators, leaving a trail of unresolved issues and loose ends. Time was certainly a factor as Russian political elites struggled to put in place new structures and processes to fill the vacuum left by the discredited and defunct Soviet system. For instance, the contemporary Dutch Civil Code, considered the most modern in the world, took nearly forty years to complete, while the Russian Civil Code was put together in less than a quarter of that time. It is not surprising that hardly before the ink was dry, the process of revising and amending new Russian law would begin.

To illustrate, the Code of Criminal Procedure was less rushed than most, but it nonetheless bears the imprint of unresolved issues. Thus, soon after its appearance, harsh criticism of some of its features was heard. Several examples: in jury trials, a judge may dissolve the jury if in his or her opinion, not subject to appeal, the jurors might hand down an 'improper verdict'. In appealing a conviction, a defendant risks receiving a longer sentence after the appellate court's *de novo* consideration of the case, and the most criticism is reserved for the greatest novelty in the new code – the introduction of quasi-plea bargaining based on American practice. Some jurists see in this a regression to the spirit of Stalin's chief prosecutor Andrei Vyshinsky, for whom an uncorroborated confession was the 'queen of evidence'. As one scholar has predicted, 'further petitions and queries to the Constitutional Court are inevitable' (Lediakh 2005).

Implementation problems

Implementation of laws and court decisions is widely regarded as the Achilles heel of Russian legal development. The problem takes various forms, from delayed or incomplete implementation to obstructed implementation and, ultimately, to implementation failure. Given the abrupt end to the USSR and Russia's takeover of a bureaucracy in disarray, the problem is understandable, although no less disagreeable for a country relying on law and courts struggling to move forward from a dark past.

The success rate of implementation has improved from the most erratic years of the Yeltsin presidency, but much remains to be done in this area of legal development. All the courts have suffered the problem, from the Constitutional Court down to the district court, but steps to assist judicial execution have been taken. A system of bailiffs attached to both the general and commercial courts has helped, and President Putin has lent his authority and executive resources to ensure implementation of Constitutional Court decisions. In substantive law, for most of the 1990s tax legislation was characterized by staggering shortfalls in revenue collection in an atmosphere of general tax avoidance. With the completion of tax law codification, the strengthening of the tax police and the introduction of a flat-rate tax, the situation has markedly improved.

In the area of procedural law, the jury is still out on the implementation of the progressive new due-process rights not only in the courthouse but down in the local police lock-up as well. However, on at least one issue successful implementation seems assured. The constitution provides that anyone detained has the right to an attorney from the moment the cell door swings shut (Art. 48.2), a right now further defined in the Code of

Criminal Procedure. The fundamental law also provides for free legal assistance to those in need (Art. 48.1). During the 1990s, since the country could not afford a public defender service, all private attorneys were – so to speak – drafted for legal aid work. Many ducked the obligation since remuneration was nominal or nil, leaving millions who lived in poverty adrift if they were hauled into court or sought legal relief.

In 2002, the first post-Soviet law on the Bar addressed this implementation difficulty, but in a manner faintly reminiscent of Soviet administrative solutions. All attorneys have now been organized into a single national Bar overseen by the Ministry of Justice, with sections in each province. Although the burden of *pro bono* clients still depresses attorneys' income, under the new law on the Bar they now risk disbarment if the duty is shirked.

Finally, there is the ongoing saga of the implementation of the constitutional principle of joint jurisdiction (Art. 72). Progress has been made on land and taxes. As part of the deal in brokering passage of the Land Code, the Kremlin agreed to considerable local discretion in implementing the most politically sensitive issue of purchase and sale of agricultural land. With the end to tax separatism in the runaway provinces by Putin's presidential envoys and final completion of the Tax Code, a system of tax federalism is now in place.

On the many other outstanding issues requiring cooperation, Putin empanelled a high-level commission to study the question of delimitating federal and subject powers in areas of joint responsibility, and drafting appropriate enabling legislation. The commission has drawn up a number of draft laws and submitted them to the State Duma, but much remains to be done in the area of joint jurisdiction with many unsettled issues still to be sorted out if Russia is to continue its long transition from Soviet sham federalism to a democratic and equitable federation.

Selective prosecution

A persistent shortcoming in the rule of law that has characterized Putin's term in office has been his carefully targeted selective prosecutions, in particular of the great business titans or 'oligarchs'. As a group, these individuals are all potentially legally vulnerable for past behaviour, given the way they acquired their vast wealth and power in the wake of the Soviet break-up. Still, for a few of the most vociferous ones to be singled out for prosecution offends a hallowed principle of rule of law jurisprudence enshrined in Article 19 of the Russian constitution, 'All are equal before the law and courts.'

Aside from the Kremlin's motivation in pursuing its latest target, the Yukos chief executive Mikhail Khodorkovsky, hardly a blameless soul, the due-process violations in his case are troubling, and reminiscent of post-Stalin-era political trials of dissidents when the fix was in and the verdict predictable. In fairness, it should be noted that this type of ad hoc behaviour is not peculiar to Russia. President Richard Nixon's so-called 'enemies list' and his administration's selective prosecution of the 'Chicago 7' come to mind. The difference of course is that the United States has a well-developed political immune system and ready antidotes that Russia's political and legal culture have yet to engender.

Aberrant police behaviour

Of all of Russia's problems in trying to create a comprehensive rule of law system, the most resistant to improvement has been police behaviour, especially at the level of the beat cop. Underpaid, poorly trained and ill-equipped for serious crime fighting, Russian cops often perpetrate a petty crime wave of their own, including protection rackets targeting street vendors, extorting and pocketing traffic 'fines', and extracting small bribes from people detained for failing to carry their passport and other minor infractions. Corruption is so endemic among the police that special labour camps are designated for rank-and-file and senior police officials to serve their time when caught.

For individuals actually charged with a crime, reports indicate that nearly half of all detainees were beaten by precinct cops in the course of questioning during the last years of the 1990s. Beyond the police lock-up lies the investigative prison where suspects are frequently held for inordinate lengths of time awaiting trial, sometimes longer than the maximum sentences they might receive, in conditions of extraordinary overcrowding, abominable filth and rampant disease (Piacentini 2004). Fortunately, this aspect of the law enforcement problem has attracted the attention of President Putin, who has called for speedier justice to reduce the population of pre-trial detention centres. Going beyond rhetoric, he has been inclined to provide the judiciary with more funding to fill vacancies and take on additional judges to better handle the caseload and reduce backlog. Most recently Putin noted with satisfaction that the transfer of arrest authority to the judges has resulted in far fewer arrests and detentions. It must be hoped that these modest trends will continue, and gain greater momentum in the future.

Recent concerns

The rising tide of terrorist acts within Russia during the past five years, and especially the attack on the Beslan primary school in September 2004, has brought forth some worrisome trends in terms of the rule of law. The

Beslan tragedy, in the manner of the controversial United States Patriot Act in the wake of 9/11, has stimulated a number of radical proposals for dealing with extremism. These include a witness protection programme for those testifying in terrorist cases, denying the right to trial by jury for individuals charged with terrorism, and significantly increasing sanctions for terrorism including restoration of the death penalty in such cases. Other illiberal solutions include reviving the Soviet-style system of police informers, and detaining the relatives of terrorists during negotiations for release of their hostages. There is opposition to some of these more extreme ideas, but another large-scale terrorist act could weaken resistance.

The very surfacing and discussion of these proposals reflect an increasingly restrictive trend in Russian legislation concerning individual rights. In June 2004, a new law restricting the scope of public demonstrations was passed. In its original version, the bill would have facilitated the authorities' suppression of nearly all such actions. Fortunately, President Putin intervened with the result that a more 'liberal' yet still restrictive bill became law. Also, during spring and summer of 2004 there was much discussion about a possible revision of the legislation concerning the election of regional chief executives and of the State Duma. Shortly after Beslan, Putin embraced both ideas, putting them forward as legislative initiatives designed to assist the struggle against political terrorism. Both proposals have elicited a great deal of criticism from liberal legislators, public intellectuals, and even the chief justice of the Constitutional Court. On the other hand, it has also been pointed out that nearly half of the member states of the European Union appoint regional chief executives, while a number of stable democratic countries elect their legislatures on a PR system. What use the authorities will make of their new powers remains to be seen.

Conclusion

We began by asking how well certain constitutional promises are being fulfilled in Russia. The answer is a mixed one, but fundamentally positive. Property rights have been strengthened by the completion of the Civil Code, the passage of civil and commercial procedural legislation, the legalization of the purchase and sale of land, the introduction of the flat-rate tax, the success of the new JP courts in resolving civil suits, and the improving rate of judicial execution in cases of administrative justice in both the general and commercial courts.

With the passage of the Code of Criminal Procedure, the due-process promises of the constitution have now been enabled in the form of operative procedural law. As already mentioned, the downward trend in arrests is a promising development. In addition, based on the initial experiment, the countrywide expansion of jury trial should increase the opportunity for good lawyers with strong cases to win more acquittals.

Finally, in 1998 the necessary enabling legislation was passed permitting Russian criminal defendants who have exhausted all domestic remedies to forward appeals to the European Court of Human Rights. Since then, nearly 15,000 Russian applications for review have gone to Strasbourg, although only a very small number have met the court's strict requirements for hearing a case on its merits. Of the three cases decided to date, all have gone against the Russian government, including a decision that the length and conditions of an applicant's five-year, pre-trial detention had violated his rights.

Of still greater significance for the prospects of a unified rule of law system is the attention now being paid to European case law on human rights. As an American justice official who has worked with Russian lawyers in this area recently observed, 'Russia's highest courts have embraced this caselaw and made it their own. By so doing, European standards on a variety of fundamental issues have been imported into Russian law' (Kahn 2004: 9).

Chapter 9

Reforming the Federation

GORDON HAHN

The success or failure of Russia's transformation into a stable state with a viable market democracy will depend much on the creation of an effective and balanced federal system. The challenge is historically unprecedented. No state of Russia's size and complexity has ever needed to develop national identity, democratize, introduce a market economy and build a state simultaneously. Russia's size dwarfs those of other states, and its multitude of some 150 nationalities is rivalled by few. Russia incorporates almost every religion and is the only state that borders the Confucian, European, Arab and Islamic civilizations. Indeed, the fault-line between the turbulent Islamic world and Russia's Orthodox civilization runs through Russia's North Caucasus and Volga mega-regions.

The national identity of non-Russians, meanwhile, is growing, and as a consequence Russians will feel, if they do not already, that they are less welcome in the titular non-Russian national autonomies. In addition, the non-Russian nationalities, especially the Muslims in the North Caucasus, have much higher birth rates than do ethnic Russians. No empire has ever been transformed into a democratic federation. The fall of the Soviet regime, the collapse of the Soviet state and the birth of the Russian Federation itself were partly the results of the failure to establish a real federation during Mikhail Gorbachev's *perestroika* reforms. Russia, the core of the USSR's 'internal empire', mirrors its predecessor not only in its territorial, ethnic and confessional incongruence but its weakened asymmetrical, 'national-territorial' administrative structure. Two Chechen wars are but the latest of a series of threats that challenge the territorial integrity of the state itself.

To some degree, first post-Soviet Russian president Boris Yeltsin's ad hoc federation-building efforts corresponded with what much social science and historical experience suggest are effective mechanisms for containing communalism (the drive for self-determination based on ethnic, national, linguistic, religious and/or regional 'identity groups') and separatism (external self-determination in a new state) in complex and incongruent multi-communal states through the provision of 'internal self-determination' or autonomy to regions and communal groups. Putin's approach, although it addresses some deficiencies in Yeltsin's system, constitutes an anti-federative counter-reform that risks mobilizing communalism, including Islamist nationalism, terrorism and separatism (the federal structure, as it presently exists, is shown in Table 9.1).

Federalism and multi-communal states

The state-building challenge is particularly difficult for states like Russia that are vast and/or communally complex, with numerous minority 'identity communities' living in territorial concentration or national-territorial administrative units. However, there is no shortage of remedies, including territorial, national-territorial, corporate and consociational federalism. Large incongruent states are more likely to be multinational and federal. As Kahn (2002) points out, except for China, the largest states in the world (Argentina, Australia, Brazil, Canada, India, Russia and the United States) are federal, except for China. Indeed, even China is developing elements of federation – decentralization and divided sovereignty – as it reforms economically. With the reincorporation of Hong Kong and the desire to reintegrate with Taiwan, China has recognized the federative principle of divided sovereignty and, moreover, political autonomy.

Traditional federalist theory envisages territorial and relatively symmetrical decentralization. Various elaborations posit the need for communal-territorial federation or regional autonomy (self-rule or self-governance) to assuage ethno-national aspirations and undercut separatism by providing the governance units in regions with concentrated minority cultural, ethnic and/or religious populations partial or full sovereignty in certain spheres of life, particularly those most closely related to their group identity. Arend Lijphart (1984) recommends consociational federalism: giving special power-sharing rights at the centre to national minorities or their regional autonomies such that consensual rather than majority rule is exercised. According to Lijphart, tyrannies of the majority frustrate ethno-national minorities' aspirations to protect their cultural, linguistic and confessional identities from assimilative policies and their territories' natural resources from expropriation by the centre. Democratic socialists Otto Bauer and Karl Renner proposed for the Austro-Hungarian Empire a rarely applied 'corporate federalism' or non-territorial cultural autonomy for minority communities to allow extraterritorial self-governance on cultural, religious and linguistic issues. The state's integration into international and international-regional organizations, internal regional autonomy in some foreign relations, and alternative voting schemes that force intercommunal coalitions may also be appropriate.

Table 9.1 *Russia's republics and regions (according to the 1993 constitution)*

Republics (21)	Leningrad Oblast
Republic of Adygeya	Lipetsk Oblast
Altai Republic	Magadan Oblast
Republic of Bashkortostan	Moscow Oblast
Republic of Buryatia	Murmansk Oblast
Chechen Republic	Nizhnii Novgorod Oblast
Chuvash Republic	Omsk Oblast
Republic of Dagestan	Orel Oblast
Ingush Republic	Orenburg Oblast
Kabardino-Balkar Republic	Penza Oblast
Republic of Kalmykia-Khalmg-Tangch	Perm Oblast*
Karachai-Cherkess Republic	Pskov Oblast
Republic of Karelia	Rostov Oblast
Khakass Republic	Ryazan Oblast
Republic of Komi	Sakhalin Oblast
Republic of Marii El	Samara Oblast
Republic of Mordovia	Saratov Oblast
Republic of North Ossetia	Smolensk Oblast
Republic of Sakha (Yakutia)	Sverdlovsk Oblast
Republic of Tatarstan	Tambov Oblast
Republic of Tuva	Tomsk Oblast
Udmurt Republic	Tula Oblast
	Tver Oblast
Krais or territories (6)	Tyumen Oblast
Altai Krai	Ulyanovsk Oblast
Khabarovsk Krai	Vladimir Oblast
Krasnodar Krai	Volgograd Oblast
Krasnoyarsk Krai	Vologda Oblast
Primorskii Krai	Yaroslavl Oblast
Oblasts or regions (49)	*Federal cities enjoying status*
Amur Oblast	*equivalent to a Region (2)*
Arkhangel Oblast	Moscow
Astrakhan Oblast	St Petersburg
Belgorod Oblast	
Bryansk Oblast	*Autonomous region (1)*
Chelyabinsk Oblast	Jewish Autonomous Oblast
Chita Oblast	
Irkutsk Oblast	*Autonomous districts (10)*
Ivanovo Oblast	Agin Buryat
Kaliningrad Oblast	Chukchi
Kaluga Oblast	Evenk
Kamchatka Oblast	Khanty-Mansi
Kemerovo Oblast	Komi-Permyak*
Kirov Oblast	Koryak
Kostroma Oblast	Nenets
Kurgan Oblast	Taimyr
Kursk Oblast	Ust-Orda Buryat
	Yamal-Nenets

* Merged from 2005 into a single Perm territory.

As Keating (2001) notes, in the postindustrial, transnational, regional integration era states are increasingly likely to feature a mix of federative and confederative arrangements and divided and multiple sovereignties and identities. In any particular multicommunal state a specific mix of mechanisms that take into account its historical, ethno-national, confessional and previous institutional peculiarities is best suited for assuaging self-determination aspirations and perceived wrongs, balancing interests, and inducing political moderation and stability. Indeed, under the pressure of a collapsing Soviet state apparatus after Gorbachev's belated attempt to federalize its unitary system, Yeltsin acquiesced in the formation of a loose 'asymmetrical federalism' in order to placate national minorities like the Chechens and Tatars. The emerging federal system, though weakly institutionalized, included various autonomy and consociational mechanisms.

The legacy of the Soviet state and Russia's revolution from above

Yeltsin's revolution from above against Gorbachev's reforming Soviet communist regime inadvertently encouraged ethno-national and regional assaults from the Russian federation's periphery against the new post-Soviet Russian regime. Intense internal infighting among elite factions of the party-state apparatus set in motion by Gorbachev's early ideological and institutional reforms was waged through the political weapon of institutional reorganization. Horizontally, the reformist Gorbachev transferred significant power from the conservative party apparatus to state organs like the soviets and the new USSR executive presidency, beginning the process of separating the party and state apparatuses. Vertically, he supported some decentralization of power from Moscow to the republics ostensibly to realize the false promise of federalism in the Soviet Constitution. Yeltsin, in attempting to push Gorbachev to reform faster and to undermine his power, used the RSFSR proto-state's apparatus to push for a full division of the party state, and creation of a loose Soviet confederation that would leave the centre with limited powers on domestic issues. To achieve these goals, Yeltsin led the new RSFSR Supreme Soviet to adopt a 'Declaration on the Sovereignty of the RSFSR' in June 1990 which de jure and gradually de facto established RSFSR and thus Yeltsin's control over the natural, financial, infrastructural and property resources on RSFSR territory. He also backed a 'financial revolution' against the centre, the Baltic and Georgian national revolutions, and the 'parade of sovereignties' in the other union republics, signing economic treaties with them to circumvent Gorbachev's union state apparatus.

In response, Gorbachev won adoption of an amendment to the Soviet constitution in April 1990 giving the autonomous national republics in the RSFSR a status equal to that of the union republics as 'subjects' or members of the union. This extended the 'parade of sovereignties' to the regional level within the RSFSR and other Soviet Union members with national-territorial administrative structures (Georgia and Ukraine). Party hardliners also tried to play this game, urging party organizations in the national autonomies to push for extended sovereignty and even secession from the RSFSR and the secessionist union republics. Yeltsin countered by coopting the movements for sovereignty in Russia's national autonomies. Two months after his election as Chairman of the RSFSR Supreme Soviet and the RSFSR's Declaration of Sovereignty, Yeltsin travelled to Tatarstan, which had the strongest nationalist movement at the time. In the capital Kazan on 5 August 1990 he told Tatars and in effect Russia's other regions to 'take as much sovereignty as you can swallow'.

The parade of sovereignties marched across Russia, bringing a wave of sovereignty declarations and 'levelling up' within Russia's then purely formal '*matryoshka*' territorial-administrative structure. Under Stalin different ethno-national groups had been made the titular nationalities of administrative-territorial units and were nested within other territorial units while at the same time they had equal 'representation' in certain party and state structures and had, in some ways, equal status and 'rights', at least formally. Now, the RSFSR's autonomous republics sought the status of union republic (which was formally in ways equal to that of the RSFSR), the lesser autonomous regions sought autonomous republican status, and the lowly autonomous *okrugs* or districts sought autonomous region status. In Tatarstan, Yeltsin's gambit allowed the republic's leader, Tatarstan Communist Party First Secretary and Supreme Soviet Chairman Mintimer Shaimiev, to unite moderate Tatar nationalists, Russians and moderate communists behind extended sovereignty rather than secession. This undercut Tatar independence movements and assuaged the fears of ethnic Russians and communists.

The Russian revolution from above's compromise with its regional native elites prevented or at least forestalled separatism (except in Chechnya), civil war, and even the dissolution of Russia during the communist regime's demise. However, the underdeveloped RSFSR proto-state initially was largely unable to contain the sovereignty movement from above that it had encouraged across Russian territory. Yeltsin's declaration encouraged two serious national liberation movements (Chechnya and Tatarstan), but in most regions former communist leaders and *nomenklatura* officials retained power and resisted much of Yeltsin's democratic revolution from above, creating an uneven or 'asymmetrical democratization'. Even some 'ethnic Russian' regions, the nonautonomous regions and territories, joined the sovereignty parade, breaking up not only the Union's but the RSFSR's common economic space. In order to halt this disintegration, Yeltsin proposed a 'Federation Treaty', much as Gorbachev had a union treaty to save at least some rump of the USSR. From here a spectrum of degrees of autonomy or sovereignty emerged: from de facto independence in Chechnya between 1996 and 1999 to loose confederal and federal relations. Yeltsin's emerging federal state included at least three major forms of federative 'asymmetry', a complexity unprecedented in the annals of federalism: 'official asymmetry' or constitutionally based treaty federalism, 'unofficial asymmetry' between federal and regional laws and constitutions, and the 'administrative-structural' asymmetry of Russia's nested or *matryoshka* national-territorial subdivisions.

The first of these asymmetries developed from the refusal of both the republics of Chechnya and Tatarstan to sign the 1992 Federation Treaty, and the latter's decision to return to the fold under conditions negotiated with federal authorities. Chechnya took a completely 'unofficial' and unconstitutional separatist path, while Tatarstan won officially recognized autonomy in an essentially confederative relationship with the rest of the federation. In Chechnya, President Dzhokar Dudaev rose to power by way of an illegal putsch, declared Chechnya's secession from the Russian Federation, stockpiled weapons bought from the decaying Soviet military fractured by the revolution from above, and sought contacts with Muslim and Arab states through Chechen émigré groups. Chechnya soon found itself in civil war and went through several stages in relation to the federation, from de facto and arguably de jure independence under the 1996 Khasavyurt agreement that ended the first post-Soviet Chechen war to a second war, military occupation, and direct federal rule in 2000.

Russia's thirty other national autonomies took different paths. The influential and titular Muslim national republic of Tatarstan (as well as Bashkortostan) was able to forge a loose confederal relationship with Moscow, leading the way in building Russian federalism's treaty-based 'official asymmetry'. In February 1994 it was the first to sign with Moscow a bilateral federal–regional treaty on sharing competences and powers after two years of difficult negotiations. Such power-sharing treaties, according to Article 11.3 of Russia's 1993 constitution, may redistribute between Moscow and a region the joint federal–regional competences and powers listed in Article 72. However, the Tatarstan treaty went further, redistributing solely federal powers to Kazan and describing the republic as 'a state united with the Russian Federation' rather than a subject of the federation. This relationship, the treaty reads, is based not only upon the treaty and the Russian constitution but also the 1992 Tatarstan constitution. The republic's constitution stipulated that the republic was a 'sovereign state' and an independent subject of international law that was merely 'associated' with Russia. It also violated the federal constitution by declaring the supremacy of republic over federal law. Subsequent agreements with Moscow gave Kazan even more rights, including 75 per cent of tax revenues collected on its territory. Eventually, 45 regions, mostly the national autonomies, followed Kazan's example and signed power-sharing treaties and agreements. Another seventeen regions signed only lower-order 'agreements'. However, Russia's treaty-based official asymmetry was a purely intra-elite affair, established neither through referendums nor through joint federal–regional legislative approval as in the Indian and Spanish cases.

All of Russia's federation subjects or regions participated in 'unofficial asymmetry' by adopting regional constitutions (or charters) and legislation that violated the Russian constitution and federal laws. Unofficial asymmetry is thus distinct from official asymmetry, since it is not sanctioned by constitution, law or treaty. In part, unofficial asymmetry emerged as a result of the sequencing of constitution- and law-making between the federal and regional levels. In some cases, regional constitutions emerged before the adoption of the December 1993 Russian constitution, and in many cases regional legislatures adopted laws in spheres where federal law was still absent. Here, the distribution of powers as laid down in the 1993 constitution also proposed problems. Article 71 listed exclusively federal spheres of competence. Article 72 listed spheres of joint federal–regional jurisdiction. Article 73 allocated to exclusive regional jurisdiction only those spheres that had not been enumerated in Articles 71 and 72. This leaves little scope for exclusive regional jurisdiction. Moreover, Article 76 explicitly states that when federal and regional laws conflict over issues coming under joint federal–regional jurisdiction, federal law is supreme. These articles taken together leave any resort to joint federal–regional law-making and such mechanisms as conciliation procedures to the whim of federal authorities. This potentially centralized distribution of powers was betrayed under Yeltsin by the broad regional autonomy provided through the power-sharing treaties and the regions' head start in adopting constitutions and laws, especially among the national autonomies. Thus, tens of thousands of laws, constitutional clauses, executive orders and resolutions adopted by the regions violated the constitution and federal law, often at the expense of democratic governance, political and civil rights, and market development. As of Putin's assumption of power in 2000, 62 of the constitutions and charters of Russia's 89 regions and republics had been pronounced to be in violation of the constitution, together with some 6,000 regional laws and tens of thousands of other legal acts adopted at the regional and subregional level.

As Larisa Kapustina (2000) notes, the power grab touched on fundamental powers typically reserved for the federal authorities even in
confederal systems, such as foreign affairs, defence and national security.
The Tyva Republic, in its constitution, even asserted the power over issues
of war and peace, violating the Russian constitution's Article 71, which
reserves this power for the president and the Federation Council.
Bashkortostan, Kalmykia and Tyva adopted laws on military service. The
Tyvan law could be interpreted as giving the republic the right to form its
own army. The constitutions of Bashkortostan, Dagestan, Ingushetia,
Komi, Novgorod region, Sverdlovsk region, Tatarstan and Tuva gave
them the power to conduct foreign policy. The pre-Putin Tatarstan constitution, as noted above, established a confederate relationship by stipu-
lating that the republic was merely 'associated' with the Russian
Federation. In addition, under the extensive sovereignty and official and
unofficial asymmetry of the Yeltsin era, governors and especially republican presidents appropriated many executive functions as well as control
over federal organs located in their regions. Police, tax, court and other
supposedly federal officials were subordinated to regional governments
almost entirely.

Finally, the 1993 constitution recognized the levelling up that occurred
in the course of the Soviet collapse's parade of sovereignties by codifying
and giving substance to the previously formal Soviet *matryoshka* or
nested national–territorial administrative structure inherited from the
RSFSR. The Russian Federation's adapted three-tier national–territorial
structure established a unique 'administrative–structural asymmetry'
under which lower-level administrative–territorial governance units
possessed federation subject status, direct channels to the federal government, and special rights and exceptions that other federation subjects did
not enjoy. For example, the Khantsy-Mansi and Yamalo-Nenets national
districts, which are located within Tyumen region and send some of their
tax revenues to Tyumen's coffers, are federation subjects just as the region
itself is. They each have two senators in the Federation Council, as does
the region, and their residents elect their own legislatures and governors
and those of the region. Associated with nested asymmetry under both the
Soviet and new Russian constitutions is the designation of two different
nationalities as the titular nationalities of a single unit of government,
including among others the Kabardino-Balkaria and Karachaevo-
Cherkessia republics.

Given the multiple hyper-asymmetry of Yeltsin's nascent federalism
and the political and financial impact of two Chechen wars, some 'gathering in' of Russia's regions and streamlining of the federation were likely
under Putin.

Putin's federative counter-reforms

Upon assuming the presidency in May 2000 Putin placed at the top of his agenda the strengthening of the Russian state as a precondition for the successful modernization of the Russian economy. This, in the view of Putin and his closest associates, required a turn towards a soft form of authoritarian rule in order to provide the central state apparatus with autonomy from societal interests, especially oligarchic business, ethno-political and regional interests. Besides subduing the financial–industrial oligarchs, the priority strategy was Putin's federative reform – strengthening the Russian state's 'executive vertical' and reintegrating Russia's 'legal space'. Putin's federative policies in effect dismantled most of the asymmetry inherited from Yeltsin; recentralized administrative, budgetary and ownership authority back to Moscow; and eliminated many federative mechanisms for containing communalism. Specific reforms included the creation of seven federal super-districts; changes in federal–regional interbudgetary relations; the institutionalization of a mechanism to harmonize regional law with federal law and thereby eliminate Russian federalism's 'unofficial asymmetry'; the abrogation or revision of federal–regional bilateral treaties and agreements in order to do away with 'official asymmetry'; a move to merge the small, sparsely populated autonomous districts with regions so as to eliminate Russia's nested 'administrative–structural asymmetry'; the reorganization of the Federation Council; and the weakening of a consociational conciliation procedure for resolving federal–regional conflict over federal legislative bills.

The federal districts

The creation of seven federal *okrugs* or districts (FO) in summer 2000 was intended by Putin to assist federal officials in accomplishing the two main goals of his federative reforms: (1) the reintegration of Russia's 'executive vertical' (or executive chain of command), and (2) the reintegration of Russia's constitutional/legal space. During the Yeltsin era most federal agencies' local branches began to function as regional governmental bodies. The regional branch offices of federal ministries and agencies, including prosecutors, tax officials and even the courts came under the control of regional governors and republican presidents. They vetoed the appointment of federal officials in the regions, manipulated financial flows from Moscow, and controlled judges by taking over the provision of some funding and resources to the ostensibly federal courts. To combat this problem, the seven FOs, each encompassing anywhere from six to fifteen regions and with their own apparatus of officials, have federal branch agencies for monitoring and coordinating the federal agencies' branches in their regions. The FOs are led by presidentially appointed 'authorized representatives' (*polpredy* or envoys), providing FO-level offices and officials with special authority over regional officials. Each *polpred* and FO has established different structures and functions in accordance with the needs of the particular FO's regions and their own professional and political interests, since the presidential decree promulgated in July 2000 which outlined their functions did not address their structures. As regards functions, the decree tasks FOs with reintegrating the country's executive vertical by ensuring that federal agencies at the regional level function in accordance with federal executive branch policies and directives. Thus, offices were created for the Internal, Finance, Tax and Foreign Ministries, the Accounting Chamber, the General Prosecutor, and other federal departments in all the FOs. For example, for reintegrating Russia's legal space a key FO function was the coordination of federal prosecutors in the regions. Thus, a deputy of the federal General Prosecutor's office was appointed to each FO headquarters and given his own staff. The FOs and FO prosecutors' offices now coordinate the work of federal and regional prosecutors in opposing and, if necessary, challenging in courts those regional constitutions and laws that contradict federal constitutional and legal provisions.

The envoys also set up various councils of federal officials in their districts, of businessmen, investment advisers and others. These bodies function as much as corporatist institutions for coopting real and potential opposition forces as public liaison and advisory bodies. For similar reasons, the FOs created numerous public reception offices in each region and in large cities for ostensibly collecting complaints and suggestions from citizens, responding to their special needs, and maintaining a presence 'on the ground'. In reality, these offices are used as much to rally the citizenry around Kremlin-backed causes, in particular its preferred candidates for 'elected' office, including Putin and his 'party of power' United Russia. The FOs played a direct role in the corrupt, unfair and rigged elections that established and characterize Putin's soft, stealth-like authoritarianism.

Overall, there is little doubt that the FOs were successful in coordinating the work of federal law enforcement organs in bringing regional laws and constitutions into conformity with federal law and the constitution. In April 2002 Putin credited his envoys with successfully completing the process of harmonizing regional and federal laws and permanently controlling the legality of the former. The *polpredy* have been fairly effective in reasserting Moscow's control over federal agencies and the appointment of their officials in the regions, especially with regard to law enforcement organs and the courts. *Polpredy* also have been effective in helping the federal General Prosecutor coordinate regional federal prosecutors' offices and work, which in turn helped rein in overly aggressive and regionally controlled branches of the Ministry of Internal Affairs.

The envoys have also acted to interfere in regional politics, including election campaigns. Their bureaucratic–authoritarian adventures in this regard have had important successes for the establishment of Putin's soft authoritarian rule under the domination of a single party, the pro-Kremlin United Russia, and its president over all other actors in the political system. The first significant success in elections was the Southern FO's blatant administrative interference in Ingushetia's 2002 presidential election. The FO in the politically sensitive North Caucasus, surely at Moscow's behest, arranged the annulment of one leading candidate's registration and a criminal investigation into another in order to win the election for the Southern FO's Federal Security Service (FSB) chief. On the other hand, Far East FO envoy Konstantin Pulikovsky has been a dismal failure in securing victory for federally backed candidates, and Volga FO envoy Sergei Kirienko was unable to ensure the reelection of the incumbent governor of Nizhnii Novgorod. During the Sverdlovsk regional elections and in St Petersburg in general, the Urals and Northwest FO envoys, Pyotr Latyshev and Viktor Cherkesov, respectively – both former FSB officers – used corruption investigations and insinuations of laxity towards organized crime to discredit the administrations of the opposition-oriented governors of these two key regions, Eduard Rossel and Vladimir Yakovlev. Massive state-administrative resources were deployed in the end to drive the latter out of office and win the election of Northwest FO envoy Valentine Matvienko, who was appointed as envoy specifically as her springboard to the governorship not least of all by affording her access to the FO's and city administration's resources (the FO headquarters are located in the heart of St Petersburg). The FOs also assisted United Russia in party-building and in slanting the electoral playing field in its favour during the 2003 State Duma election campaign and to Putin's advantage in the 2004 presidential elections.

Aside from the issue of the legality of much of the FOs' political activity is the issue of the constitutionality of the FOs' very existence. The FOs can be considered as another state administrative level and territorial subdivision. As such, they should be enshrined in Russia's constitution, which mentions all state organs by name and lists all the federation subjects or regions, the highest-level territorial subdivision of administration in the country until the formation of the FOs. One element lacking in the FOs' state-administrative status is a lack of their own budget funds or the power to direct budget funds towards one or another function. In his April 2002 address to both houses of the Federal Assembly, Putin proposed giving the FOs the power to monitor budget flows from

Moscow to the regions, but this did not appear to include the power to actually administer the distribution of federal budget transfers.

In sum, the FOs have had an ambiguous effect on federal democracy. On the one hand, they have somewhat strengthened bureaucratic discipline and rationality. On the other hand, they provided cover for authoritarian–bureaucratic interference in regional politics and elections, assisted the presidential apparatus in establishing corporatist structures for managing and limiting pluralism, and helped the Kremlin to build a corporatist–bureaucratic political party.

Eliminating Russian federalism's asymmetry

Putin's federative reforms essentially have eliminated all three of Russian federalism's asymmetries extant upon his rise to the presidency: unofficial asymmetry, official asymmetry and administrative–structural asymmetry.

Eliminating unofficial asymmetry

The expansion of unofficial asymmetry under Yeltsin left Putin with a state that was part federal and part confederal, with the additional rights under the latter institutional arrangement enjoyed mostly by the national republics. In order to rein in unofficial asymmetry between various regions' rights *vis-à-vis* the federal authorities, Putin instituted in July 2000 a mechanism for federal intervention under the amended law 'On General Principles of the Organization of Legislative (Representative) and Executive Bodies of State Power of the Subjects of the Russian Federation'. This allows the Russian president to remove regional chief executives or disband regional legislative bodies and call for elections after a series of court decisions and a presidential warning. Russia's president may also end the term of wayward governors or republican presidents if evidence that they have committed grave crimes is presented to him by the Prosecutor General. In the case of regional legislatures, the president must also get final approval from the State Duma to disband a legislature. The amended law stipulated that all regional laws and acts found to be in violation of federal laws or the constitution before 1 August 2000 had to be brought into accordance with federal norms by 1 February 2002.

Prior to Putin's reforms prosecutors managed to force amendments to regional laws and constitutions in order to bring regional laws into conformity with federal law, but this was the exception rather than the rule. Typically, regional authorities ignored prosecutors' protests and court decisions striking down the constitutionality of regional laws. With bolstered presidential support for legal harmonization in the regions, prosecutors became more aggressive and successful as they set about challenging regional laws and constitutions in regional parliaments and the courts from late 2000 onwards. According to the most recent figures, of the slightly more than 6,000 laws reported by prosecutors to be in violation of federal norms at the beginning of the harmonization process in 2000, some 5,800 had been brought into conformity with federal law by April 2002. To be sure, new regional laws and acts are passed that violate federal law, and thousands more at local level. However, since 2002 the rate of harmonization has remained at about 90 per cent compliance, signifying that a permanent and relatively well-functioning system for winning court challenges against regional violations of the constitution and federal laws has been established. Also, by April 2002 all but ten of the more than sixty regional constitutions that were found by courts at various levels to be in violation of the federal constitution had been brought into conformity. As of early 2004, however, the constitutions of the republics of Tatarstan and Bashkortostan remained in violation of the constitution.

Legal harmonization has had an ambiguous impact on the political system. Although it has reintegrated Russia's legal space and thereby streamlined administration (officials no longer have a choice of picking which laws they will follow or enforce), the centralized allocation of authority in the constitution's Articles 71–3 mentioned above means that harmonization is leading to a rather hyper-centralized distribution of power. For example, federal law now determines the rate for traffic fines in Tatarstan.

On the other hand, Putin's legal and constitutional harmonization process has had a positive influence on democracy in the regions. Before Putin's federative reforms a third of Russia's 89 regions were authoritarian, with constitutions and laws that violated the constitution and its provisions on democracy and civil rights. Authoritarian regimes seem to be the rule, rather than the exception, in the national autonomies, especially in the republics of Kalmykia, Kabardino-Balkaria, North Ossetia (Alania) and Bashkortostan. According to a 1999 study, ten of the eleven regions with the least media freedom were national republics. Regional violations of relatively democratic federal legislative and constitutional norms clearly undermined the fundamental principles of democratic governance, including the separation and balance of executive and legislative powers, and voters' and minorities' political and civil rights. Putin's concerted harmonization drive, for example, put an end to blatant regional violations of the fundamental democratic principle of the separation and balance of executive and legislative power by forcing the repeal of regional clauses in constitutions and laws that allowed regional governors and republican presidents to appoint the heads of city and city district administrations and allowed such local officials to sit in regional parliaments. Unfortunately, other Putin policies unrelated to federalism and addressed in this and the following chapter have more than negated this democratic gain.

Eliminating official asymmetry

Putin also moved to eliminate Russia's official asymmetry and treaty-based federalism by abrogating or allowing the expiration of all 42 federal–regional power-sharing treaties and many of their attendant agreements. By late April 2002, less than two years after Putin's inauguration, approximately 30 of the 42 federal treaties had been allowed to expire or had been abrogated. The issue of renegotiating new treaties with Tatarstan, Bashkortostan and several other republics had not been resolved. In his April 2002 address to the Federal Assembly, Putin acknowledged the constitutionality of such treaties and agreements, since they are enshrined in the constitution's Article 11. Moreover, he suggested that in future power-sharing treaties be approved by both houses of the federal legislature. This requirement was passed into law in 2003. This would be a small but important step towards democratically institutionalizing such treaties and Russia's treaty-based asymmetrical federalism as was done for the asymmetrical systems of India and Spain. Days after Putin's address, presidential administration deputy head in charge of the federative reform process, Dmitrii Kozak, announced that the first 28 treaties annulled met their fate because they had a 'political declarative character' and provided no legal norms. He added that Moscow would not insist all remaining treaties be abrogated but such treaties should be preserved for special cases involving regions with unique historical experiences with Russia. The next days saw the treaties with Leningrad region and Krasnodar and Altai territories annulled. However, in November 2003 a federal commission was created to prepare a new approach to drafting such treaties.

Abrogating treaties would eliminate the official asymmetry allowed by the constitution and risk mobilizing Tatars and perhaps other non-Russians. The constitution's Article 72 provides a sufficiently wide range of spheres over which authority can be split between Moscow and the regions in different ways such that considerable federative asymmetry and regional autonomy can be preserved. It appears the Kremlin may be willing to renegotiate treaties toward these ends with the most ethno-political national republics and perhaps with the most economically powerful Russian regions, so long as the new agreements conform to the constitution and federal law. By late 2003 and throughout 2004, Tatarstan, Bashkortostan and Chechnya were negotiating new power-sharing treaties with Moscow (discussed below). In sum, the future of Russian federalism's official asymmetry remains doubtful. It is sure to be much less robust than that negotiated in the environment of institutional fluidity extant during the Soviet revolution from above and the collapse of the Soviet state of the early 1990s.

Eliminating administrative-structural asymmetry

Most recently, in 2003 Putin moved cautiously to begin a process of eliminating Russia's administrative–structural asymmetry and *matryoshka* federalism. Although the Kremlin has claimed the process has emerged from below in the nested autonomous districts and their 'neighbouring' regions, it is clear that the policy emanates from Moscow but is one that accords with a certain consensus there and in the regions that the present system is ineffective from the point of view of both political representation and economic development. In 2002 officials began discussing the need to adopt a new law 'On the System of Accepting into the Russian Federation and the Formation within it of a new Subject of the Russian Federation'. This law, adopted in early 2003, established a system for calling and conducting referendums in federation subjects considering merger.

Subsequently, the newspaper *Gazeta* in May 2003 outlined a Kremlin plan that would reunite Perm region and Komi-Permyak autonomous district (which had been combined until 1992) by the end of 2005, hatched at a secret meeting in the Presidential Administration chaired by the administration deputy head Vladislav Surkov. Statements by a series of federal-level officials allied with the Kremlin calling for a reduction in the number of federation subjects to 30–40 followed. Several trips by the Komi-Permyak governor and Perm region governor to the Kremlin, and a trip by President Putin to Perm, overcame early resistance to such a merger. By the end of 2003, simultaneously with the 7 December Duma elections, referendums held in these two subjects approved a merger and the formation of a united Perm territory by 2005. Some 84 per cent of those who took part in the referendum in Perm region voted for merger, and 89 per cent in Komi-Permyak autonomous district. Oddly enough, the Komi Republic, in which the autonomous district is located, did not need to approve the merger by a referendum or any other procedure. According to reports, the formation of an Irkutsk territory will follow, to be followed by the merger of all remaining eight autonomous districts and the Jewish autonomous region in which they are nested or to which they are adjacent. The merger of the oil- and gas-rich Yamalo-Nenets and Khantsy-Mantsy autonomous districts, nested in Tyumen region, may prove to be a serious political challenge.

Federal–regional inter-budgetary relations

Putin overturned the Yeltsin era system of inter-budgetary relations between the federal and regional governments, which were uneven and asymmetrical as well. Under Yeltsin the ratio of tax revenue distribution between the federal and regional levels of government hovered around 50/50. The first Putin-era consolidated budget in 2001 saw a 56/44 federal–regional ratio, unbalanced in favour of the federal authorities. In 2002 revenue-sharing favoured the federal authorities by a ratio of 62/38, and by 2003 the ratio was 63/37. The 2001and 2002 Putin budgets violated the Russian Budget Code, which then required 50/50 revenue-sharing. Moreover, the federal–regional bilateral treaties and agreements are being allowed to expire without renewal or abrogated under pressure from Moscow, eliminating asymmetrical fiscal federalism. The recentralization of budget revenues was initiated on the generally correct principle that regional governments were misdirecting funds sent from Moscow and that the federal authorities should direct tax revenues to the poorer regions and not be giving more advantages to rich regions or favouring autonomies because of the concentrated populations of ethnic minorities.

Disbalance and 'symmetricization' of fiscal federalism is a pivotal issue for state stability. Although budget federalism under Yeltsin was roughly balanced at about a 50–50 federal–regional distribution of tax revenues, there were great disparities between the amounts of funds different regions were allowed to exempt from sending to Moscow. The federal–bilateral treaties and attendant agreements between Moscow and an increasing number of regions allowed some to keep as much as 75 per cent of tax revenues collected in the region, while others were forced to contribute more than 50 per cent to the federal budget. The national republics, especially Tatarstan, Bashkortostan and Yakutia (Sakha), were the greatest beneficiaries of this inter-budgetary asymmetry. This allowed Moscow to buy off these ethno-politicized republics, especially those with large 'Muslim' nationalities. Radical ethno-nationalist movements abated in the mid-1990s (except in Chechnya) because the leaderships in such regions could argue credibly that the dangers of trying to secede from Russia were not worth the risks, given the fiscal and other forms of autonomy won in the power-sharing treaties and agreements.

The local self-administration reform that was approved in 2003 and which is to be gradually implemented from 2006 envisages a new redistribution of revenues (and authority) between not only the federal and regional levels of government, but also the municipal and local levels. The distribution ratio has yet to be decided, making a final assessment of Putin's inter-budgetary system premature. Reports are that a federal–regional–local distribution of 40/30/30 is likely, but the sources for local self-administration budgets have yet to be specified. Federal and regional authorities are battling over the future distribution of tax revenues. The former propose that 60 per cent of income tax revenues go to the regions and 40 per cent to the localities. The latter propose 50 per cent for the regions, 20 per cent for the localities, and 30 per cent for levelling fiscal disparities between regions. The regions are also demanding transportation tax revenues. Ongoing tax reforms are also affecting the balance of power within fiscal federative relations. For example, the repeal of the sales tax in 2003, which went exclusively to regional coffers, shifted the ratio further in favour of the federal authorities. In sum, reforms of budget federalism and their effect remain an open question. All that is clear for the moment is that regions that donate more to the federal budget than they receive are more independent than those that receive more than they donate, and that under Putin the number of donor regions has decreased from eighteen to eight.

Eliminating consociational mechanisms

Putin further diminished the regions' influence in federal law-making, weakening an important consociational mechanism. Under Yeltsin, an element of consensus rule was deployed within the federal legislative process through a form of minority veto. Any federal legislative bill was moved to a federal–regional 'conciliation procedure' if in more than 30 of the 89 regions the federal or executive branch protested. Putin first raised the bar for the veto. A legal amendment adopted in 2003 required that both branches of 30 regions challenge a bill before it went to conciliation. This is virtually impossible to achieve given the Kremlin's cooptation of the regional governors and republican presidents through various carrots (third terms) and sticks (administrative resources and efforts to compromise them). Subsequently, in April 2004 the Constitutional Court ruled as legal the passage of a new Land Code despite two-branch protests from 35 regions. Consequently, the federal parliament can now exclude regional legislatures from the federal law-making process and pass bills without taking into account opinion in the regions.

The Chechen quagmire and Putin's federative counter-revolution

The ongoing war in Chechnya, like most wars, has had a deleterious effect on democracy. It has had the same effect on the nascent Russian federalism of the 1990s. More specifically, the failure of the Russian elite to fashion an effective military and political policy to quell the extremist Chechen separatists led to a radical re-Islamicization in Chechnya replete with internationally tied terrorism. Putin's policy has consisted of four elements: (1) giving the army, police, military intelligence and loyal Chechen forces freedom to prosecute the war while overlooking their massive human rights violations and economic criminality in order to fulfil his promise to 'wipe out the terrorists in the john'; (2) refusal to negotiate with any Chechen actors that were independent of the Russian central elite; (3) some exaggeration of the level of direct involvement and operational and financial role of international Islamo-fascists in the Chechen separatist movement; and (4) the 'Chechenization' of administration and, if possible, much of the fighting in the republic. The consequent brutalizing of the population, the defeat of the Chechens militarily and the absence of any possibility for negotiations helped produce the Chechens' resort to unprecedented atrocities facilitated as well by the Chechen cult of 'blood revenge' and a growing ideological affinity with Islamist elements involved in similar separatist movements and general radicalization of the Muslim world near Chechnya. The Chechen separatists' radical re-Islamicization that was consolidated after the first Chechen war produced a mounting wave of terrorism throughout Russia, especially after Chechen terrorists' October 2002 seizure of about a thousand hostages in a Moscow theatre leading to an estimated 120 deaths.

In parallel, the federal authorities did their best to reestablish an administration of loyal Chechens by holding presidential elections and a referendum on a constitution in 2003. In votes that could in no way be considered free or fair, an official figure of 80 per cent elected former chief mufti Akhmed Kadyrov as the republic's president and 90 per cent approved a new republican constitution. After Kadyrov's assassination in May 2004, Alu Alkhanov was elected his successor with 73 per cent of the vote in a similar ballot. By late 2003, Chechnya, like Tatarstan and Bashkortostan, was negotiating a new power-sharing treaty with Moscow. However, in the wake of the curtailment of Tatarstan's sovereignty and the adoption of a Chechen constitution promising the war-torn republic autonomy, any Moscow–Chechnya power-sharing treaty that affords Grozny considerable autonomy in spheres where Kazan has lost it risks provoking Tatar ire. The lesson drawn by some might be: war, not compromise, ultimately wins autonomy from Moscow.

In 2003 and 2004 a wave of mounting terrorism culminated in a summer of terror in 2004. The wave of terror reached a horrific climax at a primary school in Beslan, North Ossetia at the start of September 2004. Chechen, Ingush and other terrorists loyal to internationally wanted Chechen terrorist and former Chechnya–Ichkeria vice-premier Shamil Basaev took hostage and then brutally massacred hundreds of children as they ran for their lives. After Beslan, Putin proposed a series of measures to address the growing emergency. Although they appeared unlikely to be effective against terrorism, several will impinge directly on federalism. In the most important of these, Putin proposed and, because of his control over the Federation Council, is likely to succeed in getting passed by parliament legal amendments allowing Russia's president to appoint regional governors and republican presidents, rolling back fifteen years of Soviet/Russian reforms. The only democratic check on this power would consist in the regional parliament's power to confirm his nominee. However, should a regional parliament twice reject his nominee, the amendments would allow the president to disband that parliament, forcing elections. This will allow the president to place regional chief executives tightly under his control. Since they appoint half of the Federation Council's senators, this will also give Putin additional control over this body.

Two other aspects of Putin's post-Beslan proposals will affect what remains of Russian federalism: (1) the election of the federal parliament's lower house, the State Duma, solely on the basis of party lists and (2) the formation of a loosely defined 'Public Chamber'. The former will mean the end of the election of half the Duma's deputies from 225 single-seat districts and thus a further diminution of local representation. The latter appears to be an attempt to create the perception of compensation for the first two proposed measures. However, in reality it is likely part of a scheme to construct a corporatist system for Russia's emerging soft authoritarian regime. Such a form of rule consists of the state's organization of society's key social groups both as a method for controlling their participation in politics and for the creation of 'transmission belts' between state and society so that the preferences of society can be known and taken into account in policy-making on the state's terms and not dictated by powerful autonomous social actors. This interpretation is supported by the Chamber's purely advisory function.

Conclusion: assessing Putin's federative reforms

Russia's size and history, emerging threats along its borders, and the growing gap between its economy and the globalizing international economy all incline Russian rulers toward federative symmetry if not unitary centralization. The cumulative effect of Putin's pre- and post-Beslan federative policies constitute counter-reforms which have gutted the basic institutional building blocks of what was a nascent federative and democratic order in Russia. Putin's pre-Beslan policies moved beyond dismantling administrative–structural, unofficial and inter-budgetary asymmetries and reducing official asymmetrical federalism to undermin-ing a key pillar of any federative system. The Federation Council's reor-ganization has no relation to 'symmetricizing' Russian federalism and is a clear setback for both democratization and federalization in Russia. In combination with the elimination of Yeltsin's institutionalized consocia-tional mechanism, all regional checks on the federal branch, the 'Russian' regions and the ethnic Russian majority have been dismantled. Consequently, the political system already could have been considered substantially 'defederalized'. His post-Beslan reforms consolidate the defederalization process.

As President Putin began his federative reforms, Michael Hechter (2000), hypothesizing that attempts by multinational imperial and federal executives to extend 'direct rule' over peripheral regions may provoke nationalism, found positive correlations between both regional autonomy and an absence of ethnic conflict in multinational states and between the imposition of direct rule and the mobilization of ethno-nationalism. Putin's counter-reforms risk a similar mobilization of nationalist movements in the republics, especially the titular 'Muslim' republics of Tatarstan, Bashkortostan, Dagestan and Ingushetia. Much of the legitimacy of moderately nationalist, pro-federalist and soft authori-tarian regimes like that of Tatarstan president Mintimer Shaimiev rests on its victories securing autonomy from Moscow in the 1990s. With recen-tralization, political credit is bound to accrue to more radical nationalists and Islamists. Although the turn to soft authoritarianism under Putin may temporarily limit ethno-politicization, radical nationalists will be in a position to capitalize on any redemocratization of the Kremlin's election and media practices outlined in other chapters, particularly if some elements of the democratization of regional constitutions forced by Putin's legal harmonization policy remain intact.

In addition to managing the difficult North Caucasus and Volga mega-regions, Moscow is struggling to hold on to its Far East, so distant, desti-tute, depopulated, and deluged with illegal Chinese immigrants and businesses. An economic crisis or worsening domestic or international security environment could deplete fatally Russia's capacity to manage these multiple challenges. In sum, Russia's integrity remains threatened by ethnic and religious communalisms and its national-territorial struc-ture. Putin or his successors will have to rebuild a federation-based system in order to deal with these challenges.

Chapter 10

Politics in the Regions

DARRELL SLIDER

As the previous in this book has shown, Vladimir Putin is attempting to make fundamental changes in the relationships between regions and the central authorities. On the face of it, increasing the role of the federal government might be expected to have a positive impact on life in the regions. The uniform enforcement of the constitution and federal laws in all regions could reduce the scope for local officials to violate citizens' human rights. The federal authorities could act to ensure freedom of the press and honest elections. Increased central intervention could guarantee the operation of a free market by reining in monopolies, eliminating unnecessary bureaucracy and attacking corruption. Yet, as other chapters in this volume have also shown, these are not goals that Putin has placed at the top of his agenda. Reasserting central authority is not being pursued in order to develop Russia's democracy, establish the rule of law, or to facilitate transparency and competition in the economic sphere.

Political life outside the capital follows its own dynamic, and the nature of this dynamic differs in every region. Variations between regions are perhaps more extreme than in any other existing federation. Regions differ in the extent to which they depend on agriculture or a particular industrial or raw materials sector. For example, textiles dominate in Ivanovo, oil processing in Bashkortostan, farming in Orel, coal mining in Kemerovo, and the defence industry in Udmurtia. Politically, as demonstrated in national and regional elections, the provinces differ markedly in their relative support for communists, reformers and nationalists. Other politically significant variation is caused by the presence of non-Russian ethnic groups, particularly in the 21 ethnically based 'republics'.

This diversity greatly complicates the analysis of the state of affairs in Russian regions. There is no 'typical' region that could be used to show common patterns or tendencies. Nevertheless, all regions shared the formative impact of the communist political–economic system and responded to a set of incentives that was implicit in Yeltsin's policies towards the regions in the 1990s. Important changes in regional political institutions had their origins in the political crisis of October 1993 and the new constitution that followed. Political trends in the regions paralleled those in the centre: there was a consolidation of power in the hands of regional executives, most often called governor in the *oblasts* (regions) and *krais* (territories), and president in the republics. This consolidation took place at the expense of elected regional assemblies, most of which were dissolved. By the late 1990s, governors and republic presidents were increasingly referred to in the Russian press as 'feudal lords' who ran their territories as fiefdoms.

Regional political institutions

In the Soviet period, regional politics were defined by a uniform, hierarchical pattern, at least on the surface: the Communist Party designated regional party first secretaries who were the principal decision-makers at that level. As Jerry Hough (1969) demonstrated in his classic work on Soviet regional politics, the provincial party bosses acted much like 'prefects' in the French administrative system: they were agents of the 'centre' that carried out its policies. At the same time, they were accountable for the region's performance and had considerable discretionary power in performing their duties. Promotions to the Central Committee and Politburo often came from the ranks of regional party leaders. Both Mikhail Gorbachev and Boris Yeltsin first achieved national prominence while serving lengthy stints as regional party first secretaries – in Stavropol and Sverdlovsk, respectively. Separate from the party structure was a hierarchy of legislative–executive bodies, called soviets (the Russian word for 'council'). Until the 1990 elections, regional soviets were large bodies that met infrequently and provided little more than formalized participation in decision-making. The soviets also served as the institutional home for provincial administrators – the *ispolkom* or executive committee that constituted the core of regional government. The *ispolkom* included departments that provided or supervised education, healthcare, services, local industry and infrastructure, housing, police, and other local agencies.

Regional legislatures were chosen in competitive elections for the first time in Russia in 1990. While still called soviets, they benefited from Gorbachev's democratization and began to play a more assertive role in policy formation. They continued, however, to be large, unwieldy bodies with few permanent members and staff. A presidium, headed by a chairman, often dominated the setting of their agenda. The failed August 1991 coup marked a turning point, not just for the Soviet Union and Russia, but also for subnational Russian politics. Yeltsin disbanded the communist party hierarchy that controlled the regions and confiscated party property, which included the chief administrative buildings in every region and city. He then set out to separate the legislative and executive institutions that had been combined in the soviet structure. Yeltsin initially considered holding elections to a new post of 'chief of administration' in the provinces, but when it became evident that Communists might win many of these posts, elections were postponed 'for the period of radical economic reform'.

In other regions, Yeltsin used direct appointments to fill the vacuum left by the removal of the regional party first secretaries. In a number of cases, Yeltsin's appointments encountered serious local opposition, and he often compromised to allow local favourites to remain in power – including many from the old communist *nomenklatura*. When Yeltsin disbanded the party hierarchy that controlled the regions, he confiscated party property, which included the chief administrative buildings in every region and city. The new appointees as chief administrators moved into the old party offices and buildings; in virtually every regional capital this represented the best office space – especially in telecommunications, given that they were equipped with direct phone lines to the Kremlin separate from the regular phone system. Though Yeltsin was creating a new administrative structure separate from the soviets, he left in place the regional soviets that had been elected in 1990. This led to a number of bitter conflicts between newly appointed executives and Soviet-era regional legislatures – a direct parallel to the conflict between Yeltsin and the Russian Congress of People's Deputies in 1992–93.

From the beginning, there was a marked difference between the republics within the federation (not to be confused with the fourteen former union republics that, like Russia, became independent when the USSR collapsed) and other entities. The leaders of Russia's 21 republics followed Yeltsin's own example and were able to legitimize their standing through popular election as early as 1991, usually to the newly created post of president. Thus, from 1991 there were both republic presidents and a Russian president. The first set of republic leaders tended to come from the old regional party and economic *nomenklatura*. Among these were many who continued to dominate their regions in 2004: Mintimer Shaimiev of Tatarstan, Murtaz Rakhimov of Bashkortostan, Leonid Potapov of Buryatia, Magomed Magomedov of Dagestan (who ruled, uniquely, as chairman of the republic parliament), Sherig-ool Oorzhak of Tuva, and Alexander Volkov of Udmurtia. In a few republics, the first set of elections brought to power new, postcommunist elites who also have survived politically. The most controversial was Kirsan Ilyumzhinov, a young millionaire with money of unknown provenance and a passion for chess, who set up an autocratic regime that has been described as a new 'khanate'. Another new republic leader was Yeltsin's former justice minister, Nikolai Fedorov, who was elected president in his home region of Chuvashia. Fedorov proved to be one of the most progressive of regional leaders, and he was one of the few to resist openly Putin's programme of recentralization.

The first direct popular elections in other administrative units – *oblasts* and *krais* – took place in seven regions in April 1993 without Yeltsin's approval. The early winners were often communist-era regional leaders who were opposed to Yeltsin and his policies. Two years later, Yeltsin began to allow elections for governor on a case-by-case basis. By 1996, elections had been held in almost all the remaining regions. It is difficult to overstate the degree to which elections increased the power of governors. It both gave them a claim to legitimacy and made it exceedingly difficult for Yeltsin to remove them.

Political parties began for the first time to get involved in regional politics during the 1996 gubernatorial elections. Candidates favoured by Yeltsin received support from the 'party of power', Prime Minister Viktor Chernomyrdin's party Our Home is Russia (OHR). The party provided financing and expert assistance in campaigns for over twenty incumbent governors. Then Kremlin chief of staff Anatolii Chubais served as a national coordinator for these campaigns. The Communist Party of the Russian Federation (CPRF), which in previous national elections had done well in the southern provinces known as the 'red belt', put forward candidates in most regions. Among the candidates who won with Communist support was Yeltsin's nemesis from the October 1993 confrontation, former vice-president Alexander Rutskoi in Kursk. In most cases, however, political parties had little impact on the outcome of the elections. Even where they did, parties had few instruments of influence over candidates they had supported. Many of those elected were so-called *praktiki* – directors or former directors of major enterprises in the region who were not closely identified with any political movement, but who were well-known locally.

The establishment of new, provincial legislatures was marked by difficulties. Starting in December 1993 and extending into 1995, elections were held in most regions of the country for regional assemblies that had been dissolved in the aftermath of the shelling of the Russian parliament in October 1993. New names were chosen for these bodies – most often *sobranie* (assembly) or *duma*. These assemblies differed dramatically from the soviets they replaced: they were smaller and contained within them an even smaller subset of members who would be designated to act as permanent legislators (the others all had full-time jobs in business, industry or government). Officials from the regional administration and local economic elites dominated the new assemblies to a much greater extent than was true in the old soviets. In over 65 of the 89 assemblies, executive branch officials and enterprise directors or farm managers made up over half the members. Almost all continued to hold their posts, since this was the source of their real power, rather than devote themselves to full-time legislative activity. This virtually guaranteed substantial conflicts of interest; it also meant that assemblies would meet infrequently. The same pattern characterized the next set of elections that took place between 1996 and 1999. Here too, political parties were noticeable by their absence.

The sharp conflicts between regional assemblies and chiefs of administration that were common in the early 1990s diminished as a result of the institutional changes just described. Once governors were elected (rather than appointed by Yeltsin), there were fewer cases of political/ideological mismatches between legislative and executive branches. Also, the changes in composition of the assemblies meant that a majority was beholden to the governor or republic president, either for their government careers or for the economic well-being of their enterprises. There were few truly independent deputies, and often assemblies had no organized political opposition. Most assemblies could be accurately described as 'in the governor's pocket' (in Russian, *karmannye*).

Through most of the 1990s, regional political institutions developed in a legal vacuum. General principles were set out in the 1993 constitution on executive and legislative institutions, but a law elaborating these relationships was not passed until 1999. The delay was mostly due to opposition by regional leaders who made use of the Federation Council to veto the draft law four times before the Duma was finally able to override their veto. In the meantime, constitutions were adopted in the republics and charters (*ustavy*) in the oblasts which set the basic relationships between the organs of power. Given the political balance of forces in the regions and regional assemblies in the mid-1990s, the institutional arrangements favoured the executive. The 1999 law reinforced the dominance of the executive over the legislative branch. One measure, for example, permitted a legislature to override an executive veto only if it had the support of two-thirds of the total number of deputies who were supposed to be elected to the assembly. Many legislatures had empty seats due to insufficient turnout in some – usually urban – districts, and deputies who were not full-time legislators were frequently absent. Thus, it was very difficult for a legislature to assert itself effectively against a governor or republic president.

Components of governors' power

Resources at the disposal of the governor provided enormous advantages which allowed them to both dominate regional politics and help win reelection. These instruments are commonly known in Russia as 'administrative resources'. Regional leaders had the power to dictate the activities of police, the courts, prosecutors, enterprise directors and local officials. Leading media, both television and newspapers, were most often under the control of the regional administration. In those regions where there was an opposition or independent newspaper, its distribution was extremely limited. In several regions (for example, in Ulyanovsk, Samara and Kalmykia) journalists had no alternative but to have their newspaper published outside their region and then smuggle it back. There have been numerous cases of blatant attempts to curtail the expression of opposition views, including closing newspapers, withholding necessary newsprint and supplies, conducting repeated 'tax audits', and intimidating – or even killing – journalists. Suppression of the regional press achieved its intended result: it undermined accountability and prevented the exposure of corruption.

Governors also typically possessed a range of economic levers that could be used for political purposes. The method by which initial privatization of industrial enterprises was carried out in the 1990s had the effect of turning over control to local economic and political elites. The inside track to gaining effective control over enterprises was given to enterprise managers who had long-standing ties to the regional political elite, thus forging a variety of crony capitalism at the regional level. Local officials frequently altered the procedures for privatization to provide additional advantages to the local economic elite – such as closing share auctions to outside bidders, and creating regional share funds. Further consolidation of local control began in 1996 as the national government began turning over their shares in privatized federal-level enterprises to local government as a substitute for budgetary financing. The result of this transfer was, if not a controlling share, then a substantial voice in enterprise affairs through a place on the board of directors.

In the aftermath of the August 1998 financial crisis, regional elites tightened their grip over the local economy through strategies that relied on cooperative local courts to take control over key enterprises. A new bankruptcy law adopted in 1998 allowed even small debts to be used as a basis for 'restructuring' enterprises; with the help of the regional courts, the governor could arrange for the enterprise to be declared bankrupt and, with the help of the local police, install his choice as manager – by force, if necessary. Enterprises were pressured to provide financial or in-kind assistance to the region, for everything from construction projects to supporting local schools. Often this took the form of 'voluntary' contributions to off-budget funds controlled exclusively by the governor. In the new conditions of an emerging market economy, of course, these contributions represented a burden on the economic well-being of an enterprise; they were the equivalent of a regional tax, but one that often would not officially appear on the financial balance sheet. In return, favoured enterprises were given preferential treatment in other areas, such as the awarding of government contracts or the writing off of enterprise debt.

Moscow mayor Yuri Luzhkov provides a vivid example of how a regional leader can entrench himself in power. Even though Moscow is a city that has tended to be one of the most liberal in national elections, Luzhkov has proved to be anything but a reformer. The city government maintains tight control over the Moscow economy, which is heavily regulated and taxed, and it is assumed that the construction projects for which Luzhkov is famous are rife with corruption. According to official declarations made in order to get on the ballot at election time, Luzhkov lives very modestly and has not benefited from his position of mayor of Russia's richest city. Yet in 2004, when the Russian edition of *Forbes* magazine presented its list of the hundred richest businessmen, the only woman on the list was Yelena Baturina – Luzhkov's wife. She heads a construction empire that got its start with city contracts and then expanded to control a large percentage of Russia's cement output. *Forbes* estimated her wealth at $1.1 billion. Although Moscow is perhaps the freest city in Russia in terms of independent media availability, there is little critical reporting or commentary on the mayor and his administration. Luzhkov has been particularly adept at filing lawsuits in local courts against newspapers that allege corruption, and he always wins.

The relative power that is derived from administrative resources is most apparent at election time. The governor's team typically mobilizes the entire administrative apparatus in support of his reelection. Local police are used to verify signatures on petitions to register opposition candidates. Politically subservient district chiefs of administration are ordered to increase voter turnout. Governors typically dominate both regional election commissions and the courts that adjudicate disputes connected with elections. Local economic elites are often pressed into giving illegal cash or in-kind contributions to the governor's campaign and are threatened with reprisals if they supported an opponent. Dmitri Oreshkin, a leading analyst of regional elections, has estimated that administrative resources are responsible for an average shift in the vote of as much as 20–25 per cent (Oreshkin and Kozlov 2003).

Putin and regional politics

Putin's regional reforms had a major impact on the relationship between the centre and the regions; it was particularly successful in reducing the role of governors in national politics. As members of the Federation

Council, they had become figures of national importance who could wield power by vetoing legislation that had been approved by the Duma. Overall, though, Putin's reforms, at least until September 2004, were less successful at changing the internal politics of Russian regions.

One of Putin's first acts was to establish procedures that would allow for the removal of recalcitrant governors. In July 2000 the Duma approved Putin's proposed additions to the October 1999 law on regional political institutions to hold provincial authorities accountable for policies that violate the Russian constitution and national legislation. According to the amendments, regional officials (both executives and legislatures) must answer for any actions that cause 'massive and crude' violations of civil and human rights that threaten the unity and territorial integrity of the country, national security, or the 'unity of the legal and economic space' of the Russian Federation. This proved to be a purely symbolic victory, since removal of a governor or the dissolving of a legislature required multiple steps and the involvement of the court system. As of 2004, the mechanism had never been used.

A new control mechanism was just beginning to be applied in the latter part of 2003 and 2004. Federal prosecutors initiated criminal charges against sitting governors in Tver, Kamchatka, Saratov, Altai Republic and Yaroslavl. (Under Yeltsin, after governors became elected officials, serious charges were brought against governors only after they had lost their post. The lesson in this for regional leaders was to hold on to their posts by any means possible.) The charges usually centred on the improper use of federal budgetary funds allocated to the regions. If convicted, the result could be not only removal from office, but also a lengthy prison term. Much like the case against the oil giant Yukos, where the company was accused of activities that were widespread among Russian enterprises, the charges directed against these governors could easily be levied against any sitting governor. Inadequate funding often meant that governors were forced to make choices that violated federal budgetary priorities. The selective use of the law to put pressure on, and perhaps ultimately remove, regional leaders is very consistent with the Putin-era approach to 'the discipline of law', and it is designed to send a message of vulnerability to all.

Another direct and constitutional way to restrict the arbitrary power of governors would be to enforce a system of term limits. If regional leaders are allowed to stay in power for 15–20 years, the result is likely to be both political stagnation and corruption. A law passed at the end of the Yeltsin administration, in 1999, introduced a two-term limit to parallel that of the Russian president. As passed, however, the law did not specify how the term limits would be applied to sitting governors. If applied to terms already served, the law would have prevented most republic presidents from running again, and most governors would be limited to only one more term in office. The ambiguity was tested only in late 2000. In February 2001, governors successfully lobbied Putin's party in the Duma to 'clarify' the law so that the counting would begin only with elections held after October 1999, thus allowing 70 regional leaders to run for a third or even a fourth term. (The term in office, usually either four or five years, was set by legislatures in the regions.) The Duma returned to this question in March 2003, and again sided with regional 'heavyweights'.

The failure to enforce term limits had a profound impact on regional politics. Russia's most powerful regional leaders were also those who had been in power the longest, and they tended to be the most resistant to control from Moscow. As of 2004, some of the longest-serving leaders (up to 15 years) included many republic presidents mentioned earlier; Shaimiev in Tatarstan, Rakhimov in Bashkortostan, Magomedov in Dagestan, Potapov in Buryatia, Oorzhak in Tuva. Among governors, those who have dominated their regions longest include Yegor Stroev of Orel (governor for 15 years), Viktor Ishaev of Khabarovsk, Viktor Kress of Tomsk, Mikhail Prusak of Novgorod, Vladimir Chub of Rostov, Leonid Polezhaev of Omsk, Konstantin Titov of Samara (all in office for 13 years), Yuri Luzhkov (12 years), and Eduard Rossel of Sverdlovsk (11 years).

It was when governors were up for reelection that they were potentially the most vulnerable. During Putin's first term, the ability of the Kremlin to determine the outcome of elections varied substantially from region to region. At one extreme was the case of Chechnya, under Putin a republic that was largely administered by the Russian police and armed forces. The October 2003 Chechen presidential elections, which resulted in the victory of Akhmad Kadyrov, were perhaps the most vivid example of mobilizing administrative resources to the benefit of the Kremlin's candidate. Putin himself got involved, making opposing candidates 'offers they could not refuse' to get them to withdraw from the race. By election day, the field had been cleared of all of Kadyrov's serious competition. On election day, journalists in Chechnya reported finding polling stations nearly empty, yet the officially reported voter turnout was an amazing 81 per cent. International observers – who included representatives of a number of democratically challenged countries from the CIS such as Belarus and Uzbekistan, as well as members of the Arab League – agreeably endorsed the Kadyrov's landslide victory as free and fair.

When new elections had to be held for the Chechen presidency in August 2004 after Kadyrov was assassinated in May 2004, many of the same techniques were employed. This time the Kremlin's candidate was Alu Alkhanov, the Chechen interior minister. Once again, the favoured candidate's most effective opponents were either removed from the ballot on technicalities or persuaded to abandon their candidacies. Putin made a number of personal appearances with Alkhanov, both in Moscow and Chechnya, all under the guise of routine government business. The same Arab League and CIS observers were invited back to monitor the elections, and again an abnormally high turnout of around 85 per cent was reported. A reporter for the newspaper *Kommersant* was allowed to vote four times. No one was surprised that Alkhanov received almost 75 per cent of the vote. The obvious stacking of the odds, of course, can only work to undermine the legitimacy and popular acceptance of the newly elected leader.

To what extent was the Kremlin able to affect elections in other regions? Elsewhere the political realities required more subtle tactics, and they often proved inadequate to overcome the administrative resources available to sitting governors. A clear case showing the limits of Kremlin power was the May 2000 election in Putin's home town of St Petersburg. The one governor who stood out as a personal enemy of Putin was Vladimir Yakovlev, whom Putin had called a 'Judas' for his decision to oppose reformist mayor Anatolii Sobchak in 1996. In the 2000 election, the Kremlin openly supported Valentina Matvienko, who at the time was a deputy prime minister, to take on Yakovlev. When it became clear that her candidacy had little chance against Yakovlev and his administrative resources, Putin avoided embarrassment by asking Matvienko to withdraw from the race. Yakovlev won reelection easily, with almost 73 per cent of the vote. Ultimately, in 2004, Yakovlev was dislodged from his post by behind-the-scenes pressure and 'an offer he could not refuse' – to become deputy prime minister in charge of infrastructural reform (later Putin's representative in the troubled southern federal district and then in September 2004 minister of regional development). The Kremlin was thus able to shift the administrative resource advantage in an early election, and finally gained a victory for Matvienko

There were other cases where the Kremlin was able to decisively tip the scales towards a favoured candidate. One trend under Putin, which parallels his cadre preference for *siloviki* in other institutions, was the increasing number of gubernatorial candidates with military or secret police backgrounds. Among the regional leaders elected during Putin's first term were Vladimir Shamanov in Ulyanovsk (a controversial army commander from the war in Chechnya), Georgii Shpak in Ryazan (a well-known paratroop general), Boris Gromov in Moscow region (an army general during the Soviet occupation of Afghanistan and later deputy defence minister), and Admiral Vladimir Yegorov in Kaliningrad (former Baltic fleet commander). Former FSB officers include Vladimir Kulakov in Voronezh, Viktor Maslov in Smolensk, and Murat Zyazikov in Ingushetia. As one might expect, the skills acquired in military–security posts in the Soviet period were not particularly appropriate preparation to serve as governor of a region, and several have been spectacular failures (Shamanov and Zyazikov, in particular).

Another element in Putin's initial strategy to change regional politics involved the creation of a new political party – United Russia (see Chapter 5). As we have noted, political parties, with the partial exception of the CPRF, were not major actors in regional politics. Local parties had been created in some regions to serve as the political machine of governors, a device for dominating the regional political landscape. These parties had few links to national parties, but were designed to allow governors a more institutionalized form of control over regional legislatures. One way to put pressure on governors would be to create a new national party that would allow the centre to monitor regional developments, to develop cadres for future leadership posts in the regions, and to provide a check on executive powers through control over regional legislatures. The goal was to encourage the development of a 'party vertical' that would penetrate into each regional legislature and, through a regional parliamentary majority, turn the legislature into an additional mechanism for circumscribing the power of governors. Through changes in electoral laws and the law on parties, regionally based party groups could be marginalized in order to pave the way for United Russia. An important element of this strategy was a law adopted in July 2002 that changed the method by which regional legislatures would be chosen. In almost all regions, legislatures were chosen from single-member districts; the new law required that at least half the deputies be chosen by party list from national political parties.

United Russia began a major push to establish itself in the regions, and it did so without relying on governors. A Putin ally from his days in St Petersburg, Alexander Bespalov, was placed in charge of the party's expansion, and there was a clear attempt to draw into the party political figures in the region independent of the regional administrations. In some cases, powerful opponents of a governor were chosen to be regional leaders. By early 2003, however, with the approach of parliamentary elections and the end of Putin's first term, the attitude of the Kremlin towards regional leaders and party development changed dramatically. The most likely explanation is that the Kremlin came to recognize that it needed the active support of regional leaders and their administrative resources if it was to succeed in the national elections to be held in December 2003 (for the Duma) and March 2004. Bespalov was removed from his post in United Russia, and the Kremlin took direct control over building alliances with governors and republic presidents.

In the months before the Duma elections, many governors were brought into the top leadership council of United Russia (though at the time they could not legally be members of any party), and when the regional party lists were drawn up 28 were placed in prominent spots for United Russia. At the same time, other governors were actively dissuaded from joining the party lists of other parties. Of course, no governor ever intended to leave his post to become a Duma deputy, but the presence of governors on the party list undoubtedly helped the party draw a larger percentage of the national vote (the 28 regions represented over half the Russian population). Governors' assistance was especially vital in helping United Russia win seats in single-member districts, since administrative resources are of greater value in races within their region. This regional strategy made an important contribution to United Russia's emergence as a party with a constitutional (two-thirds) majority in the Duma. The price, however, was a loss of control over many regional party organizations as the governors' people were now placed in charge.

In September 2004, after the terrorist attack on a school in the North Ossetian city of Beslan, Putin used the 'war on terror' as a justification for making several major changes in regional political life that would strengthen his ability to influence developments. An idea that had been floated earlier in the Putin presidency, direct appointment of regional executives and the end of popular elections, was now to be imposed on the regions by a new law. The only democratic element in this procedure would be the theoretical capability of regional legislatures to reject the president's choice. In Duma elections, single-member district deputies would be eliminated, and the whole Duma would be chosen by party list. This would eliminate the necessity, apparently much resented by the Kremlin in 2003, of bargaining with governors to help obtain the victory of loyal candidates in the districts. While this would allow Putin to choose who would be governor (just like in Chechnya), it would not provide any additional tools for controlling a governor's behaviour within his or her region. Also, it was apparent that powerful governors or republic presidents who were loyal to Putin had nothing to fear. In fact, one result of the new method of selection was that the very weak provisions to introduce term limits would now be jettisoned completely. There was immediate speculation that one of the factors considered was the need to keep Shaimiev in the post of president of Tatarstan, while Luzhkov could now remain mayor of Moscow for a full five terms.

Local government

Thus far, we have discussed political institutions at the regional level. There were also dramatic developments at lower levels – in cities and rural districts (*raiony*). After October 1993, Yeltsin placed virtually all functions of local government in the hands of local chiefs of administration, usually appointed by governors or republic presidents. This was true even for most city mayors, though exceptions were made for mayors who had been elected earlier. Republic/*oblast* executive control over local government was meant to be a temporary measure, and the 1993 constitution established a framework for the democratization and empowerment of local government. In August 1995 the Duma passed a new law on local self-government. It mandated the popular election of local assemblies – organs that were supposed to have wide-ranging powers, including independent tax and budgetary authority. Local executives (mayors or *raion* chiefs of administration) could be either popularly elected or chosen by a representative assembly from among its elected members. Elections to local government bodies were completed in most regions by late 1997. In most rural districts, either chiefs of administration who had been appointed by the governor or chairmen of large collective farms were most likely to win. In any event, because rural districts tended to be dependent on the region for budgetary allocations (taxes collected in the cities were redistributed to the rural districts), financial levers preserved the dominance of governors and republic presidents.

The story was different in the larger cities, however, particularly the regional capitals. Both appointed and elected mayors often came into conflict with governors or republic presidents. Mayors represent a different constituency than governors. Urban voters are typically more supportive of reformist politicians than voters in a region as a whole. Since most cities are net donors to regional budgets, mayors have an interest in fiscal decentralization. The relationship between the holders of the two posts was poorly defined, and disputes quickly emerged over privatization, control over state and city property, tax receipts and budgets, subsidies, and other issues. Frequently the mayor of the largest city in a region became the only serious political opponent to a sitting governor or republic president. Though usually at a relative disadvantage, mayors had their own administrative resources that included city newspapers and television and city election commissions, as well as the support of many local enterprises. In the 1990s, mayors took the place of regional leaders in Karelia, Vologda, Smolensk, Irkutsk and Nizhnii Novgorod. For a brief period, when 'young reformers' were ascendant during the Yeltsin period, the Kremlin attempted to mobilize mayors as a tool for leverage over governors.

Governors engaged in sustained political warfare with city leaders. In this, governors had had the advantage of control over the budgetary weapon. Over time, local government had been assigned a greater portion of the burden of supporting healthcare, education, communal services (such as heat and water) and public transportation, but regional governments often selectively disburse funds for maximum political effect. The mayor of the capital city of Khabarovsk, a relatively progressive region, resigned in despair from his post in June 2000, complaining that he was 'tired of being treated like a whipping boy, tired of the endless search for money for coal purchases and for funds to keep the city functioning properly' (quoted in *Rossiiskaya gazeta*, 24 June 2000). His city regularly operated under a deficit of up to 50 per cent of the city budget because the regional government withheld adequate funding.

Putin sought to make fundamental changes in the relationship between this 'third level of administration' and the regions. A commission headed by then Putin aide Dmitri Kozak worked out a framework for a new division of responsibilities between the federal centre, regions and local governments. One of the purposes of this effort was to eliminate conflicts between mayors and governors by defining more precisely their respective responsibilities. It was apparent to mayors, who were mostly shut out of the drafting process, that the new law would favour governors. The Kozak reforms formed the basis for a new law on local government passed in September 2003, but it was not scheduled to go into effect until 2006, with some provisions delayed until 2008.

An important element of the new framework is a massive redrawing of administrative boundaries, which is to be carried out by officials under the control of governors. The old system of local government relied on Soviet-era administrative-territorial divisions, and many entities had no local government bodies. Henceforth, there will be a comprehensive and uniform scheme of 'municipal formations', resulting in a larger number of entities (over 24,000). One issue in the territorial division is how the productive assets will be distributed, and mayors of big cities suspect that the outcome will deprive them of key revenue sources.

The governor of Stavropol, Alexander Chernogorov, sought and received Putin's approval to become the first region to begin an 'experimental trial' of the new system in January 2005. In September 2004 district and other territorial administrative entities were replaced with new municipal governments. Rather than hold elections, Stavropol's leadership chose to form the new councils by taking representatives from existing bodies. Chiefs of administration in the cities and municipalities would not be elected mayors, but rather 'city managers' hired on a contract basis. The choice of Stavropol is an instructive one, since Chernogorov was known as one of the chief enemies of local self-government in the late 1990s, when he had argued that elected officials were too hard to deal with and made governing the region impossible.

Much about the future of local government remains uncertain and will depend on the details of the division of powers and finances. Putin has promised local officials that he will put an end to the practice of unfunded mandates – making local government organs responsible for a wide range of functions and then not providing the necessary financial support. A massive effort is under way to identify specific functions that are to be assigned to each level of government; for example, the federal centre could be responsible for universities, the regions for secondary and professional schools, and municipalities could be assigned the responsibility for primary schools. Given the rapid deterioration of Russia's infrastructure, it is virtually certain that the amount allocated to local government will be only a fraction of what is needed to guarantee the normal provision of necessary services.

Overall, the prospects for effective local government appear bleak in the Putin era. In his speech introducing the September 2004 measures, Putin urged governors to 'exert greater influence on the formation of organs of local government'. One can easily imagine governors demanding the same powers of appointment over local executives that Putin will exercise over governors. Regional leaders had already taken actions to demonstrate their preeminence in the regions. While governors still lacked the power to dismiss elected mayors, they were increasingly active in using all possible forms of pressure to remove autonomous mayors in order to create their own 'power vertical' at a regional level. In a parallel with recent federal pressure on governors, in many regions governors have used their influence with regional prosecutors to arrange for them to bring criminal charges against mayors. Alexander Tkachev of Krasnodar, a regional leader who is among the closest to Putin, has been the most active in demonstrating his predominance, and has successfully removed mayors who had been elected in all three of the largest cities in his region.

Conclusion

Regional elites took advantage of the changes in Russia in the 1990s to pursue their own interests in ways that undermined Russia's progress towards creating a law-based democracy. In the process, they succeeded in consolidating their hold on power, both economic and political. Part of the blame belongs to Yeltsin and his failings at the national level. Lax control from the centre – the legacy of Yeltsin's increasing political weakness – was compounded by the advent of elections of governors, which made even more tenuous the centre's control over the political situation in the regions.

Putin was unable to do much to reverse the situation within the regions. One can imagine two approaches with very different implications for democratic development. The first, what might be termed an 'organic' approach, would use the instruments available to the centre to stimulate the gradual growth of democratic institutions and practices that would limit the powers of regional leaders. These would include reforming the judicial system in the regions, developing truly national political parties (not a single 'party of power', but multiple parties), strengthening legislative institutions at the regional level, and supporting democratically elected mayors in towns and cities who might be more interested in pursuing reforms than governors and republic presidents. Measures could also be taken that would provide greater guarantees for independent media in the regions and that would stimulate and protect the growth of civic associations, particularly those whose purpose was to uphold human and civil rights. Election reform spurred by the Central Election Commission could establish the independence of regional election commissions from local authorities and combat the most outrageous attempts at fraud and manipulation. The result would be self-governing entities more capable of reforming themselves while also enjoying the legitimacy that comes from free and fair elections.

Putin has rejected this approach in favour of a hierarchical bureaucratic approach that is more in keeping with the Soviet experience and his own background in the KGB. Putin has favoured a series of measures that would impose stricter discipline on the regions in order to make them subservient to federal control. The main goal appears to be stability, which he understands as the absence of conflict, controversy, opposition and debate. Putin's attitude towards democracy in the regions reminds one of the Soviet attitude towards a market economy: it is chaotic, inefficient and uncontrollable – and therefore inappropriate for Russia at its current stage of development.

At the same time, Putin has ceded to regional leaders much leeway to run their regions as they see fit. Putin has come to accept that he needs the cooperation of sitting governors in order to govern effectively. After passing through an initial period of trepidation and uncertainty about their fates, governors and republic presidents have come to feel as secure in their posts under Putin as they did under Yeltsin. It remains to be seen whether Putin's decision to replace popular elections with presidential appointment will change this state of affairs significantly. The vast majority of Russian regions were governed prior to 2000 with little of the democratic veneer that was at least outwardly visible in national politics. Docile legislatures, heavy pressure on the press, harassment of opposition groups and NGOs, ruthless takeovers of leading enterprises, unfettered bureaucracy and corruption: all were common in Russia's regions in the 1990s. What Putin has accomplished is to add a new level of acceptability to these authoritarian methods. Governors and republic presidents can now point to Putin's policies at the national level as a justification to continue practices that clearly threaten democratic development and the rule of law in their regions. These 'little Putins', while part of a newly strengthened 'vertical' and more subservient to the Kremlin than in the past, remain extraordinarily powerful actors within their regions.

It is not surprising, then, that Russians have become increasingly alienated from regional and local politics. A public opinion survey conducted in mid-2004 by the Public Opinion Foundation found that 76 per cent of the population believed that organized crime had penetrated both executive and legislative institutions in the regions in which they lived, and 63 per cent thought that it happened often. Elections that were held for mayor of the Far Eastern city of Vladivostok in July 2004 were illustrative of how cynically democratic institutions could be manipulated. As the candidates were being registered, 'doubles' appeared from nowhere as local citizens were recruited because they had a name that was similar to that of a leading candidate. (Moscow newspapers described this tactic as 'the attack of the clones'.) Such candidates succeed in confusing a small percentage of votes, which is enough to determine the outcome in a close race. One candidate, Duma deputy and former mayor Viktor Cherepkov, who came in second in the initial round of voting, was disqualified from the run-off by a local court. The ruling cited a minor violation of election rules: Cherepkov had sent some of his registration materials by Duma post on Duma stationery, thus 'taking advantage of his official position'. The court, in other words, viewed this technical violation as more important than the expressed will of the voters. A few days before, someone had attempted to remove Cherepkov more brutally – he was injured by a grenade that was set off as he left his campaign headquarters. The election was won by Vladimir Nikolaev, the young head of a local fishing fleet who had been jailed in the past for fraud. Local television in the weeks before the election gave access only to Nikolaev, who was supported by United Russia. According to one report, Nikolaev's men went to each of the local stations and compensated them for the revenues they would lose by refusing to run campaign ads. In the end, turnout was low, and 37 per cent of those who bothered to vote cast their ballot for 'none of the above'.

Will Vladimir Putin's 2004 'September revolution' restore legitimacy to government and political life in the regions? It is certainly possible that the personal popularity of Putin will be partially transferred to the governors and republic presidents he appoints. A major unanswered question, however, is the source of candidates for these positions. As Russian critics of the plan have pointed out, only partly facetiously, there are not enough KGB operatives from 1980s Leningrad to fill 89 top posts. If, as seems likely, most current leaders will simply be reappointed to their posts by Putin in the interests of 'predictability and stability' then the implications would be profound. Unelected elites would be deprived of local sources of legitimacy that come from popular, even if deeply flawed, elections.

Corruption, which is already extremely high in the regions, is likely to increase as local elites become even more deeply entrenched. Early discussions of Putin's plan indicate that the effective power of regional leaders will increase within their regions, while of course their dependence on the Russian president would also increase. De facto checks and balances within regions would be obliterated. The likely extension of Putin's plan to cover all local administrative posts, including mayors of large cities, would reduce the scope of political life in the regions and give powers to governors that in the past were typically allowed only to autocratic republic presidents in regions such as Bashkiria and Tatarstan. The only popular elections that would remain would be elections for regional assemblies, and by late 2004 these were already being conducted under new rules that increase the role of national parties that are at least nominally under the Kremlin's control, especially United Russia. The locus of conflict between regional and federal elites will likely shift to a struggle for control over local branches of national parties. Another likely source of new gubernatorial powers (and corruption) will be the weakening and rapid phasing out of Putin's presidential envoys in the seven federal districts and the concurrent concentration of regional leaders' powers over federal organs of authority in their regions, especially police, prosecutors and tax authorities. Independent channels of information that might give the Kremlin a realistic view of what is happening in the regions will become fewer and fewer. In short, Putin's 'reforms' are likely to subvert the future development of Russian democracy and federalism.

Chapter 11

Putin's Economic Record

PETER RUTLAND

'We are a rich country of poor people. And this is an intolerable situation.'

(Vladimir Putin, 28 February 2000)

Vladimir Putin's record in the consolidation of democracy in Russia has attracted strong Western criticism, while his economic record has drawn some praise. In 2004 the Russian economy experienced its sixth year of steady growth, accompanied by moderate inflation, a balanced budget and a massive trade surplus. This economic recovery goes a long way towards explaining Putin's continuing popularity among Russian voters.

But observers are divided over whether Russia's economic recovery can be sustained. Putin's defenders argue that the Russian president has created a stable political environment, a vital precondition for businesses to invest. They note his firm commitment to a market economy and his systematic pursuit of structural reforms in taxation, basic legislation and government administration.

Critics attribute the macroeconomic stabilization to the rise in global oil prices. They argue that Putin has failed to complete the structural transformation that was left unfinished by Boris Yeltsin. Russia is saddled with an inefficient, politicized economy. Putin has done little to combat corruption, and has avoided the hard choices in economic reform, leaving energy monopolies like Gazprom and the electricity giant United Energy Systems largely untouched. The drift towards authoritarianism, symbolized by the October 2003 arrest of Yukos oil company head Mikhail Khodorkovsky, has scared off investors.

The truth lies somewhere between these two positions. Putin has done a much better job with the economy than many had feared when they heard that a KGB veteran had ascended to the presidency. But Russia is still quite some way away from a dynamic and healthy economic system.

The legacy of the Yeltsin years

The collapse of the Soviet Union in 1991 ushered in a confusing and chaotic decade. The Russian economy was in free fall, with goods shortages in 1991 followed by 2,500 per cent hyper-inflation in 1992. Inflation fell to 25 per cent in 1996, but GDP dropped for seven years in a row, a cumulative decline of 40 per cent from the 1990 level.

The collapse of economic institutions

Russia experienced a political and economic breakdown at the end of the 1980s, and in the subsequent chaos the rules of the game were changing from year to year. This uncertain environment rewarded economic and political actors who exploited the instability by focusing on short-run gains, subverting and destroying institutions. The chaos of democratization enabled insider elites to hijack the reform process, seizing and stripping state assets for their own private gain.

At the same time, Boris Yeltsin argued that the need to impose unpopular economic stabilization measures justified the creation of an authoritarian presidency. The pro-capitalist reformers and their Western supporters agreed with this position, effectively sacrificing democracy for market reform. Hence they supported Yeltsin's dissolution of the Russian parliament in October 1993, and they used their financial and media resources to ensure Yeltsin's reelection in June 1996. The reformers focused on crushing the communist challenge rather than building new institutions for a future liberal and democratic Russia.

Yeltsin's government itself was divided between reformists and conservatives, and between different factions struggling for a share of the privatization pie. It never really functioned as a collective decision-making body. Like the Soviet government before it, it was a sprawling bureaucracy, taking orders from the narrow leadership circle in the Kremlin. Public policy was driven by the vagaries of these political battles, and not by the needs of society.

The rule of law collapsed, with no reliable judicial system or legitimate political institutions. Businesses turned to organized crime groups (the 'Mafia') to provide security against extortionists; to enforce contract discipline on their customers; and to protect their ownership rights. Most businesses had their own *krysha* ('roof'), meaning a criminal group offering protection, or built up their own security services. This 'demand' for the services offered by organized crime coincided with an available 'supply'. Criminal groups had preserved their code of behaviour during Soviet times, mainly in prison. This created a criminal 'social capital' that was used to provide a service for the newly emergent market economy. Government security agencies, such as the police and Federal Security Service, also entered this market, providing protection for a fee.

From central planning to crony capitalism

Russia emerged from the post-Soviet decade with a market economy in which most prices are set by supply and demand and privately owned businesses account for two-thirds of the economy. However, it is an economy dominated by a small group of business leaders, the 'oligarchs', most of whom acquired their wealth through their political ties to the Yeltsin government during the privatization campaigns of 1992–95. In fifteen years Russia went from a society where entrepreneurship was a crime to one that had 36 billionaires, the third largest number in the world (*Forbes*, 15 March 2004).

The Soviet economy of 1991 was unlike any other on the planet. It had a large industrial base, developed over more than two generations according to the logic of central planning, whose objectives were national security and social transformation. What would happen when such an economy was exposed to the forces of supply and demand? There was no such thing as a 'world market price' for nuclear submarines or space stations – the items in which Russia had developed a 'comparative advantage' during the Cold War. After 1991 Russian manufacturers were devastated by imports, and only a few industries like automobiles and aircraft struggled to survive behind high protective tariffs.

Russia's energy wealth was another distinctive feature, but it proved to be a mixed blessing. Russia's vast natural resources encouraged myopic, rent-seeking behaviour by Russian elites, and discouraged them from embracing economic liberalization. Oil production collapsed from 600 to 300 million tonnes a year between 1990 and 1995, and between 1985 and 1999 not a single kilometre of new oil pipeline was built. Even after 1992 the government kept oil and gas fields out of the hands of foreign investors. The natural gas monopoly Gazprom used export revenues to subsidize domestic consumers, creating a mini-planned economy based on cheap energy. Thanks to electricity prices fixed at one quarter of those in Europe, metal producers enjoyed an export boom.

The privatization of Russian industry began with the distribution of vouchers to ordinary citizens and workers in 1992–94, followed by cash or investment pledge auctions in 1995–97. Management insiders managed to gain control of most companies during the first phase. In the second phase politically favoured outsiders won ownership of some of Russia's most lucrative oil and metal producers. Some of these new 'oligarchs' had earned their first millions by starting their own businesses in foreign trade, currency exchange or commodity-broking. Others had used their connections to spin off businesses from state-run trade and banking organizations.

The August 1998 crash: a turning point

In 1997 the GDP grew for the first time since 1990, by a measly 0.7 per cent, while inflation fell to 12 per cent. But the macroeconomic stabilization was illusory. Yeltsin's administration bought political support by boosting federal spending while exempting powerful regional leaders and industrialists from federal taxes. These irresponsible policies led to a yawning budget deficit – 10 per cent of GDP in 1996 (see Table 11.1) – that was covered by international borrowing.

The Asian financial crisis in 1997 caused a slump in world oil prices, eroding Russia's current account surplus. That together with the budget deficit led to a run on the rouble in August 1998 and a dramatic devaluation, accompanied by a default on government debt and the collapse of nearly all private banks. The crash discredited the liberal reformers, and made the Russian government and people very wary of repeating such financial instability in the future.

Ironically, the 75 per cent rouble devaluation that followed the August 1998 crash was the best thing that happened to the Russian economy in a long time. It cut imports, because they immediately became much more expensive, and gave Russian farmers and manufacturers a chance to recapture their old markets. The new government that came in after the crash led by Prime Minister Yevgenii Primakov increased taxes on energy producers, while cutting subsidies. (Before 1999, for example, the republics of Tatarstan and Bashkorkostan had even refused to allow a branch of the federal treasury to be opened on their territory.) For the first time in a decade, the federal budget moved into balance. Federal spending recovered from a low of 9.2 per cent of GDP in 1998 to reach 17.1 per

Table 11.1   *The Russian central government budget, 1996–2003*

	1996	*1997*	*1998*	*1999*	*2000*	*2001*	*2002*	*2003*
Revenue	35.1	37.2	31.7	34.6	38.7	38.5	38.1	36.1
Spending	45.1	45.9	37.0	35.1	35.2	35.4	37.8	34.9
Balance	–10.1	–8.7	–5.3	–0.5	3.5	3.1	0.3	1.2

Note: Figures show government revenue and spending as a percentage of GDP; federal, regional and off–budget funds combined.
Source: OECD (2004).

cent in 2001, while federal spending was 14.1 per cent and 14.8 per cent respectively (see Table 11.1, which shows federal and regional budgets combined).

Putin takes the helm

When Putin became president he was a virtual unknown, leaving Western observers scrambling for insights into his political views. On the economic front, there were two unknowns in particular: his commitment to market reform, and his dependence on the oligarchs who had dominated decision-making during the waning years of the Yeltsin administration.

Many supposed that Putin was a tool of the oligarchs, since Boris Berezovsky had played a pivotal role in Putin's recruitment by the Kremlin. However, within weeks of Putin's inauguration as president the Kremlin launched a vigorous campaign against the two most powerful oligarchs: Berezovsky and Vladimir Gusinsky. Through financial machinations and threats of criminal prosecution both men were stripped of their television stations and forced to flee the country. Clearly, Putin was nobody's puppet.

The remaining oligarchs were worried that they would be next. They feared that the KGB men who rose to power with Putin wanted to strip the capitalists of their ill-gotten gains. Putin tried to reassure the oligarchs that it would be business as usual, so long as they stayed away from national politics. He proclaimed a policy of 'equidistance' from the oligarchs, although some figures (such as Vladimir Potanin, head of the Interros metals group) seemed to be treated more favourably by the Kremlin than others.

As for market reform, Putin campaigned for the presidency by promising stability: no more experiments, no miracle cures. This essentially meant a policy of continuity: that he would stick to Yeltsin's pro-market policies. Putin's firm commitment to market reform was unexpected, since public support for market reform had steadily eroded. According to an Ebert Foundation survey in 2000, 70 per cent of Russians favoured more state planning, and 63 per cent approved of confiscating the property acquired by the 'New Russians'. It was easy to imagine a scenario in which Putin would try to reintroduce state planning, raise tariffs and use energy revenues to reequip Russian industry. But in his first state of the federation address in July 2000 Putin reaffirmed his commitment to the market. He admitted that he used to favour protectionist tariffs but now saw such a policy as ineffective and a recipe for corruption.

A reform agenda

Putin's first presidential term saw the passage of important new reform legislation. However, measures that aroused public anxiety, such as pension reform or utility price increases, were postponed. Likewise steps that threatened powerful interests, such as banking reform, made only glacial progress. It was not clear whether the slow pace of change was because Putin did not want more radical measures, or because he lacked the political authority to push them through.

In January 2000 Putin gave German Gref, a lawyer from St Petersburg, the task of developing an economic strategy. The Gref plan had four main themes: defining a new social contract; modernizing the economy; reforming public administration; and identifying a new international role. The plan's release was delayed for months, since Prime Minister Mikhail Kasyanov was understood to be unhappy with its liberal tone.

The plan proposed to slash personal income tax from a top rate of 35 per cent to a flat rate of 13 per cent, and this was done in 2001. It was hoped that the new low rate would encourage employees to declare their incomes, since half of all income went unreported. At the same time medical, employment and pension contributions were fused into a unified social tax, fixed at 36 per cent of wages, which remained a strong disincentive to full income declaration. Income tax revenue rose, but not as much as reformers had hoped. In 2002 profits tax was also cut, and a package of debureaucratization measures included a bill reducing the number of business activities requiring licences from 500 to 104.

Large sections of Russian law were still based on Soviet-era legislation, since Yeltsin could not push new laws through the opposition-dominated parliament. Having forged a working arrangement with the Communists in the State Duma in 2000, Putin's government passed a number of important laws, including revisions to the Labour Code, pensions, the judiciary, the Tax Code and the banking sector. There was still resistance, however, to the attempt to push a new land code through parliament in October 2001. For the first time the code allowed land to be sold, but parliament insisted on excluding most farmland from the law, leaving it up to the regions to set their own rules. The new Labour Code, introduced in December 2001, made it easier for employers to hire and fire workers (which had previously required union approval), but otherwise preserved some of the worker-friendly features of the 1971 code. The Federation of Independent Trade Unions supported the new code; the Communist Party did not.

The main challenge was the need to reform the 'natural monopolies' – the railways, Gazprom and the UES electricity giant – which were still under state control. In 2001 Putin replaced the long-standing head of

Gazprom, Rem Vyakhirev, with a young economist from St Petersburg, Aleksei Miller. Gazprom's $15 billion exports made it Russia's largest cash earner and the second largest employer after UES. It has had more than its share of scandal, with new revelations surfacing in 2001 about dubious transactions through its subsidiary Itera. Nevertheless, Putin rejected suggestions that Gazprom be reformed. During his first term only one monopoly was restructured: the railway ministry was broken up into private regional companies in 2002.

Putin tried to move ahead with reform of UES, but retreated in the face of stiff resistance and the sheer complexity of the task. UES was Russia's largest employer, with revenues of $16 billion. It provided another $7–10 billion in subsidies to domestic customers through artificially low prices. Former privatization chief Anatolii Chubais had headed UES since 1998 and he prepared a plan to privatize the company and create a national electricity market. The government agreed to this reform in November 2001, and the bill passed its first reading in the State Duma in October 2002. But it then ran into opposition from regional governors and rival oligarchs, supported by Chubais's opponents inside the government. Only Putin's firm support for Chubais and the latter's relentless energy kept the proposal alive. Actual implementation of the plan was postponed until after the 2003–04 election cycle.

UES could only be privatized if the new companies had a chance of making a profit. This meant that utility prices would have to be raised and customers in arrears would have to be cut off. Efforts to introduce such measures triggered public unrest, especially in energy-deficient regions such as the Russian Far East. Utility price increases were postponed, causing UES to fall even further behind in its long-overdue investment programme.

As with the natural monopolies, the reform of the bank sector proceeded at a snail's pace. In 2002 the traditionally minded head of the Central Bank, Viktor Gerashchenko, was replaced. But there was no progress in restructuring or improving regulation of the commercial banks, which had been devastated by the 1998 crash. The foreign trade Vneshtorgbank was not privatized as promised. In 2002 the 12 per cent ceiling on foreign ownership in banks was abolished, and a law on mortgage collateral adopted. Seventy per cent of deposits were still lodged at the state-owned savings bank. A long-overdue law introducing deposit insurance for private banks was passed in November 2003. Steps to tighten bank regulation in preparation for deposit insurance triggered a run on several banks in April 2004. Even the leading Alfa Bank was besieged by panicky depositors, in a worrying echo of earlier bank crises.

Economic performance

Thanks to the 1998 rouble devaluation and the tight monetary and fiscal policies of the Primakov government, the economic tide had already begun to turn when Putin became prime minister in August 1999 and acting president on 31 December 1999. His main achievement has been to keep the Russian economy on this steady course. During the Yeltsin era, there had been a major financial crisis every two or three years. This did not happen under Putin. Real incomes fell in 1999–2000, but by 2004 real wages were 28 per cent above pre-1998 levels, and the number living in poverty has fallen by a third. The recovery was helped by the revival of world oil prices, with Urals crude going from $12 in 1997 to $37 by mid- 2004. The government made sure taxes and bills to state companies were paid on time, and non-cash settlements (barter and debt swaps), which reached 50 per cent in 1998, fell to 30 per cent in 2000 and 11 per cent in 2004.

According to World Bank calculations, Russia is now a middle-income country. Its gross national income per capita in 2002 was $2,130, compared to a world average of $5,120. Adjusting for domestic price levels (or purchasing power parity) its per capita income was $8,080, putting Russia above the world average and in 83rd place, just ahead of Botswana and Uruguay. But Putin's goal was to see Russia back in the front ranks of the world powers, something that would need more rapid and sustained GDP growth.

Table 11.2 presents the basic macroeconomic data, which represent the best side of Putin's economic record. GDP grew at an average of 6.8 per cent in 1999–2004. The government ran a budget surplus every year after 2000, while bringing inflation down to 10 per cent in 2004. A huge current account surplus enabled it to meet its international debt obligations. Foreign currency reserves rose to $85 billion by 2004.

Many critics argue that the recovery was entirely due to the world oil price. The official statistics office has oil and gas accounting for 8 per cent of GDP. Correcting for transfer pricing, the World Bank puts it at 19 per cent (World Bank, *Russian Economic Report*, February 2004). The World Bank estimates that a 10 per cent rise in oil prices translates into 0.7 per cent growth in GDP. Oil and gas accounted for 54 per cent of export earnings in 2003.

Still, the Organization for Economic Cooperation and Development estimates that oil accounts for only about one-third of the growth since 1998. Russian manufacturing became more competitive, thanks to what the OECD (2004) calls 'passive restructuring' – gradually shedding labour, as opposed to plant closures. In the first five months of 2004, manufacturing grew faster than energy and minerals: by 8 versus 6.8 per cent respectively. Telecommunications grew by 57 per cent and railcar

Table 11.2   *Basic economic indicators, 1998–2003*

	1998	1999	2000	2001	2002	2003
Real GDP growth	−5.3	6.3	10.0	5.1	4.7	7.3
Investment	−12.4	6.3	18.1	10.3	3.0	12.9
Unemployment	13.2	12.4	9.9	8.7	8.8	8.0
Budget surplus/deficit (as % of GDP)	−5.3	−0.5	3.5	3.1	0.3	1.2
Inflation	85	37	20	19	15	12
Exchange rate (R/$)	10	25	28	29	31	31
Exports ($bn)	75	76	105	102	107	136
Imports ($bn)	58	40	45	54	61	75
Current account ($bn)	17	36	60	58	46	61
Foreign exchange reserves ($bn)	12	13	28	37	48	77
Average real wages	−10	−22	18	19	17	26

Note: Figures show percentage annual change, unless otherwise indicated. Unemployment is based on International Labour Organization criteria – surveys, not officially registered unemployed.
Source: OECD (2004).

manufacturing (serving oil exports) by 51 per cent, but even automobiles and farm and construction machinery rose by 14–16 per cent. Manufacturing exports grew by 27 per cent, much of it driven by increased demand from the CIS. In addition to energy and manufacturing, the service sector, which is relatively immune to import competition, was the third leg of the economic recovery, accounting for 46 per cent of Russian GDP by 2004.

Apart from benefiting from high oil prices, Russia also increased the volume of oil production and oil exports, which went from 135 million tonnes in 1999 to 225 million in 2003. Most of this growth came from the private companies Yukos, Sibneft and TNK. However, there was little efficiency growth in the oil sector, and most investment went into increasing export capacity rather than prospecting for new reserves. The gas monopoly Gazprom did even worse. Employment in the natural gas sector rose by 90 per cent, while labour productivity fell by 40 per cent between 1997 and 2002.

Russia had long been the world's number one natural gas exporter. In September 2003 Russia overtook Saudi Arabia as the world's number one oil producer, pumping 8.5 million barrels a day against the Saudis' 8.47 mbd (Russia, however, exported only 5 million barrels a day as compared with Saudi Arabia's 7 million). Excess revenues were transferred into a stabilization fund that had reached $15 billion by the end of 2004.

After the 1998 crash the government tightened controls on export earnings and hiked the oil export tariff from 5 euros a tonne in September 1999 to 27 euros a year later. In December 1999 copper, nickel and zinc tariffs were doubled to 10 per cent and a new 5 per cent gas export tax was introduced, the latter alone worth $500 million in 2000. Some regional tax shelters persisted until they were closed in November 2003. The Sibneft oil company, for example, saved some $450 million in taxes by nominally basing operations in the far eastern republic of Chukotka, where its head Roman Abramovich had been elected governor.

With dollar reserves increasing from the trade surplus, Russia stopped taking IMF loans and began paying off its international debts. Prime Minister Kasyanov successfully negotiated a rescheduling and some cancellation of Russia's debts in 2000. Russia brought down its foreign debt from $156 billion in 2001 (88 per cent of GDP) to $105 billion (33 per cent of GDP) in 2004.

Apart from the surge in oil exports, another crucial factor in the Putin recovery has been sound fiscal policy (see Table 11.1). However, the government lacked the monetary instruments to sterilize the inflow of cash from the trade surplus (the 'Dutch disease'), and struggled to bring inflation down to single digits. The rouble continued to strengthen against the dollar, and by 2004 the competitive advantage of the 1998 devaluation had almost entirely disappeared. The stronger rouble made the government confident enough to take a step towards fuller convertibility, by easing some currency controls and cutting the proportion of export earnings that must be converted into roubles from 50 to 25 per cent in July 2003.

By 2002, in recognition of Russia's financial and political stability, Western agencies raised Russia's investment rating, and Western speculative capital returned to the Russian stock exchange (RTS). Foreign direct investment was $4.7 billion in 2003 – modest compared to China's $54 billion, but higher than in previous years. The Russian government was reluctant to open lucrative sectors such as financial services and the oil and gas industry to foreign investors. Instead, foreign capital has flown into less politically contentious sectors, such as food-processing and retailing. Foreign investors were not generally allowed to take a majority stake in strategic industrial projects in oil and gas. The major exception is the joint ventures to develop the Sakhalin oil and gas fields that started small-scale production in 1999 and will come fully on-stream in 2007. In the Sakhalin case, technical challenges involved in off-shore drilling gave the Russians little choice but to bring in foreign expertise.

The main problem on the investment front was not so much attracting foreign investors, but persuading Russia's oil and metals barons to invest their profits inside Russia. Although capital formation increased by 18 per cent in 2003, faster than in previous years, it still only amounted to 18 per cent of GDP, perhaps half what Russia needs to overhaul its ageing industrial infrastructure.

In addition, capital flight – the transfer of export revenues and domestic profits outside Russia – ran at $10–20 billion a year throughout the 1990s. There were hopes that the Putin stabilization would cause a reversal of this trend. In the second quarter of 2003, for the first time in a decade, capital inflow exceeded capital outflow, to the tune of $3.7 billion. But this reversed in the third quarter, which saw a $7.7 billion outflow after the arrest of executives in the Yukos oil company (see below).

Although Putin's political status seems secure, persisting social problems take the shine off the economic recovery. The boom benefited the rich and the small but growing middle class. 'Middle class' refers to the 30 million or so people (out of a total population of 145 million) who live in families earning at least 7,000 roubles ($230) per month. Although unemployment has been held to 10 per cent, the wages of many workers hover at the subsistence level. The average wage in September 2004 was 6,976 roubles ($235) and average pension 1,877 roubles ($65), although this was up from the equivalent of $21 in 2001. Between 1999 and 2002, the proportion of people living in poverty, according to official estimates, fell from 42 to 20 per cent. Still, at the end of 2003 23 million people, 16 per cent of the population, were living below the poverty line, then set at 2,143 roubles ($70). Poverty rates were twice as high in rural areas as in towns. According to a May 2004 survey, 89 per cent of respondents spent more than a half of their income on food. Nevertheless, 45 per cent said that they lived quite well.

Social inequality has meanwhile reached Brazilian levels, in a country that used to be highly egalitarian. The income ratio (the top 10 per cent compared with the bottom 10 per cent) stands at 14 to 1. The bottom 20 per cent received 6 per cent of total income while the top 20 per cent received 46 per cent. Regional inequality is also very large. The top six of Russia's 89 regions (Moscow, Tyumen, St Petersburg, Sverdlovsk, Tatarstan and Samara) account for fully half of the overall economy. Average annual income was above $6,500 a head in Moscow and below $1,000 in the dozen poorest regions.

During the Yeltsin years, arrears in the payment of state pensions and wages were a major social and political problem. Putin made sure that most state aid recipients were paid on time, though problems persisted for several years in the poorer regions. Public sector wage arrears occasionally caused protests, for example doctors in Irkutsk went on hunger strike in 2002. By 2003, state finances were in better shape and Putin even managed a 33 per cent increase in public sector pay in October 2003, just in time for the State Duma election. Some 6 million workers were still owed roughly $1.5 billion in wage arrears, although only 10 per cent of them were in the state sector.

An unfinished agenda

Making Russia rich

In his state of the federation address in May 2003 Putin laid down the challenge of halving poverty by 2007 and doubling GDP by 2010, something that would require annual growth in excess of 7 per cent. At the same time he admitted that 'Our economic foundation, although it has become much sounder, is nevertheless unreliable and very weak', in part because 'the monopolists are suffocating the competitive sector of our economy'.

Sceptics ridiculed the idea of doubling GDP as a throwback to Soviet-style plan targets. Putin loyalists saw it as a stimulus to press ahead with structural reform. The presidential address was delivered a month late, apparently because of disputes between Prime Minister Mikhail Kasyanov and ministers from the liberal St Petersburg group about the feasibility of Putin's growth target. Kasyanov also criticized finance minister Alexander Kudrin for proposing tax cuts that could cause a fiscal deficit and inflation.

After some fierce and occasionally public confrontations, Kudrin prevailed over Kasyanov. From 1 January 2004 VAT was cut by 2 per cent to 18 per cent, the securities tax was lowered from 0.8 to 0.2 per cent, and the regional 5 per cent sales tax introduced in 1998 was abolished. From 2005 the unified social tax on wages will be cut from 36.5 per cent to 26 per cent. Oil and gas taxes were increased, but the cuts left the pension fund with a $2.6 billion deficit, which will be plugged with money from the oil stabilization fund.

The government's medium-term economic strategy, released in August 2003, postponed doubling the GDP by 2013–14 rather than 2010, as the president had initially demanded. It also dropped the proposal in the original January draft for introducing competition in the natural gas market and increasing gas and electricity tariffs by 100 per cent and 50 per cent respectively. In January 2003 the Federal Energy Commission set a ceiling of 14 per cent for utility rate increases for that year, but regional energy commissions raised rates by double that amount, causing public unrest. In a bizarre twist, even the pro-government United Russia party organized protests against utility tariff increases in April 2003.

The Yukos affair

The year 2003 saw a pivotal development that was a blow to those who still believed that Russia was in transition to Western-style 'market democracy' when Putin launched an attack on Russia's top businessman, Mikhail Khodorkovsky, and used this to achieve a sweeping victory for the pro-presidential United Russia party in the December 2003 State Duma election.

While the natural gas and electricity sectors had been privatized through the creation of a single, state-controlled monopoly, Russia's oil industry was broken up into a dozen independent companies, most of them in the hands of private owners. In June 2003 the state launched a criminal investigation of the top executives in the largest oil company, Yukos. Initially, the accusations focused on fraud in a 1994 privatization deal, but then widened to include money-laundering and tax evasion to the tune of $5 billion.

The head of Yukos, Mikhail Khodorkovsky, refused to concede defeat and flee the country, as previous oligarchs who had fallen foul of the Kremlin had done. As a result, on October 2003 he was arrested, denied bail, and charged with offences that could keep him behind bars for ten years. In June 2004 the company was presented with additional charges for tax arrears from 2000–02, with the total of back taxes rising to $17 billion. Yukos was effectively forced into bankruptcy.

Khodorkovsky was singled out for attack precisely because he was the most successful and ambitious of the oligarchs. Yukos had brought its accounting practices up to Western standards, and in April 2003 it announced that it would merge with Russia's fifth largest oil company, Sibneft. The head of Sibneft, Roman Abramovich, moved to England that summer, following his purchase of the Chelsea soccer team. It was expected that the combined Yukos–Sibneft would be sold to a Western oil major, probably Exxon. Another factor attracting the wrath of the Kremlin was the plan Khodorkovsky had put together to build a $1.8 billion pipeline between Angarsk in Siberia and Daqing in China, jointly with the China National Petroleum Corporation. This would have broken the monopoly of the state-owned Transneft corporation on Russia's oil exports, and it rivalled a Russian government proposal to build a pipeline to the port of Nakhodka, in order to export oil to Japan. In the wake of Khodorkovsky's arrest, the merger with Sibneft was reversed. The China export pipeline was dropped in favour of the Nakhodka route, to be built by Transneft and the Kremlin-friendly Lukoil company.

Finally, Khodorkovsky made no secret of his political ambitions. He was generously funding political parties across the spectrum, from the liberal Yabloko to the Communists. Experts speculated that Yukos could end up controlling a third of the seats in the State Duma that would be elected in December 2003. Putin decided to eliminate this political rival by unleashing an anti-corruption campaign. This handily provided a popular theme for the pro-presidential party, United Russia, which swept to victory in the elections and established firm control over the State Duma.

The Yukos affair had important political repercussions. It brought about the departure from the Kremlin of the remaining top officials who had been held over from the Yeltsin years. Chief of staff Aleksandr Voloshin resigned straight after Khodorkovsky's arrest in October 2003 and Prime Minister Kasyanov was replaced in February 2004.

The arrest of Russia's richest man (Khodorkovsky's personal wealth was estimated at $8 billion) and the near destruction of its largest and most successful private company grabbed the attention of Western observers, who feared that Russia was turning its back on the market economy. Western governments reacted with alarm, though most investors seemed to buy the Kremlin's argument that Khodorkovsky had overstepped the mark by launching a direct political challenge to Putin.

Corporate governance

Leaving aside the exceptional case of Yukos, corporate governance throughout Russia's newly minted private sector leaves much to be desired. By 2004 only a dozen of the leading firms had adopted international accounting standards and traded their shares on the stock exchange.

A study of the ownership structure of Russian industry released by the World Bank (2004a) found that the 23 largest private corporations accounted for about 30 per cent of industrial sales and 11 per cent of employment. This is a remarkably high degree of industrial concentration by international standards. Moreover, most of those firms seemed to be controlled by a single individual or group of individuals. The level of concentration had actually increased in the wake of the 1998 crash, as weaker conglomerates collapsed.

The World Bank report also noted a vast 'hidden' sector of state-owned defence and other plants, which continue to receive subsidies and which account for a quarter of industrial output. Nearly half of Russian companies report that they are running at a loss. Many of them only survive thanks to state subsidies (such as toleration of tax and utility arrears); many are probably under-reporting income in order to evade taxation.

Western observers were divided over the viability of oligarchic capitalism. Some, such as Anders Aslund (1995), praised Khodorkovsky and his ilk as robber barons whose aggressive methods would drag the Russian economy into the twenty-first century. Others such as Reddaway and Glinski (2001) and Goldman (2003) saw the oligarchs as glorified crooks who preferred to play politics and reap the benefits of monopoly.

Stock ownership in Russian firms is extremely concentrated, posing an endemic problem for minority shareholders. And in many cases, actual control is not related to formal stock ownership. More legal reforms are needed. Prime Minister Mikhail Fradkov, appointed by Putin in February 2004, complained that 'many companies, including large ones, do not disclose their real owners, do not disclose an exhaustive list of affiliated firms and people, and continue to act, not always legally, through offshore zones' (Interfax, 4 June 2004).

In 1998 a new bankruptcy law was introduced, intended to make it easier to sue debtors (under the 1992 law, debts had to exceed assets). The new law was used by unscrupulous businessmen holding modest unpaid bills to tie up major companies in bankruptcy proceedings in obscure regional courts. Sometimes the goal was blackmail, at other times entrepreneurs used the procedure to seize ownership of companies they coveted. Regional governors also used bankruptcy to repel outsider owners and evade federal taxes. In dozens of cases rival court decisions were resolved through pitched battles among private (and public) security agencies. Eventually in 2002 an amendment to the law closed most of the loopholes.

The Russian government still holds a large stake in a broad range of Russian industries. Periodically the state sold off its stake in select industries, and these sales were often reminiscent of the corrupt loans-for-shares auctions of the 1990s. A case in point was the auction of Russia's sixth largest oil company, Slavneft, in December 2002. Rival bids were blocked, including one from a Chinese oil company, and the auction was rigged to ensure victory for the $1.86 billion bid from TNK and Sibneft. (Sibneft's owner Roman Abramovich was seen as close to Premier Kasyanov at this time.)

For much of the 1990s, the government did not try to exercise any systematic influence over the privatized companies in which it held shares. Putin made a coordinated effort to regain control over these companies by having trusted aides appointed to their boards, in some cases as chief executive. In the wake of the Yukos affair Putin moved to tighten Kremlin control still further. In the summer of 2004 two deputy heads of the presidential staff were appointed to chair the board of directors of Transneft oil pipeline and Rosneft oil companies, while other presidential staffers joined the boards of Aeroflot and Russian Railways.

Knocking at the door of the World Trade Organization

Russia first applied for entry to the World Trade Organization (WTO) in 1993. A decade later Russia, the seventeenth largest trading nation in the world, stood by as countries such as Kyrgyzstan and Moldova were allowed into the 144-member organization. China was granted membership in 2001 due to its massive presence in international trade, despite the fact that its currency was non-convertible; the state still controlled the banking system and much of heavy industry; the rule of law was non-existent; and intellectual property protections were minimal.

Economic interests inside Russia were divided over WTO entry. Reformers saw it as vital to promoting competitiveness and breaking up the cosy monopolies that had come to dominate the Russian economy. The oil and metal oligarchs were in favour – for them it would mean cheaper capital and easier access to Western markets. But other groups who feared foreign competition (such as farmers, bankers and automobile producers) opposed the move. The sensitivity of these issues was illustrated in 2002, when middle-class drivers objected to the introduction of a 30 per cent tariff on used car imports, intended to protect motor industry jobs.

Putin repeatedly stated that WTO admission was a top priority, but a number of obstacles continued to block Moscow's application. Unfortunately for Russia, the tide had begun to turn against free trade. In September 2003 the Cancun round of WTO talks collapsed because of the refusal of Europe and the USA to cut farm subsidies. The European Union was also preoccupied with absorbing the ten poor East European countries that had joined that organization in May 2004.

The government claimed that Russia already met most of the conditions for joining the WTO, thanks to a decade of legislative reform and trade liberalization. In May 2002 the European Union officially designated Russia as a market economy, and the USA followed suit in June. Later that year the International Financial Action Task Force removed Russia from its blacklist of money-laundering countries, after the Duma passed the required legislation.

However, there were a number of important issues still troubling Western negotiators. The EU's main complaint was that Russia provided unfair subsidies to domestic manufacturers through state control of energy exports and the system of dual energy pricing. For example, at the end of 2003 the price of natural gas for Russian industry was $23 per 1,000 cubic metres, while exported to Europe the same gas cost $130. The domestic oil price was $17.45 a barrel, while the export price was $29.

But Moscow refused to budge on energy liberalization. When Putin hosted a visit by German Chancellor Gerhard Schroeder in October 2003, he lashed out at 'European bureaucrats' blocking Russia's WTO entry. He said:

> Such a tough position towards Russia is unjustified and dishonest. It's an attempt to twist our arms, but Russia's arms are getting stronger and the EU won't succeed in twisting them. We intend to retain state

control over the gas transportation system and over Gazprom. We are not going to divide Gazprom. The European Commission had better forget about its illusions.

A breakthrough came in April 2004, when Putin brokered a deal with EU negotiators. In return for Russia supporting the Kyoto protocol on greenhouse gas emissions, the EU would drop its demands for energy liberalization and offer full support for Russian entry to the WTO. But there remained a number of issues that Moscow would have to resolve before other countries, such as the USA, would approve Russian WTO membership.

First, there was disagreement over farm subsidies. Russian state subsidies for agriculture, about $1.5 billion a year, were well below WTO levels, but Moscow wanted to preserve the right to pay up to $14 billion subsidies in the future.

Second, there were ongoing disputes over tariffs and quotas. Russia's average tariff level (10.7 per cent) was acceptable, but the WTO urged Russia to cut import tariffs on some items – for example, automobile tariffs should be cut from 25 to 5 per cent. Russia periodically found its exports of metals and other goods subject to anti-dumping tariffs. In March 2002 for example the US imposed a 30 per cent tariff on Russian steel imports from Russia and other countries (the USA eventually abandoned this tariff under WTO pressure in December 2003), and at the end of that year the EU imposed quotas on Russian grain exports. In retaliation, Russia periodically introduced quotas on certain foreign imports, such as US meat and poultry imports.

Third, there were complaints that there were still too many barriers to foreign investors in Russia. Telecommunications, banking and insurance were still largely protected from majority foreign ownership. It was reported that as part of the deal with the EU, Russia promised to liberalize the telecommunications market by 2007, but did not budge on financial services. Few foreign companies have been allowed to take a majority stake in leading oil and gas companies. Foreign ownership of Gazprom shares was capped at 20 per cent. Out of 28 production-sharing agreements proposed by foreign partners, only three were in operation, all approved prior to 1998 (agreements of this kind are a way of reducing investment risk by guaranteeing a pre-tax share of revenues). There was much talk of an 'energy partnership' with the USA. But at the US–Russia Energy Summit in Houston in October 2002, US companies said they wanted protection from changes in tax codes and regulatory policies before they invested further in Russia.

Fourth, there were doubts over the reliability of Russian customs and law enforcement. A new customs code was signed into law in May 2003, which should help. But implementation is weak. A study by the US Business Software Alliance found that Russia's piracy rate, contrary to government claims, actually rose in 2003 to 89 per cent, a level only exceeded by China and Indonesia (pirated DVDs of new Hollywood releases are openly sold in the underpass beneath Lubyanka square, just yards from the FSB headquarters).

Given all these problems, it seems likely that Russia's slow-motion negotiations with the WTO will continue, but actual entry will be postponed until 2006–07 at the earliest.

Future prospects

Although Russia's political trajectory under Putin is quite clear, its economic path is less certain. It has been suggested, for instance, that 'Mr Putin is attempting a Russian version of the Chinese model, strengthening political controls while opening the country up to market forces' (Strobe Talbott in the *Financial Times*, 27 September 2004). Others suggest that Putin has little interest in a competitive market, and instead wants to move back towards a state-controlled economy, or even a form of 'state capitalism'.

It is not clear how far Putin wants to go down the path of state regulation. He has been very selective in choosing which oligarchs to attack: business leaders who remained loyal to the Kremlin and avoided ties with opposition politics have been left alone. Putin has not dismantled the system of oligarchic capitalism as such. Rather, as Aleksei Zudin (2001) argues, it has been rearranged from a horizontal pluralism of competing groups, with the Kremlin as a referee, to a vertical hierarchy, with Putin at the head.

It is an open question whether this hybrid system, in which an intrusive state bureaucracy watches over private oligarchs, can be maintained over time. It is probably *politically* feasible. But is it *economically* feasible? The sustainability of the Putin recovery hinges on major investment and structural reforms to increase the competitiveness of Russian industry. But the politically closed nature of the 'power vertical' is not conducive to creating the competitive environment needed for sustained economic growth. As new oilfields and export pipelines are developed, and telecommunications licences put up for auction, the oligarchs will compete fiercely among themselves, knowing that political favouritism will most likely determine the outcome. In such conditions the political risk premium may make oligarchs less willing to reinvest their profits and expand their business. These political uncertainties are a particular barrier for foreign investors, who have few friends and many antagonists in the Kremlin.

Chapter 12

Social Policy in Post-Soviet Russia

JUDY TWIGG

Not many Russians want a return to the Soviet period, and for understandable reasons. But underlying the current nostalgia for the order and stability of Soviet days are fond – and perhaps exaggerated – memories of that era's system of cradle-to-grave social welfare. The social contract between the Soviet state and its citizens offered physical and financial security in exchange for individual freedom and token support for the regime. The Soviet government claimed to provide free and universally accessible healthcare, housing, education and childcare, and guaranteed employment and retirement pensions. Although the quality of these services was dismal compared to their Western counterparts, the basic elements of this social contract were maintained. A rudimentary package of health services was freely available; all children received an effective primary and secondary education, resulting in almost 100 per cent literacy rates; everyone had a roof over their heads, even if this meant sharing a communal apartment with a dozen other families; and the pension system ensured that the elderly and disabled were fed and cared for. The Soviet social safety net may have been a shabby one, but it was comprehensive and intact, and people relied on it.

Now, during the transition to a market economy, the state has significantly and rapidly withdrawn from even this meagre level of basic social services, leaving a vacuum that thus far has not been replaced by a new social welfare system. Although the Russian government can arguably claim to have succeeded in establishing at least the elements of a democracy and a free market, it has failed a large number of its citizens in an area most of those citizens still consider a state responsibility. The old state-funded system struggles to survive in an environment where funding has evaporated, policy is ineffective, and a functional privatized or self-help system has not yet emerged.

Instead, the country has starkly bifurcated into a small number of 'haves' and a significant majority of struggling 'have-nots'. Highly visible pockets of extravagance, most concentrated in and around Moscow, may trick the untrained eye into believing that Russia has emerged from the chaotic 1990s into a period of unparalleled prosperity. The number of Russian millionaires grew by 5 per cent in 2003 and now amounts to 84,000 people (MosNews.com 2004). A dizzying array of dazzling new shopping centres and high-class restaurants pepper the capital. Behind this garish new wealth, a small but growing nascent middle class – undeniably the hope for Russia's future socioeconomic stability – struggles to emerge from its infancy. Difficult to ignore, however, is the huge swathe of the population either trapped in poverty or hovering precariously just above it. Russia is now two starkly different nations, able to draw on vastly different sets of resources to cope with the social challenges this chapter will address: poverty, crime, health and education.

Poverty

According to official statistics, poverty in Russia is on the decline. In 1999, 35 per cent of Russians had incomes below the subsistence minimum level, compared with 23 per cent in 2003. But while the overall percentage of Russians in absolute poverty has declined, the demographic and geographic distribution of wealth continues to divide Russia into two separate and markedly unequal societies. For a start, the rise in living standards that has contributed to the reduction of poverty in the last five years has occurred almost exclusively in the country's larger cities. In small cities, 57 per cent of the population fall below the poverty line; 38 per cent of rural residents are considered poor. Indeed, poverty and despair in some of Russia's more far-flung regions has produced an epidemic of dying villages. The 2002 census shows that 17,000 out of a total of 155,000 rural settlements on the Russian map have been completely abandoned, and another 38,000 have ten or fewer inhabitants and are likely to disappear in the coming months (Agence France Presse 2003).

The gap in all regions between rich and poor is also remarkable. In the first half of 2004, over 46 per cent of all income was earned by the richest 20 per cent of citizens, while the poorest 20 per cent received only 5.4 per cent (Dzis-Voinarovsky 2004). While this income gap is comparable to that in some Western industrial democracies, and indeed is not as great as it was during the transition period of the 1990s, it still represents a monumental change from the relative equality of the Soviet period, and has resulted from a shift in socioeconomic circumstance unparalleled in its rapidity. To the extent that this income and wealth bifurcation divides the cities from the rural areas, and in particular Moscow from the remainder of the country, envy and resentment are growing. A 2004 survey in 39 Russian regions shows that 74 per cent (compared with 44 per cent in

1993) of Russians resent Muscovites, with over 80 per cent of respondents agreeing that Moscow's prosperity comes at the expense of the regions (RFE/RL, 2004c). Optimists predict that Moscow's wealth will soon and inevitably trickle down through the provinces, but others worry that two distinctly separate economic cultures are solidifying.

More than 40 per cent of young families in Russia fall below the poverty line for the first time when they have a child, and the most potent predictor of poverty is the birth of an additional child to a family. Many of these situations involve mothers raising sons or daughters on their own, so that poverty is frequently a feminine and childhood trait. About 70 per cent of families with children in Russia fall below the official poverty threshold (ITAR-TASS 2003). And this official poverty line in many cases is barely enough to sustain human existence. Novgorod region, for example, raised its subsistence minimum early in 2004 to $2.30 per resident per day; one Russian publication immediately observed that the average British house cat costs its owner almost the exact same amount of money (RFE/RL 2004b).

A diverse array of factors has given rise to poverty in Russia. The country has more than its share of the 'traditional' impoverished: single mothers, pensioners, the disabled and the chronically unemployed. The rate of unemployment is high, despite the plethora of jobs worked 'off the books' so that employers and workers can evade taxes. Almost half of those classified as poor continue to work at full-time jobs, most of those paid by the state budget but not providing a living wage – highly educated and skilled teachers, doctors and managers. Currently over a quarter of the Russian workforce is concentrated in education, healthcare, public administration and the military, all dependent on a government salary (Bulgakov 2004).

Services the state formerly provided free of charge, moreover, are now consuming an increasing share of low-income workers' paychecks, reducing dramatically the amount available for household discretionary spending. A 2003 poll, for example, indicated that an overwhelming majority – 81 per cent – find the constant growth of prices on food and other essential goods to be their biggest concern, followed closely (68 per cent) by increasing housing prices (Interfax 2003a). And as many as 87 per cent of Russians spend at least half of their income on food (RFE/RL 2004a). The state has periodically attempted to mitigate the poverty problem, announcing occasional rises in the minimum monthly wage, pension and wage for state-sector workers. Seldom, however, have these increases kept pace with inflation, so that the spending power of the impoverished or near-impoverished family continues to wane.

Perhaps the most notable characteristic of the distribution of wealth in Russia is the small size of the middle class. A graph displaying household income levels in the United States looks markedly like a classic bell curve, with over 75 per cent of Americans falling comfortably between poverty and grand prosperity. In Russia, by contrast, economic class is a much more difficult set of labels to assign. At the poles, 1 or 2 per cent of Russians are unquestionably extremely wealthy, while about 10 per cent clearly have no resources whatsoever on which to draw (savings, income, property or education). In the middle, about 20 per cent may, at a stretch, fit a standard definition of middle class based not only on income level but also on some mix of education and skill level, property ownership, consumption patterns, and long-term personal economic planning and outlook. The remaining 70 per cent fall into a category unique to today's Russia. While not victims of grinding poverty, their position is consistently precarious. They have jobs, but those jobs are unstable and pay poorly. Depending on a wide variety of factors – macroeconomic circumstance, hard work, just plain luck – they could eventually either advance to the middle class or sink into destitution. By and large, when statistics indicate that average real incomes in Russia are growing, the increases are not affecting this vast, undefinable 'below-middle' class. Instead, the growth takes place to the benefit of people working in the competitive private sector, and also (to a lesser extent) to those in the lowest income brackets who can benefit from improved state social programmes (Skorobogatko 2003).

Many members of this below-middle class display spending and consumption patterns that belie their low official incomes. The Soviet-era practice, for example, of under-the-counter 'bonuses' to teachers and doctors persists, enabling these professionals considerably to enhance their standards of living. But this phenomenon does not extend consistently beyond Moscow and St Petersburg; in the provinces, most of the population is simply too poor to afford these side payments.

Despite the frustration of remaining just out of reach of the middle class, and despite the humiliation of living a life where income and living standard are such a gross mismatch to education level and skill, this below-middle class has yet to display any signs of social unrest. This fact is even more remarkable given that many of its members had risen to genuine middle-class status before the 1998 financial crisis but have since remained trapped in near poverty. What accounts for this social stability in the face of economic struggle and uncertainty? This vast near-middle class does have some resources on which it can draw. Most of its members have accumulated some meagre savings or property, and their education and professional skills constitute a minimal safety net. In many cases, members of this economic stratum juggle two or three part- or full-time (usually temporary) jobs in an effort to stay afloat. As in Soviet days, they can rely on networks of family, close friends, and self-provision of some home-grown foods and other goods. Even though their situation is not improving, it is also not getting significantly worse. The most common response to these stimuli is not social upheaval – who has the time and energy for that? – but rather social apathy. People feel swindled: they lost the benefits and status that were their birthright during the Soviet period, and they are not sufficiently poor to receive most of the social benefits that have been on offer in the postcommunist years. Without strong trade unions, and faced with the time-consuming challenge of eking out an everyday living, there is no time or energy for strikes and protests.

The solution to Russian poverty and near poverty is clearly a ladder for this below-middle class to climb into middle-class status. The state budget, however, cannot support 70 per cent of the population, nor should it. One of the main reasons state-sector wages remain so low is that, in conditions of a marketizing private economy, the state sector is still woefully inefficient. The key to eradicating near poverty is therefore structural reform that will render the activities of teachers, nurses and physicians more productive, bring the 'shadow' financing circulating through education and medicine into the light, and enable these skilled professionals to earn a middle-class wage commensurate with their hard work and competitiveness.

President Putin has made a war on poverty an explicit part of his policy menu, with a promise in his 2004 annual address to parliament to halve the number of people living below the poverty line within the next four years. Thus far, it appears as though the government's approach will shy away from offering people more handouts, instead focusing on creating conditions, largely through changes to the tax system, under which more and better jobs will be available and people will be able to earn more money for themselves. Putin has also explicitly targeted pensioners in his assault on poverty. This strategy makes good political sense, since pensioners represent a large and frequently well-organized voting bloc. But although many pensioners do indeed struggle economically, the state does index their incomes to inflation, and most enjoy a safety net of family and community support. Pensioners are certainly not the demographic group most dramatically and desperately afflicted by poverty.

An April 2004 poll indicated that less than one-fifth of Russian citizens believe that the government's poverty reduction goals are realistic (Interfax 2004a). The structure of the economy, with its heavy dependence on the oil and natural gas sectors and consequent vulnerability to swings in prices for these commodities, may make it difficult to sustain the kind of social-sector investment and structural reform that is so desperately needed (Brown 2004). And a rising-tide-lifts-all-boats approach may not apply to Russia, where so much of poverty and near poverty is a unique by-product of the Soviet legacy – workers in the shadow economy who remain off the books because they lack large-city residency permits, for example, or residents stuck in remote and decaying industrial towns built on the whim of communist economic planners.

Crime

The late 1980s and 1990s saw dramatic increases in Russia's crime rate. Property and other non-violent crime seems to have tracked directly with changes in the country's overall economic situation – significant acceleration of negative trends in the early 1990s, followed by a levelling off and then reduction in 1995–97, and then a renewed rise in crime after the financial crisis in the summer of 1998. The most spectacular increases have involved economic and illegal drug-related crimes, and offenders became more violent throughout the 1990s (Andrienko 2001). The overall number of crimes committed annually in Russia is about one-tenth that in the United States – about three million registered crimes compared with 30 to 40 million. And officially, Russia solves a higher percentage of its reported crimes than any other country in the world. Russia, however, has the second highest level of homicide in the world, behind only South Africa, with a rate 20 times higher than Japan, 14 times higher than France, and 3.5 times higher than the United States. Contrary to what is probably common perception, most homicides in Russia are related not to politics or business, but instead to the stresses the transition period has placed on ordinary home and family life. And although alcohol is an underlying factor in violent crime worldwide, it takes on a special significance in Russia, with about 80 per cent of murderers and 60 per cent of their victims under the influence at the time of the homicide (Andrienko 2001). As in most other countries, crime in Russia is a phenomenon involving youth, with most offenders between 20 and 33 years of age.

The validity of Russian crime statistics is questionable. Police are notorious for refusing to register crimes that they do not consider relatively easily solvable, in order to maintain high rates of arrest and conviction. The Russian public also considers street-level police officers corrupt and untrustworthy, with demands for side payments to traffic police particularly common. According to the Interior Ministry's Research Centre, almost 60 per cent of victims do not bother to report crimes to law enforcement agencies (Maksakova 2004).

Russia incarcerates more of its citizens as a percentage of its total population than any country except the United States, with 605 and 710 per 100,000 people respectively (Interfax 2003b). In Russia, this amounts to about one million people in prisons or pre-trial detention centres. Over the last ten years, four million people, or 2.5 per cent of the working-age male population, have passed through the penal system (Russian Regional Report 2004). The prison population grew by 50 per cent during the 1990s. Prison facilities are notoriously overcrowded, with pre-trial detention centres often allowing less than one square metre per person, forcing detainees to sleep in shifts. Claustrophobic quarters and substandard food, clothing and medicine have made the Russian prison system one of the country's primary incubators for infectious disease, including HIV and most notably tuberculosis. Russian prisoners are about 60 times more likely to contract TB than the general population, and the general mortality rate in the prisons is about 30 times the national average (Andrienko 2001). There have been confirmed cases of prisoners dying from oxygen deprivation.

Recent years have seen several attempts to reform the penal system. Most of these have been linked to a transfer of the Main Penitentiary Directorate from the Interior Ministry to the Justice Ministry. Amendments passed to the Criminal Code in 2004, for example, were predicted to result in a 20 per cent drop in the total number of prisoners over the following year, due largely to an increase in the number of cases qualifying for early parole, a shortening of average sentences, and the transfer of non-violent offenders to milder prison conditions or sentencing with fines rather than incarceration. A 2003 reform that gave defendants for the first time the right to a jury trial has resulted in acquittal rates rising from 0.4 to almost 20 per cent in some regions (Farquharson 2003; Yablokova 2003a). Trial by jury is scheduled to be in place throughout the country, expanding from its current use on an experimental basis in a handful of regions, by 2007. And since July 2002, accused persons can no longer be held in pre-trial detention centres indefinitely while awaiting trial; courts must now review the arrest of all suspects within a 48-hour period, and they are to dismiss the case and release the prisoner if no convincing grounds are found for the detention. From mid-2002 to mid-2003, the absolute number of arrests dropped dramatically, and courts mandated the release of about 10 per cent of those detained. Officials hope that these trends will continue, resulting ultimately in a reduction of overcrowding and more efficient and just processing of those who remain.

One particular face of Russian lawlessness that has attracted considerable attention in the computer virus-afflicted West is cybercrime. In 2003, computer-related crime in or emanating from Russia doubled to over 11,000 reported cases. Hacking and virus-writing are rapidly shifting from a mischievous hobby of bright teenagers to a lucrative profession of skilled programmers working with and for established criminal interests (Blau 2004). According to international providers of information technology security services, organized crime in Russia is increasingly using the internet as a resource for implementing mass identity theft and financial fraud. The 1998 financial crash left many talented computer professionals across Russia out of work, and many of these underemployed specialists now troll the Web searching for security vulnerabilities in American and European corporate computer networks – often at the behest of criminal organizations that have set up recruitment networks at university maths and physics departments. Although hacking is illegal in Russia, it is considered a victimless crime when it involves, for example, copycatting foreign software that young programmers could never afford to purchase legally. No hackers are currently imprisoned in Russia, perhaps not surprising given that the hacking has been directed almost exclusively at Western individuals and firms rather than Russian companies or organizations. In a society where violent crime remains such a serious plague, law enforcement authorities and the public alike tend to dismiss cybercrime as a secondary problem.

Health and demographic concerns

In recent years, the Russian government and media have paid considerable attention to the declining quantity and quality of Russia's population. Russian deaths annually exceed births by nearly one million. Even with significant migration into the country to compensate partially for the positive ratio of deaths to births, Russia's population has been declining by about 750,000 people a year for well over a decade. Demographic predictions are always uncertain, but virtually all forecasts estimate dramatic and continued declines for decades to come, with the most startling speculating that there may be only 70 to 100 million Russians left by the year 2050 (RFE/RL 2003a).

The most alarming and unique contributor to these demographic trends has been the skyrocketing of young and middle-aged male mortality throughout the 1990s and continuing into the present. In 2003, the death rate among Russia's working-age population was up to 350 per cent higher than the European Union average, and 50 per cent higher than the average in developing countries (Interfax 2004b). Put another way, the Russian workforce has declined by twelve million over the last ten years, with the loss of men five times higher than that of women (Rosbalt 2003). Life expectancy for men plunged from 64.2 years in 1989 to 57.6 in 1994, including an astonishing one-year drop (from 1992 to 1993) of more than three years, from 62.0 to 58.9. This figure rebounded to 61.3 in 1998, regaining more than half of its earlier loss, but dropped again after the 1998 financial crisis and has remained around 59 despite the recent economic recovery.

Across the age and gender spectrum, but particularly for men, the explanation for excess death in the 1990s and early 2000s lies predominantly in two categories: cardiovascular disease (heart attack, stroke and so on), and 'external causes' (such as injuries, suicide, homicide and poisonings). Many factors, of course, have contributed to this appalling increase in mortality: poor diet, lack of exercise, environmental degradation, high rates of tobacco use (40 per cent of Russian boys are smokers by the age of 19) and, most importantly, the unprecedented economic and social stress brought on by the sudden and unpredictable transition from communist rule. But it is impossible to overlook alcohol as an important underlying factor driving all of these causes of death. About 40 per cent of men who die from causes other than cancer die while drunk, and more than half that number die in an extreme state of intoxication, with a significant concentration of deaths on Saturdays or Sundays due to heavy drinking at weekends (Twigg and Schecter 2001). Adult Russian men consume, on average, 160 to 180 half-litre bottles of vodka a year, equivalent to a bottle almost every other day. About 40,000 Russians die of alcohol poisoning every year, compared to about 150 in the United States (Nemtsov 2003). The Ministry of Health estimates that 40 per cent of adult Russian men and 17 per cent of women are seriously affected by drinking, although over the last ten years alcoholism has been growing at a faster rate among women than among men.

Although 'softer' alcoholic beverages such as beer have become more popular in recent years (Russia is second only to China as the fastest-growing beer market in the world), they appear to be supplementing rather than replacing harder liquor. One popular modern proverb says that 'Drinking beer without vodka is a waste of money' (Shakina 2003). Beer still does not fall into the official category of alcoholic beverages in Russia, excluding it from the long-standing ban on the advertising of vodka and wine. Until recently, therefore, it seemed as though every other advertisement on Russian television and billboards promoted a particular beer (the remainder, coincidentally, seemed to be for cigarettes). And beer can legally be sold around the clock to people of any age, producing an epidemic of young 'beer alcoholics' – teenagers who have become alcoholics by drinking only beer. One recent survey of 14- to 19-year-olds throughout Russia revealed that over 40 per cent of youth drink beer at least once a week (Pilkington and Omel'chenko 2004).

Mikhail Gorbachev tried to tackle the drinking problem through his now infamous anti-alcohol campaign (there is a full account in White 1996). In effect for less than two years, the 1985 policy raised prices on state-produced vodka and sharply limited the hours and places at which alcoholic beverages would be available. Widespread anger and frustration resulted, along with an array of unintended consequences including a marked increase in cases of alcohol poisoning due to consumption of unsafe home brew, a sharp fall in state revenues from excise duties on alcohol sales, and the disappearance of sugar (an essential ingredient for moonshine) from retail shelves. Jokes abounded. In one, a man queues for vodka for several hours before deciding, exasperated, that it would be easier to shoot Gorbachev. He marches off to the Kremlin but returns minutes later. The line to shoot Gorbachev, he explains, was even longer (Ferreira-Marques 2004).

But the anti-alcohol campaign did produce a temporary rise in Russian life expectancy for the first time since the 1960s. Since then, the government has seemed reluctant to tackle the alcohol problem, having shied away in 2003 from draft legislation that would have increased penalties for drink-driving, and actually doubling the legal limit for alcohol in a driver's bloodstream from 50 to 100 millilitres (RFE/RL 2003c). The only concrete step forward has been a law restricting beer advertising, which came into force in September 2004. It prohibits beer ads on television and radio between 7 in the morning and 10 in the evening, and in close proximity to schools, sports arenas and cultural facilities. It also requires advertisers to allocate at least 10 per cent of broadcast time or ad space to warnings about the potential dangers of beer drinking. Already, however, legislators are mulling changes to the law, which was hugely unpopular among brewers and broadcasters.

On the other side of the lifespan, birth rates have plummeted from 2.2 children per woman of childbearing age in the late Soviet period to 1.24 in 1997 and 1.3 in 2003, almost 40 per cent below the population replacement rate of 2.1. This pattern, in particular the slight but seemingly stable increase in the last several years, might be interpreted optimistically: Russian families delayed childbearing during the turbulent 1990s, but now the improved economic climate has made prospective parents feel more confident about adding the burden and responsibility of a new baby. But part of this increase is due to a temporary demographic blip: Russia is currently experiencing a rise in the number of 20- to 29-year-old females, a reflection of birth cohort size increases in the past but one that will evaporate by 2010. And reliable estimates attribute at least part of the dismal birth rate to involuntary infertility, with 15 to 20 per cent of all married couples unable to reproduce – almost three times the figure for the United States (Eberstadt 2004). The prevalence of infertility is currently increasing by more than 3 per cent annually. These alarming figures are due in part to a skyrocketing rate of sexually transmitted infections – new incidents of syphilis increased by 77 times from 1990 to 1997 – and also to the practice of multiple abortions. Although the abortion rate has declined significantly in recent years, it remains the most common form of contraception in the country and is free on demand at most hospitals and clinics within the first trimester. With very little social stigma attached to it, twice as many abortions as live births were experienced in Russia in the early 1990s, although that number fell to about 130 abortions for every 100 births in 2003 (RFE/RL 2003b). This still amounts to almost two million terminated pregnancies annually, with 40 per cent of those botched by the healthcare system to the point that the woman requires antibiotics or hospitalization.

Another set of alarming health threats looms just over the horizon: infectious disease. While such illnesses accounted for a very small percentage of the increased mortality of the 1990s, by many estimates tuberculosis and, especially, HIV/AIDS threaten the economic productivity and perhaps even political stability of the country over the next twenty years. As of late 2004, over 290,000 HIV-positive persons had been officially reported since the beginning of the epidemic in the mid-1990s, of whom 1,057 had AIDS and 4,780 had died of AIDS-related causes. Most observers estimate that the true figure for HIV infections is considerably higher, by a factor of three to ten. Because the vast majority of cases are among injecting drug users, there are considerable disincentives for HIV-positive persons to report themselves to the authorities. The rate of increase of HIV in Russia from 1999 to 2002 was among the highest in the world, and evidence over the last few years points to a spread outward from drug users to their heterosexual partners, and perhaps from there into the general population. The face of HIV in Russia is a young one, with 80 per cent of cases among people aged 15 to 29 (Galvin and Feshbach 2004).

Despite the establishment of federal and regional AIDS centres in the late 1980s, the Russian response to HIV to date has been lamentably insufficient. The highest levels of the government, for a start, have remained stubbornly silent on the issue. The government's early response was dominated by inefficient mass testing (known as 'screening'), rather than the kinds of education and prevention efforts, targeted at the groups known to be most vulnerable to the infection, that are internationally accepted as best practice. Less than $4 million a year is spent at the federal level on earmarked HIV and AIDS programmes, or about thirty cents a person. Many government practices on both HIV and sexually transmitted infections continue to stigmatize people who engage in high-risk behaviour, such as injecting drug users and commercial sex workers. There is very little treatment, publicly funded or otherwise, of HIV/AIDS patients with anti-retroviral therapy, and the dominant approach to this therapy in Russia again does not conform to international standards.

A World Bank study warns that GDP growth could be reduced by 4 to 11 per cent by 2020 as a result of HIV/AIDS, in the absence of a scaled-up response to the crisis (Rühl *et al.* 2002). A recent estimate from the

International Labour Organization holds that, if left unaddressed, the AIDS epidemic in Russia will claim between 1.3 and 4.4 per cent of the population, including as many as 5.4 per cent of working-age men and women. The World Health Organization reports that AIDS could lead to a four-year drop in life expectancy for Russian men by 2015. According to the working group US–Russia Against HIV/AIDS, around eight million Russians will be infected with HIV by 2010, a prevalence rate of close to 10 per cent (RFE/RL 2004d). As these HIV sufferers develop full-blown AIDS, the toll they exact on the healthcare system – and on the state budget – will be overwhelming. Although international donors like the World Bank and the Global Fund to Fight AIDS, Tuberculosis and Malaria are now funnelling considerable assistance into the country, pressure and funding from the outside will be insufficient as long as the government refuses to acknowledge the scope of the problem and act accordingly.

Abuse of injecting drugs has been the primary vector spreading HIV. According to the United Nations Office on Drugs and Crime and the Russian Ministry of Education, 2 to 3 per cent of the working-age Russian population uses drugs, as do four million young people between the ages of 11 and 24 (Walters 2004). Among these groups, as many as four million are addicts, and Russian users tend to move from 'soft' drugs like marijuana to 'harder' drugs like heroin and methamphetamines much more rapidly and at a younger age than those in other societies. The illegal drug trade in Russia is worth between $5 and 10 billion a year, while the country spends only about $90 million annually to combat drug abuse (RFE/RL 2003d; Bullough 2004). Illegal drug use in Russia stems from both supply-side phenomena – its proximity to producing regions such as Central Asia and its own highly developed chemical industries, easily exploited by synthetic drug manufacturers – and demand-side pressures among a population seeking escape from the stresses of socioeconomic transition (Mainville 2003).

In March 2003, President Putin established the Federal Anti-Drug Service, ultimately planned to employ a staff of 40,000 people (including 30,000 members of the now defunct Tax Police), more than twice the number that have thus far dealt with illicit drug issues in all the country's law enforcement agencies combined. Taking over the duties of the Interior Ministry's narcotics department, the agency has thus far earned a mixed reputation. While it has been accused of violent tactics in raids on Moscow nightclubs, for example, it has been praised for its role in shifting towards a crackdown on drug dealers while encouraging small-quantity users to seek treatment. The latter philosophy seems consistent with amendments to the Criminal Code passed in early 2004 that make possession of small quantities of drugs punishable by fine rather than by prison sentence (considerably easing the way for effective needle exchange and other harm reduction programmes), but imposing significantly harsher sentences for dealing and selling to minors (Schreck 2004).

Russia's system of healthcare is ill-equipped to deal with these burdens. Chronically underfunded during Soviet times, and with public funding cut to barely more than half of Soviet levels today, Russian hospitals and clinics exist on a shoestring. Russian medical officials claim that up to 40 per cent of the country's excess mortality is preventable with better-quality and accessible healthcare, yet the government continues to spend only about 3 per cent of its GDP on health – less than half the average of developed countries. To its credit, in 1993 the Russian government recognized the precarious situation of health having constantly to compete with higher-priority items for budget allocations. It instituted a system of nationwide compulsory medical insurance that, while not correcting for the structural deficiencies (overhospitalization and overspecialization) that still plague the health services, has still provided medicine with a pool of protected revenue that has insulated it partially from the vagaries of the annual budget cycle.

Nevertheless, the overall quality of healthcare remains low. A shockingly high percentage of health facilities have no hot water or sewage systems, and sanitary and sterilization procedures are frequently far below Western norms. Patients suffer long waits even for urgently needed care, and a long list of medications is not only unaffordable but unavailable at any price. Perhaps most disturbing, a higher quality of services, in a system where free medical care is constitutionally guaranteed, is now routinely provided only to the small number of people with the ability to pay for it. State-owned clinics openly (and illegally) demand money for basic diagnostics, routine attention from ward nurses and orderlies, anesthetics and other drugs, and the like. Almost two billion dollars are paid each year in bribes in public hospitals (Agence France Presse 2004). Perhaps inevitably, healthcare has succumbed to market forces – a necessary step towards improvements in quality and efficiency of service delivery, to be sure – but in a chaotic and uncontrolled manner that has left the most vulnerable parts of the population unprotected.

Education

The Soviet Union bequeathed to Russia a well-developed, comprehensive system of pre-school through to university education. This system, however, has proven inflexible in response to the changing economic structures of a transition economy. In 1992, the education sector was decentralized, with responsibility for financing and managing schools devolved to regional and local authorities. As was the case with decentralization in many other sectors, this transfer of responsibility was not accompanied by requisite funding and appropriate definition of roles. As a result, overall funding for education has declined dramatically in the post-Soviet period; many regions (particularly those with significant minority ethnic populations) have launched their own local administrative and curricular reforms, creating disjunctures between federal and regional approaches; and educators' pay has plummeted, prompting many of the most competent teachers and administrators to seek more lucrative opportunities elsewhere (Chowdhury and Verbina 2003). The Russian education and science minister claims that the public school system is short of more than 20,000 teachers (ITAR-TASS 2004). Significant gaps have formed between the regions with the best systems of education and those with the worst, with sixteen regions spending at least a third more per student on compulsory education than the eighteen regions that spend the least. Overcrowded, poorly lit and underequipped classrooms led to the development of chronic illnesses, including intestinal and psychological problems, among more than 15 per cent of schoolchildren in 2003 ('Top Doctor' 2004).

Despite these problems, the number of Russians above fifteen years of age with a secondary education has increased by 10 per cent since 1989, to 90 per cent. The number of college and university undergraduates doubled during the 1990s, and the number of women with a higher education now exceeds the number of men for the first time ever. Illiteracy rates (among people ten years of age and older) have shrunk fourfold, to 0.5 per cent, since 1989 (RIA Novosti 2003). New-found academic freedom and access to international scholarship represent important gains. The number of university-level institutions jumped from 517 state-sponsored schools in 1990 to 1,337 in 2000, including 365 new private ones (Holley 2003). Still, during the 2003–04 academic year over 15,000 Russian children did not receive basic primary or secondary education. And many observers worry that the explosion of new university-level institutes and departments represents a rush toward shifting and temporary academic fads, creating a surplus of graduates in some fields and undermining the overall quality of the education system. Already fifteen universities from around the country have been stripped of their accreditation due to poor teaching and curricula and substandard facilities (RIA Novosti 2004).

Amidst the chaos, an enormous shadow market for educational services has developed, according to some estimates equivalent to 1.5 per cent of GDP (Chowdhury and Verbina 2003). Campus space, for example, is now routinely leased to private companies, providing an essential source of additional institutional income but also lining the pockets of corrupt administrators. Teachers and professors routinely tutor future applicants, moonlight at institutions other than their primary employers, or commit outright extortion to guarantee admissions or good grades. A national survey conducted in 2001 found education to be the third most corrupt institution in the country, after healthcare and law enforcement (Yablokova 2003b). Although higher education remains nominally free of charge to anyone who qualifies for admission, fully half of college and university students now pay – either by attending one of a growing array of private institutions, or bribing their way into and through public ones. 'Admission' to the most prestigious departments at the top schools, such as Moscow State University, now costs as much as $50,000, and a passing grade for exams in these departments runs from $100 to $200. Of course, there are some professors who refuse to carry out this extortion. But there is no rule requiring that exams must be taken from the primary professor conducting a course, so students can simply pay a different instructor for a passing grade. Many observers naturally fear that, in this environment, the perceived importance and status of education will diminish. In the chaotic 1990s, many people observed that economic success was achieved by luck and lawlessness rather than through intellect and hard work. Now, if it continues to be possible essentially to purchase a diploma from even the most prestigious institutes, the value of study and academic pursuits is degraded.

In an effort to combat the corruption problem, the Education Ministry has introduced a unified entrance examination for admission to universities across the country. Almost half of the regions have put the exam in place, with almost a million students having taken it so far. In 2005, all Russian high school graduates will take the test, with a three-hour section on maths, one on Russian, and three more on subjects specific to each student. Whereas places in the most prestigious Moscow and other large-city institutes used to be available only to students who could travel to those urban areas to take written and oral entrance exams specific to each school (and very probably, who could also afford the necessary bribes to secure admission, since the tests were not standardized and frequently varied from student to student), now a sufficiently high score on the national exam guarantees students a place in the department of their choice. Moscow State University, Russia's premier institution of higher education, has fiercely opposed this innovation, claiming that it does not sufficiently evaluate applicants' credentials. Of course, Moscow-area faculty worry that the lucrative business of entrance fees will grind to a halt, and Moscow-resident students are dismayed that the guaranteed admission offers to students from the provinces will nudge them from their former admissions advantage. In fact, the spigot of bribe money will probably not be shut down completely but simply shift in location, since the exams will be scored locally and probably by teachers that the students and their families know.

Separate and unequal

Russia is increasingly a country of contradiction. The commodity-fuelled economic prosperity of recent years has unquestionably improved the living conditions of millions of Russians. The younger generation in particular is more optimistic about their own and the country's future than at any other moment in modern times. Yet average Russian citizens, including those benefiting from the recent upturn, continue to fret about the rifts that split Russia along so many dimensions: rich versus poor, young versus old, healthy versus sick, ethnic Russians versus non-Slavs, urban versus rural, Moscow (it seems) versus everywhere else. Seemingly opposite mentalities – fatalism and apathy together with an increasingly energetic and positive outlook toward the foreseeable future – coexist, often within the same household or even within the same individual.

Perhaps this paradox is inevitable in a society that has endured so much, not only during the 1990s, but over the whole of the twentieth century. The Russians have proven to be an extraordinarily patient, tolerant and resilient people. History has taught them caution, but only in recent years are they being encouraged (indeed, forced) to fend for themselves in lieu of reliance on a paternalistic state. The final element of this withdrawal of the state – and the ultimate test of people's tolerance – may prove to be the controversial 2005 reform that replaces the bulk of Soviet-era privileges for needy groups (free or subsidised housing, transportation, medicine and the like for pensioners, students and others) with supposedly equivalent cash payments. Some analysts predict that this policy, with the cash benefit unlikely to be sufficient to cover the old handouts, will finally produce the long-feared social explosion (it has already led to demonstrations). But equally likely is more of the same, where already abused people adapt to further insult through time-tested sets of resourceful coping strategies.

In the long run, social policy and its beneficiaries will have to adapt to market conditions. This means that the old, inefficient Soviet-era social benefit structures will require, across the board, institutional restructuring that will permit talented doctors, nurses, educators, law enforcement officers and administrators to deliver services through effective, stable and routinized channels, free of perverse incentives and corruption. Putin has instituted, on paper, reforms in virtually all social sectors that appear to be reasonable steps in this direction. And if the government permits it, there are plenty of civil society organizations able and willing to fill gaps in the safety net and play a significant role in the implementation of social programmes. But Russia has become all too accustomed to phantom policies that never materialize in practice.

Whether a strong Russian state can actually craft and implement structural reform – reform that moves beyond handouts that the state never could afford – is the key to the country's ability to weather the multifaceted health, demographic and other human capital storms looming over the horizon.

Chapter 13

Foreign Policy

MARGOT LIGHT

In the first few years after Russia became independent, its foreign policy was characterized by incoherence which reduced its effectiveness, decreased its influence, and confused its citizens and its international partners. What Russian policy-makers said was different from what they did, and different officials sometimes said very different things, so that Russia seemed to have not one, but several foreign policies. Incoherence is not uncommon in the foreign policies of new states. But was Russia a new state? It was accepted as the legal heir to the Soviet Union. On the other hand, except for a brief period before the Soviet Union disintegrated, the constitution and institutions of the RSFSR had never previously performed serious foreign policy functions. Moreover, the constitution adopted in 1993 established very different institutions from those that had formerly existed. In many respects, therefore, the Russian Federation was a new state with all the associated problems of setting up institutions to deal with foreign policy, establishing how they should relate to one another and deciding what goals the state should pursue in its relations with the outside world.

It is also not unusual for the foreign policy of a country that has lost an empire to be unpredictable. But it was unclear that Russia *had* lost an empire. Russians took no responsibility for the policies of either the tsarist empire or the Soviet Union. However, there was general agreement within the country that Russia lost its identity when the Soviet Union disintegrated. Attempts to redefine Russia's identity affected the coherence of foreign policy, and so did the numerous concepts and doctrines adopted by the Russian government to define its foreign, military and security policies. Further problems emerged as a result of confusion about Russia's status in the international political system.

There was also considerable uncertainty about the nature of the post-Cold War international system. It was unclear whether the Cold War bipolar system had been replaced by unipolarity, or by a new kind of multipolarity. 'Europe' had to be redefined; did it stretch from the Atlantic to the Urals? Or from Vancouver to Vladivostok? This was not simply a geographical abstraction; it was a practical and political problem for both sides of the former bipolar divide. It also became evident that the tacit rules about international relations that had developed during the Cold War had ceased to operate. It was unclear how the 'new world order' was to be regulated. Defining the international system and working out how it was to operate also affected Russian foreign policy.

In January 1996, when Yevgenii Primakov became foreign minister, the contours of a more predictable foreign policy began to be established. Primakov had been a journalist and academic specializing in the Arab world before becoming Russia's head of foreign intelligence in the wake of the collapse of the USSR. He set about improving the coordination between institutions with foreign policy interests. Although discordant voices can still be heard, predictability and pragmatism characterize the foreign policy of President Vladimir Putin's Russia. This chapter will consider the reasons for the initial incoherence by examining the domestic context – the structure and processes of decision-making and the establishment of a new identity – of Russian foreign policy. The following two sections will explore how it was reflected in Russia's policy towards the 'near abroad' (Russian policy-makers initially used this term to refer to the other Soviet successor states) and 'far abroad' (other foreign states), and how it was gradually replaced by a more stable foreign policy. The chapter concludes with a brief consideration of how Russian foreign policy is likely to develop in the next few years.

The domestic context of Russian foreign policy

The incoherence that characterized Russian foreign policy in the first decade of independence was caused by the structural features and processes of decision-making and exacerbated by confusion about the identity of Russia and its role in the world.

Foreign policy decision-making: structures and processes

In established states foreign policy continuity results to a large extent from the bureaucratization of policy-making. What this means is that there is a well-organized and widely accepted division of responsibility with clear channels of communication between institutions and individuals. A great deal of day-to-day policy results from the application of standard operating procedures rather than being the outcome of active decision-making. None of these conditions pertained in Russia immediately after the USSR disintegrated. The division of responsibility between government institutions was unclear and often contentious, and channels of communication had yet to be established. Two further factors exacerbated the confusion over responsibility and authority and the absence of established channels of communication. The first was the character of the president, the second the nature of Russian politics itself.

The constitution that the Russian Federation inherited from the RSFSR did not specify how power was divided between the legislative bodies and the executive, and it was even more vague about the relationship between the two branches of the executive, the government ministries and the president. It gave the legislative bodies the right to determine the general framework of foreign policy, and made the president and his government, particularly the Ministry of Foreign Affairs (MFA), responsible for implementing it. The president was empowered to negotiate on behalf of the Russian Federation, and he headed the Security Council, a consultative body established in May 1992 to make recommendations about internal and external security matters. There was a great deal of confusion, however, about who communicated to whom and whose views had precedence.

The 1993 constitution redistributed foreign policy power in favour of the executive, making the president responsible for determining the basic guidelines of policy, representing Russia abroad, appointing diplomats and Security Council members, and conducting international negotiations. International treaties had to be ratified by the Duma and the Federation Council, and the Duma was given the right to scrutinize foreign policy, while the Federation Council was accorded jurisdiction over the use of Russian troops abroad. However, the new constitution did not clarify how authority was to be divided between the MFA and the president, and it encouraged a proliferation of administrative structures serving the president. In 1995 the power ministers, including the ministers of foreign affairs and defence, were made directly subordinate to the president.

The confusion about responsibility and authority and the absence of established channels of communication explains some of the incoherence in Russian foreign policy. But the situation was exacerbated by the personality of the president and his management style. President Boris Yeltsin appointed a number of aides and advisers who often made statements and travelled abroad on his behalf, rarely coordinating their activities with either the Security Council or the MFA. Moreover, the president was prone to making impromptu policy announcements that took his own staff, his government and his interlocutors by surprise. On numerous occasions, foreign policy officials were forced to reinterpret what the president had said or to insist that his audience had misunderstood him. Before the position was abolished at the end of 1993, Vice President Rutskoi was also prone to making foreign policy statements that contradicted the president's view, while Ministry of Defence statements sometimes appeared to challenge official policy. Malcolm points out that 'the part played by different institutions [was] dependent much less on constitutional provisions . . . than . . . on shifts of power and allegiance among the individuals and groups participating in a fierce and at times violent political struggle' (Malcolm *et al.* 1996: 129).

President Yeltsin's management style included playing advisers and institutions off against one another. Moreover, he thought nothing of dressing down his ministers, including the foreign minister, in public. He was usually playing to a domestic audience, forgetting that he was also visible abroad. This undermined the status of the foreign minister at home and made him a far less credible interlocutor with foreign governments. It also weakened the authority of the MFA and made it difficult for it to coordinate policy. When Primakov replaced Andrei Kozyrev as foreign minister in 1996 the status of the MFA rose (for a list of foreign ministers to date see Table 13.1). Primakov also improved the level of cooperation between the various institutions that dealt with foreign policy. Nevertheless, coordination remained an intermittent problem, and it still occasionally undermines the coherence of Russian foreign policy.

The second factor that aggravated the incoherence was the conflictual nature of politics in Russia. The conflict was, in part, a struggle for power (between institutions as well as individuals), but it also reflected a dispute over the kind of economy Russia should have, and the distribution and timing of the costs and pain of reform. It affected all aspects of policy-making and it politicized foreign policy, turning it into an arena in which wider political struggles took place. Parliament wanted to exercise influence over foreign policy and to make the executive accountable. Often, however, its primary purpose was to oppose the president, and it used foreign policy as one of its instruments. The general atmosphere was one of confrontation and, as a result, president and government dismissed parliamentary criticism as illegitimate and hostile. At times the Supreme Soviet, and later the Duma, seemed to have its own, separate foreign policy. So, often, did the military, and neither of these policies had much

Table 13.1   *Russian foreign ministers, 1990–2004*

Appointed by	Name	Dates of appointment
President Yeltsin	Andrei Kozyrev	June 1990 (as foreign minister of RSFSR) to January 1996
	Yevgenii Primakov	January 1996 to September 1998, when he was appointed prime minister
	Igor Ivanov	September 1998 to March 2004
President Putin	Sergei Lavrov	March 2004 to present

in common with the policies of the president and the MFA. In 1993 the political confrontation ended in the dissolution of the Supreme Soviet and the adoption of a new constitution.

The 1993 constitution did not reduce the political conflict (or, at least, not until Putin replaced Yeltsin as president in 2000). Duma deputies soon began to use foreign policy debates as much to express general opposition to the government and the president as to influence policy. More seriously, they frequently adopted resolutions that appeared to contradict Russia's official foreign policy. They also postponed ratifying treaties, often simply to mark their disapproval of the executive but sometimes because they hoped to change government policy. They did not often succeed since the Duma's tendency to turn foreign policy into an area of confrontation undermined its influence on policy. The problem for Russia's foreign partners, however, was to work out whose policy was likely to prevail. In other words, even though the Duma undermined its own impact, it contributed to the incoherence of Russian foreign policy (the more important agencies involved in foreign policy formulation in the different branches of government are set out in Table 13.2).

Identity and concepts

In addition to these structural, personal and political factors, confusion also arose from uncertainty about the identity of Russia and what its foreign policy should be. The identity of Russia and the idea of Russian statehood have always been closely associated with the existence of an empire. Most Russians found it difficult to accept that some areas of the USSR were no longer part of Russia. It was not just a question of nostalgia for past greatness, though that too played a part in making Russian foreign policy erratic. The loss of the empire led to confusion about Russia's role in the world. The establishment of new, independent states on Russia's western border separating Russia from the rest of Europe revived an old debate: was Russia part of Europe, or had the loss of empire turned it into an Asian or Eurasian power? Some believed that, since Europe represented progress and prosperity, Russia must be European despite the distance that now separated it from the rest of the continent. Others claimed a unique Eurasian role for Russia, bridging Europe and Asia.

The loss of the empire also raised the question of Russia's status in the international system. Russia had inherited the Soviet Union's international treaty obligations, and took over its seat on the United Nations Security Council and its diplomatic institutions and nuclear capabilities. To all intents and purposes, therefore, Russia inherited its international status. But it had few of the traditional attributes of power: its economy

Table 13.2   *The Russian foreign policy decision-making process*

President's Office	Government	Legislature
President	Ministry of Foreign Affairs	State Duma Committee for International Affairs
President's Aide for Foreign Policy and International Relations	Ministry of Defence	State Duma Committee for Defence
President's Aide for Issues of the Development of Relations with the European Union	Ministry of Economics and Trade	State Duma Committee for Security
Presidential Directorate on Foreign Policy	Federal Security Service (FSB)	State Duma Committee for CIS Affairs and relations with Compatriots
Security Council	Foreign Intelligence Service	Council of Federation Foreign Affairs Committee
Presidential Commission for Military Technology Cooperation of the Russian Federation with Foreign States	Various coordinating committees	Council of Federation Committee on Defence and Security
State Council		Council of Federation Committee on the Commonwealth of Independent States

was close to collapse, it did not have an extensive sphere of influence and, although still vast, it was far smaller than the USSR. Russia was clearly not a superpower; indeed, it was questionable whether it could be considered a great power. Yet to ordinary people as well as politicians, it was unthinkable that Russia could be anything less than a great power. The insistence that Russia should be accorded the respect due to a great power became an important rhetorical theme in statements and discussions about foreign policy. However, the mismatch between the perception of great power status and the reality of Russia's declining power contributed to the incoherence of foreign policy.

Many intellectuals believed that Russia's identity could be established by defining the principles of its foreign policy. They demanded that the government should provide a framework for its foreign policy in the form of a doctrine or concept. By April 1993 when the first foreign policy concept was adopted, a broad consensus had been reached about Russia's status and its foreign policy priorities. The concept portrayed a far less benign view about Russia's external environment than the rather idealistic and uncritically pro-Western policy Russia was pursuing at that time. It asserted a prominent international role for Russia, particularly in the 'near abroad', and criticized attempts to squeeze Russia out of foreign markets and to turn it into a supplier of energy and raw materials. While it did not express aggression towards the outside world, it revealed considerable suspicion of Western intentions towards Russia. The first military doctrine, adopted in October 1993, adopted a harsher stance about Russia's national interests than the foreign policy concept.

The view of Russia's place in the world expressed in the foreign policy concept and military doctrine did not serve to make Russian foreign policy more coherent. For one thing, the disparate foreign policy views expressed by the legislature, the military and various presidential spokesmen did not reflect the contents of either document. Nor was it easy to relate the practice of Russian policy to the priorities expressed in the documents. Moreover, a series of subsequent official doctrines and concepts caused confusion. A national security concept was adopted in December 1997, for example, only to be replaced by a new one in January 2000. A new military doctrine was formulated in April 2000, while the President ratified a new foreign policy concept in June 2000 (the texts of all three documents can be found at http://www.ln.mid.ru/ns-osndoc.nsf/osndd). These later doctrines were responses to perceived changes in Russia's internal and external environment, but what alarmed Russia's foreign partners was that they seemed to indicate a significant hardening of Russian foreign policy. The feature of the 2000 national security concept that aroused most anxiety outside Russia was that it envisaged looser conditions under which Russia might resort to nuclear weapons. For Russians themselves, the most important feature of the new national security concept and the military doctrine is that they envisage the use of military force inside the country, retroactively legitimizing army action in Chechnya.

Western policy-makers were confused. They could understand the external factors that made Russians feel more vulnerable, although they disagreed that they represented a threat to Russian security. But what was striking about the new concepts and doctrines was that they defined domestic problems as far more threatening to Russian security than external factors. The 2000 national security concept, for example, identifies the critical state of the economy as a potential cause of separatist aspirations and, therefore, a serious threat to Russia's federal structure.

The criminalization of Russian society and the lack of a rule-based state are also acknowledged to be factors that might undermine Russian security.

These domestic threats had nothing to with foreign countries, so Western policy-makers could not understand why the Russian government had responded with a more assertive foreign policy stance. In fact, popular perceptions hold the West responsible for Russia's economic failures and there are officials who agree with this interpretation. The new doctrines also emphasize the danger of terrorism and they link internal threats of terrorism and separatism to external efforts to undermine Russia's sovereignty and territorial integrity. If domestic threats are perceived to have external causes, there is a logic to the more assertive foreign policy stance that emerges in the new doctrines and concepts. Russia is by no means unique in blaming intractable domestic problems on external factors, but it is unusual in adopting so many concepts and doctrines in which this becomes apparent.

The uncertainty about whether Russia is a new state beset with problems or simply a smaller version of the Soviet Union contributed to confusion about Russia's status in the international political system. With regard to its immediate neighbours, the Russian leadership did not always appear to accept the sovereignty and independence of the other successor states. This provoked accusations of neo-imperialism, although the origin of the problem probably lay in the absence of any experience of treating them as foreign states. As far as the sovereignty and independence of Russia itself were concerned, the concepts and doctrines were adamant that other foreign states and international organizations had no business interfering in Russia's domestic affairs. In relation to the major industrial nations represented in the Group of Seven (G7) in particular, Russian leaders invariably insisted that Russia is a great power and should be treated as a great power. There seemed to be nostalgia for the respect that the Soviet Union enjoyed in the past. The problem was that the insistence on great-power status frequently alternated with demands for economic assistance, and the combination of being a supplicant for aid while wanting to be accepted as a great power, together with a tendency to indulge in 'declaratory' politics, made Russian foreign policy seem very inconsistent.

With time, the structural problems began to improve: the relationship between the various ministries with foreign policy interests was gradually sorted out, cooperation between the different branches of the state improved, and channels of communication became established and accepted. The status of the MFA rose when Primakov became foreign minister and the confrontation between the legislature and executive abated after the 1999 parliamentary elections. Most importantly, the personality features associated with President Yeltsin which affected the coherence of foreign policy are no longer a factor. President Putin's background, history and personality are very different from those of his predecessor. He has a better relationship with his ministers and with the Duma and a very different management and foreign policy style. Although he believes in a strong state, and is a more overt nationalist (though he calls it patriotism) than Yeltsin and is even more insistent about Russia's great-power credentials, he is realistic about the state of Russia's economy and he recognizes the relationship between the economy and international power. Moreover, he appears to be aware of the inconsistencies in Russian foreign policy and the harm it does to Russia's national interest. Indeed, the new foreign policy concept promises a consistent and predictable foreign policy, which is based on 'a reasonable balance between objectives and possibilities for attaining these objectives'.

Pragmatism is the recurring theme of the foreign policy statements of Putin and his government. Foreign minister Igor Ivanov, for example, claimed that 'Russian diplomacy has always won when guided by realistic, pragmatic considerations' (Ivanov 2001: 8). In his 2002 address to the Federal Assembly, Putin declared that 'Russia's foreign policy will continue in the future to be purely pragmatic, based on our possibilities and national interests'. When Sergei Lavrov was appointed Russian foreign minister in March 2004, he announced that 'Russia will display flexibility and readiness to compromise in the work for its national interests' (ITAR-TASS, 17 March 2004).

Russian policy towards the 'near abroad'

The mismatch between what policy-makers say and what they do has been particularly striking with regard to Russia's relations with its immediate neighbours. Strengthening relations with the countries of the Commonwealth of Independent States (CIS) is listed, in the doctrines and concepts as well as in speeches, as 'an unconditional foreign policy priority' (Press release, Russian President Putin's State of the Nation Address to the Federal Assembly, 16 May 2003). In practice, however, Russia has appeared reluctant to translate rhetoric into policy.

Russia and multilateral relations in the CIS

The CIS was established in December 1991 and by the end of 1993 it consisted of all the successor states except the Baltic republics. An elaborate institutional structure was set up to further 'the development and strengthening of relations of friendship, good neighbourliness, inter-ethnic accord, trust and mutual understanding and cooperation' between its members (Preamble, Charter of the Commonwealth of Independent States, 1993). However, few of these aims have been realized.

One reason why the CIS has had limited success in integrating its members is that it does not have supranational powers. It operates on the basis of consensus, permitting any member to opt out of a decision to which it objects. A second reason is that, in size and military and economic power, Russia is by far the largest member. Consequently, even the most enthusiastic participants fear Russian hegemony. Russian policy-makers fuel their anxiety by asserting that protecting the 25 million ethnic Russians and Russian-speakers who live in the other successor states is a vital national interest. Although these declarations have not been translated into active policy, they suggest that Russia might intervene in the affairs of its neighbours. A third reason is that the variable pace at which the successor states have reformed their economies makes integration very difficult. But Russian ambivalence has been the main obstruction. Although Russian policy-makers frequently support integration verbally, they have done little to promote it.

A succession of vehicles for integration have been created, starting with an economic union in 1993 (Ukraine did not join but became an associate member in 1994), a free trade area in 1994 (ratified by all members except Russia), and a Belarus–Kazakhstan–Russia customs union in 1995, renamed the free trade zone in 1996. It became the Eurasian Economic Community (EURASEC) in 2000, with Belarus, Kazakhstan, Kyrgyzstan, Russia and Tajikistan as full members, Moldova, Ukraine and Armenia obtaining observer status in 2002–03. None of these agreements has resulted in a functioning free trade regime or customs union, however, primarily because of Russia's insistence on a long list of exclusions and quotas.

Russia has been more active in organizing the collective defence of the CIS, but here too the unified military force that was initially envisaged has never been formed. A Collective Security Treaty was signed in Tashkent in 1992 by Russia, Belarus and Armenia. Moldova, Ukraine and Turkmenistan acceded to it in 1993, but effectively seceded when the treaty was renewed in 1999. Five of the six signatories agreed to establish joint peacekeeping forces; in effect, however, CIS peacekeeping forces are primarily Russian, and this raises suspicion that Russia uses them for neo-imperialist purposes. A treaty providing for the collective defence of the Commonwealth's external borders was concluded in May 1995, but Azerbaijan, Moldova, Turkmenistan, Ukraine and Uzbekistan did not accede to it or to the treaty establishing a common air defence system in February 1996 (by 1998, however, Turkmenistan, Ukraine and Uzbekistan had joined the latter).

The existence of a number of parallel multilateral regional organizations suggests that Russian policy-makers are not alone in being ambivalent about the CIS. The Central Asian states, for example, are members of the Central Asian Cooperation Organization, of the Economic Cooperation Organization (Azerbaijan is also a member) and also, with the exception of Turkmenistan, of the Shanghai Cooperation Organization (which includes Russia and the People's Republic of China). The Organization of the Black Sea Economic Cooperation consists of the littoral states, as well as Armenia and Azerbaijan. In 1997 the four countries that have been most resistant to closer CIS integration, Azerbaijan, Georgia, Moldova and Ukraine (joined in 1999 by Uzbekistan), established GUUAM as a counterweight to Russia's perceived hegemonic ambitions in the post-Soviet space.

President Putin has somewhat reduced the gap between Russia's rhetoric about integration and its policy. On his initiative, for example, the six original Tashkent treaty members formed a rapid reaction force in May 2001, primarily to deal with incursions into Central Asia by Islamic militants. All CIS members with the exception of Turkmenistan also established an Anti-Terrorist Centre, which opened in Bishkek in September that year. In 2002 the Tashkent treaty was upgraded to the Collective Security Treaty Organization (CSTO). In September 2003, again in response to a Russian proposal, the presidents of Russia, Belarus, Ukraine and Kazakhstan agreed to form a single economic space, which was envisaged to progress in three stages, from a free trade regime to a customs union, and finally to a single economic space in 2007 with freedom of movement for services, capital and workforce (*Russia Journal*, 19 September 2003). According to Trenin (2004), 'operation CIS' will be a major objective of Putin's second term.

Russia's bilateral relations with the successor states

Russia has been far more active in advancing its bilateral relations in the near abroad than in promoting multilateral integration within the CIS. Given the dependence of the former Soviet states on Russian energy, achieving economic influence by forgiving debts in return for shares in local businesses has proved a more cost-effective way of fulfilling Russia's economic and political aims than investing in multilateral integration. Separate, bilateral agreements on border control and bases have, by and large, satisfied Russia's security aims, providing it with the means to defend itself at the external borders of the former USSR.

Russia's most difficult bilateral relations have been with Latvia, Estonia and Ukraine. The status of the very large Russian minorities in Latvia (34 per cent) and Estonia (30 per cent) has been a cause of constant tension. Despite threats to keep Russian troops in the two countries in protest at the treatment of Russian minorities, however, their withdrawal was completed on schedule in 1994. The Russian government continues to complain regularly about the infringement of human rights in the two countries but it maintains normal diplomatic relations with both of them.

Most Russians perceived the loss of Ukraine, and of the Crimea to Ukraine, as a grievous blow. Moreover, Ukraine is the most reluctant member of the CIS, the most apprehensive about Russian hegemony and an increasingly important partner to Western countries. Not surprisingly, therefore, Russian–Ukrainian relations have sometimes been difficult. The most contentious issue – the division of the Black Sea fleet and the location and status of naval bases for the Russian fleet – was resolved in May 1997. Other difficulties remained, however, including heavy debts incurred by Ukraine to Russia for its energy supplies and the division of the Azov Sea. In November 1999 President Kuchma proclaimed Ukraine's 'European choice' (the aspiration to join the European Union and cooperate closely with NATO), and appeared to be distancing Ukraine from Russia and the CIS. However, after a domestic political crisis in 2001, Ukrainian policy shifted towards Russia and Kuchma's agreement to join the single economic space in 2003 appeared to confirm the shift.

Russia's closest relationship in the near abroad has been with Belarus. In 1996, the two presidents declared that Russia and Belarus would establish a Community of Sovereign Republics. A year later the Community was converted into a Union of Sovereign Republics and in 1999 a confederal Russian–Belarusian state was proclaimed, with an elaborate institutional structure (a Higher State Council, a Council of Ministers, a bicameral parliament, a Supreme Court and an Accounting Chamber). Since Belarus has adopted few economic and political reforms, however, and since the harmonization of the two countries' legal and economic systems is a prerequisite to the formation of a confederal state, there has been little real progress in implementing the Union.

President Putin has shown little enthusiasm for the Russia–Belarus Union. Indeed, rather than a confederation, he appears to favour a unified federal state in which Belarus would, in effect, be incorporated into the Russian Federation. This is unacceptable to President Lukashenko.

Russia and internal and interstate conflicts in the CIS

When the USSR disintegrated in 1991, three violent conflicts were already taking place in the South Caucasus, and three more soon erupted on

Russia's periphery in Tajikistan, Georgia and Moldova. Perceived as a threat to Russian security, Russia became involved both in peacekeeping (either on its own behalf or as part of CIS forces) and in attempting to mediate between the conflicting parties. Russian policy-makers claimed that Russia has a duty to ensure security in the post-Soviet space and demanded that the UN and other international organizations should recognize this responsibility. This was hotly disputed in the successor states, and Russia was accused of using or instigating the conflicts to further its neo-imperialist goals. Some of the conflicts did, indeed, prove useful (Georgia, for example, was persuaded to join the CIS when Russian help was required to bring the Georgian–Abkhazian conflict to an end). But it was also the case that there was no credible alternative peacekeeper, since the UN was unlikely to intervene in any part of the former USSR, and the Organization for Security and Cooperation in Europe (OSCE), while active in mediating conflicts, does not have peacekeeping troops at its disposal.

In Tajikistan the dispute was essentially a conflict between rival clans for political power, but when refugees and forces supporting the defeated clan fled into Afghanistan and began to organize armed incursions across the border, the spectre was raised of another Afghan war. Russian border troops were rushed in to seal the border and the Russian army, together with small contingents from Kazakhstan, Kyrgyzstan and Uzbekistan, began to monitor the ceasefire agreements that were reached. The Russian government also helped to mediate a peace agreement in May 1997. This did not completely eliminate the violence and, following an Islamist insurgency in 1999 that initially targeted Kyrgyzstan (Uzbekistan was the ultimate goal), there was little pressure on Russia from the Central Asian governments to withdraw its troops. However, Russia no longer exercises sole influence in Central Asia; in 2001 Kyrgyzstan, Tajikistan and Uzbekistan granted the USA and its allies access to their bases for the 'war on terrorism' in Afghanistan. In November 2003 Russia opened an air force base in Kant in Kyrgyzstan, just a few kilometres from the Ganci air base (at Manas International Airport) of the US-led coalition forces.

The conflicts in the South Caucasus were over the right of minorities to self-determination, which erupted when the central governments reduced the degree of autonomy the disputed areas had enjoyed under the Soviet constitution. In Nagorno-Karabakh, a predominantly Armenian enclave within Azerbaijan that had requested a transfer from Azerbaijani to Armenian jurisdiction in 1988, the conflict escalated into a war between Armenia and Azerbaijan in which Armenia annexed the Azerbaijani territory that had previously separated Nagorno-Karabakh from Armenia itself. There has been a cease fire since 1994, but the conflict has not been resolved. A draft settlement proposed by the 'Minsk Group' of the OSCE (which includes Russia) provides for the autonomy of Nagorno-Karabakh, the return of occupied territory, and assured access from Karabakh to Armenia. However, Armenia, Azerbaijan and Nagorno-Karabakh have not been able to make the necessary compromises to finalize a settlement.

There were three separate conflicts in Georgia. The first, essentially a struggle for political power, began before the USSR disintegrated and ended when Eduard Shevardnadze, previously first secretary of the Georgian Communist Party and then Soviet minister of foreign affairs, returned to become president of Georgia in March 1992. The other two were secessionist conflicts between the central Georgian government and South Ossetia and Abkhazia. In South Ossetia a cease fire was agreed after two years of sporadic fighting, which is policed by Georgian, Russian and South Ossetian troops. OSCE attempts to mediate have stalled because a mutually acceptable compromise on South Ossetia's status has not been found. When Mikhail Saakashvili became president of Georgia in January 2004, he pledged to restore Georgia's territorial integrity. Relations between Georgia and South Ossetia, and between Russia and Georgia, deteriorated and they remain tense.

Russia intervened far more directly in the conflict between Georgia and the Autonomous Republic of Abkhazia. By September 1993 Georgian troops (and the ethnic Georgian population of Abkhazia) had been evicted from Abkhazia and the Georgian state seemed on the brink of collapse. Under CIS auspices and with some UN cooperation, Russia peacekeeping forces intervened and Russia has also been involved in trying to reach a political settlement. As in South Ossetia and Nagorno-Karabakh, however, negotiations have reached an impasse over Abkhazia's future status. Georgia and Russia have been in intermittent dispute about the presence of Russian peacekeepers, the difficulty of returning Georgian refugees to Abkhazia, and Russia's delay in implementing an undertaking given at the OSCE summit in 1999 that it would withdraw from its remaining military bases in Georgia. The Russian government also accuses Georgia of harbouring Chechen terrorists in the Pankisi Gorge region. In 2002 the USA sent military advisers to train Georgian forces to conduct anti-terrorist operations. In the South Caucasus, therefore, as in Central Asia, Russia no longer exercises uncontested hegemony.

Russia was also directly involved in the conflict that erupted in the Moldovan region of Transdniestria in 1992 when the majority ethnic Russian population declared its independence as the 'Dnestr Republic'. Soldiers stationed in the area, from the Russian 14th Army, were accused of fighting with the separatists. When a ceasefire was agreed in June 1992,

Russian troops were entrusted with keeping the peace. Protracted negotiations have failed to resolve the issue of Transdniestria's future status. In 2002 the OSCE proposed a federative solution, guaranteed by Russia, Ukraine and the OSCE and monitored by OSCE peacekeeping troops. The Moldovan government appeared to be prepared to accept the proposal, but Transdniestria continued to insist on a confederation. Here, too, Russia has not fulfilled its undertaking to the OSCE to withdraw its military equipment from Transdniestria.

Russia has, of course, also been involved in a secessionist conflict of its own in Chechnya. The Russian government's insistence that it is a domestic conflict and that external intervention would infringe Russia's sovereignty has, by and large, been accepted in the international system. Nevertheless, the 1994–96 war had profound consequences for post-Cold War international relations. First, it made the Russian government more wary of supporting separatist movements in the near abroad. Second, it increased the anxiety within other successor states that Russia might use force to reinstate the USSR. Third, it enhanced an already widely held perception that Russia had become more belligerent. As a result, the governments of the former socialist Central and East European countries petitioned more zealously for early membership of NATO, and were met with a more sympathetic response. The ferocity of the second war, which began in 1999, and Russia's apparent disregard for human rights in Chechnya, exacerbated the perception that Russia had become aggressive. In 2001 international criticism of Russian policy in Chechnya subsided for a while in the interests of ensuring Russian cooperation in the war on terrorism. However, Russia's relations with its neighbours and with the wider world are deeply affected by its policy in Chechnya.

Russian policy towards the 'far abroad'

The contradiction between the insistence that Russia is a great power and should be treated with the respect that status warrants, and Russia's need, in the early years particularly, for economic assistance, together with a tendency to indulge in 'declaratory' politics, contributed to the incoherence in Russia's policy towards the 'far abroad', above all towards the United States and Europe. West European governments and Presidents Bush Senior and Clinton were aware of Russian sensibilities and careful not to reject the claim to great-power status. However, strains began to appear in Russian–Western relations when Russian leaders, disappointed that its initial orientation to the West did not bring the expected benefits, began to revive relations with some former Soviet allies. At the same time, Western countries, having initially concentrated on Russia, turned their attention to the other successor states, arousing anxiety in Russia that foreign powers would make inroads into an area which they regarded as their own sphere of influence. Although political and economic cooperation continued, a number of contentious issues created tension between Russia and Western countries, particularly the USA.

Sources of tension: arms control and NATO expansion

Russian–US relations began with a flourish, when the second Strategic Arms Reduction Treaty (START) was signed in January 1993. It envisaged each side reducing its nuclear arsenals to 3,500 warheads, as well as a 50 per cent reduction in US submarine-launched nuclear warheads and the elimination of all multiple warheads and of Russia's heavy land-based intercontinental missiles. However, the Duma postponed the ratification of START 2. In part postponement was simply an instrument in the domestic political conflict, but it also signalled the Duma's conviction that President Yeltsin was repeating the Soviet leadership's mistake in making too many concessions to the West, and its opposition to NATO expansion and to any modification of the 1972 Anti-Ballistic Missile (ABM) Treaty.

The issue of NATO expansion has been a persistent irritant in Russian–Western relations. The Russian government was happy to join the North Atlantic Cooperation Council (NACC, succeeded in 1997 by the Euro-Atlantic Partnership Council), established as a forum for consultation and cooperation between NATO and the former socialist countries. It was much less happy about joining NATO's 'Partnership for Peace' (PfP) in 1994, demanding special terms in its PfP agreement that would reflect Russia's great-power status. The inclusion of former socialist states in NATO was anathema to Russians and expansion was perceived as a threat to Russian security. Russia–NATO relations were formalized in 1997 by the adoption of the Founding Act on Mutual Relations, Cooperation and Security between the Russian Federation and the North Atlantic Treaty Organization. Russian objections to NATO expansion did not abate, but despite their protests, the Czech Republic, Hungary and Poland joined NATO in 1999. At the same time, NATO announced an 'open door' policy to membership by other countries and adopted a new strategic doctrine, which envisaged the alliance undertaking military operations in non-NATO countries when necessary. Since NATO had already launched an attack on Serbia, Russians perceived the doctrine as a direct threat to Russian security. Cooperation in the NATO–Russian Permanent Joint Council set up by the Founding Act was suspended and official public statements on foreign policy were fiercely critical of NATO.

Apart from the issue of NATO enlargement (blamed almost entirely on the USA), Russian–US relations were affected by a disagreement about the 1972 ABM treaty, which limits Russia and the United States to one anti-missile system each. The USA wanted to modify or abrogate the treaty and to develop a national or ballistic missile defence (NMD or BMD) system. The Russian government was adamantly opposed to any modification of the ABM treaty, believing (as did many European governments) that it was the foundation of the strategic deterrence that had kept the world safe from nuclear war. They also believed that the deployment of even a limited US NMD system would undermine Russian deterrent capabilities (Pikayev 2000).

The Conventional Forces in Europe (CFE) treaty, which had marked the end of the Cold War in 1990, also fell victim to increasing tensions in Russian–Western relations. When the USSR disintegrated, the conventional forces permitted it by the CFE agreement had to be divided between the European successor states. By then, however, the Russian government believed that the forces it was permitted on its southern flank were inadequate to deal with the security threats arising from the conflicts on its periphery. NATO members were reluctant to renegotiate the treaty and the Russian leadership interpreted their reluctance as a refusal to recognize Russia's legitimate security interests. The issue had still not been resolved by November 1995, the deadline for full compliance with the treaty. By then Russians had good grounds for arguing that deploying conventional arms on the territory of an enlarged NATO would contravene CFE. NATO became more flexible about renegotiating the terms and a new CFE agreement was adopted at the OSCE summit in November 1999.

Political and economic relations

The decision to expand NATO and the argument about the ABM treaty convinced many Russians that the USA wanted to undermine Russian security. Since American advisers had played a prominent role in dictating Russia's economic reform, the USA was also blamed for the hardships it produced, and the corruption that accompanied it. Other issues began to affect Russian–US relations, for example US objections to Russian arms sales, and Russian opposition to US policy in the Balkans and towards Iraq. The Gore–Chernomyrdin Commission which presided over US–Russian economic relations continued to operate, but Russians became increasingly bitter about the 'unipolarity' which they believed the United States wanted to impose upon the international system.

Well before the USA and its allies acquired bases in Central Asia for the 'war on terrorism', Caspian Sea energy resources and the route by which they reached world markets had become a contentious issue in Russian foreign policy. Russia controlled the pipelines through which the oil and gas were exported and the Russian government was determined both to ensure that it had a major share of Caspian assets and to retain the leverage controlling the pipelines gave it over Azerbaijan, Kazakhstan and Turkmenistan, the other former Soviet littoral states. The multinational oil companies involved in extracting the resources and the countries in which their headquarters are based, particularly the USA, were equally determined to diversify the transport routes. The other littoral states wanted to reduce Russia's leverage, while surrounding countries like Georgia were keen to provide lucrative transit facilities. To US delight and Russian displeasure, a legal framework was agreed in 1999 for the construction of a pipeline from Baku, in Azerbaijan, via Tbilisi, in Georgia, to the Turkish Mediterranean terminal at Ceyhan.

Russians had far more benign perceptions of Europe than of the USA, and Russian–European multilateral and bilateral relations were not affected by NATO expansion or the CFE difficulties. Like NATO, the European Union (EU) also planned to enlarge. It tried to ensure that Russia was not sidelined by the process, concluding a Partnership and Cooperation Agreement (PCA) with the Russian Federation in June 1994 which aimed to develop closer political links, foster trade and investment, and support economic and political reform. When the PCA came into force in December 1997, it created a dense network of permanent institutions and political consultations between the EU and Russia, including regular six-monthly EU–Russia summits. The EU was already a major aid donor to Russia and in 1999 the EU adopted a Common Strategy on Russia, which committed EU members to cooperate on policy towards Russia.

Russian–EU relations have not been completely free of conflict. EU members were appalled by Russian policy towards Chechnya, and Russians, in turn, were offended by EU criticism of what was, in their view, a domestic matter. As enlargement approached, Russians became increasingly apprehensive about the effects on cross-border movement between Russia and the accession countries. Movement between Kaliningrad, which would become an exclave in the EU, and the rest of Russia was a particularly contentious issue, and there were also concerns about possible adverse consequences for Russian–East European trade. Nevertheless, the EU is extremely important to Russia: it is Russia's main trading partner, accounting for more than 50 per cent of its export trade. And, since Russia was the EU's fifth largest trading partner in 2003, both sides retain a commitment to develop the relationship, despite the tensions that arise in the relationship.

Russian policy-makers developed good bilateral relations with

European states, in particular with Germany and France. They also began to revive relations with former Soviet partners such as Cuba, North Korea and Iraq, and to improve relations with the People's Republic of China, Japan, India and Iran. The diversification of Russia's foreign policy did not, however, create the multipolarity the Russians had hoped would counter US unipolarity.

President Putin and the 'far abroad'

On the face of it, President Putin's relationship with the USA has been no more successful than that of President Yeltsin. Although he persuaded the Duma to ratify START 2 in April 2000, President Bush was determined to develop an NMD system and in December 2001 he announced his intention unilaterally to withdraw from the ABM treaty. Putin responded by declaring Russia's withdrawal from START 2, but this was a largely symbolic gesture. In May 2002 a new US–Russian strategic arms limitation treaty was concluded, limiting each side to a nuclear arsenal of 1,700–2,200 warheads, but Putin did not manage to prevent a second round of NATO expansion. Despite fierce Russian opposition, the Baltic states were admitted to NATO together with Slovakia, Slovenia, Bulgaria and Romania in May 2004.

Nor has Putin produced markedly better results in diversifying Russian foreign policy. The high point of Russia's rapprochement with China was reached with a Friendship and Cooperation Treaty in July 2001, but this has not provided a counterbalance to US predominance. The niche he identified for Russia as an intermediary between pariah states and the international political system was demolished by President Bush's denouncement of Iran, Iraq and North Korea as the 'axis of evil' in January 2002.

In fact, however, Putin has also presided over a marked improvement in Russian–Western relations and has raised Russia's international stature. Following the terrorist attacks on the World Trade Center and the Pentagon on 11 September 2001, he supported the US-led coalition against international terrorism, and Russian–US relations improved. In May 2002 Russia and the nineteen NATO member countries signed the Rome Declaration, establishing a NATO–Russia Council to replace the Permanent Joint Council. Russia has an equal voice in the NATO–Russia Council on issues such as combating international terrorism, peace-keeping, civil emergency planning, defence modernization and preventing the proliferation of weapons of mass destruction. In 2002, Putin achieved a long-standing Russian ambition, when Russia became a full member of the G7, turning it into the G8.

These successes do not mean that there are no disputes in Russia's relations with the West. Putin (together with President Chirac and Chancellor Schroeder) strongly objected to the war against Iraq in 2003, for example. But having protested robustly about events of which they disapprove or which they believe undermine Russian security, once they occurred, Russian officials now temper their comments. Consequently Russian foreign policy is more realistic and pragmatic. Putin appears to have achieved the 'reasonable balance between objectives and possibilities for attaining these objectives' which the 2000 foreign policy concept calls for.

Conclusion

By 2004, many of the inconsistencies and discordant voices in Russian foreign policy had disappeared. The CIS had survived, and there were signs that Russia had become less ambivalent about the costs of further integration. It is an open question whether the new CIS institutions established under Putin's initiative will be more effective in advancing integration than the existing institutions. Moreover, it is clear that the CIS is unlikely to become a credible counterpart to the EU and/or NATO in the foreseeable future.

Whether or not the USA retains its presence in Central Asia and the Caucasus, Russia will continue to identify the other successor states as areas of vital interest. Russian leaders will not be able to be indifferent to the fate of diaspora Russians, and the threat of international terrorism will continue to enhance the perception that Russia can only be defended by protecting the external borders of the former USSR. As long as there are conflicts in the 'near abroad', the conviction that the integrity of the Russian Federation is under threat will remain. Moreover, Russia's economic and strategic interests in the Caspian Sea will continue as long as there are resources to be extracted.

In Russia's relations with the 'far abroad', the optimism of the immediate post-Cold War period about Russian–Western relations will not be recaptured. Russia will continue to develop a multi-vector policy, but Putin, a realist, recognizes that Russia's status in the international system benefits from cooperation with the West. This does not mean that Russia will necessarily approve of Western policies, and nor will Western leaders necessarily support Russian policies. There are a number of contentious issues that are likely to put the relationship under strain, perhaps particularly Russia's policy towards Chechnya and the domestic changes that have recently been proposed to counter the threat of terrorism.

Chapter 14

The Democratization of Russia in Comparative Perspective

ZVI GITELMAN

Contrary to what most residents of English-speaking countries might assume, democracy has not been and is not now the 'normal' form of government. Democracy made its first appearance in the modern world only a little over two hundred years ago when first the American and then the French revolutions inaugurated it. A look at a map of today's world shows that democracy is the dominant form of government in the twentieth and twenty-first centuries only in North America and Western Europe, Oceania, India, Israel, but in very few countries in Asia, Africa and Latin America. According to Samuel Huntington (1991), in 1990 about two-thirds of the countries of the world did not have democratic regimes. Beginning in the mid-1970s, as Huntington sees it, a 'third wave' of democratization has swept over southern and Eastern Europe as well as Latin America. (The first two 'waves' were in 1828–1926 in Europe and the United States, and in 1943–62 in Europe, East Asia and parts of Latin America.) Nevertheless, despite the collapse of authoritarian communist regimes the proportion of democracies has not grown appreciably. It remains true that across both time and space, democracy has been the exceptional form of government rather than the rule.

Democracy, like other forms of government, should not be seen as an absolute, but as a spectrum. Political systems are not easily classified as either democratic or non-democratic. There are more and less democratic political systems and organizations, and the same system may vary over time in the extent to which it is democratic. For example, the gradual expansion of the franchise in England in the mid-nineteenth century, granting women the right to vote in the United States after the First World War and the passage of the Civil Rights Act of 1964 granting African-Americans full legal equality and protection of the law moved those countries toward the more democratic end of the spectrum.

The idea that democratic forms of government are expandable and retractable is crucial for our discussion of Russia or any other postcommunist country. Especially after only a little more than a decade of post-communist political life, preceded by seven decades of communism and centuries of tsarist autocracy, the proper question is not so much whether Russia *is* democratic or not, but whether it is *becoming* more or less democratic. There has been considerable debate over whether the Russian Federation has evolved into a democratic state. When the communist regimes of the Soviet Union and Eastern Europe collapsed in 1989–91, many in the West made the facile assumption that democratic systems would replace them, as if there were no alternatives to communism other than democracy. In hindsight, we realize that no single type of system has replaced communism and that the formerly communist states in Eastern Europe and the territories of the former Soviet Union range from those that seem fully democratic to the distinctly undemocratic. Some have been admitted to the European Union, while others seem to be a way off from meeting the criteria for admission, which include commitments to democratic practices as defined by the Union's members. One scholar maintains that while 28 states have abandoned communism, only nine have become liberal democracies (McFaul 2002).What explains why some postcommunist states have moved considerable distances toward democracy (Poland, Hungary, the Baltic States and most recently Georgia as well as others) while other countries (Azerbaijan, Belarus, Romania, the Central Asian republics) have not, and still others have moved only hesitantly in this direction (Moldova, Albania, Armenia)? What, after all, is democracy? How and why among a group of states, all of which started from the same communist base, do some appear to be democracies today and others do not?

What is democracy?

Democracy is a system of government that meets three essential conditions: (i) meaningful, extensive and non-violent competition for power at predictable intervals; (ii) the opportunity for all to participate in politics; (iii) civil and political liberties 'sufficient to ensure the integrity of political competition and participation' (Diamond *et al*. 1988: 4). What differentiates democratic governments or organizations from others is that anyone can aspire to leadership, and can dissent from leaders' opinions and preferences. Moreover, leadership is responsive to the rank and file.

A more elaborate set of criteria for democracy is posited by Robert Dahl. These are: freedom to form and join organizations; freedom of expression; the right to vote; eligibility for public office; the right to compete for electoral support; alternative sources of information; free and fair elections; and institutions for making government policies depend on votes and other expressions of preference (Dahl 1971). Both definitions encompass the sources of authority for government, the purposes served by government, and the procedures for constituting it. These are the critical issues for democracies. Huntington (1991), like many before him, believes that what distinguishes democracy from other forms of government is the emphasis on procedure – contestation and participation. To have genuine contestation and participation a system must provide for freedom of expression and assembly, for without such freedoms, genuine contestation and participation cannot occur.

Transition, democratization and consolidation

Analysts have identified three stages of post-1991 politics in Russia and other formerly communist states: transition, democratization and consolidation. There is no consensus on the importance or utility of any of the three terms. Some argue that while a transition from communism has been made, it is not clear to what the transition has been. Others point to the return to power in Hungary, Poland, Lithuania and Central Asia of former communists – though by the twenty-first century they had once again lost power in the first three – and the vigorous competition given to Boris Yeltsin by a coalition of Communists in the 1996 Russian presidential election and their dominance of the Duma until President Putin gained the overwhelming support of the Duma in recent elections as evidence that the transition from communism is by no means assured. Communist or quasi-communist parties remain competitive in several of the post-communist states and it is not impossible that they will return to power through democratic means. While some claim that the transitions from communism are paralleled by transitions from authoritarian governments in southern Europe (Greece, Portugal, Spain) and Latin America (Argentina, Brazil) and that there are critical features common to these transitions, others argue that the transitions are different in important ways. For example, in southern Europe the only issue was democratization, whereas in Eastern Europe and the former Soviet Union it has been the creation of a new economy, class systems, international relations and even states themselves (Schmitter and Karl 1994; Bunce 1995).

There are similar disagreements over the most effective way of 'democratizing' a political system. Should economic and political reform be introduced simultaneously, and, if not, which should come first? What is the most effective and long-lasting way of democratizing – by agreement among elites, by pressures 'from below' (among ordinary people), or by some combination of these? What should be the role of external actors – states, international organizations, private groups – in spurring the growth of democracy? Can democratization be accomplished in a relatively short period, or does it require slow, organic growth over many years if it is to be firmly implanted (Linz and Stepan 1996)? Obviously, these issues are relevant to many parts of the world. For example, these questions would presumably be highly relevant to the current American administration's purported attempt to bring democracy to Iraq, or to the Palestinian Authority which is wrestling with the legacy of corruption and authoritarianism bequeathed to it by Yasser Arafat.

Analysts realize that democratization may be temporary and superficial. Therefore, they have considered how and when a democracy can be 'consolidated'. Some reject the very notion that there is some point at which a democracy can be assumed to be permanent or 'consolidated'. After all, the argument goes, if democracy is a process and not a result, 'if the democratic project can never be completed, then how can we understand the term "consolidation" with its implication of democracy as an end state?' (Bunce 1995: 125). What are the measuring rods of consolidation – the absence of large-scale protest against the system or presence of relatively durable coalitions, and widespread support for the institutions and procedures of democracy? Concretely, how would an observer know whether Ukraine, Moldova, Albania or Russia – or Iraq and Afghanistan – can be considered viable democracies where democratic systems will persist for a very long time?

Huntington suggests that a democracy is consolidated when citizens learn that 'democracy rests on the premise that governments will fail and that hence institutionalized ways have to exist for changing them. . . . Democracies become consolidated when people learn that democracy is a solution to the problem of tyranny, but not necessarily to anything else' (1991: 263). In other words, when people persist in supporting a democratic system even though the particular government is not meeting their expectations, democracy is consolidated. More concretely, Huntington proposes a 'two-turnover test' for measuring democratic consolidation. If the party or group that takes power in the initial election loses a subsequent election but turns over power peacefully, and if the new winners, in turn, surrender power to the winners of the next election, the democratic system can then be considered consolidated. Moreover, he notes, 'A striking feature of the first fifteen years of the third wave was the virtual absence of major antidemocratic movements in the new democracies' (1991: 263). However, this has not been true in Russia where unreconstructed communists, nationalist authoritarians (including even some monarchists), and other anti-democratic groupings have secured significant proportions of the vote in parliamentary and presidential elections. Perhaps in no other European former Soviet republic, except Belarus and perhaps Ukraine, have authoritarian alternatives been as visible and popular as in Russia.

The prospects for democracy in Russia

Though there is a broad consensus on *what* democracy is, there is no agreement on *how* a system becomes democratic. What are the prospects of Russia becoming democratic? This, too, is a matter of considerable debate. The debate centres on the importance of economics and of political culture, that is, a group or nation's subjective orientation towards and understanding of politics. Nearly half a century ago, Seymour Martin Lipset argued that democracies emerge only in societies that are relatively prosperous (Lipset 1959, 1994). He continues to believe that 'economic well being comes close to being a necessary condition for democracy. The poorer a polity, the less amenable its leaders . . . will be to giving up power, their only source of status and wealth' (Lipset 1998). Potentially always one of the world's richest countries, Russia remains poor by European standards and her economic status should not be conducive to democracy.

Nevertheless, as a Russian political scientist points out, India, a poor country, is a democracy, while Singapore, a rich one, is not (Melville 1999). Moreover, due to the steep increase in world petroleum prices, Russia has been able to take advantage of its being first or second in the world in the volume of oil production and has greatly increased its national income, curbed inflation, and raised the standard of living of many of its citizens, though Russia's new wealth is heavily concentrated in Moscow and in the hands of relatively few people. But even after four straight years of relatively rapid economic growth, Russia's GDP was still only $346 billion in 2003, less than that of the Netherlands. Personal incomes rose by up to 16 per cent, but again they were very unevenly distributed across the republics and regions. Thus, country-wide a middle class that is said to be the social backbone of democratic systems is emerging only slowly and thus far it has not acquired a distinctive political profile or voice.

Lipset (1998) suggests that relatively high levels of education and low income disparities are other requisites for the emergence of democracy. In addition, he sees democracy requiring 'a supportive culture, the acceptance by the citizenry and political elites of the principles underlying freedom of speech, media and assembly; rights of political parties, rule of law, human rights, and the like. Such norms do not evolve overnight'.

Some believe that culture is quite stable and puts its stamp on state institutions, creating an inertia difficult to reverse. They would argue that in the light of Russia's autocratic past, there is a 'natural tendency' towards non-democratic forms of government. Others see political culture as more malleable. As William Zimmerman points out, there are two variants of this approach, one holding that 'the core attitudes that constitute a political culture are driven by societal and technological change and evolve as society changes'. The other variant stresses the role of institutions and incentive structures. 'If the institutions are right, political culture follows, rather than drives, successful institutionalization. . . . Change the institutions, change the political culture' (Zimmerman 1995: 631). Institutional change was seen as the way to democratize Germany after the First World War, but it proved insufficient to overcome that country's authoritarian heritage. Following the next world war, the Allies attempted to change not only Germany's (and Japan's) institutions but also its political culture, including family patterns and attitudes towards authority and towards peoples of different religions, races and cultures. This attempt to alter the political culture directly, rather than relying on institutions, seems to have been more effective. Perhaps it was so because, unlike the aftermath of the First World War, Allied troops occupied the country and supervised the transformation of its political culture.

The German experience may provide some lessons for those interested in changing Russian political culture in a more democratic direction. Constitutional lawyers, political scientists, educators and human rights activists, from within Russia and without, have been attempting to alter both Russia's institutions and, to a lesser extent because it is much more difficult and a longer-term undertaking, its political culture. But, unlike Germany and Japan in 1945, Russia has not had democratic rule imposed on it by occupying powers who invested a great deal in the political resocialization of the population. Militating against rapid democratization are Russia's history and traditions of authoritarian rule; disunity among democratic politicians who have not been able to unite in a single electoral list, let alone a political party, over the course of several parliamentary and presidential elections; prolonged economic crisis; and the training and experience of most of the leaders of the formerly Soviet states. As one observer points out, despite the collapse of the Soviet state and its economy, there has been 'remarkable elite stability' (Solnick 1999). Unlike Poland, Hungary, the Czech Republic, Slovakia and the Baltic states – but like the Central Asian states, Romania, Serbia and other states that have not moved very far towards democracy – the postcommunist leadership in Russia has come largely from the former elites and not from the democratic opposition (Kryshtanovskaya and White 1996). One of Moldova's postcommunist presidents had been first secretary of the Moldavian Communist Party (1989–91) and a member of the Politburo of the CPSU; the presidents of Kazakhstan, Turkmenistan, Uzbekistan, Georgia and Azerbaijan (until November 2003 in the two last cases) were first secretaries of their republics' communist parties before the fall of the Soviet Union; and many more were prominent at the regional level.

Moreover, unlike Hungarian, Polish and even Czech Communists, Russian Communists did not have several years of experience in negotiating with an opposition and at least partly accommodating it. Thus, their authoritarian reflexes were largely undisturbed. One of the criticisms of Boris Yeltsin's rule was that under a democratic veneer it was quite authoritarian. But, some argued, presidential power and dominance of the other branches of government was needed in a period of transition to democracy because only a strong presidency could push Russia along the road away from its authoritarian past. Yet, when Yeltsin resigned in favour of Vladimir Putin, the latter took advantage of the ongoing conflict in Chechnya to rationalize the need for an extension of presidential power. Since late 1999, little has been heard of limiting that power. Instead, Putin went after the few media that were critical of him and his government by arresting Vladimir Gusinsky, head of the largest independent media conglomerate, and by curbing the power of the regional governors. Gusinsky, like other oligarchs such as Boris Berezovsky and Leonid Nevzlin, fled abroad to avoid what they consider to be political persecution under the guise of legal prosecution. In October 2003, Federal Security Bureau officers in Novosibirsk pulled Mikhail Khodorkovsky, chairman of the Yukos oil company and reputedly Russia's richest man, from his charter plane and arrested him. He was charged with seven counts of tax evasion and embezzlement, acts supposedly committed in the early 1990s when Russian laws were poorly defined. Ironically, it was widely agreed that Yukos was the most transparent among Russia's major companies and that Khodorkovsky had done more than any other oligarch to bring order to Russian business practices and to eliminate corruption. Many suggested that the real reason for Khodorkovsky's arrest was that he was financing politicians opposed to Putin and that he himself had ambitions of running for the presidency of the Russian Federation.

President Putin has attempted several times and in different ways to limit the powers of the regional governors. To be sure, many of the latter rule their regions like feudal fiefs, but Putin's drive to reduce the number of Russian regions, and to curb the powers of the governors, was designed to enhance central power, not to democratize the regions. Following the atrocity at Beslan in the Caucasus in September 2004 in which over 300 people, including many children, were killed in the clash between Chechen hostage-takers and Russian forces, Putin proposed replacing popular elections and other regional leaders with people appointed by the federal government in Moscow. Like President Bush in the United States, Putin argued that the threat of terrorism demanded more centralized government and a stronger executive. It should be noted that in Holland, Spain, France and Britain, where terrorist actions have also occurred, there have been similar calls to limit such rights as freedom of expression and of assembly. It seems that peoples who are terrorized are willing to put more power in the hands of a leader, as George Bush's advisers realized in the 2004 presidential campaign when they correctly counted on Americans 'feeling safer' with a single-minded leader than with one who would weigh alternatives.

Certainly, Putin projects strength and determination. His proposals and actions have gone much further than those of American and West European leaders. Thus, if we measure Russia under Putin against criteria for democracy such as free and open competition for office and power, and civil and political liberties 'sufficient to ensure the integrity of political competition and participation' (Diamond *et al.* 1988: xvi), the Russian Federation falls short. Moreover, where once the Duma was controlled by the Communists and thus presidential power would run into some, at least symbolic, opposition, in 2003 the party supporting Putin, United Russia, secured more than 37 per cent of the party-list votes for the Duma, nationalist parties had about 20 per cent, and the Communists only about 13 per cent, whereas they had been the largest single party in the Dumas of the 1990s. Liberal parties such as Yabloko and the Union of Right Forces, as we have seen in earlier chapters, failed to pass the 5 per cent threshold and won very few single-member seats. At least in the short run, the government would hear fewer dissenting voices and independent opinions.

Putin's steadily high ratings in opinion polls, even in the wake of the *Kursk* submarine disaster in the summer 2000, the seizure of a Moscow theatre by Chechen terrorists in October 2002 resulting in the deaths of more than a hundred, as well as the Beslan massacre indicate that a large number of Russians favour a strong and even somewhat dictatorial leadership. Moreover, disunity among democratic politicians has not only weakened their influence in the institutions of governance, but has diminished their appeal as people worthy of support and of office-holding.

The authoritarian traditions of Russia and most of the other Soviet successor states mean that people are not used to democratic behaviours and values, such as welcoming pluralism in thinking and behaving, tolerating dissent, and supporting seemingly less efficient methods of democratic decision-making. They do not easily see the advantages of debate, discussion and non-conformity, and not deferring to a class of 'superiors'. Recent surveys certainly show that Russians have far less favourable attitudes towards democracy than people in scores of other countries. Studies in the early 1990s carried out by scholars with little familiarity with Soviet culture and traditions optimistically concluded that there was broad support for democracy among the population of the Russian Federation (Gibson and Duch 1994). The World Values Survey, however, which compares over 60 countries, found in 1999–2000 that whereas over all the countries 89 per cent of respondents gave a positive account of democracy, in Russia only 56 per cent did so (Inglehart 2000). Russians were very dissatisfied with their government's performance; they were less trusting and tolerant, less healthy and less happy than people in many other countries. Inglehart finds that such attitudes are correlated with scepticism about democracy. 'Culture seems to shape democracy far more than democracy shapes culture. This is bad news for anyone seeking a quick and easy solution to the problems of democratization.' Since, he argues, 'cultural factors are ultimately more decisive than economic ones' in bringing democracy about, an improvement in the Russian economy would not by itself substantially increase the prospects for democracy (Inglehart 2000).

The Russian Federation has failed to develop stable, respected and vigorous political institutions such as political parties, non-commercial interest groups, an independent judiciary and an effective legislature. Much of this may be attributable to the desire of Yeltsin and especially Putin, both of whom made their careers in the Soviet apparatus, for personalistic regimes. Second, there are no precedents in the living memory of Russians for such democratic institutions, unlike the Czech Republic and even Poland and Hungary. Third, many Russian citizens have a deep-rooted cynicism about political life, a rational response to Soviet circumstances, and this has led them to adopt apolitical postures. For example, in the elections to the governorship of St Petersburg and to the governorship of the Leningrad region, only 29 per cent of eligible voters cast a ballot, and 11 per cent of those who did vote selected 'against all candidates'. Moreover, citizens' post-Soviet experiences of widespread corruption, self-serving and cynical politicians, and political murders have reinforced their belief that little changes or can change. The euphoria of 1988–90 when people listened attentively to debates in the Supreme Soviet and took a genuine interest in political life was dissipated by coup attempts, an inebriated and ineffective president and, very importantly, widespread corruption.

But there are forces that could impel Russia in the other direction. They include the revulsion that is felt by many about the communist political and economic systems; Western pressure for democratization and the desire by many to be accepted as part of 'Europe'; growing exposure to the cultures and political systems of the West; and the democratic strains in the Russian political tradition upon which even Russian nationalists can draw. Indeed, most surveys taken in Russia in the last decade show that democratic attitudes and support for a market economy are strongest among the young, those who have had the least experience of communism and the most of the West. Roughly speaking, younger cohorts are more inclined towards pluralism of opinions, are sceptical about the existence of a 'single truth', optimistic about the future of democracy in Russia and reluctant to return to communist practices in economics, culture and politics. The university-educated are also more likely to support democratic values than those with less education. They tend to be more favourable towards the market economy, and more willing to gamble that political and economic change will be ultimately for the better. They are less inclined to retain an oppressive but familiar political system and a stagnant but minimally providing economic system. On the other hand, middle-aged men, farm workers, the unemployed and underemployed, and those dependent for their livelihood on one of the enormous industrial 'dinosaurs' that can no longer be justified in economic terms are understandably desperate. It is among such people that the 'solutions' proffered by non-democratic politicians such as Vladimir Zhirinovsky or Gennadii Zyuganov, or a variety of nationalists and even neo-fascists find their greatest appeal. Some have concluded, therefore, that since it is among the younger people that support for democracy is strongest, all other things being equal, time is working in favour of broader mass support for democracy in Russia.

Huntington (1991) lists several factors that influence whether or not a country will go in a democratic direction. These include prior democratic experience; a high level of economic development; a consensual and non-violent transition; and absence of severe social and economic problems. Russia has had only fleeting prior democratic experience. On economic development Russia would rank much higher than the Central Asian successor states, and ahead of Moldova, Belarus and Ukraine and the republics of the Caucasus, but behind the three Baltic republics. Indeed, those people who are worse off economically within Russia are generally the least favourable towards reform and democracy. The transition in Russia was largely consensual, though both in 1991 and 1993 some violence accompanied major changes. Unfortunately, Russian continues to face serious problems, including crime, corruption, capitalist-style poverty, homelessness, dramatic increases in the gap between the rich and poor, high rates of divorce and alcoholism – the latter contributing to a shocking decline in longevity, especially among men – and unemployment. To the extent that these are associated with 'democracy', as opposed to communism – in other words, that people believe that these social and economic problems appeared only with the dissolution of the Soviet state – popular support for political democracy is weakened.

Moreover, the prolonged, demoralizing and costly war in Chechnya is a multifaceted problem: the Chechens have humiliated the armed forces and political leadership, divided Russia's politicians, thrust the vexed problem of the nature of the federation and centre–periphery relations into the forefront of Russians' consciousness and, worst of all, cost thousands of lives. The humiliation of Russia has another dimension, the loss of empire and of control over a huge multi-republic state. Not only has

Russia lost her status as a world superpower, but she has lost control of Eastern Europe and of the roughly 140 million non-Russians in the old Soviet Union. Perhaps this is why President Putin intervened openly in Ukraine's presidential election in 2004, backing the preferred choice of that country's Russian-speaking population, while most West European leaders and the Americans favoured his Western-oriented challenger. Ukraine became for Putin a third area of contestation with the USA, the others being Iran (where Russia has continued to assist that country's nuclear energy programme), and Iraq (where Russia joined France, Germany and many others in opposing American military intervention). The confrontation over Ukraine signalled that the Russian Federation is a regional power and will exercise its power in its 'sphere', certainly in the former Soviet republics in Europe apart from the Baltic. Such a position appeals to Russians' pan-Slavism and their desire to stand up to the USA and restore their international dignity. Not surprisingly, they are also interested in securing what they regard as a pro-Russian government in Ukraine and the other countries of the 'near abroad'.

Democratization in Russia in comparative perspective

Analysts agree that Russia is not a consolidated democracy, but there is no consensus on how to 'label' its political system. Many point to the 'hybrid' nature of a regime that exhibits both democratic and non-democratic characteristics (Bunce 2000). One scholar describes Russia not as a democracy but as a system with a 'durable division of power among a fairly stable group of elite actors' (Solnick 1999: 799), though this was written before Putin began his campaign against the oligarchs and regional governors. Other writers have called the Russian system 'soft Bonapartism', a 'personalist, populist, plebiscitary regime that rests on the administrative and coercive apparatuses of the state and that by seemingly elevating itself above society, acts as an arbitrator and preserver of the new bourgeoisie's interests as a whole' (Gill and Marwick 2000: 257). Should Putin continue successfully to erode the power of the 'new bourgeoisie' and other elites, analysts may begin to perceive the system in different terms.

Obviously, it is very difficult to predict how the Russian system will evolve even in the near future. Can one extrapolate from the experiences of other democratizing societies in order to make an educated guess about the direction in which Russia will go? Some have suggested that the way in which the transition from authoritarianism was made originally is critical to the prospects for democracy. Transitions may be led by existing elites or by the opposition. They may result from the overthrow of the regime or from its collapse from within. They may be consensual ('pacted') or produced by conflict. Elite-led transitions are less likely to lead to democratization since the elites were the leaders of an authoritarian system, and this is certainly the case in Russia and many of the other successor states, as noted earlier. The transition in Russia was not exclusively the result of an internal collapse, though that was the long-term cause, but violence was rather limited and the process of transition did not leave the deep scars it might have. This is, of course, propitious for democracy. The transition also had elements of both conflict and consensus. Therefore, the transition process itself does not point clearly towards or away from the consolidation of democracy in Russia.

According to Linz and Stepan, in order to become consolidated democracies need five interacting areas: a lively civil society, a relatively autonomous 'political society' (institutions and procedural rules), the rule of law, a functioning state bureaucracy, and an 'economic society' (norms, institutions and regulations that mediate between the state and the market) (Linz and Stepan 1996: xiv, 11). A democracy is 'consolidated' when no major group tries to overthrow the democratic system, a strong majority of the public believes that democratic procedures and institutions are the most appropriate way to govern collective life, and conflicts are resolved within the democratic process.

Once again, the evidence from Russia is mixed. Some observers see a civil society emerging, one in which autonomous groups mediate between the state and the citizenry, though the most powerful groups seem closely tied not just to the state but to a particular government and even a particular person, whether Yeltsin or Putin or a local ruler. One element of civil society is stable, visible political parties that serve to aggregate and articulate the political interests of the citizenry. With the possible exception of the weakened Communist Party, Russian political parties (as we saw in Chapter 5) seem to be ad hoc coalitions of electoral candidates. They lack permanent structures, clear ideologies and programmes, and stable constituencies. Political institutions are still being moulded, as might be expected. The shape of the executive and legislature, relations between the nearly ninety units of government and the federal centre, and other basic institutional arrangements are not yet stabilized. The rule of law seems to be taking hold (as we noted in Chapter 8), though as in most other spheres, few would assert that it is firmly established. The state bureaucracy is problematic for several reasons: Soviet-era habits are still prevalent, and corruption is widespread, although apparently less than in Ukraine and other postcommunist states. Relations between the state and the market seem to be volatile, especially as the market is not yet fully developed. Local and foreign businessmen complain of what they see as capricious economic regulation and exploitative taxation, favouritism, and irrational and unpredictable state economic policies.

Part of the problem of both political and economic institutionalization may lie in the choice made between parliamentary and presidential forms of democracy. Linz and Stepan argue that the choice of parliamentary or 'semi-presidential' constitutions in Greece, Spain and Portugal gave those new democracies 'greater degrees of freedom' than if they had chosen American-style presidentialism as their constitutional framework. Parliamentarism is generally more conducive to democratic consolidation than presidentialism because it gives the political system greater efficacy, the capacity to construct majorities and the 'ability to terminate a crisis of government without it becoming a crisis of the regime' (Linz and Stepan 1996: 141). Hungary, the Czech Republic and Slovenia have adopted the parliamentary system and 'it is perhaps no accident' that they are closer to consolidation than any postcommunist country with a directly elected president who has significant powers. The three major Slavic republics of the former Soviet Union, Russia, Ukraine and Belarus, all have presidential forms, as do the Central Asian states.

In addition to the choice of presidentialism, there are other choices made by Russia which have militated against rapid democratization. Several policies of the late Soviet period weakened the state but did not create new democratically legitimated central state structures. Gorbachev's programme of *perestroika* and *glasnost* was one of these. The previously hollow institutions of Soviet federalism provided the framework for the political mobilization of ethnicity. That was more effective than ideological mobilization in a state in which political alternatives had not been open to discussion for the better part of a century. Appealing to one's 'primordial' ethnic identity was a far more effective short-term strategy than trying to win support for a new, complicated political programme, even had such programmes existed. Moreover, many of the nationalisms which emerged from under the façade of Soviet 'proletarian internationalism' and 'friendship of the peoples' were exclusivist, militant and intolerant, and not very compatible with democratic thinking and acting. Local and regional elections shifted the focus from civic to ethnic issues, spurring the disintegration of the state. Most of the successor states have put independence ahead of democratization and have therefore emphasized collective over individual rights, and economic ahead of political restructuring. According to Linz and Stepan, had political reform and consolidation preceded economic reform, the state would have been stronger and better able to implement the economic reforms.

This raises the question of whether the sequencing of political and economic reform influences the success of democratization. Linz and Stepan argue that in Spain, the primacy of political reform, followed by socioeconomic reform and only then economic reform, was probably the optimal sequence for the consolidation of democracy. However, most analysts of the postcommunist states argue for the simultaneity of economic and political reform as the optimal strategy. Linz and Stepan feel that political reform should precede economic reform because democracy legitimates the market, not the reverse. Democratic regulatory state power is needed to make the market work. 'Effective privatization . . . is best done by relatively strong states that are able to implement a coherent policy . . . Effective privatization entails less state scope but greater state capacity . . . A state with rapidly eroding capacity simply cannot manage a process of effective privatization' (Linz and Stepan 1996: 436). Furthermore, if there is a strong popular commitment to the new democratic forms of government, this can be a cushion against the blows of economic restructuring. The postcommunist Polish system seems to have enjoyed this advantage. Painful economic restructuring was tolerated by a public firmly committed perhaps not so much to democracy as to not returning to communist dictatorship. By now, it is clear that the Polish economy has succeeded in making the transition to the market, and economic success now serves as legitimation of the political system with which it is associated. Support for specific achievements of a system can grow into 'diffuse support', that is, a generalized support of the system which gives it the slack to survive temporary setbacks.

Comparable survey data show that the postcommunist polities of Hungary, Poland and the Czech Republic get much more popular support than do those of Russia, Belarus and Ukraine:

> Respondents in the six former Warsaw Pact countries of East Central Europe gave a mean positive rating of 62 to the post-Communist political system (a rise of 16 points over the positive rating they gave to the Communist political system). In sharp contrast, in the three former Soviet Union countries (Russia, Ukraine, and Belarus), a mean of only 29 gave the post-Communist political system a positive rating (a decrease of 26 points from those who gave the Communist system a positive rating). (Linz and Stepan 1996: 446)

In addition, there is a much lower willingness to defer material gratification in the former Soviet Union than in East Central Europe, possibly because of greater pessimism regarding the economy, state disintegration and armed conflicts, shame and humiliation over the loss of empire and the disintegration of the Soviet state.

Thus, it seems reasonable to conclude that democracy is better established in the northern tier of East Central Europe (Poland, Czech Republic, Hungary), in the three Baltic states and in Slovenia than it is in

Russia, but in this respect Russia is ahead of Belarus, the Central Asian states, and perhaps other former Soviet republics. Even where reform communists have returned to power, they have accepted the rules of the game both in the elections themselves and in the way they have been exercising power. They have been accepted by the parties they defeated and by the public and thereby strengthened confidence in the fairness of democratic procedure. But more than the East European parties, a Russian communist party or coalition is likely to revert to practices of earlier times. Some even advocate a return to Stalinism.

There is no reason to assume either that democracy can never be firmly established in Russia or that it must inevitably be. It is reasonable to expect that postcommunist states will reach different degrees of democratization or not democratize at all. We come back to the idea that democracy is a spectrum, and the states emerging from the Soviet Union, though they all seemed to start at the same point, are likely to range themselves across this spectrum. Scholars will continue to debate the determinants of democracy and why one country reaches one point on the spectrum and another reaches a different point. Political culture, level of economic and cultural development, external influences and social problems are all factors in the equation. But perhaps the most important is elite choices. Precisely in periods of transition, elites make fateful choices among alternative directions in which they can lead their countries. As Linz and Stepan note, 'Democratic institutions have to be not only created but crafted, nurtured and developed' (1996: 457). Russia seems to have been halted, at least temporarily, at the creation stage. This is due in large part to the contradictory nature of Yeltsin's impulses, which alternated between those of a populist democrat and those of the provincial party boss he once was. A range of freedoms never enjoyed by Russia's citizens was not only introduced but has been more or less maintained, but neither Yeltsin nor Putin has even tried to form an institutionalized constituency for democracy (a party, for example). Yeltsin's seemingly arbitrary hiring and firing of assistants, advisers and ministers was more reminiscent of a royal court than of a modern democracy. Putin's intolerance of political competitors and growing appetite for control have moved Russia further away from consolidated democracy, at least for now. If one were to draw up a balance sheet of democratization in Russia to date, on the positive side one might list broad freedom of expression but not in the most popular public media; the right to organize; a broad franchise; no ethnic discrimination emanating from the government and governmental tolerance and sometimes even support for non-Russian cultures; freedom of travel and of emigration; and the lifting of most restrictions on private economic activity. On the other side of the balance sheet would be presidential control of much of the media, especially television; the imbalance of power within the federal government which gives the president overwhelming power *vis-à-vis* the legislature; the '*nomenklatura* privatization' which gave favoured individuals privileged access to vast resources; and the too close ties between many interest groups and the government. The preoccupation with Chechnya, the genuine though perhaps waning strength of the communist constituency and the failure of the democrats to unite and articulate a clear and appealing programme are other roadblocks on what might otherwise have been a smoother path to democracy.

Over 150 years ago, the Russian novel *Dead Souls*, written by Nikolai Gogol, whom Ukrainians claim as one of their own, concluded with this by now well-known observation:

> And you Russia – aren't you racing headlong like the fastest troika imaginable . . . And where do you fly to, Russia? Answer me! . . . She doesn't answer. The carriage bells break into an enchanted tinkling, the air is torn to shreds and turns into wind; everything on earth flashes past, and, casting worried, sidelong glances, other nations and countries step out of her way.

At the beginning of the twenty-first century it is still not clear where Russia is racing. While outsiders continue to cast 'worried, sidelong glances' they cannot permit themselves to merely 'step out of her way'. Though no longer a superpower, Russia remains the largest state in the world, a country of some 145 million, and a great power with which the rest of the world is still obliged to come to terms.

Guide to Further Reading

The listing that follows suggests a number of items that students and others may find useful to consult on the themes that are covered by each chapter of this book. Current developments in Russian politics and related themes are regularly considered in academic journals such as *Europe–Asia Studies* (eight issues annually); the *Journal of Communist Studies and Transition Politics* (quarterly); *Post-Soviet Affairs* (quarterly); *Communist and Post-Communist Studies* (quarterly); and *Problems of Post-Communism* (six issues annually). Legal and constitutional issues across the postcommunist countries generally are given particular attention in the *Review of Socialist Law* (quarterly) and the *East European Constitutional Review* (quarterly). The *Current Digest of the Post-Soviet Press* (weekly) is a digest of translations from newspapers and journals; the *BBC Summary of World Broadcasts* (from 2001 superseded by Global Newsline) and the *Foreign Broadcast Information Service* (daily) include radio and television broadcasts as well as periodical material. Pockney (1991) and Ryan (1993) provide useful collections of statistics on social and economic developments over the Soviet and early post-Soviet periods.

Electronic resources may be most conveniently consulted through one of the gateways that provide a specialist service. See, for instance, the websites maintained at the University of Pittsburgh (www.ucis.pitt.edu/reesweb/), at the School of Slavonic and East European Studies in London (www.ssees. ac.uk/russia.htm), and the Centre for Russian Studies of the Norwegian Institute of International Affairs (www.nupi.no/). The official internet site of the Russian presidency (www.president.kremlin.ru/) may also be consulted. The daily news service maintained by Radio Free Europe and Radio Liberty is available in a searchable form at www.rferl.org/newsline. A very useful ongoing collection of journalistic writings on Russian politics and society is *Johnson's Russia List* (website and email newsletter, by subscription).

Chapter 1   Politics in Russia

There are a number of good overviews of the Soviet system. These include Gooding (2001), Keep (1996), Kenez (1999), Malia (1994), Marples (2002), Sakwa (1998), Sandle (1997), Service (1997), Suny (1998) and Westwood (2002). The Gorbachev period is covered by Brown (1996), by Gorbachev himself (1987) and by Sakwa (1990). Arnason (1993) provides a good analysis of the overall failure of the Soviet system, while Cox's edited book (1998) presents a number of debates about the academic study of the fall. More detailed analyses can be found in Kotkin (2001) and Kotz and Weir (1997), and a fine overview in White (2000a). General analyses of contemporary

Russian politics can be found in Barany and Moser (2001), Brown (2001), Lane (2002), McFaul *et al.* (2004), Remington (2004) and Ross (2004), Sakwa (2002), White (2000b), . A full biography of Yeltsin is provided by Aron (2000) and his leadership is compared with Gorbachev's by Breslauer (2002), while the Putin period is analysed by Herspring (2005), Sakwa (2004) and Shevtsova (2005), with his own views presented in Putin (2000).

Chapter 2   Putin and the Hegemonic Presidency

For comprehensive discussions of the Putin presidency, see Flikke (2004), Herspring (2005) and Sakwa (2004). For overview treatments of the politics of the Yeltsin and Putin regimes and their policy programmes, see Shevtsova (1999 and 2005). On the development of the Russian presidency up to the Yeltsin period, see Huskey (1999); for a discussion of the dynamics of presidential popularity, see Mishler and Willerton (2003); and for an analysis of presidential decree issuance, see Protsyk (2004). For information on the backgrounds and careers of Yeltsin and Putin, see Aron (2000) and the autobiographical volumes by Yeltsin (1990, 1994 and 2000) and Putin (2000). Freeland (2000) and Hoffman (2002) provide in-depth treatments of the Russian oligarchs and their role in the post-Soviet political process, while Kryshtanovskaya and White (2003) detail the mounting role of security– intelligence officials under Putin. For discussions of Soviet-period institutions and policies see Bialer (1981) and Hough and Fainsod (1979), and on the informal politics of the later Soviet period Willerton (1992). Breslauer (2002) provides a comparison of the Gorbachev and Yeltsin leadership styles, while Brown and Shevtsova (2001) compare these leaders and Putin. Broader comparative discussions of the opportunities and dilemmas of strong presidential systems are provided in Linz and Valenzuela (1994) and Mainwaring and Shugart (1997). The central institutions of government are considered more directly in Shevchenko (2004).

Chapter 3   Parliamentary Politics in Russia

On representative institutions since the late Soviet period see McFaul (2001) and Remington (2001b), and on the contemporary Duma and Federation Council see Remington (2000, 2001a, 2002, 2003a and 2003b), Troxel (2003) and Smith and Remington (2001). For a comparative perspective, see Ostrow (2000). The Russian constitution of 1993 is available in a number of convenient editions, and may be consulted electronically at a number of locations; an easily followed English language version is available at www. departments.bucknell.edu/russian/const/constit.html.

Chapter 4   The Electoral System

On the difference between electoral democracies and competitive authoritarian regimes generally, see Diamond (1999, 2002) and Levitsky and Way (2002). On the evolution of Russia's electoral politics more generally, see McFaul (2001) and McFaul *et al.* (2004). Fuller analyses of Russian elections since the collapse of the Soviet Union include Belin and Orttung (1997), Colton and Hough (1998), Colton and McFaul (2003), Marsh (2002), Moser (2001), Rose and Munro (2002), Treisman and Gimpelson (2001), White *et al.* (1997), Wyman *et al.* (1998). A convenient set of results is available in Munro and Rose (2001).

Chapter 5   The Political Parties

Much of the literature on elections and electoral behaviour is relevant to the study of Russian parties, including Colton (2000) and White *et al.* (1997). There are detailed studies of party politics in the late 1990s in Löwenhardt (1998) and Wyman *et al.* (1998) and White (2005) is comprehensive. On individual parties see March (2002, 2004), Urban and Solovei (1997) on the Communist Party, and Hale (2004) on Yabloko. Hutcheson (2003) is a pioneering study of local-level party politics; see also Golosov (2004). Mair (1997) is a thoughtful study of postcommunist party politics within a broader comparative framework.

Chapter 6   A Russian Civil Society?

For background on the growth of civil society in the late tsarist period, see Bradley (2002), Clowes *et al.* (1991) and Conroy (2005). There are many writings on social organizations in the Soviet Union. The best source on developments during the period from the October 1917 Revolution to the 1930s is Il'ina (2000). An essay summarizing information on social organizations in the Soviet system is Evans (forthcoming). Golenkova (1999), Kholodkovsky *et al.* (1998) and Khoros *et al.* (1998) represent some of the major Russian scholarly writings about civil society in Russia during the 1990s. Strong Western scholarly studies of specific types of non-governmental organizations in postcommunist Russia include Sperling (1999), which is an indispensable starting place for reading on the topic, Henderson (2003), Henry (2005) and Sundstrom (2002, 2005). The issues of the journal *Demokratizatsiya* for spring and summer 2002 (vol. 20, nos 2 and 3) and the forthcoming book edited by Evans *et al.* (2005) are all devoted to the subject of civil society in contemporary Russia. Howard (2003) provides a comparative dimension.

Chapter 7   Media and Political Communication

Among the best work on the Soviet and post-Soviet media, particularly in understanding the late Soviet and early Russian media, is Mickiewicz (1980, 1988, 1999). Other work on the *glasnost* era includes Remington (1988) and Wedgwood Benn (1992). For a discussion of the media in other post-Soviet countries, see McCormack (1999). On the role of media in elections and campaigns, see particularly the reports that were produced by the European Institute for the Media immediately after Duma elections (1993–99) and Russian presidential elections in 1996 and 2000 (see European Institute for the Media 1994, February 1996, September 1996, March 2000, August 2000). The Organization for Security and Cooperation in Europe's Office for Democratic Institutions and Human Rights has produced reports on the media performance in Russian elections; for the most recent see http://www.osce.org/documents/odihr/. The rankings by Freedom House (http://www.freedomhouse.org/) and the Committee to Protect Journalists (www.cpj.org) provide insight into the Russian media sphere. Other useful resources include the Russian branch of Internews, a non-governmental organization that supports media freedom worldwide   (www.internews.org)   and   the   First   Channel (http://www.1tv.ru/)

Chapter 8   In Search of the Rule of Law

For useful background studies on Russia's political and legal transitions, see Sakwa (2002) and Smith (1996). For a comprehensive study of Russia's constitutional development from 1991 to 2002, consult the *magnum opus* of van den Berg (2001, 2002–3). Judicial reform and development are covered in Jordan (2000), Solomon and Fogelsong (2000), Smith (2001), and the Justice of the Peace courts in particular in Solomon (2003). The role of the West in assisting law reform in Russia is discussed in Sharlet (1997, 1998) and on the theory of legal transplants, see Watson (1974). On all aspects of the Russian legal system, the magisterial study of Butler (2003) is a principal source, as well as Burnham *et al.* (2004). The problem of the runaway provinces and Putin's restoration campaign is discussed in Sharlet (2001, 2003). On the Constitutional Court and criminal procedure, see Bariknovskaya (2000) and Lediakh (2005), while the new Code of Criminal Procedure is extensively discussed in Smith (2005). For a study of the Bar in general, and particularly the issue of legal aid to the indigent, see Huskey (2005). Finally, on the important role of the European Court on Human Rights in stimulating rule of law development in Russia, see Kahn (2004).

Chapter 9   Reforming the Federation

The classic literature on the theory of federalism includes Friedrich (1968) and Riker (1964). Contemporary theory on federalism and other mechanisms for containing nationalism may be found in Hechter (2000). Lijphart (1984 and 1996) has produced the best studies of consociationalism in federal systems and touched on issues of corporate federalism or cultural autonomy. Keating (2001) incorporates the concepts of multiple sovereignties and identities in looking at multinational states and the European Union. Theory and detailed case studies of ethno-national mobilization and self-determination movements are expertly explored in Gurr (2000). On the importance of the Soviet legacy of pseudo-federalism and Russia's eternal nationality problem, see Connor (1984) and Walker (2003). There are as yet few book-length treatments of post-Soviet Russian federalism in English, but see Kahn (2002) and Pascal (2003). On the problem of the post-Soviet Chechen wars and post-Soviet state-building in the Russian Federation, Evangelista (2002) is helpful.

Chapter 10   Politics in the Regions

Books by Johnson (2000) and Woodruff (1999) shed light on how regions took advantage of the economic chaos of the Yeltsin period. Several useful case studies of particular regions are presented in Ross (2002), along with discussions of federalism, voting and political parties. Golosov (2004) provides an overview of politics and party development, mostly covering the 1990s Local government, both from an historical perspective and in the form of regional case studies, is examined in Evans and Gel'man (2004), and the relationship between civil society and localities is explored in Lankina (2004).

Chapter 11   Putin's Economic Record

The most reliable sources on the Russian economy are the periodic reports published by the World Bank, International Monetary Fund and Organization for Economic Cooperation and Development, and available on their websites. For current information there is the Economist Intelligence Unit and the Bank of Finland *Russian Review* (www.bof.fi) and newspapers like the *Moscow Times*. Russian government websites include the statistics agency Goskomstat (www.gks.ru/eng), the Ministry of Economy and Trade (www.economy.gov.ru), and the Ministry of Energy and Industry (www.mte.gov.ru). For vivid accounts of life among the oligarchs, see Brady (1999), Freeland (2000) and Khlebnikov (2000).

Chapter 12   Social Policy in Post-Soviet Russia

The best broad treatments of Russian social issues and policy have been those issued by international organizations, including the annual Human Development Reports of the United Nations Development Programme in the Russian Federation (see, for example, UNDP 2003) and a similar overview issued by the Organization for Economic Cooperation and Development (OECD 2001). Twigg and Schecter's edited volume on social capital also remains relevant (2003). Beyond these multi-subject compilations, the best English-language work focuses on the health and demographic situation. Murray Feshbach (2003) provides a comprehensive and pessimistic treatment of Russia's health crisis, which would be well supplemented by the World Bank's assessment of HIV/AIDS (2003), Lee Reichman's account of tuberculosis in Russia (2002), and the RAND corporation's publications on demographic dynamics (DaVanzo and Grammich 2001; DaVanzo *et al.* 2003).

Chapter 13   Foreign Policy

General accounts of Russian foreign policy may be found in Donaldson and Nogee (1998), Trenin (2001) and Webber (1996). For more detailed analyses of the domestic context of Russian foreign policy, see Ivanov (2002), Light (2000), Malcolm (1996) and Shearman (2001). On Russian policy towards the near abroad, see Jonson (1999), Lynch (2000), Olcott *et al.* (1999), and Sakwa and Webber (1999). On Russia's relations with the 'far abroad', Russian–US relations are covered by Kubicek (1999–2000) and Lieven (2002), while Baranovsky (1997), Baranovsky (2000), Light *et al.* (2000) and Pinder and Shishkov (2002) deal with Russian–European relations and Menon (1997) and Sherman (2000) examine Sino-Russian relations. Lo (2003) concentrates on Putin's foreign policy.

Chapter 14   The Democratization of Russia in Comparative Perspective

Among the better-known works on the nature of democracy are Dahl (1971), Diamond *et al.* (1988) and Lipset (1959, 1994). On democratization generally, see Huntington (1991), O'Donnell *et al.* (1986), Przeworski (1991) and Rustow (1970). An attempt to synthesize the experiences of Latin America, the former Soviet Union and southern and Eastern Europe is Linz and Stepan (1996). On transitions from authoritarianism, see Bunce (1995), Schmitter and Karl (1994), Terry (1993) and Zimmerman (1995). Reconsiderations of Russia's path to democracy are found in Bunce (2003) and McFaul *et al.* (2004).

References

Agence France Presse (2003) '50,000 Ghost Towns Draining Russia's Budget', 25 April.

Agence France Presse (2004) 'Bribe Your Way Back to Health in Russia's Hospitals', 10 February.

Alexander, Nikitin and Buchanan, Jane (2002) 'The Kremlin's Civic Forum: Cooperation or Co-optation for Civil Society in Russia?', *Demokratizatsiya*, vol. 10, no. 2 (Spring), pp. 147–65.

Andrews, Josephine T. (2002) *When Majorities Fail: The Russian Parliament, 1990–1993*. Cambridge: Cambridge University Press.

Andrienko, Yurii (2001) *Explaining Crime Growth in Russia during Transition: Economic and Criminometric Approach*. Moscow: Centre for Economic and Financial Research (CEFIR).

Arnason, Johann P. (1993) *The Future that Failed: Origins and Destinies of the Soviet Model*. London: Routledge.

Aron, Leon (2000) *Boris Yeltsin: A Revolutionary Life*. London: HarperCollins.

Aslund, Anders (1995) *How Russia Became a Market Economy*. Washington, DC: Brookings Institution.

Barany, Zoltan and Moser, Robert G. (eds) (2001) *Russian Politics: Challenges of Democratization*. Cambridge, Cambridge University Press.

Bariknovskaya, Elena (2000) 'How the Constitutional Court is Reforming Criminal Procedure: The Nikitin Case', *East European Constitutional Review*, vol. 9, no. 4 (Fall), pp. 99–101.

Baranovsky, Vladimir (2000) 'Russia: a part of Europe or apart from Europe?', *International Affairs*, vol. 76, no. 3 (July), pp. 443–58.

Baranovsky, Vladimir (ed.) (1997) *Russia and Europe: The Emerging Security Agenda*. Oxford: Oxford University Press/Stockholm International Peace Research Institute.

Barnes, Andrew (2001) 'Property, Power, and the Presidency: Ownership Policy Reform and Russian Executive–Legislative Relations, 1990–1999', *Communist and Post-Communist Studies*, vol. 34, no. 1, pp. 39–61.

Bartle, John (2003) 'Measuring Party Identification: An Exploratory Study with Focus Groups', *Electoral Studies*, vol. 22, pp. 217–37.

Belin, Laura and Orttung, Robert W. (1997) *The Russian Parliamentary Elections of 1995*. Armonk, NY: M. E. Sharpe.

Berg, P. van den (2001) 'Russia's Constitutional Court: A Decade of Legal Reforms, Part 1: Summaries of Judicial Rulings', *Review of Central and East European Law*, vol. 27, nos. 2–3, pp. 175–566.

Berg, P. van den (2002–3) 'Russia's Constitutional Court: A Decade of Legal Reforms, Part 2: The Constitution of the Russian Federation Annotated', *Review of Central and East European Law*, vol. 28, nos 3–4, pp. 273–653.

Bialer, Seweryn (1981) *Stalin's Successors*. Cambridge and New York: Cambridge University Press.

Bjorkman, Tom (2003) *Russia's Road to Deeper Democracy*. Washington, DC: Brookings Institution Press.

Blau, John (2004) 'Viruses Nip Russia after Cold War', *IDG News Service*, 25 May.

Bradley, Joseph (1994) 'Dobrovol'nye obshchestva v Sovetskoi Rossii, 1917–1932 gg.', *Vestnik Moskovskogo Universiteta, Seriya 8, Istoriya*, no. 4, pp. 34–44.

Bradley, Joseph (2002) 'Subjects into Citizens: Societies, Civil Society, and Autocracy in Tsarist Russia', *American Historical Review*, vol. 107, no. 4 (October), pp. 1094–1123.

Brady, Rose (1999) *Kapitalizm: Russia's Struggle to Free its Economy*. New Haven, CT: Yale University Press

Breslauer, George W. (2002) *Gorbachev and Yeltsin as Leaders*. Cambridge and New York: Cambridge University Press.

Brown, Archie (1996) *The Gorbachev Factor*. Oxford: Oxford University Press.

Brown, Archie (ed.) (2001) *Contemporary Russian Politics: A Reader*. Oxford: Oxford University Press.

Brown, Archie and Shevtsova, Lilia (eds) (2001) *Gorbachev, Yeltsin and Putin: Political Leadership in Russia's Transition*. Washington DC: Carnegie Endowment for International Peace.

Brown, Mark M. (2004) 'Balancing Social and Economic Goals', *Moscow Times*, 18 March.

Bulgakov, Dimitry (2004) 'In War on Poverty, Victory Is Hard To Measure', *Moscow Times*, 22 April.

Bullough, Oliver (2004) 'Drug Trade Earns $10Bln per Year, Top Official Says', Reuters, 25 June.

Bunce, Valerie (1995) 'Should Transitologists be Grounded?', *Slavic Review*, vol. 54, no. 1, pp. 111–27.

Bunce, Valerie (2000) 'Comparative Democratization: Big and Bounded Generalizations', *Comparative Political Studies*, vol. 33, no. 6/7, pp. 703–34.

Bunce, Valerie (2003) 'Rethinking Recent Democratization: Lessons from the Post-Communist Experience', *World Politics*, vol. 55, no. 2 (January), pp. 167–92.

Burnham, William, Maggs, Peter B. and Danilenko, Gennady M. (2004) *Law and the Legal System of the Russian Federation*, 3rd edn. New York: Juris Publishing.

Butler, W. E. (2003) *Russian Law*, 2nd edn. Oxford: Oxford University Press.

Carothers, Thomas (2002) 'The End of the Transition Paradigm', *Journal of Democracy*, vol. 13, no. 1, pp. 5–21.

Chaisty, Paul (2001) 'Legislative Politics in Russia', in Archie Brown (ed.), *Contemporary Russian Politics: A Reader*. New York: Oxford University Press.

Chaisty, Paul (2003) 'Defending the Institutional Status Quo: Communist Leadership of the Second Russian Duma, 1996–99', *Legislative Studies Quarterly*, vol. 28, no. 1, pp. 5–28.

Charter of the Commonwealth of Independent States (1993) Available from http://www.cis.minsk.by/russian/osn_dokum/cis_doc2.htm.

Chowdhury, Abdur and Verbina, Inna (2003) 'Reforming Russia's Education System', *Transition: The Newsletter about Reforming Economies*, vol. 14, nos 1–3 (January/February/March), p. 43.

Clowes, Edith, Kassow, Samuel D. and West, James L. (eds) (1991) *Between Tsar and People: Educated Society and the Quest for Public Identity in Late Imperialist Russia*. Princeton, NJ: Princeton University Press.

Cohen, Stephen F. (2004) 'Was the Soviet System Reformable?' *Slavic Review*, vol. 63, no. 3 (Fall), pp. 459–88.

Collier, David and Levitsky, Steven (1997) 'Democracy With Adjectives: Conceptual Innovation in Comparative Research', *World Politics*, vol. 49, no. 3 (April), pp. 430–51.

Colton, Timothy J. (2000) *Transitional Citizens: Voters and What Influences Them in the New Russia*. Cambridge, MA: Harvard University Press.

Colton, Timothy and Hough, Jerry (eds) (1998) *Growing Pains: Russian Democracy and the Election of 1993*. Washington, DC: Brookings Institution.

Colton, Timothy J. and McFaul, Michael (2003) *Popular Choice and Managed Democracy: The Russian Elections of 1999 and 2000*. Washington, DC: Brookings Institution.

Committee to Protect Journalists (2004) *World's Worst Places to Be a Journalist. Report*, 3 May. Available from www.cpj.org.

Connor, Walker (1984) *The National Question in Marxist–Leninist Theory and Strategy*. Princeton NJ: Princeton, University Press.

Conroy, Mary S. (2005) 'Civil Society in Late Imperial Russia', in Alfred B. Evans, Jr, Laura A. Henry and Lisa McIntosh Sundstrom (eds), *Change and Continuity in Russian Civil Society: A Critical Assessment*. Armonk, NY: Sharpe.

Cox, Michael (ed.) (1998) *Rethinking Soviet Collapse: Sovietology, the Death of Communism and the New Russia*. London: Cassell Academic.

Dahl, Robert A. (1971) *Polyarchy, Participation and Opposition*. New Haven, CT and London: Yale University Press.

Danspeckgruber, Wolfgang (ed.) (2002) *The Self-Determination of Peoples: Community, Nation, and State in an Interdependent World*. Boulder, CO: Lynne Reinner.

DaVanzo, Julie, and Grammich, Clifford (2001) *Dire Demographics: Population Trends in the Russian Federation*. Santa Monica, CA: RAND Corporation.

DaVanzo, Julie Oliker, Olga and Grammich, Clifford (2003) *Too Few Good Men: The Security Implications of Russian Demographics*. Santa Monica, CA: RAND Corporation.

Diamond, Larry (1999) *Developing Democracy: Toward Consolidation*. Baltimore, MD: Johns Hopkins University Press.

Diamond, Larry (2002) 'Thinking About Hybrid Regimes', *Journal of Democracy*, vol. 13, no. 2 (April), pp. 21–35.

Diamond, Larry, Linz, Juan and Lipset ,Seymour Martin (eds) (1988) *Politics in Developing Countries: Comparing Experiences with Democracy.* Boulder, CO: Lynne Rienner.

Donaldson, Robert H. and Joseph L. Nogee (1998) *The Foreign Policy of Russia: Changing Systems, Enduring Interests.* Armonk NY and London: M.E. Sharpe.

Dzis-Voinarovskiy, Nikolai (2004) 'The Poor Get Poorer, the Rich Get Richer', *Novye izvestia*, 4 August.

Eberstadt, Nicholas (2004) 'The Emptying of Russia', *Washington Post*, 13 February.

Elgie, Robert (ed.) (1999) *Semi-Presidentialism in Europe.* Oxford: Oxford University Press.

European Institute for the Media (1994) *The Russian Parliamentary Elections: Monitoring of the Election Coverage of the Russian Mass Media.* Düsseldorf: European Institute for the Media.

European Institute for the Media (February 1996) *Monitoring the Media Coverage of the 1995 Russian Parliamentary Elections.* Düsseldorf: The European Institute for the Media.

European Institute for the Media (September 1996) *Monitoring the Media Coverage of the 1996 Russian Presidential Elections.* Düsseldorf: The European Institute for the Media.

European Institute for the Media (March 2000) *Monitoring the Media Coverage of the December 1999 Parliamentary Elections in Russia. Final Report.* Düsseldorf: European Institute for the Media.

European Institute for the Media (August 2000) *Monitoring the Media Coverage of the March 2000 Presidential Elections in Russia. Final Report.* Düsseldorf: European Institute for the Media.

Evangelista, Matthew (2002) *The Chechen Wars: Will Russia Go the Way of the Soviet Union?* Washington, DC: Brookings Institution.

Evans, Alfred B. Jr. (2005) 'Civil Society in the Soviet Union?', in Alfred B. Evans, Jr, Laura A. Henry and Lisa McIntosh Sundstrom (eds), *Change and Continuity in Russian Civil Society: A Critical Assessment.* Armonk, NY: Sharpe.

Evans, Alfred B., Jr, Laura A. Henry and Lisa McIntosh Sundstrom (eds) (2005) *Change and Continuity in Russian Civil Society: A Critical Assessment.* Armonk, NY: M.E. Sharpe.

Evans, Alfred B. Jr and Gel'man, Vladimir (2004) *The Politics of Local Government in Russia.* Lanham, MD: Rowman & Littlefield.

Evans, Geoffrey and Whitefield, Stephen (1995) 'The Politics and Economics of Democratic Commitment: Support for Democracy in Transition Societies', *British Journal of Political Science*, vol. 25, no. 4 (October), pp. 485–514.

Farquharson, Marjorie (2003) 'After One Year, New Russian Criminal Procedure Code Is Showing Results', RFE/RL Newsline, 31 July.

Ferreira-Marques, Clara (2004) 'Teetotal Crusaders Fight to Keep Russia Sober', Reuters, 18 March.

Feshbach, Murray (2003) *Russia's Health and Demographic Crises: Policy Implications and Consequences*. Washington, DC: The Chemical and Biological Arms Control Institute.

Firsov, B. M. and Muzdybaev, K. (1975) 'K stroeniyu sistemy pokazatelei ispol'zovaniya sredstv massovoi kommunikatsii', *Sotsiologicheskie issledovaniya*, no. 1, pp. 113–20.

Fish, M. Steven (2000) 'The Executive Deception: Superpresidentialism and the Degradation of Russian Politics', in Valerie Sperling (ed.), *Building the Russian State: Institutional Crisis and the Quest for Democratic Governance*. Boulder, CO: Westview Press.

Fish, M. Steven (2001a) 'Conclusion: Democracy and Russian Politics', in Zoltan Barany and Robert Moser (eds), *Russian Politics: Challenges of Democratization*. Cambridge: Cambridge University Press.

Fish, M. Steven (2001b) 'When More Is Less: Superexecutive Power and Political Underdevelopment in Russia', in Victoria E. Bonnell and George W. Breslauer (eds), *Russia in the New Century: Stability or Disorder?* Boulder, CO: Westview Press.

Fitzpatrick, Catherine A. (2004) 'Russian NGOs Slam Putin's Reforms as "Unconstitutional" ', *RFE/RL Political Weekly*, vol. 4 (24 September), no. 37, www.rferl.com.

Flikke, Geir (ed.) (2004) *The Uncertainties of Putin's Democracy*. Oslo: Norwegian Institute of International Affairs.

Freedom House (2004) 'Freedom of the Press 2004: Table of Global Press Freedom Rankings'. Available from www.freedomhouse.org.

Freeland, Chrystia (2000) *Sale of the Century: Russia's Wild Ride from Communism to Capitalism*. London: Little, Brown and New York: Times Books and Crown Business.

Friedrich, Carl J. (1968) *Trends of Federalism in Theory and Practice*. New York: Praeger.

Galvin, Cristina and Feshbach, Murray (2004) 'Russia in denial over its AIDS epidemic', *The Irish Times*, 23 August.

Garnett, Sherman W. (ed.) (2000) *Rapprochement or Rivalry? Russia–China Relations in a Changing Asia*. Washington, DC: Carnegie Endowment for International Peace.

Gibson, James and Raymond Duch (1994) 'Postmaterialism and the Emerging Soviet Democracy', *Political Research Quarterly*, vol. 47, no. 1 (March), pp. 5–39.

Gill, Graeme (2002) *Democracy and Post-Communism: Political Change in the Post-Communist World*. London: Routledge.

Gill, Graeme and Marwick, Roger (2000) *Russia's Stillborn Democracy? From Gorbachev to Yeltsin*. New York: Oxford University Press.

Goldman, Marshall (2003) *The Piratization of Russia. Russian Reform Goes Awry*. New York: Routledge.

Golenkova, Z. T. (ed.) (1999) *Grazhdanskoe obshchestvo: teoriya, istoriya, sovremennost*. Moscow: Institut sotsiologii RAN.

Golosov, Grigorii V. (2004) *Political Parties in the Regions of Russia: Democracy Unclaimed*. Boulder, CO: Lynne Rienner.

Gooding, John (2001) *Socialism in Russia: Lenin and His Legacy, 1890–1991*. Basingstoke: Palgrave.

Gorbachev, Michael S. (1987) *Perestroika: New Thinking for Our Country and the World*. London: Collins.

Gurr, Ted R. (2000) *Peoples versus States: Minorities at Risk in the New Century*. Washington, DC: United States Institute of Peace.

Hahn, Gordon M. (2001a) 'Putin's Federal Reforms: Integrating Russia's Legal Space or Destabilizing Russian Federalism', *Demokratizatsiya*, vol. 9, no. 4 (Fall), pp. 498–530.

Hahn, Gordon M. (2001b) 'Putin's "Federal Revolution": Administrative Versus Judicial Methods of Federal Reform', *East European Constitutional Review*, vol. 10, no. 1 (Winter), pp. 60–7.

Hahn, Gordon M. (2002) *Russia's Revolution from Above, 1985–2000: Reform, Transition, and Revolution in the Fall of the Soviet Communist Regime*. New Brunswick NJ: Transaction Publishers.

Hahn, Gordon M. (2003a) 'The Impact of Putin's Federative Reforms on Democratization in Russia', *Post-Soviet Affairs*, vol. 19, no. 2 (April–June), pp. 114–53.

Hahn, Gordon M. (2003b) 'The Past, Present, and Future of the Russian Federal State', *Demokratizatsiya*, vol. 11, no. 3 (Summer), pp. 343–62.

Hahn, Gordon M. (2004) 'Putin's "Stealth Authoritarianism" and Russia's Second Revolutionary Wave', *Radio Free Europe/Radio Liberty Regional Analysis*, 21 April.

Hale, Henry (2004) 'Yabloko and the Challenge of Building a Liberal Party in Russia', *Europe–Asia Studies*, vol. 56, no. 7 (November), pp. 993–1020.

Hardt, John (ed.) (2003) *Russia's Uncertain Economic Future*. Armonk, NY: Sharpe.

Hechter, Michael (2000) *Containing Nationalism*. Oxford: Oxford University Press.

Hellman, Joel (1998) 'Winners Take All: The Politics of Partial Reform in Post-Communist Transitions', *World Politics*, vol. 50, no. 2 (January), pp. 203–34.

Henderson, Sarah L. (2003) *Building Democracy in Contemporary Russia: Western Support for Grassroots Organizations*. Ithaca, NY: Cornell University Press.

Henry, Laura A. (2005) 'Russian Environmentalists and Civil Society', in Alfred B. Evans, Jr, Laura A. Henry and Lisa McIntosh Sundstrom (eds), *Change and Continuity in Russian Civil Society: A Critical Assessment*. Armonk, NY: Sharpe.

Herspring, Dale R. (ed.) (2003) *Putin's Russia: Past Imperfect, Future Uncertain*. Lanham, MD: Rowman & Littlefield.

Herspring, Dale R. (ed.) (2005) *Putin's Russia: Past Imperfect, Future Uncertain*. 2nd edn. Lanham, MD: Rowman & Littlefield.

Hoffman, David E. (2002) *The Oligarchs: Wealth and Power in the New Russia*. New York: Public Affairs.

Holley, David (2003) 'Russian Underworld Extends to Higher Education', *Los Angeles Times*, 31 March.

Horowitz, Donald L. (1985) *Ethnic Groups in Conflict*. Berkeley and Los Angeles: University of California Press.

Hough, Jerry F. (1969) *The Soviet Prefects: The Local Party Organs in Industrial Decision Making*. Cambridge, MA: Harvard University Press.

Hough, Jerry F. and Fainsod, Merle (1979) *How the Soviet Union is Governed*. Cambridge, MA: Harvard University Press.

Howard, Marc Morjé (2003) *The Weakness of Civil Society in Post-Communist Europe*. Cambridge: Cambridge University Press.

Hudson, George E. (2003) 'Civil Society in Russia: Models and Prospects for Development', *Russian Review*, vol. 62, no. 2 (April), pp. 212–22.

Huntington, Samuel (1991) *The Third Wave: Democratization in the Late Twentieth Century*. Norman and London: University of Oklahoma Press.

Huskey, Eugene (1999) *Presidential Power in Russia*. Armonk, NY: Sharpe.

Huskey, Eugene (2005) 'The Bar's Triumph or Shame? The Founding of Chambers of Advocates in Putin's Russia', in Ferdinand Feldbrugge and Robert Sharlet (eds), *Public Policy and Law in Russia*. Leiden and Boston: Brill.

Hutcheson, Derek S. (2003) *Political Parties in the Russian Regions*. London and New York: RoutledgeCurzon.

Il'ina, Irina N. (2000) *Obshchestvennye organizatsii Rossii v 1920-e gody*. Moscow: Institut rossiiskoi istorii RAN.

Inglehart, Ronald (2000) 'Political Culture and Democratic Institutions: Russia in Global Perspective'. Paper presented at the annual meeting of the American Political Science Association.

Interfax (2003a) 'Price Growth Is Russians' Biggest Concern', 6 May.

Interfax (2003b) 'Russia Registers 3m Crimes a Year', 21 May.

Interfax (2004a) 'Most Russians Do Not Believe Poverty Can Be Halved in Four Years', 5 April.

Interfax (2004b) 'Death Rate among Working Russians Higher Than Elsewhere', 18 August.

ITAR-TASS (2003) 'Nearly Three-Quarters of Russian Families with Children Live in Poverty', 23 June.

ITAR-TASS (2004) 'Russian Schools Experience Severe Shortage of Teachers', 30 August.

Ivanov, I. S. (2001) 'The New Russian Identity: Innovation and Continuity in Russian Foreign Policy', *Washington Quarterly*, vol. 24, no. 3 (Summer), pp. 7–13.

Ivanov, I. S. (2002) *The New Russian Diplomacy*. Washingtron, DC: Nixon Center/ Brookings Institution Press.

Johnson, Juliet (2000) *A Fistful of Rubles. The Rise and Fall of the Russian Banking System*. Ithaca, NY: Cornell University Press.

Jonson, Lena (1999) *Keeping the Peace in the CIS: The Evolution of Russian Policy*. London: Royal Institute of International Affairs.

Jones, Luong P. and Weinthal, Erika (2002) 'Environmental NGOs in Kazakhstan: Democratic Goals and Nondemocratic Outcomes', in Sarah E. Mendelson and John K. Glenn (eds), *The Power and Limits of NGOs: A Critical Look at Building Democracy in Eastern Europe and Eurasia*. New York: Columbia University Press.

Jordan, Pamela (2000) 'Russian Court: Enforcing the Rule of Law?', in Valerie Sperling (ed.) *Building the Russian State*. Boulder, CO: Westview Press.

Kahn, Jeffrey (2002) *Federalism, Democratization, and the Rule of Law in Russia*. Oxford: Oxford University Press.

Kahn, J. (2004) 'Russia's "Dictatorship of Law" and the European Court of Human Rights', *Review of Central and East European Law*, vol. 29, no. 1, pp. 1–14.

Kapustina, Larisa (2000) *Evolyutsiya otnoshenii tsentr-regiony i stsenarii razvitiya federativnykh otnoshenii v Rossii*. Available from federalmcart. ksu.ru/conference/seminar5/kapustina.htm.

Keating, Michael (2001) *Plurinational Democracy: Stateless Nations in a Post-Sovereignty Era*. Oxford: Oxford University Press.

Keep, John L. H. (1996) *Last of the Empires: A History of the Soviet Union, 1945–1991*. Oxford: Oxford University Press.

Kenez, Peter (1999) *A History of the Soviet Union from the Beginning to the End*. Cambridge: Cambridge University Press.

Khlebnikov, Paul (2000) *Godfather of the Kremlin: Boris Berezovsky and the Looting of Russia*. New York: Harcourt.

Kholodkovsky, K. G. *et al.* (1998) *Grazhdanskoe obshchestvo v Rossii; struktury i soznanie*. Moscow: Nauka.

Khoros, V. G. *et al.* (1998) *Grazhdanskoe obshchestvo: mirovoi opyt i problemy Rossii*. Moscow: Editorial URSS.

Kolosov, Vladimir, Petrov, Nikolai and Smirnyagin, Leonid (eds) (1990) *Geografiya i anatomiya parlamentskikh vyborov*. Moscow: Progress.

Konstitutsiia Rossiiskoi Federatsii (1994) Moscow: Yuridicheskaya literatura.

Kotkin, Stephen (2001) *Armageddon Averted: The Soviet Collapse 1970–2000*. Oxford: Oxford University Press.

Kotz, David and Weir, Fred (1997) *Revolution from Above: The Demise of the Soviet System*. London: Routledge.

Kryshtanovskaya, O. V. (2003) *Anatomiya rossiiskoi elity*. Moscow: Solov'ev.

Kryshtanovskaya, Olga and White, Stephen (1996) 'From Soviet Nomenklatura to Russian Elite', *Europe–Asia Studies*, vol. 48, no. 5 (July), pp. 711–34.

Kryshtanovskaya, Olga and White, Stephen (2003) 'Putin's Militocracy', *Post-Soviet Affairs*, vol. 19, no. 4 (October–December), pp. 289–306.

Kubicek, P. (1999–2000) 'Russian Foreign Policy and the West', *Political Science Quarterly*, vol. 114, no. 4 (Winter), pp. 547–68.

Kulik, Anatolii (2001) *Perspektivy razvitiya partiino-politicheskoi sistemy v Rossii: kruglyi stol 'Ekspertiza'*. Moscow: Gorbachev-Fond. Available from www.gorby.ru.

Lane, David (ed.) (2002) *The Legacy of State Socialism and the Future of Transformation*. Lanham, MD: Rowman & Littlefield.

Lankina, Tomila (2004) *Governing the Locals: Local Self-Government and Ethnic Mobilization in Russia*. Lanham, MD: Rowman & Littlefield.

Lapidus, Gail W. and Tsalik, Svetlana (eds) (1998) *Preventing Deadly Conflict: Strategies and Institutions*. New York: Carnegie Corporation.

Lediakh, Irina A. (2005) 'Russia's Constitutional Court and Human Rights', in Ferdinand Feldbrugge and Robert Sharlet (eds) *Public Policy and Law in Russia*. Leiden and Boston, Brill.

Levitsky, Steven and Way, Lucan (2002) 'The Rise of Competitive Authoritarianism', *Journal of Democracy*, vol. 13, no. 2 (April), pp. 51–65.

Lieven, Anatol (2002) 'The Secret Policemen's Ball: the United States, Russia and the International Order after 11 September', *International Affairs*, vol. 78, no. 2 (April), pp. 245–59.

Light, Margot (2000) 'Democracy, Democratization and Foreign Policy in Post-Socialist Russia' in Hazel Smith (ed.), *Democracy and International Relations: Critical Theories/Problematic Practices*. Basingstoke: Macmillan.

Light, Margot, John Löwenhardt and Stephen White (2000) 'Russian Perspectives on European Security', *European Foreign Affairs Review*, vol. 5, no. 4 (Winter), pp. 489–505.

Lijphart, Arend (1984) *Democracies: Patterns of Majoritarian and Consensus Government in Twenty-One Countries*. New Haven, CT: Yale University Press.

Lijphart, Arend (1996) 'The Puzzle of Indian Democracy: A Consociational Interpretation', *American Political Science Review*, vol. 90, no. 2 (June), pp. 258–68.

Linz, Juan J. and Valenzuela, Arturo (eds) (1994) *The Failure of Presidential Democracy*. Baltimore, MD and London: Johns Hopkins University Press.

Linz, Juan and Stepan, Alfred (1996) *Problems of Democratic Transition and Consolidation*. Baltimore, MD: Johns Hopkins University Press.

Lipset, Seymour Martin (1959) 'Some Social Requisites of Democracy', *American Political Science Review*, vol. 53, no. 1 (March), pp. 69–105.

Lipset, Seymour Martin (1994) 'The Social Requisites of Democracy Revisited', *American Sociological Review*, vol. 59, no. 1 (February), pp. 1–22.

Lipset, Seymour Martin (1998) 'Excerpts from Three Lectures on Democracy', *Transitions*, Spring, accessed at www.ou.edu.

Lo, Bobo (2003) *Vladimir Putin and the Evolution of Russian Foreign Policy*. London: RIIA and Blackwell.

Löwenhardt, John (ed.) (1998) *Party Politics in Post-Communist Russia*. London: Cass.

Lynch, Dov (2000) *Rusian Peacekeeping Strategies in the CIS: The Cases of Moldova, Georgia and Tajikistan*. Basingstoke: Macmillan.

Mainville, Michael (2003) 'Russia's First City of Art, Culture, Heroin', *Toronto Star*, 29 June.

Mainwaring, Scott and Shugart, Matthew (eds) (1997) *Presidentialism and Democracy in Latin America*. Cambridge and New York: Cambridge University Press.

Mair, Peter (1997) 'What is Different about Post-Communist Party Systems?', in Mair, *Party System Change: Approaches and Interpretations*. Oxford: Clarendon Press, ch. 8, pp. 175–98.

Maksakova, Nina (2004) 'The Sky, the Prosecutor, and the Prison Bars', *Moskovskaya Promyshlennaya Gazeta*, August.

Malcolm, Neil, Pravda, Alex, Allison, Roy and Light, Margot (1996) *Internal Factors in Russian Foreign Policy*. Oxford: Oxford University Press.

Malia, Martin (1994) *The Soviet Tragedy: A History of Socialism in Russia, 1917–1991*. New York: The Free Press.

Manikhin, Oleg (2003) *Rossiiskaya demokraticheskaya partiya 'YABLOKO'*. Kratkii istoricheskii ocherk. Moscow: Integral-Inform.

March, Luke (2002) *The Communist Party in Post-Soviet Russia*. Manchester: Manchester University Press.

March, Luke (2004) 'The Putin Paradigm and the Cowering of Russia's Communists', in Cameron Ross (ed.), *Russian Politics under Putin*. Manchester: Manchester University Press.

Marples, David (2002) *Motherland: Russia in the Twentieth Century*. Harlow: Longman.

Marsh, Christopher (2002) *Russia at the Polls: Voters, Elections, and Democratization*. Washington, DC: CQ Press.

McCormack, Gillian (ed.) (1999) *Media in the CIS*, 2nd edn. Düsseldorf: European Institute for the Media.

McFaul, Michael (1997) *Russia's 1996 Presidential Election: The End of Polarized Politics*. Stanford, CA: Hoover Institution Press.

McFaul, Michael (2001) *Russia's Unfinished Revolution: Political Change from Gorbachev to Putin*. Ithaca, NY: Cornell University Press.

McFaul. Michael (2002) The Fourth Wave of Democracy and Dictatorship: Noncooperative Transitions in the Post-Communist World', *World Politics*, vol. 54, no. 2 (January), pp. 212–44.

McFaul, Michael, Petrov, Nikolai and Ryabov, Andrei (2004) *Between Dictatorship and Democracy: Russian Post-Communist Political Reform*. Washington, DC: Carnegie Endowment for International Peace.

Melville, Andrei (1999) 'Post-Communist Russia: Democratic Transitions and Transition Theories', in Lisa Anderson (ed.), *Transitions to Democracy*. New York: Columbia University Press.

Menon, Rajan (1997) 'The Strategic Convergence between Russia and China', *Survival*, vol. 39, no. 2 (Summer), pp. 101–25.

Mereu, Francesca (2004) 'Kremlin Looking for Loyal NGOs', *Moscow Times*, 25 June, p. 1.

Mickiewicz, Ellen P. (1980) *Media and the Russian Public*. New York: Praeger.

Mickiewicz, Ellen P. (1988) *Split Signals: Television and Politics in the Soviet Union*. New York: Oxford University Press.

Mickiewicz, Ellen P. (1999) *Changing Channels: Television and the Struggle for Power in Russia*. 2nd edn. Durham, NC: Duke University Press.

Miller, Arthur H. and Klobucar, Thomas F. (2000) 'The Development of Party Identification in Post-Soviet Systems', *American Journal of Political Science*, vol. 44, no. 4 (October), pp. 667–85.

Miller, Arthur H., Gwyn Erb, William M. Reisinger and Vicki L. Hesli (2000) 'Emerging Party Systems in Post-Soviet Societies: Fact or Fiction?', *Journal of Politics*, vol. 62, no. 2 (May), pp. 455–90.

Mishler, William and Willerton, John P. (2003) 'The Dynamics of Presidential Popularity in Post-Communist Russia: How Exceptional is Russian Politics?', *Journal of Politics*, vol. 65, no. 1 (December), pp. 111–41.

Moser, Robert (2001) *Unexpected Outcomes: Electoral Systems, Political Parties, and Representation in Russia*. Pittsburgh PA: University of Pittsburgh Press.

MosNews.com (2004) 'Russia Has Either 11,000 or 84,000 Millionaires', 17 June.

Munro, Neil and Rose, Richard (2001) *Elections in the Russian Federation*. Glasgow: Centre for the Study of Public Policy, University of Strathclyde.

Nemtsov, Alexander (2003) 'Every Third Death Alcohol-Related', *Izvestiya*, 1 October.

Nikitin, Alexander and Jane Buchanan (2002) 'The Kremlin's Civic Forum: Cooperation or Co-optation for Civil Society in Russia?', *Demokratizatsiya*, vol. 10, no. 2 (Spring), pp. 147–5.

North, Douglass (1990) *Institutions, Institutional Changes and Economic Performance*. Cambridge: Cambridge University Press.

Oates, Sarah (2004) 'The Mass Media, Elections and the Failure of Democracy in Russia'. Paper presented at the annual meeting of the American Political Science Association, Chicago, USA.

Oates, Sarah and Roselle, Laura (2000) 'Russian Elections and TV News: Comparison of Campaign News on State-Controlled and Commercial Television Channels', *Harvard International Journal of Press/Politics*, vol. 5, no. 2 (Spring), pp. 30–51.

Obshchestvennaya ekspertiza: anatomiya svobody slova (1999) Moscow: Nauka.

O'Donnell, Guillermo (1994) 'Delegative Democracy', *Journal of Democracy*, vol. 5, no. 1 (January), pp. 55–69.

O'Donnell, Guillermo, Schmitter, Philippe C. and Whitehead, Laurence (eds) (1986) *Transitions from Authoritarian Rule*, 4 vols. Baltimore, MD: Johns Hopkins University Press.

O'Donnell, Guillermo (1993) 'On the State, Democratization and Some Conceptual Problems (A Latin American View with Glances at Some Postcommunist Countries)', *World Development*, vol. 21, no. 8, pp. 1355–69.

OECD (Organization for Economic Cooperation and Development) (2001) *The Social Crisis in the Russian Federation*. Paris: OECD.

OECD (Organization for Economic Cooperation and Development) (2004) *Economic Survey: Russian Federation 2004*. Paris: OECD.

Olcott, Martha Brill, Anders Åslund and Sherman W. Garnett (1999) *Getting it Wrong: Regional Cooperation and the Commonwealth of Independent States*. Washington, DC: Carnegie Endowment for International Peace.

'O politicheskikh partiyakh' (2001) *Sobranie zakonodatel'stva Rossiiskoi Federatsii*, no. 29, art. 2950, 11 July.

Oreshkin, Dmitrii and Kozlov, Vladimir (2003) 'Voting under the

Governors' Wing: "Administrative Resource" as a Foundation of an Election Strategy', *Nezavisimaya gazeta* (9 September), p. 10.

OSCE (Organization for Security and Cooperation in Europe/Parliamentary Assembly International Election Observation Mission) (2003) *Statement of Preliminary Findings and Conclusions, Russian Federation State Duma Elections.* Available from www.osce.org.

OSCE (Organization for Security and Cooperation in Europe/Office for Democratic Institutions and Human Rights) (27 January 2004) *Russian Federation: Elections to the State Duma. OSCE/ODIHR Election Observation Mission Report.* Available from www.osce.org.

Ostrow, Joel M. (2000) *Comparing Post-Soviet Legislatures: A Theory of Institutional Design and Political Conflict.* Columbus, OH: Ohio State University Press.

Pascal, Elizabeth (2003) *Defining Russian Federalism.* Westport, CT: Praeger.

Pavlovsky, Gleb (2004) 'Russian Civil Society Hampered by Weak "Grass Roots" ', *Rossiiskaia gazeta,* 22 July, in BBC Monitoring Reports, 26 July.

Peregudov, Sergei (2003) *Korporatsiya, obshchestvo, gosudarstvo.* Moscow: Nauka.

Piacentini, Laura (2004) *Surviving Russian Prisons. Punishment, Economy and Politics in Transition.* Cullompton: Willan.

Pikayev, Alexander A. (2000) 'Moscow's Matrix', *Washington Quarterly,* vol. 23, no. 3 (July), pp. 187–94.

Pilkington, Hilary and Omel'chenko, Elena (2004) *'Everyday' but not 'Normal': Drug Use and Youth Cultural Practice in Russia.* University of Birmingham: Economic and Social Research Council.

Pinder, John and Yuri Shishkov (2002) *The EU and Russia.* London: Kogan Page.

Pockney, B. P. (1991) *Soviet Statistics since 1950.* New York: St Martin's.

Popov, S. A. (2003) *Partii, demokratiya, vybory.* Moscow: Omega-L.

'Programma' (2001) *Kommunisticheskaya partiya Rossiiskoi Federatsii v rezolyutsiyakh i resheniyakh s"ezdov, konferentsii i plenumov TsK (1999–2001).* Moscow: Izdatel'stvo ITRK, pp. 4–21.

Protsyk, Oleh (2004) 'Ruling with Decrees: Presidential Decree Making in Russia and Ukraine', *Europe–Asia Studies,* vol. 56, no. 5 (July), pp. 637–60.

Przeworski, Adam (1991) *Democracy and the Market: Political and Economic Reforms in Eastern Europe and Latin America.* Cambridge: Cambridge University Press.

Putin, Vladimir (2000) *First Person.* London: Hutchinson and New York: HarperCollins.

Putin, Vladimir (2004a) 'Full Text of Putin's State of the Nation Address to Russian Parliament', RTR Russian TV, BBC Monitoring, 26 May.

Putin, Vladimir (2004b) 'Russia's Rulers and Public Must Unite against Terrorism', RTR Russian TV, BBC Monitoring, 13 September.

RFE/RL (Radio Free Europe/Radio Liberty/Daily Report) (2003a) 'Demographer Says Migrants to Form Bulk of Country's Future', vol. 7, no. 109, part I, 11 June.

RFE/RL (2003b) 'Number of Children Continues to Decline', vol. 7, no. 188, part I, 2 October.

RFE/RL (2003c) 'Ministry of Health Revises Drunk-Driving Rules', vol. 7, no. 139, part I, 24 July.

RFE/RL (2003d) 'Education Minister Releases Statistics on Drug Use', vol. 7, no. 94, part I, 20 May.

RFE/RL (2004a) 'As Poll Paints Not-So-Rosy Picture', vol. 8, no. 93, part I, 18 May.

RFE/RL (2004b) 'It's a Cat's Life', vol. 8, no. 11, part I, 20 January.

RFE/RL (2004c) 'Divide Between Moscow and Regions Continues to Grow', vol. 8, no. 170, part I, 7 September.

RFE/RL (2004d) 'AIDS To Cut Population and Workforce By Almost 5 Percent in Four Decades', vol. 8, no. 101, part I, 28 May.

Reddaway, Peter and Glinski, Dmitri (2001) *The Tragedy of Russia's Reforms: Market Bolshevism against Democracy.* Washington, DC: United States Institute of Peace Press.

Reichman, Lee B. (2002) *Timebomb: The Global Epidemic of Multi-Drug-Resistant Tuberculosis.* New York: McGraw-Hill.

Remington, Thomas (1988) *The Truth of Authority: Ideology and Communication in the Soviet Union.* Pittsburgh, PA: University of Pittsburgh Press.

Remington, Thomas F. (2000). 'The Evolution of Executive–Legislative Relations in Russia since 1993', *Slavic Review,* vol. 59, no. 3 (Autumn), pp. 499–520.

Remington, Thomas F. (2001a) 'Putin and the Duma', *Post-Soviet Affairs,* vol. 17, no. 4 (October–December), pp. 285–308.

Remington, Thomas F. (2001b) *The Russian Parliament: Institutional Evolution in a Transitional Regime, 1989–1999.* New Haven, CT: Yale University Press.

Remington, Thomas F. (2002) 'Putin, the Duma, and Political Parties', in Dale Herspring (ed.), *Putin's Russia: Past Imperfect, Future Uncertain.* Boulder CO: Rowman & Littlefield.

Remington, Thomas F. (2003a) 'Coalition Politics in the New Duma', in Vicki L. Hesli and William M. Reisinger (eds), *The 1999–2000 Elections in Russia: Their Impact and Legacy.* Cambridge: Cambridge University Press.

Remington, Thomas F. (2003b) 'Majorities without Mandates: The Federation Council since 2000', *Europe–Asia Studies,* vol. 55, no. 5, pp. 667–91.

Remington, Thomas (2004) *Politics in Russia,* 3rd edn. London: Pearson Longman.

RIA Novosti (2003) 'Russia Getting Better Educated', 23 October.

RIA Novosti (2004) 'President Worried by Deteriorating Education Standards', 23 July.

Riker, William (1964) *Federalism: Origin, Operation, Significance.* Boston, MA: Little, Brown.

Rosbalt (2003) 'Russian Workforce Declines by 12 Million over Last Ten Years', 5 September.

Rose, Richard (1998) *Getting Things Done with Social Capital: New Russia Barometer VII*. Glasgow: Centre for the Study of Public Policy, University of Strathclyde.

Rose, Richard and Munro, Neil (2002) *Elections without Order: Russia's Challenge to Vladimir Putin*. Cambridge: Cambridge University Press.

Rose, Richard, Munro, Neil and White, Stephen (2001) 'Voting in a Floating Party System: The 1999 Duma Election', *Europe–Asia Studies*, vol. 53, no. 3 (May), pp. 419–43.

Ross, Cameron (ed) (2002) *Regional Politics in Russia*. Manchester: Manchester University Press.

Ross, Cameron (ed.) (2004) *Russian Politics under Putin*. Manchester: Manchester University Press.

Rühl, Christof, Pokrovsky, Vadim and Vinogradov, Viatchslav (2002) *The Economic Consequences of HIV in Russia*. Moscow: World Bank, 15 May.

Russian Regional Report (2004) 'Krasnodar Groups Discuss Ways to Monitor Correctional Facilities', vol. 9, no. 12, 6 July, pp. 1–3.

Rustow, Dankwart (1970) 'Transitions to Democracy: Toward a Dynamic Model', *Comparative Politics*, vol. 2, no. 2 (January), pp. 337–63.

Ryan, Michael (1993) *Social Trends in Contemporary Russia: A Statistical Source-Book*. London: Macmillan.

Sakwa, Richard (1990) *Gorbachev and His Reforms, 1985–90*. Hemel Hempstead: Philip Allan.

Sakwa, Richard (1998) *Soviet Politics in Perspective*, 2nd edn. London: Routledge.

Sakwa, Richard (2002) *Russian Politics and Society*, 3rd edn. London and New York: Routledge.

Sakwa, Richard (2004) *Putin: Russia's Choice*. London and New York: Routledge.

Sakwa, Richard and Mark Webber (1999) 'The Commonwealth of Independent States, 1991–1998: Stagnation and Survival', *Europe–Asia Studies*, vol. 51, no. 3 (May), pp. 379–415.

Sanders, David, Burton, Jonathan and Kneeshaw, Jack (2002) 'Identifying the True Party Identifiers: A Question Wording Experiment', *Party Politics*, vol. 8, no. 2, pp. 193–205.

Sandle, Mark (1997) *A Short History of Soviet Socialism*. London: UCL Press.

Schmitter, Phillipe and Karl, Terry Lyn (1994) 'The Conceptual Travels of Transitologists and Consolidologists: How Far Should They Attempt to Go?', *Slavic Review*, vol. 53, no. 1 (Spring), pp. 173–85.

Schreck, Carl (2004) 'No More Jail Terms for Drug Possession', *Moscow Times*, 14 May.

Schumpeter, Joseph A. (1976) *Capitalism, Socialism and Democracy*. London: George Allen & Unwin.

Service, Robert (1997) *A History of Twentieth-Century Russia*. Harmondsworth: Penguin.

Shakina, Marina (2003) 'Commentary: Calling Time on Vodka?', RIA Novosti, 27 August.

Sharlet, Robert (1997) 'Bringing the Rule of Law to Russia and the Newly Independent States: The Role of the West in the Transformation of the Post-Soviet Legal Systems', in Karen Dawisha (ed.), *The International Dimension of Post-Communist Transitions in Russia and the New States of Eurasia*. Armonk, NY: Sharpe.

Sharlet, Robert (1998) 'Legal Transplants and Political Mutations: The Reception of Constitutional Law in Russia and the Newly Independent States', *East European Constitutional Review*, vol. 7, no. 4 (Fall), pp. 59–68.

Sharlet, Robert (2001) 'Putin and the Politics of Law in Russia', *Post-Soviet Affairs*, vol. 17, no. 3 (July–September), pp. 195–234.

Sharlet, Robert (2003) 'Resisting Putin's Federal Reforms on the Legal Front', *Demokratizatsiya*, vol. 11, no. 3 (Summer), pp. 335–42.

Shearman, Peter (2001) 'The Sources of Russian Conduct: Understanding Russian Foreign Policy', *Review of International Studies*, vol. 27, no. 2 (April), pp. 249–63.

Shevchenko, Yuliia (2004) *The Central Government of Russia: From Gorbachev to Putin*. Aldershot: Ashgate.

Shevtsova, Lilia (1999) *Yeltsin's Russia: Myths and Realities*. Washington DC: Carnegie Endowment for Peace.

Shevtsova, Lilia (2003) *Putin's Russia*. Washington, DC: Carnegie Endowment for International Peace.

Shevtsova, Lilia (2005) *Putin's Russia*, 2nd edn. Washington, DC: Carnegie Endowment for International Peace.

Shleifer, Andrei and Treisman, Daniel (2001) *Without a Map. Political Tactics and Economic Reform in Russia*. Boston, MA: MIT Press.

Skorobogatko, Tatyana (2003) 'Ordinary Russians Yet to Notice the Upturn', *Moscow News*, 3–9 September.

Smith, Gordon B. (1996) *Reforming the Russian Legal System*. Cambridge: Cambridge University Press.

Smith, Gordon B. (2001) 'Russia and the Rule of Law', in Stephen White, Alex Pravda and Zvi Gitelman (eds), *Development in Russian Politics*, 5th edn. Durham, NC: Duke University Press, pp. 108–27.

Smith, Gordon B. (2005) 'Putin, the Procuracy, and the New Criminal Procedure Code', in Ferdinand Feldbrugge and Robert Sharlet (eds), *Public Policy and Law in Russia*. Leiden and Boston: Brill.

Smith, Steven S. and Remington, Thomas F. (2001) *The Politics of Institutional Choice: Formation of the Russian State Duma*. Princeton, NJ: Princeton University Press.

Sobyanin, Aleksandr and Sukhovolsky, Vladislav (1995) *Demokratiya, ogranichennaya falsifikatsiyami: vybory i referendumy v Rossii v 1991–1993 gg.* Moscow: Evraziya.

Solnick, Steven (1999) 'Russia's 'Transition': Is Democracy Delayed Democracy Denied?', *Social Research*, vol. 6, no. 3 (Fall), pp. 789–824.

Solomon, Peter H. (2003) 'The New Justices of the Peace in the Russian Federation: A Cornerstone of Judicial Reform', *Demokratizatsiya*, vol. 11, no. 3 (Summer), pp. 381–96.

Solomon, Peter H. and Fogelsong, Todd S. (2000) *Courts and Transition in Russia: The Challenge of Judicial Reform*. Boulder, CO: Westview Press.

Sperling, Valerie (1999) *Organizing Women in Contemporary Russia: Engendering Transition*. Cambridge: Cambridge University Press.

Spravochnyi material k politicheskomu otchetu TsK KPRF VII S"ezdu KPRF (2000) Moscow: TsK KPRF.

Squier, John (2002) 'Civil Society and the Challenge of Russian Gosudarstvennost'', *Demokratizatsiya*, vol. 10, no. 2 (Spring), pp. 166–82.

Stepan, Alfred (2000) 'Russian Federalism in Comparative Perspective', *Post-Soviet Affairs*, vol. 16, no. 2 (April–June), pp. 133–76.

Sundstrom, Lisa McIntosh (2002) 'Women's NGOs in Russia: Struggling from the Margins', *Demokratizatsiya*, vol. 10, no. 2 (Spring), pp. 207–29.

Sundstrom, Lisa McIntosh (2005) 'Soldiers' Rights Groups in Russia: Civil Society through Russian and Western Eyes', in Alfred B. Evans, Jr, Laura A. Henry and Lisa McIntosh Sundstrom (eds), *Change and Continuity in Russian Civil Society: A Critical Assessment*. Armonk, NY: Sharpe.

Suny, Ronald G. (1998) *The Soviet Experiment: Russia, the USSR, and the Successor States*. Oxford: Oxford University Press.

Szacki, Jerzy (1995) *Liberalism after Communism*. Budapest: Central European University Press.

Terry, Sarah Meiklejohn (1993) 'Thinking About Post-Communist Transitions: How Different Are They?', *Slavic Review*, vol. 52, no. 2 (Summer), pp. 333–7.

'Top Doctor Bemoans State of Schools' (2004) *Moscow Times*, 24 August.

Triesman, Daniel and Gimpelson, Vladimir (2001) 'Political Business Cycles and Russian Elections, or the Manipulation of the "Chudar"', *British Journal of Political Science*, vol. 31, no. 2 (April), pp. 225–46.

Trenin, Dmitri (2001) *The End of Eurasia: Russia and the Border Between Geopolitics and Globalization*. Washington, DC: Carnegie Endowment for International Peace.

Trenin, Dmitri (2004) 'Moscow's Realpolitik', *Nezavisimaya Gazeta*, 16 February.

Troxel, Tiffany A. (2003) *Parliamentary Power in Russia, 1994–2001: President vs Parliament*. New York: Palgrave Macmillan.

Twigg, Judyth L. and Schecter, Kate (2001) 'The Russia Initiative: Social Cohesion', *The Russia Initiative: Reports of the Four Task Forces*. New York: Carnegie Corporation of New York.

Twigg, Judyth L. and Schecter, Kate (eds) (2003) *Social Capital and Social Cohesion in Post-Soviet Russia*. Armonk, NY: Sharpe.

UNDP (United Nations Development Programme in the Russian Federation) (2003) *Human Development Report, Russian Federation, 2002/2003*. Moscow: UNDP.

Urban, Joan Barth and Solovei, Valerii D. (1997) *Russia's Communists at the Crossroads*. Boulder, CO: Westview Press.

Volokhov, A. E. (2003) *Noveishaya istoriya Kommunisticheskoi partii: 1990–2002*. Moscow: Impeto.

Walker, Edward W. (2003) *Dissolution: Sovereignty and the Breakup of the Soviet Union*. Lanham, MD: Rowman & Littlefield.

Walters, Greg (2004) 'UN Drug Chief Urges Russia to Take Action', *Moscow Times*, 28 June.

Watson, Alan (1974) *Legal Transplants: An Approach to Comparative Law*. Charlottesville VA: University of Virginia Press.

Webb, Paul, Farrell, David and Holliday, Ian (eds) (2002) *Political Parties in Advanced Industrial Democracies*. Oxford: Oxford University Press.

Webber, Mark (1996) *The International Politics of Russia and the Successor States*. Manchester: Manchester University Press.

Weber, Max (1995) *The Russian Revolutions*, translated and edited by Gordon C. Wells and Peter Baehr. Cambridge: Polity Press.

Wedgwood Benn, David (1992) *From Glasnost to Freedom of Speech: Russian Openness and International Relations*. London: Royal Institute of International Affairs.

Westwood, John (2002) *Endurance and Endeavour: Russian History, 1812–2001*, 5th edn. Oxford: Oxford University Press.

White, Anne (1999) *Democratization in Russia under Gorbachev, 1985–91: The Birth of a Voluntary Sector*. New York: St Martin's.

White, Stephen (1983) 'Political Communications in the USSR: Letters to Party, State and Press', *Political Studies*, vol. 31, no. 1 (January), pp. 43–60.

White, Stephen (1996) *Russia Goes Dry. Alcohol, State and Society*. Cambridge and New York: Cambridge University Press.

White, Stephen (2000a) *Communism and its Collapse*. London: Routledge.

White, Stephen (2000b) *Russia's New Politics*. Cambridge and New York: Cambridge University Press.

White, Stephen (2005) 'Russia's Client Party System', in Paul Webb and Stephen White (eds), *Political Parties in Transitional Democracies*. Oxford: Oxford University Press.

White, Stephen, Sarah Oates and Ian McAllister (2005) 'Media Effects and Russian Elections', *British Journal of Political Science*, vol. 35, no. 2 (April), pp. 191–208.

White, Stephen, Rose, Richard and McAllister, Ian (1997) *How Russia Votes*. Chatham NJ: Chatham House Publishers.

Willerton, John P. (1992) *Patronage and Politics in the USSR*. Cambridge and New York: Cambridge University Press.

Woodruff, David (1999) *Money Unmade: Barter and the Fate of Russian Capitalism*. New York: Cornell University Press.

World Bank (2003) *Averting AIDS Crises in Eastern Europe and Central Asia: A Regional Support Strategy*. Washington, DC: The World Bank.

World Bank (2004a) *From Transition to Development*, draft (April). Available from www.worldbank.org.ru.

World Bank (2004b) *Russian Economic Report*, no. 8, 30 June.

Wyman, Matthew, White, Stephen and Oates, Sarah (eds) (1998) *Elections and Voters in Post-Communist Russia*. Cheltenham: Edward Elgar.

Yablokova, Oksana (2003a) 'First Moscow Jury Rules 'Not Guilty''', *Moscow Times*, 19 August.

Yablokova, Oksana (2003b) 'Education Minister Raises the Standard', *Moscow Times*, 10 June.

Yeltsin, Boris (1990) *Against the Grain: An Autobiography*. London: Cape and New York: Summit Books.

Yeltsin, Boris (1994) *The Struggle for Russia*. New York: Random House. Also published as *The View from the Kremlin*. London: HarperCollins.

Yeltsin, Boris (2000) *Midnight Diaries*. New York: Public Affairs and London: Weidenfeld & Nicolson.

Zakaria, Fareed (1997) 'The Rise of Illiberal Democracy', *Foreign Affairs*, vol. 76, no. 6, pp. 22–43.

Zakaria, Fareed (2003) *The Future of Freedom*. New York: Norton.

Zaslavsky, S. E. (2003) *Politicheskie partii Rossii. Problemy pravovoi institutsionalizatsii*. Moscow: Institut prava i publichnoi politiki.

Zevelev, A. I., Yu. P. Sviridenko and V. V. Shelokhaev (eds) (2000) *Politicheskie partii Rossii: istoriya i sovremennost'*. Moscow: Rosspen.

Zimmerman, William (1995) 'Synoptic Thinking and Political Culture in Post-Soviet Russia', *Slavic Review*, vol. 54, no. 3 (Autumn), pp. 630–41.

Zudin, Aleksei (2001) 'Neokorporatizm v Rossii?', *Pro et Contra*, vol. 6, no. 4, pp. 171–98.

Zudin, Aleksei I. (2003) 'Rezhim V. Putina: kontury novoi politicheskoi sistemy', *Obshchestvennye nauki i sovremennost*, no. 2, pp. 67–83.

Index

Abortions, incidence of 213–14
Abramovich, Roman 7
'Administrative resources', in elections 78, 173, 174
Alcohol, as social problem 212–13
Alkhanov, Alu 165, 176–7
All-Russian Communist Party of the Future 84
Andropov, Yuri 3
Anti-alcohol campaign, under Gorbachev 3
Anti-Corruption Council 28
Argumenty i fakty (Arguments and Facts) 119
Armenia, Russian relations with 233–4
Azerbaijan, Russian relations with 233–4

Banking 192
Belarus, Russian relations with 232
Berezovsky, Boris 7, 72, 75, 77, 122
Beslan, hostage-taking incident in 9, 37, 145–6, 165–6, 247
Bespalov, Alexander 178
Brezhnev, Leonid I. 2–3

Cabinet of Ministers 28–9
Capital flight 196
Censorship 121
Chechnya, media coverage of 123
Chechnya, separatist conflict in 72, 153, 164–6, 176–7, 235, 250
Chekisty, in Putin leadership 13
Cherepkov, Viktor 184
Chernenko, Konstantin 3
Chernogorov, Alexander 181
Chernomyrdin, Viktor 29
Chubais, Anatolii 27, 192
Church, in Soviet period 99
Civic Forum 108–9
Civil Code 136–7
'Civil society' 96–113
    definition of 96–7
    in postcommunist period 101–13
    Putin and 108–13

reasons for weakness of 102–3
    in Soviet period 98–101
    in Tsarist period 98
Committees of Soldiers' Mothers 107
Commonwealth of Independent States (CIS) 5, 229–31
Communist Party of the Russian Federation 82–4
Communist Party of the Soviet Union 4, 80–1
Constitution, of Russian Federation 6, 45–6, 66–7, 130–3
Constitutional reform, discussion of 93–4
Constitutionalism 11–12
Corporate governance 199–200
Coup, attempted (1991) 4–5, 43–4, 120
Courts   *see* Judicial system
Crime 209–11
Criminal Code 137–8
Criminal Procedure Law 140–2, 143

Death penalty 137–8
Democracy
    consolidation of 243–4, 252
    delegative 11
    definitions of 242–3
    liberal and illiberal forms of 10
    prospects for in Russia 245–56
    quality of 10
Democratization 3–4, 241–56
'Dictatorship of law' 14
Dissidents, in Soviet period 100
Drugs 215–16
Dudaev, Dzhokar 153

Economy 186–203
    performance of 193–7
    in Putin period 190–203
    in Yeltsin period 187–90
Education 216–18
Elections 61–79
    fairness of 75–7
    of Federation Council 67–8
    media coverage of 75–6, 125–6

Elections – *continued*
  place of in political life   78–9
  in RSFSR   62–4
  in Soviet period   61–2
  of 1993   66–7, 68
  of 1995   68–70
  of 1996   70–1
  of 1999   71–2
  of 2000   73
  of 2003   74
  of 2004   74–5
Environmental organizations   106–7
Estonia   5, 231–2
European Court of Human Rights,
      Russian appeals to   147
European Union   8, 9
  Russian relations with   238–40

'Family', in Yeltsin period   7, 22, 36
Federal Assembly   40–60
  factional balance within   46–52
  federal districts   139, 156–9
  internal organization of   55–6
  legislative process within   53–5,
      56–8
  place of in political system   58–60
  in RSFSR   42–6
  in Soviet period   40–4
  under 1993 constitution   44–5
Federal system   138, 148–67
  budgetary aspects of   163–4
  in early postcommunist period
      152–5
  harmonization of legislation and
      159–61
  in Putin period   156–67
  reforms of 2004, proposed   166–7,
      179
  tension over in late Soviet period
      151–2
  treaties and   161–2
Federalism, as system of rule   149–51
Federation Council   32, 52–3
Federation Treaty (1992)   153
Fedorov, Nikolai   170–1
Fiscal policy   195
Foreign debt   195
Foreign policy   221–40
  decision-making structures   222–5,
      226
  'far abroad'   235–40
  under Gorbachev   4
  identity and concepts   225–9

'near abroad'   229–35
  Putin on   229, 239–40
Fradkov, Mikhail   29–30, 36

Gas, Russian output of   194
Gaulle, General Charles de   14
Gazprom   192
Georgia   4, 234
Glasnost   3, 118–20
Glazev, Sergei   84
Gorbachev, Mikhail   1, 3
  evaluation of reforms of   5
  and *glasnost*   118–19
  political reforms of   21, 41–2, 62,
      101
Governors, election and powers of
      32, 132–4
Great Patriotic (Second World) War   2
Gref, German   31, 35–6, 191
Group of Seven (G7), Russian
      membership of   239
Gryzlov, Boris   85, 91
Gusinsky, Vladimir   7, 70, 75, 77,
      86–7, 122, 247

Health and health care   211–16
HIV/AIDS, incidence of   214–15

Illarionov, Andrei   36
Ilyumzhinov, Kirsan   170
Impeachment, of Russian president
      24, 48–9
Income differentials   196, 205–6
Internet, Russian use of   121
Ivanov, Igor   27

Judicial system, reform of   133–5, 210

Kadyrov, Akhmed   165, 176
Kasyanov, Mikhail   29, 36
Khakamada, Irina   87
Kharitonov, Nikolai   74–5
Khodorkovsky, Mikhail   7, 77, 87,
      198–9, 247
Khrushchev, Nikita   2
Kirienko, Sergei   87
Kompromat   125
Kozak, Dmitri   31, 36
Kudrin, Aleksei   31, 35
Kyrgyzstan   233

Land law   140
Latvia   4, 5, 231–2

Law 130–47
  continuing obstacles to rule of
    142–7
  under Putin 139–47
  under Yeltsin 135–8
Lenin, Vladimir 1
Liberal Democratic Party of Russia
    81, 87–8
Lithuania 4, 5
Local government 179–82
Luzhkov, Yuri 71, 174

'Managed democracy' 9, 10, 13, 35
Matvienko, Valentina 177
Media 114–29
  and attempted coup 120
  bias in 122–3, 125–6
  consumption patterns 120–1, 123,
    124
  and elections 75–6, 125–6
  popular attitudes towards 126–8
  in postcommunist period 120–9
  in Soviet period 115–20
  trust in 127
Medvedev, Dmitri 27, 36
'Middle class' 106–7
Moldova, Russian relations with
    234–5
Moscow News 119

Nagorno-Karabakh, dispute concerning
    233–4
'Namedni' (television programme)
    124–5
Naryshkin, Sergei 31
NATO, Russian relations with 236–7,
    239
Nemtsov, Boris 87
Nikolaev, Vladimir 184
Novaya gazeta 123–4
NTV (television channel) 122, 126,
    128

'Oligarchs' 6–7, 77, 144–5, 188, 190

Parliament *see* Federal Assembly
Parties, political 80–95
  classifications of 81–2
  identification with 91
  membership of 91–2
  and Russian public 89–95
  trust in 89
Pavlovsky, Gleb 110
People's Patriotic Union of Russia 84

Perestroika 3
Perm territory 162
Peter the Great 20
Pitertsy, within Putin leadership 13
Police 145
Population, trends in 211–14
Potanin, Vladimir 7
Poverty 196, 205–9
Praktiki 171
Presidency 7, 13, 18–39
  administration of 25–7
  and federal system 32, 38
  under Putin, evaluations of 36–9
Presidential envoys 32
Primakov, Yevgenii 14, 71, 72, 222,
    224
Prime minister, position of 28–31
Prisons 209–10
Public chamber, proposed 111, 166
Putin, Vladimir 7, 9
  political forces within presidency of
    33–6
  political leadership of 22–3, 36–9
  popularity of 37–8
  regime of 13–17
  and regional leaders 76–7

Referendum (1993) 65
Regime type 11, 13
Regions, politics of 168–85
  executive institutions within
    172–4
  Putin's reforms of 174–9, 182–5
  representative institutions within
    169–72
Rodina party 84
Rogozin, Dmitri 84
Rule of Law Consortium 136
Rutskoi, Aleksandr 66, 171

Sakhalin, energy resources of 195
Sakharov, Andrei 119
Security Council 27, 223
Seleznev, Gennadii 83
Semigin, Gennadii 84
Separation of powers 12
Shaimiev, Mintimer 152
Shoigu, Sergei 85, 91
Siloviki 27, 34–5, 177–8
Slavinvest, sale of 200
Sobchak, Anatolii 22, 33–4
Social policy 204–20
  see also Crime; Health and health
    care; Poverty

Solzhenitsyn, Alexander   116
Soviets   40–1
'St Petersburg group', in Putin
        leadership   35–6
Stalin, Joseph   1–2
State Council   27–8
State Council of Legislators   28
State service, law on   93
Svoboda Slova (television programme)
        124–5

'Third wave', of democratization   8, 9
Tajikistan   233
Tatarstan   153, 155
Tax law   140
Television   *see* Media
Terrorism   145–6, 239, 247–8
Tkachev, Alexander   182
Tsarist system, political power in
        20–1
Turkmenistan   8

Ukraine, Russian relations with   8,
        232, 251
Union of Right Forces   87
Unified Energy Systems (UES)   192
United Russia party   15, 31–2, 34–5,
        178–9
United States, Russian relations with
        236–8, 239–40

Unity party   85
Uskorenie (acceleration)   3
USSR, dissolution of   4, 5
Uzbekistan   8, 233

Vladivostok, mayoral elections in
        (2004)   184
Voloshin, Alexander   27, 36

Wages   196
        see also Income differentials
Women's organizations   103–5, 107
World Trade Organization (WTO),
        Russian membership of   200–3

Yabloko party   86
Yakovlev, Vladimir   177
Yavlinsky, Grigorii   86–7
Yeltsin, Boris   4, 5, 6, 18, 21
        and federal system   151–2
        and 1996 election   201
        political leadership of   21–2
        and Russian parliament   43–6, 64
Yukos (oil concern)   86, 197–8

Zakaria, Fareed   10
Zhirinovsky, Vladimir   87–8
Zhukov, Aleksandr   30–1
Zyuganov, Gennadii   70–1, 72, 82,
        84

New Charter for
Health Care Workers